MEMORY, TRAUMA, AND HISTORY

Essays on Living with the Past

MICHAEL S. ROTH

For Georgia Jane,
With love,

COLUMBIA UNIVERSITY PRESS *New York*

COLUMBIA UNIVERSITY PRESS *Publishers Since 1893* NEW YORK CHICHESTER, WEST SUSSEX

Library of Congress Cataloging-in-Publication Data
Roth, Michael S., 1957–
Memory, trauma, and history : essays on living with the past / Michael S. Roth.
p. cm.
Includes bibliographical references and index.
ISBN 978-0-231-14568-8 (cloth : alk. paper) — ISBN 978-0-231-14569-5 (pbk. : alk. paper) —
ISBN 978-0-231-52161-1 (ebook)
1. History—Philosophy. 2. Memory (Philosophy) 3. Psychoanalysis—History. 4. Psychic trauma—Social aspects. 5. Photography—Psychological aspects. I. Title.

D16.8.R848 2011
901—dc23 2011018871

Columbia University Press books are printed on permanent and durable acid-free paper.
This book is printed on paper with recycled content.
Printed in the United States of America

c 10 9 8 7 6 5 4 3 2 1
p 10 9 8 7 6 5 4 3 2 1

All but three of the chapters in this book were first published in journals or collections. I acknowledge these publications and the permission of the publishers here:
"Remembering Forgetting: *Maladies de la Mémoire* in 19th Century France," *Representations*, 26 (1989), 49–68. © 1989 University of California Press. "Dying of the Past: Medical Studies of Nostalgia in Nineteenth-Century France," *History and Memory*, 3, no. 1 (1991), 5–29. © 1991 Indiana University Press. "Hysterical Remembering,"*MODERNISM/modernity*, 3, no. 2, (1996), 1–30. © The Johns Hopkins University Press, 1996. "Trauma, Representation and Historical Consciousness," in *Common Knowledge*, v.7, pp. 99–110. © 1998 Duke University Press. 'Trauma: A Dystopia of the Spirit," *Thinking Utopia*, ed. J. Rusen, M. Fehr, T. Rieger (Making Sense of History series) (New York: Berghahn Books, 2005). "Falling into History: Freud," Case of Emmy von N.," in *The Psychoanalytic Century: Freud," Legacy for the Future*, ed. David E. Scharff (New York: The Other Press, 2001), 5–20. "Classic Postmodernism," *History and Theory*, 43 (2004), pp. 372,–378. © 2004 Wesleyan University. "Ebb Tide," *History and Theory*, 46 (2007) , 66–73. © 2007 Wesleyan University. "The Art of Losing Oneself," *Raritan*, 27, no. 3 (Winter, 2008): 158–167. © 2008 Rutgers University Press. "Inquiry As Hope," *History and Theory*, 47 (2008), 413–420. © 2008 Wesleyan University. "Photographic Ambivalence and Historical Consciousnes," *History and Theory*, 48 (2009), pp. 82–94. © 2009 Wesleyan University. "Why Photography Matters to the Theory of History," *History and Theory*, 49 (2010), pp. 90–103. © 2010 Wesleyan University. "Ordinary Film," *Raritan*, 25 (2005), pp. 1–11. © 2005 Rutgers University Press. "Graves of the Insane, Decorated," in *Library of Dust: Photography by David Maisel* (San Francisco: Chronicle Books, 2008). "On a Certain Blindness in Teaching," *Higher Education Exchange* (1995), 8–17. "On the Limits of Critical Thinking," *The Chronicle Review*, January 3, 2010. "Good and Risky: On the Promise of a Liberal Education," *The Chronicle Review*, July 11, 2010.

To my brother, Rick Roth

Contents

Illustrations

Acknowledgments

The following colleagues and students have made significant contributions to my thinking over the many years I've worked on these essays. I am pleased to acknowledge them: Elazar Barkan, Darcy Buerkle, Marianne Calnen, Nathalie Z. Davis, Robert Dawidoff, Brian Fay, Péter Forgács, Victor Gourevitch, Matthew Jordan, Michael Ann Holly, Ethan Kleinberg, Jackson Lears, David Maisel, Elizabeth Minnich, Julia Perkins, Matt Reed, Jörn Rüsen, Carl E. Schorske, Andrew Tanaka, and Hayden White. At Scripps College, the Getty Research Institute, the California College of the Arts, and Wesleyan University I have been very fortunate to work with thoughtful and caring assistants. Claire Bridge, Elizabeth Garrett, Helen Frierson, and Joan Adams have all contributed to this book in myriad ways. I especially want to thank Lisa LaPlant and Joan Adams for their help with the final manuscript preparation.

Charles Salas studied with me as a graduate student and has for many years now been my colleague and friend. Most of the essays in this volume benefited from his close reading and suggestions, and the whole would have been much better if I had been even more attentive to his advice.

My children Jeremy Roth, Max Roth, and Sophie Weil-Roth have spent too much time watching their dad hunched over a computer, or running off to a library, or simply lost in thought. I hope this book responds to whatever curiosity they may still have about what I was doing all that time.

For many years now Kari Weil has been a tough critic and loving supporter. She ensures that I don't have to live in the past even as I try to figure out how we live with it.

I have dedicated this book to my brother, Rick Roth, the most relentlessly optimistic person I know. He is also the person I know who shows most care and love for connections to the past that matter. It will come as no surprise to him that I have no idea how he does it. "When they built you, brother, they broke the mold."

Introduction

Memory, Trauma, and History is comprised of essays that fall into five overlapping subject areas: history and memory; psychoanalysis and trauma; postmodernism, scholarship, and cultural politics; photography and representation; and liberal education. The oldest essays in this book were first drafted at the end of the 1980s, and the most recent ones in 2010. Over these twenty or so years I have continued to pursue issues emerging from those that first drew me to academic work, issues that orbit around the question of how people make sense of the past. *Memory, Trauma, and History* contains work written for academic audiences as well for more general ones.[1] All of the essays are concerned with making meaning out of history and memory, a concern which (at least academically) I first began to pursue with a project on Sigmund Freud and politics in the late 1970s, and one on which I continue to write and teach. An early version of that first project was my senior honors thesis at Wesleyan University, published almost a decade later as *Psycho-analysis as History: Negation and Freedom in Freud*. I returned to Wesleyan in 2007 to become its sixteenth president, and the most recent pieces in this collection were written after I'd assumed this position. I am not sure if this counts as a "full circle," but this professional homecoming is part of the context for *Memory, Trauma, and History*.

Since the late 1980s, attitudes toward the role of the past in the present have changed greatly—in the Academy and the wider public—and the essays here address many of these changes. I have not attempted to update the older articles, except to point in a few footnotes to some major trends in scholarship that have developed since my articles were first published. In this introduction I have provided some context for the essays, particularly in the section concerned with psychoanalysis and trauma, to address theorists, such as Giorgio Agamben, Slavoj Žižek, and Dominick LaCapra, who have tackled related topics and generated significant commentary over the last decade or so. Throughout this volume, and even in this introduction, I write about topics in relation to others tilling similar soil. If my own ideas wind up emerging in hybrid form, I hope that they are heartier for it.

Part 1: Nineteenth-Century Maladies of Memory

The essays in the first part of the book examine three kinds of memory disturbances that attracted much attention in medical and literary culture in nineteenth-century Europe, especially France: forgetting (amnesia and multiple personality), longing (nostalgia), haunted histrionics (hysteria). These *maladies de la mémoire*, as they were called, helped doctors, philosophers, neurologists, and would-be psychologists to define what it was like to have a normal memory in a period of extraordinary economic, social, and cultural change. I turned to this subject having written monographs on Freud and on French Hegelianism. In each of those earlier projects I was interested in how the conceptual machines of psychoanalysis and Hegelianism created meaning out of the past while addressing key political and ethical issues. I eschewed questions of cultural impact or influence in favor of an exploration of the theoretical implications of these modes of understanding for generating meaning from history. In *Psycho-analysis as History*, I tried to show how we could make sense of Freud's oeuvre as a theory of history, although I did not attempt to place the founder of psychoanalysis in a particular context or to show how his work developed over time. By contrast, *Knowing and History* developed a conceptual explication of French philosophers wrestling with Hegel, and added to this a historical argument about the antecedents of structuralism as well as its aftermath. This historical argument charted the change in focus from the question "what does it mean?" to a concentration on the question "how does it work?"—a shift from interest in significance to interest in structure. I sought to understand how French theoretical sophistication (and its American imitators) had become wedded to a rejection of historical thinking. The retreat from historical meaning-making that one could already see in the writings of Alexandre Kojève, Jean Hyppolite, and Eric Weil created the context for the more celebrated contributions of Levi-Strauss and Barthes, of Deleuze and Foucault. The retreat from historical meaning, I argued, came at a heavy cost because it meant that crucial questions of politics and legitimation would go unaddressed. In subsequent essays collected in *The Ironist's Cage*, I argued that an attitude of ironic sophistication was a poor substitute for meaningful theoretical or practical engagement with politics and history.[2]

In beginning the research for the essays in part 1 of this book, I was moving away from my focus on questions of high theory and toward histories of culture that raise theoretical questions less directly. The doctors and writers on whom I focused did not develop conceptually rich systems with truth claims to reckon with, but they did develop practices through which we can now see how notions of memory and forgetting, identity and desire, progress and tradition were changing in nineteenth-century France. The sciences of memory developed as a socially legitimate way of having reasonable discourse about how one becomes a normal human being. I was not interested in whether doctors *really* understood amnesia, hypermnesia, and split personality, nor did I take a stand on whether nostalgia really was a fatal illness or just a mistaken diagnostic category. I was interested instead in how professionals in France created categories of pathology to express their concerns with how one was to live with the past—or how one was to live without it. These soundings in the cultural history of memory were meant both to illuminate aspects of the history of medicine and to raise questions for us concerning how we live with the past during our own period of technological and economic transformation.

The turn in the Academy to the cultural history of memory became very powerful in the mid-1980s through the 1990s. Pierre Nora began publishing his great project *Les Lieux de Mémoire* in 1984, and the journal *History and Memory* was founded in 1989. I had become interested in the historical consideration of memory when reading Yosef Yerushalmi's concise and powerful *Zakhor* (1982), through which I first encountered an account of how modern historical understanding was a response to the loss of a shared sense of the past.[3] The tension between history and memory became an important axis of scholarship in the 1980s and 1990s, as scholars tried to understand the evolution of collective memory, and how their own works might be related to it.

For many writers on these topics, history's obligation was to offer a critical perspective on memory. If memory was immediate, many writers noted, it was also dangerously naïve. If memory was said to inhere in places and objects, this was because it was felt by somebody to be there, perhaps because they were *told* it was there, told for specific reasons. Memory, so historians often argued, was ripe for manipulation. History writing, because of the self-criticism built into its operation, brought a reflexive check on what we thought we knew about the past. Since history writing was already self-conscious with regard to possibilities of manipulation, it was less open to dangerous distortion than were claims made about the past on the basis of memory. At least that was the argument.[4]

This discourse concerning the critical virtues of history in relation to "lived memory" arose in spite of the deconstructive attacks on the truth-value of historical writing more generally. Attacks ranging from the ironically formalist writings of Hayden White on the rhetoric of history writing, to Peter Novick's contextual critique of objectivity should have made problematic any notion of history as an antidote to myth and memory.[5] But the notion of a communal, unmediated culture of commemoration was tailor-made to shore up the historian's sense of intellectual purpose and epistemological confidence. We may not be able to claim scientific objectivity, historians admitted with some satisfaction, but at least we are not merely reenacting our myths about a shared past.

Although Yerushalmi and Nora both stressed the opposition between the lived milieu of memories and the institutionalized historical profession, several writers soon began to intermingle the two in their own approaches to the past. In *History as an Art of Memory* Patrick Hutton acknowledged the tension just described, but he saw an emphasis on the claims of memory, on the arts of memory, as an antidote to the potential skepticism about connections to the past that had emerged in theorizing about historical knowledge and writing. For Hutton, it was jejune to think one could simply accept the skeptical notion that we did not care about the truths about the past since we could never be sure we arrived at such truths. "Memory is a problem in the postmodern age because of our anxieties about the implications of our loosening attachments to the collective memories that once sustained us."[6] By acknowledging our felt attachments to the past rather than just our ability to discern falsehoods about accurate representations of it, he argued, we might ease some of our skeptical anxieties.

This acknowledgment is also important to Susan Crane, who has contributed historical accounts of what we might call the memory industry in early nineteenth-century Germany, and who has now developed a more theoretical or prescriptive perspective concerning how historians can use the claims of memory within their own work. Crane, like Hutton, has argued for the presence of the historian's own voice in critical representations of the past as a way of breaking down the false dichotomy between memory and history. Rather than see memory as part of lived experience in opposition to a fully critical historical consciousness, she frames historical discourse, too, as part of the broad context of collective memory: "I am suggesting that historical research is a lived experience that the self-reflexive historian consciously integrates into collective memory. Historical representation is inadequate to this lived experience only so long as the author remains absent and the textual or site-artifact serves only the function of commemoration."[7] Crane, like Hutton, thinks the distance historians have typically taken from the context of collective memory might have more to do with professional legitimation than it does with some inherent tension between experience and critical reflection on it.

In contrast to Hutton and Crane, historians Kerwin Klein and Allan Megill have each offered strong defenses of the importance of the critical aspects of historiography as opposed to the feelings of immediacy supposedly attached to collective memory or milieux of memory. Klein is troubled by the "range of theological concepts as well as vague connotations of spirituality and authenticity" that he thinks have infected discourse about memory.[8] He finds that the use of psychoanalytic concepts for large groups of people (as if they were individuals writ large) is on shaky ground, and the connotations of "working through" or "coming to terms with the past" too close to therapeutic or new age discourse. "The new memory work displaces the old hermeneutics of suspicion with a therapeutic discourse whose quasi-religious gestures link it with memory's deep semantic past."[9] Megill's work on the relationship between memory and history has strong affinities with Klein's. "History," he writes, "ought rather to counter the harmful effects of an excessive preoccupation with memory."[10] Megill identifies memory with "affirmative historiography," and, like Klein, worries that a call for "more memory" will result in just more celebration or affirmation of aspects of the past that are in accord with present preoccupations. These two historians exude satisfaction with their profession's guarantees of rationality, and put themselves in the paradoxical position of calling for more self-criticism even as they affirm the deep reasonableness of their own intellectual practice. Clearly, self-criticism only goes so far.

The tradition of self-congratulation in which historians often participate is itself a tried and true memory practice. Connecting contemporaries to a "best practice" (within their own discipline) creates scholarly legitimation and a sense of belonging. Of course, professional history writing has often been "affirmative," be it in nationalistic works to shore up the position of a regime, or self-styled radical works meant to earn favor with an opposition party (or tenure committee). Klein and Megill have been troubled by a tendency in recent decades to search the past for heroic ancestry and self-validating victimization. This uncritical memory bath, they rightly note, allows myth building to proceed unchecked in ways that produce political formations that work against what they would regard as progressive change. But it is incorrect to think that memory practices are necessarily uncritical, or that they always give rise to great homogeneity rather than productive conflict. Commemorations, reenactments, and rituals often give rise to ambivalence and self-questioning—not just reaffirmations of the status quo. The still repeated ancient Hebrew injunction, for example, to remember that "we were slaves in Egypt" does not give rise to only four questions.

In the first three essays in this book, I am concerned less with the general relationship of history and memory than with how nineteenth-century French doctors and philosophers came to grips with what they perceived to be disorders in the way people related to their past. Nineteenth-century medical writers invented new ways to have amnesia, and this category of forgetting soon became populated with cases. So it was with nostalgia, split personality, and hysteria as well. As writers tried to make sense of these disorders—put them in some kind of order—they were, to use Ian Hacking's phrase, making up new kinds of people. And as the "kinds" were made up, people found ways to fit themselves into these categories.[11]

Part 2: History and the Psyche

Trauma has become a core issue for psychoanalysis and for history, and in this part of the book I focus on the vicissitudes of representation that extreme events pose for both fields. The tide of memory issues with which the book begins saturates this group of essays as well, since the question at the heart of the reconsideration of trauma is how a memory becomes a charismatic wound, an injury that attracts everything to it. In trauma, the recollected past causes suffering, and the traumatic event has a magnetic appeal that pulls a wide constellation of experience (often, an individual's whole life) into its orbit. But the extreme event itself resists representation; it seems to defy the meaning-making activity at the core of both the psychoanalytic and historical enterprise. The traumatic cannot be contained in representation, but it is "too big to fail"—too important to be left out of an attempt to make sense of the past at either the individual or collective level.

As E. Ann Kaplan and Ruth Leys, among others, have noted, the Freudian approach to trauma depends on the idea of a motivated unconscious.[12] People will encounter an extreme event through the desires and memories that initially formed their personalities and that remain at the core of identity, and traumatic events will in turn reconfigure those same desires and memories. Temporal continuity is radically disrupted by trauma, and the past is reconfigured even as one attempts to deflect present pain. Embodied (but often unconscious) memories resist traumatic experience although they must find ways to respond to it. Since a traumatic event is characterized, however, by its inability to be integrated into one's normal patterns of meaning-making, this response will always be inadequate, always be painful or disruptive.

In critical theory the traumatic has been framed as a window onto more general issues of representation. The inability to properly represent some events is said to show the inadequacy of representation of any and all events; the painful gap between meaning-making and experience that comes to light in the processing of trauma is said to illuminate the more general failure to make sense of experience. Trauma in this regard is linked to notions of the sublime, which have become convenient ways for theorists to have their disruption and write about it too. The sublime, like the traumatic, reminds us that the unrepresentable is always lurking if we dare pay attention to it. The sublime, like the traumatic, reminds us that efforts at meaning-making must always circumvent an intensity that would otherwise disrupt all coherence.

For several years now the Italian philosopher Giorgio Agamben has been exploring the ways in which the modern politics has rested on intense acts of exclusion or displacement that define the normal and the legal while seeming to defy them. For him, the disruption of coherence indicates what makes coherence possible in the first place. He has argued that the ban is at the root of the polity, and that the truth of modern politics, its core, is to be found in the death camps.[13] The mode of thinking that Agamben brings to a variety of subjects makes the exceptional into the truth of the rule.[14] Charting a course among points set out by Heidegger, Carl Schmitt, and Walter Benjamin, Agamben sees in "states of exception" the heart of modern political sovereignty, and the death camp is the state of exception par excellence.[15] For Agamben the death camp is a zone that reveals the sense of everything around it, even as it seems to resist the normal processes of meaning-making: "From this perspective, the camp—as the pure, absolute, and impassable biopolitical space (insofar as it is founded solely on the state of exception)—will appear as the hidden paradigm of the political space of modernity, whose metamorphoses and disguises we will have to learn to recognize."[16] The camp is, he writes, "the hidden matrix and *nomos* of the political space in which we are still living":[17]

> In this light, the birth of the camp in our time appears as an event that decisively signals the political space of modernity itself. . . . The state of exception, which was essentially a temporary suspension of the juridico-political order, now becomes a new and stable spatial arrangement inhabited by the bare life that more and more can no longer be inscribed in that order. . . . The camp as dislocating

> localization is the hidden matrix of the politics in which we are still living, and it is this structure of the camp that we must learn to recognize in all its metamorphoses into the *zones d'attentes* of our airports and certain outskirts of our cities. The camp is the fourth, inseparable element that has now added itself to—and so broken—the old trinity composed of the state, the nation (birth), and land.[18]

In this long quote one can see that the normal is not only defined by the pathological, but that the entire modern "juridico-political order" is understood by the creation of a system that produced mass death. The "extreme expression" of this system, as Agamben understands it, is the "Muselmann," the broken prisoner in a death camp who can no longer respond to his surroundings, whether a vicious attack by a guard or the opportunity to grab a scrap of food. The camp inmates saw the Muselmann as having been stripped of all dignity, or all humanness, and of having submitted totally to his situation. He had given himself to death but was still alive. Bare life.

> [T]he atrocious news that the survivors carry from the camp to the land of human beings is precisely that it is possible to lose dignity and decency beyond imagination, that there is still life in the most extreme degradation. And this new knowledge now becomes the touchstone by which to judge and measure all morality and all dignity. The *Muselmann*, who is its most extreme expression, is the guard on the threshold of a new ethics, an ethics of a form of life that begins where dignity ends.[19]

The most abject figure is now the "touchstone by which to judge and measure all morality and dignity." Agamben's rhetoric of dramatic polarization and reversal seems to have been embraced by those in academic circles eager to breathe new life into radicalism in this age of seriously diminished expectations. The truth of humanity is found in the deadened eyes of the Muselmann of Auschwitz, the prisoner who has so completely surrendered that he no longer responds to the world at all. Why make a broadly resonant symbol of this total lack of expectation? The hope is that, if we can understand our situation through the empty gaze of the most degraded death camp prisoner, we will then be in a position to change it. This hope, based on the grammar of dramatic reversal, is familiar enough from either Christianity or Marxism: the last shall be first.

The trope of dramatic reversal underlies much of the recent interest in trauma and shame. The chapters in part 2 of this book examine how the notion of trauma was a response to concerns about politics, representation, and ethics that had become prominent in critical theory at the end of the twentieth century and the beginning of the twenty-first. Agamben's mode of thinking through the extreme met receptive readers who had been wrestling with how spirit-breaking trauma might be the key to understanding contemporary experience. "The extreme situation can no longer function as a distinguishing criterion," Agamben writes. "The extreme situation's lesson is rather that of absolute immanence, of everything being in everything. In this sense, philosophy can be defined as the world seen from an extreme situation that has become the rule."[20]

For Agamben it is not just the extreme of trauma that defines our world but more specifically the extreme of shame. In *Remnants of Auschwitz* the philosopher portrays shame as a fundamental ontological position revealed by the experience of the camps. The degradation of the Muselmann gives rise to shame for those who witness it because we experience the truth that human life continues despite the total destruction of dignity, or humanness. Agamben argues against what he regards as the superficial and mistaken notion of survivor's guilt, and instead focuses on the "flush" of being seen, of being called intimately, radically, to one's death. The key to this flush is the fact that the call to intimate death, like the fact of survival, is meaningless. It just happens:

> Everyone dies and lives in place of another, without reason or meaning; the camp is the place in which no one can truly die or survive in his own place. Auschwitz also means this much: that man, dying, cannot find any other sense in his death than this flush, this shame.[21]

Agamben writes that in the process of becoming a subject the "man who experiences disgust recognizes himself in an alterity that cannot be assumed."[22] Shame is "the fundamental sentiment of being a subject."[23]

In chapter 5, "Trauma: A Dystopia of the Spirit," I discuss some of the ways that the concept of trauma has functioned in providing paths to a "moral high ground" in an age generally cynical about moral legitimation. The abjection of the traumatized has been an effective tool in political and aesthetic arenas in which claims of victimization trump all other arguments. "Trauma," I write, "replaced utopia in providing overriding legitimation." In Agamben's work, as well as in the work of many contemporary queer theorists, the idea of shame points to the most fundamental dimensions of traumatic abjection. The deep shame he has in mind doesn't go away when the concentration camp guard is there no more. Similarly, shame in contemporary queer theory is not dependent on persecution by active homophobes. As Ruth Leys has skillfully shown, shame is thought to be fundamental because it is said to be autotelic, independent of any object in the external world.[24] Shame is thus said to be an automatic bodily response, not just a reaction to something done to the subject. Perhaps that is why Agamben emphasizes that Auschwitz reveals the fundamental character of subjectivity that is still relevant today. The experience of shame is the marker of an experience of one's own difference; it points to our separateness from one another. As Douglas Crimp says in relation to viewing Warhol's films: "In taking on the shame, I do not share in the other's identity. I simply adopt the other's vulnerability to being shamed. In this operation, most importantly, the other's difference is preserved; it is not claimed as my own."[25] The primary ethical category revealed by shame is difference: we don't *share* in difference, we simply acknowledge "each identity's absolute difference from the other."[26] We are singled out by the blush of shame. This difference is not about what we believe, or how we act; it is a difference stemming from our subject positions and our bodies. It just is.

As Leys and Walter Benn Michaels have pointed out, over the last four decades the humanities in general and critical theory in particular have moved increasingly toward ideas that attack intention and agency as the core components of the subject and propose instead difference as the subject's defining characteristic. Michaels has argued that the result has been a devaluation of ideology and dispute, and their replacement by identity and affirmation.[27] I can acknowledge the traumas that have shaped your life or the shame that at times overwhelms you. But I can neither share it nor critically analyze it. The cultivation of abjection through trauma and shame has contributed to this process of dehistoricization by conceptualizing these states as structural yet individualizing components of subjectivity. As components of subjectivity they are marked "off limits" for political debate, trumping all other claims. Michaels has convincingly argued that as we pay our respects increasingly to histories of victimization, our political culture is impoverished by a cultivation of trauma and shame. That cultivation and its consequences are at the core of part 2 of this volume.

For many years now, Dominick LaCapra has charted a prudent, pluralistic course through the sea of theoretical, critical, and historical writings on trauma. With deep interests in deconstruction, psychoanalysis, and critical theory, LaCapra has been adept at recognizing both the challenge of the concept of the traumatic for historical representation and the temptation of the concept for those eager to escape the constraints of some connection to the real. On the one hand, he has articulated the ways in which traditional realist approaches to the past are inadequate when faced with the radical disruption of trauma for victims, perpetrators, witnesses, and even for historians writing about these events. On the other hand, he has resisted recent attempts to define all human experience via the category of the traumatic, or to resacralize the traumatic with notions of transcendence steeped in the awesome stimulation of the negative sublime. LaCapra has rejected both skepticism as to whether we can know what really happened in a horrific situation and identification with the experiences of victims in favor of a version of the psychoanalytic concept of "working through." This allows him to continually reexamine problems with hopes of getting some pragmatic handle on them: don't deny the possibility of understanding but don't promise too much.[28]

As will be clear from the essays in part 2, LaCapra's interests in trauma, the holocaust, and the sublime were part of larger developments in the fields of history, literature, and much of the humanities. The concept of trauma gained academic currency in the intellectual atmosphere of postmodernism and antifoundationalism—an atmosphere in which LaCapra breathed deeply. By the late 1980s it had become commonplace to ask the postmodern historian whether all representations of the Shoah were equally valid. The ethical turn in postmodernism has been an attempt to respond to this question without relying on some new epistemological foundation. As an event that destroys cognitive and emotional foundations, trauma has been a key concept in this ethical turn.

LaCapra has set up an important position for himself in the emerging field of those writing on memory, trauma, the holocaust, and the sublime. He has rejected those who want to see trauma as always and everywhere (should we still say "already"?) a structural part of experience that makes us all victims. In a parallel vein, he has rejected a dogged empiricism that would deny the structural elements of trauma that might allow for comparative analysis. Thus, he has been a thoughtful reader of Agamben as well as a persistent critic of the Italian philosopher's tendency to reach for the ontological at the expense of historical specificity. He has also criticized the overly cryptic and sometimes downright apocalyptic rhetoric of intellectuals seeking to ground their politics in a reversal of abjection. Although he finds much stimulation in the work of a thinker like Slavoj Žižek, LaCapra deplores Žižek's reliance on the Lacanian unhistorical notion of a "constitutive lack" as the key to understanding trauma. Moreover, he criticizes Žižek's rhetorical habit of bringing everything back to "terrifying excess," and for "his typical gesture of taking it to the limit every time" and seeing others as insufficiently radical. "One may affirm that there is a 'totally other' or enigmatic, excessive dimension in every other," LaCapra writes, "but not conclude that every other is totally other or reducible to terrifying excess."[29]

It's not just the "constitutive lack" that returns again and again in Žižek, it is a structure of antinomies that always reappears, whether the subject is Hollywood melodramas, psychoanalysis, contemporary politics, or the history of philosophy. Žižek uses a different trope of reversal than does Agamben, for whom there still is a core or a revelatory zone that speaks a Truth about the polity or the human. The reversals in Žižek point instead to an impossibility of knowing a Truth, a foreclosed zone of meaning, an antinomy without resolution. Or rather, what one knows is this impossibility (of sexual relations, of representation, of human rights); one has knowledge that there is no "truth about the polity or the human" because there will always be contradiction, antinomy. In Žižek's genealogy of what he calls "parallax logic," Kant set up the structure of antinomies, and Hegel draws out its consequences:

> [F]ar from overcoming the parallax logic, Hegel brings it from the Kantian "in itself" to "for itself." It is only Hegel who can think the parallax in its radicality, as the priority of the inherent antagonism over the multiple/failed reflection of the transcendent/impossible Thing.[30]

The Real is the shift from the noumenal to the phenomenal (and back again). The gap is never to be closed, or even "worked through." There is no solution to the antinomies. Or, as Žižek sometimes puts it: there is no Big Other.[31]

So what does one *do* with this recognition of a nonconnection? One uses it as a form of critique for any attempt to cover over impossible gaps with political, economic, or psychological solutions. The critiques are often amusing and insightful (rather than just redundant) because Žižek has an extraordinary talent for close rereadings of an astonishing variety of culture forms. The fact that he always returns to a structure of lack (or, we might say, skepticism) gives rise to LaCapra's criticism that Žižek is insufficiently historical. But Žižek isn't trying to be historical. He's writing philosophy with a political agenda of intellectual disruption. The gap that his Kant and Hegel, his Freud and Lacan, refuse to close is the hole that he wants to create by puncturing any set ideological position. There are countless examples in Žižek's work, but two fairly recent ones will suffice. In his essay on the neighbor, the philosopher is resisting the ethical turn in critical theory (represented by an increased interest in the philosopher Emmanuel Levinas) that tries to promote a kinder and gentler way of coexiting with others:

> In short, the temptation to be resisted here is the ethical "gentrification" of the neighbor, the reduction of the radically ambiguous monstrosity of the Neighbor-Thing into an Other as the abyssal point from which the call of ethical responsibility emanates.[32]

By "restor[ing] monstrosity to Levinasian face,"[33] Žižek disrupts any easy appeal to ethics. Similarly, in a recent essay on enforced enjoyment, he tweaks Judith Butler for her notion of liberatory postmodern "passionate attachments" by describing the rigid role-playing of master and slave often found in contemporary lesbian communities:

> Everything is turned back to front. Public order is no longer maintained by hierarchy, repression and strict regulation, and therefore is no longer subverted by liberating acts of transgression (as when we laugh at a teacher behind his back). Instead, we have social relations among free and equal individuals, supplemented by "passionate attachment" to an extreme form of submission, which functions as the "dirty secret," the transgressive source of libidinal satisfaction. In a permissive society, the rigidly codified, authoritarian master/slave relationship becomes transgressive. This paradox or reversal is the proper topic of psychoanalysis.[34]

Paradox or reversal in the service of rethinking contemporary earnestness is the "proper topic" of Slavoj Žižek.

It is this repetitive gesture of reversal that LaCapra dislikes. He prefers to tack among competing theoretical approaches to a problem or issue, critically evaluating work in emerging fields while also finding something useful in a variety of interventions. This conceptual and historical tacking is key to his version of "working through," quite the opposite of what he called Žižek's penchant for "taking things to the limit." For LaCapra, the compass that helps him navigate among positions is Freud's distinction between "acting out" and "working through." The former is a largely unconscious process through which we wind up repeating facets of our own problematic past, which LaCapra extends to a historian or theorist unconsciously reenacting issues that are embedded in the material being studied. The latter is a more conscious effort to confront one's emotional, intellectual, and erotic links to the past, and to one's subject. Instead of just repeating, one avoids acting out by working through one's ambivalent connections to the past.

> In working through, the person tries to gain critical distance on a problem and to distinguish . . . between past, present, and future. And working through is intimately bound up with the possibility of being an ethical and political agent. . . . Working-through involves coming to terms with extreme events, including the trauma that typically attends them, and critically engaging—but not simply reinforcing—the tendency to act out the past while nonetheless recognizing why acting out may be necessary and even compelling.[35]

LaCapra has insightfully recognized how the dynamic of repetition often plays out in trauma studies, and he is careful to emphasize that there is no bright line separating acting out and working through. There is always some repetition in every effort to understand the traumatic. Unlike Žižek's focus on an unbridgeable gap between our desires and our situation, which might lead him to point out that every "working through" is always already an acting out (and vice versa), LaCapra is committed to a theoretical practice that moves forward through critique and dialogue. He eschews the rhetorical reversals of the Lacanian theorist in favor of contingent conversations designed to explore how much we are repeating when we really mean to be moving in a particular direction.[36]

The contrast between the theorists of trauma and theorists of shame should not obscure how much of the work on both their parts has been done in relation to (and often against) psychoanalysis. The last two essays in part 2 of this volume deal directly with Freud and his legacy, the first by way of a discussion of one of his early case studies, the second in relation to his persistent relevance to the way we make meaning out of the past. In the now thirty years or so that I have been writing about Freud, I have been presenting psychoanalysis as a theory of history, as a body of work whose key concepts structured a story of the past "with which one could live." During these years there have been intense controversies over Freud's biography (was he a good man? was he a good scientist?), over the scientific credibility of psychoanalysis (did it produce testable hypotheses? does it work in a clinical setting?), and over the political or ethical value of the tradition of work that takes its bearings from Freud (is it sexist? does it deny the reality of violence against children?). Many of these controversies came to the fore around the Library of Congress exhibition, *Sigmund Freud: Conflict and Culture*, which I curated. The exhibition opened in Washington in 1998 after having been postponed due to concerns about the appropriateness of the nation's premier public library dedicating a full public presentation to Sigmund Freud. Political agitation over historical exhibitions, such as the Smithsonian's Enola Gay display, was in the air.[37] Many in the psychoanalytic establishment saw the Freud show as a vindication of their founder's importance and legitimacy. "His portrait will hang where the portraits of our founders have been hung," a New York clinician intoned. Critics of psychoanalysis (who also made their careers in the Freud industry) had a field day talking to the press about why the immoral charlatan who begat a pseudoscience had no business being exhibited in our nation's capital. Philosophers spoke of the corruption of science, while self-styled critical historians sought to expose issues ranging from the founder's alleged immoral cult building to claims of sexual impropriety.

As the curator, I regarded all of this as more fodder for the exhibition, the point of which would be neither to defend nor expose Freud. Rather, the show was to explore how the founder of psychoanalysis presented his key concepts as tools for making sense of history, and to make the point that, if we were to make sense of our own recent cultural history, we would have to figure out what to do with Freud. In addition to materials from the archives in Washington, London, and Vienna, the show included materials from popular culture (animated cartoons, television shows, movies) to provide examples of how Freud had permeated our world.

One of the contributors to the companion volume to the exhibition was Peter Kramer, a psychiatrist teaching at Brown whose *Listening to Prozac* had been a bestseller in 1993.[38] Kramer had argued that the new psychopharmacology could make people "better than well," and he advanced a conceptualization of mental illness that made an understanding of one's past all but irrelevant to successful treatment. *Listening to Prozac* was just the tip of the psychopharmacological iceberg, and companies that can profit from "successful" drugs have had a field day commissioning research and mounting massive public relations campaigns on behalf of their products. While philosophers of science were busy arguing about whether Freud's stories of patients produced testable hypotheses, and while critical historians were deep into their investigations concerning how hypnosis and mimetic attraction might have influenced the development of psychoanalysis (or whether Freud slept with his sister-in-law), drug companies created psychiatric disorders and the medications to treat them. No matter that if some years later there were troubling reports of at best marginal reductions in symptoms. The profit margins were still so attractive. Meanwhile, cognitive behavioral therapists and writers associated with them told us not to understand the past and why it continued to haunt us, but instead advised us to recode or rewrite it. When a bad memory comes to the surface, they suggested, learn how to turn it into something else! As Žižek puts it: "Thus the solution for the Wolf Man would have been to 'regress' to the parental *coitus a tergo* and then rewrite the scene so that what he saw was merely his parents lying on the bed, his father reading a newspaper and his mother a sentimental novel."[39]

The pharmaceutical and insurance industries have no interest in the patient pursuit of working through the past, and to be fair there is no especially good reason to bet on a dramatic alleviation of suffering through a talking cure. I make no claims as to whether or not the suffering of patients with mental illness should be treated with techniques that have evolved since Freud developed psychoanalysis by "falling into" listening to his patients. Instead, I want to underscore the contrast between the perspective of psychoanalysis and that of medical practitioners who seem to long for a naturalist explanation of mental anguish as physical illness. If there is a "chemical imbalance" or one is not "in harmony" with one's environment, perhaps balance and harmony can be restored through expert (outside) intervention. Or, if we can redescribe our seemingly strange behaviors as adaptations to some distant evolutionary dynamic, we can feel "in tune" with both nature and the scientific. The psychoanalytic perspective, by contrast, assumes no natural harmony and asserts instead that there is constitutive conflict for human self-consciousness and desire. Desire is not "sustainable" at the level of the individual. We are not "green."[40] Freud's psychoanalysis, and the transference neurosis between analyst and analysand on which it depended, never assumed that relations were naturally healthy, or that some relations were more natural than others. Human relations can never be fully satisfying, from a Freudian perspective, because our own desires are in conflict with one another, and we must always negotiate the particularities of our precarious "fit" with others. The fit is always precarious because it will be renegotiated as new desires and memories come into play. There is no natural balance for which to strive, no evolutionary train that we should be hopping aboard. That's why small gains in self-consciousness based on working through our sense of the past, making meaning out of memory, is so important in the psychoanalytic framework. Creating a past with which one can live matters because it gives one a sense of freedom, of constructing one's relationship to one's past and desires. If we no longer consider the past and its representations relevant to our well-being in the present, then we will indeed have a very different culture and politics in the future—one in which freedom through self-consciousness will count for little.

Part 3: Postmodernism and Cultural Politics

The third group of essays in this volume addresses issues related to postmodern, antifoundational theory, especially as it is connected to scholarship and politics. The opening pieces are critical reflections on key trends in contemporary scholarship in the wake of postmodernism. In the first, I explore why certain theorists or historians become "intellectual sponsors" for contemporary scholarship. Aby Warburg was resurrected as such a sponsor for a variety of cultural-contextual approaches to art. The next two essays are concerned with prominent theorists of history. The first, Keith Jenkins, remains committed to the rhetoric of antifoundationalism and radical experimentation, but he has hedged his bets by trying to reinscribe the playful celebration of contingency in a recognizably progressive political agenda. The second theorist, Frank Ankersmit, presents a more complicated story because he is trying to become a post- postmodernist by grabbing onto a notion of sublime experience as a new sort of ecstatic anchoring of scholarly and aesthetic practice. Ankersmit seems to have arrived at a perspective that envisions both the weakness of traditional empiricism and the poverty of antifoundationalism. In the concept of the sublime, he thinks he has found an antidote to the linguistic skepticism of the last few decades, but I conclude that his efforts to target an unmediated fluidity with the world are at best contradictory exhortations for more ecstasy through recognition of trauma and tragedy. By contrast, in a brief consideration of the poet Anne Carson's volume *Decreation,* I acknowledge how her consideration of "getting the self out of the way" reminds us of forms of pleasure and loss that are key facets of our aesthetic, religious, and philosophical traditions. She explores these traditions in ways that invite our interest and even participation, but she never presumes to authorize.

The final essay of part 3 examines the collection of essays on which the philosopher Richard Rorty worked at the end of his life. His book brings together his efforts to rethink the practice of philosophy as a form of cultural politics, and the reader will see that I have enormous sympathy and admiration for this project. Rorty thought that once we recognized that the philosophical task was not the creation of secure foundations for our beliefs, once we recognized that the goal of critical theory was not the accumulation of complex aporias, then we could get on to the real work of substantial thinking: energizing our efforts to make our world more just and more free. Philosophical "redescriptions" should engender conversations that enable us to act as citizens capable of creating a society that would live up to our aspirations for it. If Rorty the postmodern antifoundationalist exposed the philosophical language games that were holding us hostage to intellectual authority, Rorty the political pragmatist worked to restore a belief in democracy as the best vehicle for eroding inequality and inspiring solidarity.

Part 4: Photography and Piety

Here photography and video take center stage in essays of very different styles and lengths. The first two pieces are concerned with the ways that photography's powerful vision also creates new forms of blindness. How does the ubiquity of photographic representation affect the experiences we document with the medium's tools? Do we relate to time differently because of the power now at our fingertips to slice it or freeze it in perfect, or at least memorable, moments? How do our notions of historical representation change when traces of the past seem available to us in two-dimensional form? Given the appearance of literalism in photographic processes, are there some things that should never be represented?

In "Photographic Ambivalence," I explore how our notions of the past are inflected by photography. In the late nineteenth century, blindness to duration was conceptualized as the price paid for photographic precision. Since the late twentieth century, blindness to our own desires, or inauthenticity, has been underlined as the price of photographic ubiquity. These forms of blindness, however, are not so much disabilities to be overcome as they are aspects of modern consciousness to be acknowledged. Photography's indexicality combined with its reproducibility gives rise to photographic ambivalence. As with other forms of ambivalence, I argue that we should be less concerned with diluting its constitutive tensions than with learning to live with its conflicted possibilities.

"Why Photography Matters to the Theory of History" considers recent books by the art historians Georges Didi-Huberman and Michael Fried. The former's study is concerned with epistemological and ethical questions that arise from visual representations of the Shoah, while the latter's is concerned with the ontological possibilities explored by contemporary art photography. The books have two things in common: an argument against postmodern skepticism, and an insistence that photography has become a field in which questions of history, truth, and authenticity are being explored with particular acuity. Rather than reject even the possibility that photographs have something to tell us about the Shoah, Didi-Huberman shows that they can offer important insights into the difficulties and the possibilities of apprehending aspects of the past. Fried shows that contemporary photographic work has taken on the ambitions of high modernism by accepting the challenge of "to-be-seenness"—the challenge of acknowledging the gaze of the spectator. Photography as a "historical practice" does not escape from the difficulties of evidence and of the "constructed" nature of historical understanding; photography functions neither as a pure trace of the past, nor as a mere invitation to spectacle.

The last two essays in this section offer brief reflections on two artists whose practices are in dialogue with many of the theoretical issues concerning photography and representation. The first, "Ordinary Film," concerns *The Maelstrom*, a piece by Hungarian director Péter Forgács, who has for many years woven intricate, moving videos based on found footage (mostly home movies). I became interested in Forgács's projects as representations of the past that are also traces of it. The complexity of his storytelling is balanced with a deceptively simple presentation, creating a powerful way of telling the truth about history. The multiple temporalities at play in watching his film remind viewers of the historical whirlpool swirling around some of the most ordinary moments of daily life.

The final essay in this section was a contribution to a project by Californian photographer David Maisel. His *Library of Dust* is a large format artist book with arresting images of metal canisters containing the cremated remains of patients from the Oregon State Hospital for the Insane. Maisel had read about the controversy in Salem concerning the inadequate storage and labeling of these remains, and about efforts of relatives of the deceased to reclaim the ashes that "belonged to them." Maisel asked me to write an essay for his book that would evoke the historical context of the asylum, and I was drawn to the project's sober yet beautiful effort to memorialize people whose illnesses may have already had driven them into anonymity. The state hospital was in many ways a land of the unknown, and Maisel's photographs (at least) acknowledges this. On the other hand, no images are really capable of returning identity to these lost remains, and Maisel knows one can't get beyond the surface with the camera. *Library of Dust* is an admirable example of the productivity of the ambivalence of photography for historical consciousness.

The essays in this section all deal with the effort to turn oneself toward a relation to traces from the past that acknowledges both their otherness and the connection one can make with them. When one discovers the home movies of a murdered family, what is one's proper relation to the material? How should one act on the desire to represent the history of this family and also to acknowledge its loss? Forgács answers that question by making *The Maelstrom*, and Maisel deals with a related set of issues in *Library of Dust*. Rather than striving only for accuracy, or only for making a political or ethical argument, both artists also strive for what I have called piety, an acknowledgement of the existence of the past, and of the capacity of what-has-been to make a claim on us. The ambivalence of photographic representation—the combination of its indexicality and malleability—underscores the dimension of piety in a particularly powerful way. By using the word "piety" I do not mean to evoke some necessarily transcendent or theological aspect to one's relation to the past. I do mean to evoke recognition that we sometimes strive to relate to what-has-been in ways that are not reducible to a quest for empirical veracity or pragmatic appropriation.

Coda: Risks and Limits of Liberal Education

The brief essays that comprise the last section of this volume form a coda to the rest, dealing from a more institutional perspective with critical thinking, liberal learning, and teaching. As I mentioned at the beginning of this introduction, I became president of Wesleyan University in the summer of 2007, after having completed seven years as president of the California College of the Arts. During this period of administrative responsibility, I have continued to teach regularly and to contribute to scholarly conversations as best I can, but much of my professional time has been dedicated to institutions of liberal learning. At CCA this took the form of shaping an arts school long known for its devotion to craft to become also a center for education through the arts. The artists, designers, and architects at CCA are not only impressive practitioners, they are educators and students developing ways of thinking and making that will be reservoirs from which they will continue to draw. Wesleyan University has long been an innovator in the liberal arts, and as its president I have tried to build upon a vision of liberal learning that will remain relevant and vital in the decades to come.

A commitment to liberal learning is one of the distinctive features of American higher education. Our universities, we are often told, are the envy of the world. Most of the most highly rated research institutions are on American soil, and their focused productivity is built on the combination of flexibility and focus offered by their undergraduate divisions. Liberal education grows out of this combination, cultivating the soil for specialized achievement with the seeds of free inquiry and experimentation. Schools in this country draw talented people from around the world, and national university systems that are much more specialized—be they in the United Kingdom, China, or Singapore—are now looking to the American liberal arts for effective tools in preparing graduates for a lifetime of learning. Yet our elite colleges and universities are often plagued by self-doubt or by the lack of clear, shared objectives. Many scholars, especially in the humanities and the interpretative social sciences, find their intellectual legitimation in a critique of institutions like the very ones that support their research. Economically, many universities have been thrown into crisis as public support has waned and private funding sources have been depleted.

While institutional critique and economic pressures have taken their toll, there have also been internal critiques of liberal education from two important groups: those who desire education to be more immediately applicable to the working lives of students, and those who desire education to reflect a greater diversity of cultural sources. Both desires aim at greater relevance: the first through connecting what you learn in class to the job you are going to have after school; the second through connecting what you learn in class to a greater range of cultures and identities. These calls for relevance are closely linked to the profound change from the 1950s through the 1970s in the demographics of higher education. As a larger and larger percentage of students have expected to receive some form of college education, the pressure for "relevance" has also increased. This pressure has been intensified in our time by protracted economic crisis, cynicism, and fear about the future.

In the final essays of this volume, I call for a pragmatic, reflexive approach to the liberal arts. This is an approach that remains poised for self-criticism, but also for addressing problems and seizing opportunities. One of the regular surprises of this kind of education is the recognition of our own blindness, of our failure to see, our failure to connect with people and materials that have something to teach us. Through this kind of recognition, students and teachers learn to develop the capacity to translate from one case, one situation, to another. Remembering to look for what William James called the "whole inward significance" of another's situation is a crucial dimension to an education that takes us beyond the borders of our comfort zone. So is learning to see things by what Emerson called "animating" the world:

> We animate what we can and we see only what we animate. Nature and books belong to the eyes that see them. It depends on the mood of the person whether he shall see the sunset or the fine poem. There are always sunsets and there is always genius. But only a few hours so serene that we can relish nature or criticism.[41]

Education should deepen our ability to animate the world and not just criticize it; education should help us bring things to life. This is an enormous gift. Bringing things to life through creative intelligence is so much more important than being able to show somebody why something they thought was alive is really dead. That move will show how smart one is but does no good. When we can use our education to animate, we harness it in the service of life and not just in the service of being smart.

Emerson said, "Nature and books belong to the eyes that see them. It depends on the mood of the person whether he shall see the sunset or the fine poem." Education should help us have access to moods that open our eyes and ears. Education at its best teaches us to take the world's sights and sounds to animate our own and perhaps someone else's imagination. At its best, education develops the capacities for seeing possibilities in the world and for relishing the world around us across borders we might not have dared cross before. Education must lead us beyond these borders if it is to be more than training to assume a position that has already been allocated for us.

A reflexive, pragmatic education would enhance our capacities for freedom because it would help us to experience the world and understand ourselves without excessive dependence on unquestioned authority. There is no formula for determining how much dependence is appropriate, just as there are no firm criteria for determining how we should live with the past. The reader will see that my approach to education owes much to my perspective on history and psychoanalysis. By underscoring the reflexive dimensions of education, I mean to keep open the door of self-criticism, to remain committed to a reexamination of one's assumptions. By underscoring the pragmatic dimensions of education, I mean to embrace Dewey's insight that a commitment to inquiry should replace a commitment to Truth, and Rorty's notion that inquiry can animate hope and politics, giving us greater capacity to "reshape ourselves." The liberal learning I envision helps us live with the past without being dominated by it, while opening the possibility of sharing our lives with others. This is education for freedom, at least the kind of freedom available to us when we acknowledge that we also live with the past.

PART 1

NINETEENTH-CENTURY MALADIES OF MEMORY

1. Remembering Forgetting

Maladies de la Mémoire in Nineteenth-Century France

Thus even a happy life is possible without remembrance, as the beast shows: but life in any true sense is absolutely impossible without forgetfulness.

NIETZSCHE

A little insomnia is not without its value in making us appreciate sleep, in throwing a ray of light upon that darkness. An unfailing memory is not a very powerful incentive to the study of the phenomenon of memory.

PROUST

The attempt to understand how a culture lives with or against its past often leads to a consideration of rituals, ceremonies, monuments, and written history. When we want to know about the ways people recollect the past and represent it, we want to know about individual as well as social memory. Individual memory is notoriously difficult to comprehend, and we are currently witnessing resurgences of interest both in social memory and in the ways in which the brain stores and organizes memories. The works of Oliver Sacks and Israel Rosenfield have brought neurobiology to a popular audience, and treatments of the latest trends in brain research on memory by the press and by television have called attention to the mechanisms of memory.[1] Such public concerns with memory and with the investigation of it can be considered screens on which a culture projects its anxieties about repetition, change, representation, authenticity, and identity. By examining cultural imaginations of remembering and forgetting we can learn much about cultural investments in questions about continuity and change.

The end of the nineteenth century in France was also a period in which there was great interest in the mechanisms of memory, especially in their malfunctions. The expressions of this interest can be considered to be what

Pierre Nora and his collaborators have called a "*lieu de mémoire*." Maladies of memory attracted the curiosity of doctors, philosophers, and the popular press because they seemed to be phenomena in which one could discover the secrets of conservation and reproduction. Moreover, memory disturbances became a specific kind of problem—a problem not only of recall but of disease, the representations of which contained important lessons about the brain, the self, responsibility, and normality. In the age of the ideology of progress and of the reality of the accelerating disappearance of traditional society, conservation and reproduction were no longer to be the province only of popular memory. But the medicalization of memory included a certain amnesia. In other words, the new discourse about maladies of memory depended in part on a blindness to the status of this discourse itself. Sander Gilman has noted how in the depiction of disease, "The fear we have of our own collapse does not remain internalized. Rather, we project this fear onto the world in order to localize it, and, indeed, to domesticate it."[2] Professional as well as popular curiosity generated many tales about people who suffered from their memories or from the lack of them, as it also fed the need to explain in a rational way, or organize into acceptable categories, what seemed to be bizarre phenomena. What are we to make of these stories and explanations, which often seem to merge into a single, paradoxical series of narratives? At the very least, we should begin to notice how the representation of maladies of memory in the medical narratives of case studies project a concern with, and perhaps anxiety about, what the normal or healthy relation of past and present might be.

However the interest in memory disorders may be symptomatic of the ways contemporaries viewed the use and abuse of the past, I think we can see that in late-nineteenth-century France the discourse about conserving and reproducing the past was also a discourse about what it meant to be normal in the present. Not surprisingly, when moderns want to know about the normal relation to the past, they accumulate examples of the abnormal. Here I shall simply indicate how three *maladies de la mémoire*—amnesia, hypermnesia, and periodic amnesia—were crucial for those trying to define how much of the past we need to be able to recapture, and when too much of the past captures us. I shall sketch briefly some of the immediate contexts for the investigation of amnesia, hypermnesia, and periodic amnesia and discuss three scientific approaches to the disorders. We shall see how Théodul Ribot, professor at the Collège de France and a major figure in late-nineteenth-century French psychology and philosophy, constituted amnesia as a scientific and clinical problem, and how Albert Guillon, a clinician in Bordeaux during the same period, used the study of hypermnesia to determine when too much memory is unhealthy. Finally, we shall briefly discuss Eugène Azam's case of periodic amnesia, or multiple personality, Félida X.

A great admirer of Hippolyte Taine and Herbert Spencer, Ribot was enormously influential. The founder of the *Revue philosophique de la France et de l'étranger*, he aimed to make both psychology and philosophy more scientific. Guillon, on the other hand, never emerged from the shadow of his *maître* Emmanuel Régis, but his thesis on hypermnesia reflects some of the important trends in nineteenth-century French psychiatry. Azam was also a clinician in Bordeaux, but he became well known throughout French scientific circles because of his work on the case of Félida. All three agreed with Nietzsche's idea that forgetfulness is necessary for life "in any true sense," but they went on to specify how much forgetting made for a normal life, and when too much forgetting was a sign of disease. Their work on maladies of memory is framed by an effort to differentiate the disorders they write about from the normal workings of memory and from the order of their own observations. These figures were part of a large constellation of professionals who at the end of the nineteenth century helped create the representation of the healthy human individual as the embodiment of a particular connection between past and present. The scientistic discourse that we shall examine in this essay helped foster a forgetting that this connection was a cultural construction and not a natural discovery. The study of *maladies de la mémoire* should contribute to our comprehension of how our relations with our pasts have been conditioned by expectations about how much conservation and reproduction of the past is good for us.

Not Enough: Localizing and Ordering Amnesia

Amnesia was a disease of the nineteenth century. It was discussed at the end of the eighteenth century by Francisco Boissier de Sauvages in his classification of medical disorders, but it was the next century that first paid attention to it and gave it importance as a phenomenon that shed light on the normal functioning of memory.[3] And it was in the second half of that century that the study of amnesia became a principal vehicle for understanding the dynamics of memory. In the 1819 *Dictionnaire des sciences médicales*, the article on "*mémoire: maladies de la*" is twenty-eight pages long, while the article on "*amnésie*" has only several lines. In the 1865 *Dictionnaire encyclopédique des sciences médicales* there is a dense, seventeen-page entry on "*amnésie*," with only a few lines devoted to the entry "*mémoire*."[4] Defined as the total or partial loss of memory, amnesia is not to be confused with forgetting specific experiences of the past. Instead, amnesia is conceived as a disturbance in the *faculty* of memory—a disturbance that either prevents the mental storage of the past or that inhibits our conscious access to the *past as past* which is encoded in the brain.

There are several reasons for the abundance of nineteenth-century writing about amnesia.[5] The first is that this was the great period of professionalization of French psychiatry, and that there was suddenly much writing about many kinds of psychiatric disturbances. As Jan Goldstein has shown, classification of disorders was one of the principal vehicles for the establishment of psychiatry as a profession.[6] We can add that amnesia was a particularly important phenomenon in this regard because it was, in Ribot's phrase, both a "biological and a psychological fact." Thus we find that Ribot's *Revue philosophique* not only was the organ for his own writings on memory dysfunctions but also welcomed reports from psychiatrists, neurologists, and philosophers interested in how memory is affected by such diverse phenomena as sleep, trauma, dreams, disease, and hypnotism. In other words, understanding amnesia was the philosopher's and the clinician's route to understanding memory in a way that would show not only how the brain works but also how we know who we are. And the claims of both to have scientific knowledge of the former were used to legitimate their authority to speak on the latter.

Earlier, phrenology had an important influence on the ways in which psychology and biology were linked via the brain and skull. Phrenology was imported to Paris from Vienna in the first decade of the nineteenth century, and its founder, Franz Josef Gall, played a major role in relating specific parts of the brain to specific human characteristics. Although the phrenologist's claim that the characteristics of the brain could be determined by examining the skull was ultimately rejected, the idea that the brain was the organ of the mind remained a crucial component of physiological psychiatry until the end of the century.[7]

A decisive step in relating memory and the brain was taken in 1861 by Paul Broca, who claimed that a lesion in the left side of the brain was the cause of the loss of a specific linguistic function. The moral of Broca's case study was taken to be the following: memory images are stored in discrete sections of the brain. Trauma to a part of the brain can affect our recall of the memories contained therein. Carl Wernicke's work on auditory aphasia in 1874 added more credence to the theory that specific kinds of memories are to be found in clearly delimited portions of the brain. As Robert M. Young has noted, the "literature on cerebral localization after 1873 became so extensive that contemporary reviewers listed hundreds of references."[8] The scientific study of memory worked within the strong paradigm of cerebral localization. Understanding how the brain was put together was thought to be a key to the analysis of specific memory dysfunctions.

The doctrine of cerebral localization served well those French psychiatrists anxious to link their treatments with the more firmly established science of neurobiology.[9] A disturbance of memory would thus be caused by a lesion or an "inflammation" of a part of the brain. The cause could either be "moral" or physical, but the effect would be described in either case in relation to a particular part of the brain. When Ribot published *Les Maladies de la mémoire* in 1881, he related many cases of individuals who suffered head injuries and could not remember any events from very specific periods of time. After certain physical trauma, either experiences are not registered by the brain or access to storage areas of memory or the stored images themselves are destroyed. On the other hand, Ribot also discussed many cases of amnesia where the lines between "moral" and physical etiology are blurred:

> A shoemaker, overcome by an epileptic mania the day of his wedding, stabs his father-in-law to death. Coming to his senses after a few days, he had not the slightest knowledge of what he had done.[10]

> A young woman, married to a man she loved passionately, during labor fell into a deep coma, after which she had lost the memory of the time that had passed since her marriage inclusively. She remembered very exactly all the rest of her life until then. At first she rejected with fear her husband and child when they were brought to her. Since then, she has never recovered the memory of this period of her life, nor the events that accompanied it. Through the authority of their testimony, her parents and friends persuaded her that she was married and that she had a son. She believed them because she preferred to think that she had lost the memory of a year rather than believing that they were all imposters. But her conviction, her *conscience intime*, had nothing to do with this. She saw before her her husband and her child without being able to imagine

> by what magic she had acquired one and brought the other into the world. (61)[11]

Ribot explains the shoemaker's partial amnesia as caused by the weakened consciousness that was brought about by the epileptic mania. The artisan did not have a problem of recall because the experience of his wedding day was never registered in his brain in the first place. Instead, the events that took place during his mania were like the events that we experience in a dream. While we sleep, Ribot pointed out, our consciousness is extremely weakened. So it was for the murderous shoemaker. Although he was more than a little active on his wedding day, his activity was not accompanied by sufficiently intense consciousness of what he was doing:

> How to explain amnesia in cases where there have been states of consciousness? By the extreme weakness of these states. A state of consciousness is fixed definitively only by two means: intensity, repetition. . . . Here there is neither intensity nor repetition. (58)

The nervous system is capable of directing action without recording it because "a nervous state, sufficient for determining certain acts, is insufficient for awakening consciousness" (60). If consciousness is intense enough, memories are recorded and stored in their proper place in the brain.

The second case of wedding amnesia just described presented different problems for the philosophical psychologist. Here it was clear that the experience is at some point registered but subsequently lost to memory. Ribot describes a situation in which either memory residues or the faculty of reproducing these images is destroyed by illness. A "cerebral commotion" could be responsible for partial amnesia once one assumes that different faculties and even different memories are located in specific parts of the brain or nervous system. The significance of the memories themselves is not considered (why the marriage?), since what counted as an explanation is trauma to parts of the nervous system, not parts of one's life that might be too traumatic (passionate?) to be recollected.

Ribot's study of amnesia becomes more complex when he considers periodic amnesia. Here forgetting takes place during a certain time, and then memory returns only to be followed by new episodes of forgetting. In this regard Ribot claims that an understanding of the phenomenon would require a separate work on personality aberrations and diseases (75).[12] In cases of periodic amnesia one is justified in talking about two faculties of memory in a single individual, each located in separate parts of the brain. The first may include all of a person's experience and the second only a part, or neither faculty of memory may have access to the other. The latter is described as two-way amnesia. In other words, we see here the popular late-nineteenth-century "disease" of split personality.[13]

As Ian Hacking has pointed out, the concept of a split personality was used as a tool by positivist psychologists aiming to undermine the notion of a self independent of experience.[14] As Ribot says:

> Let us put aside the idea of a self conceived as an entity distinct from states of consciousness. It is a useless and contradictory hypothesis, an explanation worthy of psychology in a stage of infancy. . . . I join with the opinion of contemporaries who see in the conscious person a composite, a result of very complex states. (82–83)

Now that psychology is a mature, positive science, the self can be considered as the "sum of states of consciousness" (82–83). In the following passage—which provides further evidence of the importance of "oculocentrism" in modern French culture—Ribot ties the self to memory:

> The mechanism of consciousness is comparable, without metaphor [!], to that of vision. With the latter, there is a visual *point* that alone makes a perception clear and precise: around it, there is a visual *field* that decreases in clearness and in precision insofar as the point is further from the center and brought closer to the circumference. Our self at each moment—this present perpetually renewed—is in large part nourished by memory. That is to say, our present state is associated with other states that, rejected and localized in the past, constitute our person such as it appears at each instant. . . . It would seem, according to this account, that the identity of the self rests entirely on memory. (83)[15]

Thus, at every moment our sense of ourselves is dependent on the proper placement of the past *as past*. The "placement" is literally in the brain; the past *is*, and it is in us.

The idea of the *being* of the past and the problem of where to place it was later to be forcefully explored by Henri Bergson in his *Matière et Mémoire*

(1896). Bergson, however, emphatically rejects the localization of the past in the brain. He argues instead that just as our faculty of perception does not undermine the real existence of matter, our faculty of recall does not undermine the real existence of the past. For him, unlike Ribot, the "real existence of the past" is not at all dependent on the brain. Bergson compares the brain to a central telephone exchange that only allows us to connect with the past.[16] Disturbances such as amnesia and aphasia are only malfunctions in our ability to reach out and link our action with the past, not destructions of memories that are engraved in the matter of the brain.

Bergson's effort to found a *nouveau spiritualisme* is a long way from the late-nineteenth-century scientific mainstream in which Ribot successfully navigated.[17] The positivist psychologist did not attempt to carve out the relation between body and spirit but assumed that the brain is the organ of the mind. Ribot was concerned not only with the localization of memory but with distinguishing it from perception of the present, and also from the imaginary. "Localizing" experiences in the past should not, however, break the continuity of these experiences with our present. Normal identity, according to the psychologist, is based on this continuity. If at different moments we are nourished by memories that are foreign to one another—if, in other words, a person has more than one constellation of memories that are not linked together—this periodic amnesia results in the fragmentation of personality. Of course, a fragmented personality is thought to be a disease only when a unified personality with a continuous connection to the remembered past is taken as a criterion of health.

There is no continuity for the murderous shoemaker. His weakened consciousness during the mania means that there is a gap in his history—a break in the connection of past and present. This break is mended by the narrative case study, which makes sense of the discontinuity as the sign of disease. How could the artisan be responsible for his actions when he had no consciousness and, hence, no conscience during the attack? With this question amnesia entered into the debates about legal responsibility during this period. If there is no memory, then there is no *conscience*, and perhaps no responsibility. This was the argument used by the psychiatrist Auguste Motet to convince a tribunal that his twenty-eight-year-old patient with "a nervous temperament . . . and feminine allures" was not responsible for a "public offense of decency" because he had no memory of his actions during his spontaneous hypnotic trances.[18] For Ribot, there was still no explanation of why there are cases in which consciousness suddenly evaporates, since neither physiology nor psychology has any knowledge of the genesis of *conscience* (59). Alfred Fouillée took the philosopher to task on this point. For Fouillée, Ribot and those who thought like him could never understand memory and consciousness because they saw indivisible, instantaneous sensations as their component parts.[19]

> The indivisibility and the instantaneousness of consciousness is the nothingness of consciousness. The flash is seen only on condition of no longer being in us a flash, but a continuity of light having a certain duration; the indivisible flash would be invisible.[20]

Thus the problem for Ribot, a problem that Fouillée thought insoluble in the positivist paradigm, was to understand how indivisible moments can create continuity. If memory is made up of instants, how does consciousness find a *sens* in the past?[21] Ribot did not answer this question in either psychological or physiological terms, but he did make a commitment to continuity as a fundamental feature of the normal personality, and his conceptualization and organization of memory disorders affirmed (and depended on) this commitment.

Continuity was key for Ribot, and one of the primary goals of *Les Maladies de La mémoire* was to organize amnesia in such a way that the disorder would have a comprehensible order of development. We can see this most clearly in his discussion of progressive amnesia. The development of the disease that undermines the continuity necessary for normal identity could be normalized by showing how its pathological progression is in fact continuous. This malady is ideally captured in the narrative genre of the case study, which promotes the perception of continuity and closure. The disorder does not have to be forced into a narrative, since it seems to exist in narrative form. As Ribot noted, the path of the disease is very simple and instructive, "because in showing how memory is disorganized, it shows us how memory is organized" (90).

There is no need here to go into the discussion of progressive amnesia in detail, only to note that for Ribot the path of forgetting proceeds from the unstable and often recent past to the stable ideas and sentiments that we remembered long ago. In this regard he cites a case used by Taine:

> Recently we have seen in Russia a famous astronomer forget successively the events of the preceding day, then those of the year, then those of recent years, and thus so on the gap continued to grow, until finally he retained nothing but the memory of events of his childhood. One believed he was lost. But, by a sudden halt and an

> unpredicted return, the gap was filled in the inverse direction. The events of youth became visible, then those of maturity, then the most recent, and finally those of yesterday. His memory was completely restored when he died. (96)[22]

This strange little story had a simple moral for Ribot. Forgetting is not arbitrary; its development obeys laws that can be articulated by the scientist. Rather than undermining our ideas of normal memory, the bizarre tales of progressive and partial amnesia collected by Ribot and others enabled them to have a clearer and more detailed notion of the normal workings of memory than they would have had otherwise. The narrative form of the tales relieves their strangeness by conveying a sense of closure. "When we have an exact idea of what we mean by the word *memory*," he says, "all the marvelous evaporates, and the [bizarre] facts, far from surprising, appear as natural and logical consequences of a morbid influence" (106).

The seemingly bizarre type of partial amnesia to which Ribot attached the most importance was the amnesia of signs, which he distinguished from aphasia more generally. He describes disturbances of memory that are manifested in the form of linguistic disorders as above all diseases of *la mémoire motrice* (122). In other words, what is forgotten in the amnesia of signs is the constellation of means we have "for expressing our sentiments and ideas." The sentiments and ideas themselves, that is, remain intact in the brain; the disturbance amounts to our forgetting how to "translate" these ideas and sentiments into expressions (124). Intelligence, according to this model, remains unimpaired, although the *forms* of language might be lost. Ribot was aware of the difficulties in establishing the existence of ideas that have no way of being communicated, although when only certain forms of expression are affected (written or oral), he felt he was on firm ground. In any case, the amnesia of signs, if not part of complete dementia, must undermine our "interior speech" (129).

Ribot concluded his discussion of the amnesia of signs with a model of the progression of the forgetting of linguistic expression. First rational language, then emotional language are lost to memory, and in extreme cases even gestures are forgotten. The signs most vulnerable to amnesia are those that are the least frequently repeated; those that resist forgetting are those that we first learn to use and that form the basis of our linguistic functions. "The evolution of language takes place, as one should expect, in the order inverse to that of its dissolution" (134). Thus, the disorder of memory and signs is used as evidence of the order of the "natural" and individual development of language.

The philosopher/psychologist thus conceptualized and organized the maladies of memory by recalling the stages of their development. Ribot historicized amnesia in order to emplot it as a phenomenon that would illuminate our normal, healthy connection to our remembered past. The structure of the development of the disorder thus reveals an order that recalls the development of language and also the positivist account of the development of the sciences. Amnesia is not bizarre or marvelous; it consists of certain stages that must be seen in their proper narrative sequence and interrelation. Ribot's "law of regression" explained the development of a disease, but the law also affirmed its inverse: the healthy progression from simple to complex, from emotions to reason, that should explain development of our normal connections to the remembered past.

Too Much: Hypermnesia and the Disorder of the Present

Ribot did not discuss hypermnesia, "*les exaltations de la mémoire*," in detail, but he did devote a brief chapter to it. Although "one man's amnesia is another's hypermnesia," he viewed the latter as a "necessary correlative" of the former (140, 143). For the psychologist, the symptoms of hypermnesia—a "great mass of memories surging in all directions"—show again that "memory consists in memories" (140, 143). Furthermore, the disease of too much memory was important conceptually for Ribot because it allowed him to situate normality between amnesia and hypermnesia. Memory is connected to the "fundamental condition of life," conservation and reproduction (163). Conservation can be explained in reference to specific areas of the brain, and reproduction in relation to a sequence of stages. Normality depends on conservation without an excess of reproduction. Amnesia and hypermnesia allow us to fix the normal by illuminating its borders.

Albert Guillon, a naval physician, provided a detailed discussion of hypermnesia in his thesis, also called *Les Maladies de la mémoire*, published in Paris in 1897. Guillon subscribed to the view that nothing which makes an impression on our minds (*esprit*) can disappear, and viewed hypermnesia as a break in the harmony of our mental faculties. For Guillon, "disharmony" is the fundamental sign of a malfunctioning of cerebral organization, and "disharmony becomes more extreme as the disease is more serious."[23] Too much memory, or memories that we no longer control, destroy our psychological balance.

Guillon discussed many cases in this regard, for example that of Monsieur X, the reclusive and celibate bourgeois who memorized the Bible and the names of railway stations in all of Europe and parts of Asia, Africa, and America. Monsieur X

> began very young to apply himself to this study of the names of railway stations. His mother had him recite them, and admired him when he knew them well. *Today he spends long hours reading aloud and repeating their names.* Going to sleep rather late, he awakes at dawn and begins this work above all in the morning in the long, covered paths of his park. . . . If during a mealtime conversation something leads to his favorite subject, he begins his litanies and keeps at it for at least a quarter hour, speaking about railway connections. Indeed, he is very proud of this genre of knowledge. (82)[24]

But the problem of Monsieur X is not simply that his memory of train lines is too strong. Rather, the strength of this memory shows that his life, *as a whole,* is unbalanced. Never having "the least" sexual relation, he "pushes prudishness to the point of being shocked by the nudity of museum paintings" (80). More generally, Monsieur X is

> incapable of spontaneous reasoning. He has no imagination; lacks absolutely *d'esprit*, and his relationships have no charm; when he wants to apply himself to his studies, he abandons everyone and will not be disturbed by anybody. (83)

Thus, the malady of Monsieur X does not consist in his remembering too much but in his cultivation of memory having replaced a more "harmonious" life. He has been, Guillon notes, "singularly deluded by the incessant exercise" of his memory. The doctor goes on to speculate that we have here an example of real monomania, with the *idée fixe* so closely tied to memory as to deserve the name *mnémomane* (85).

Harmony, for Guillon, like continuity for Ribot, expressed his idea that an individual life has to make sense as a coherent whole. The exaltation of memory is a sign that the healthy, well-rounded personality has been lost. Indeed, in his narrating the stories of aberrations caused by too much memory, Guillon attempted to restore a meaningful order to a fractured, nonsensical life. His narrative put the unbalanced memory back into a total picture by showing the nefarious results of the exaltation. Normality and a meaningful narrative triumph as excess is placed in the proper perspective—the perspective of the healthy. Memory, not just forgetting, is threatening to the doctor seeking to affirm the normal.

The "most curious" case of hypermnesia that Guillon discussed concerned a thirty-year-old tailor who was diagnosed in an asylum as suffering from manic excitation and "delusions of grandeur." Guillon draws on the work of his teacher, Emmanuel Régis, in relating this case:

> The patient had received only the most rudimentary instruction. But, under the empire of his madness he began to write letters, memoirs, and verse in which we find again the trace of a surprising exaltation of his memory. The most remarkable fact . . . is the following: a few days after entering the asylum the patient began to write a complete history of the siege of Paris during the last war, thus of the Commune. No fact was lacking in it; the smallest anecdotal or technical details, the names of officers or of soldiers who were distinguished or killed in a particular affair . . . nothing was missing from this work, which the author entitled *Mémoires d'un vrai parisien*. But, in order to write this history so precise, so exact even in its smallest details, the patient had no books, no documents. . . . *Everything* was written from memory. (184)[25]

Guillon, given precious access to the tailor's writings by his teacher, quotes at length from the history of the Commune, a narrative "which would not be disavowed by a sane [*sensé*] historian" (186). Indeed, the manuscript, "scratched with a pencil without any mistakes" by a "*pauvre fou* in his cell, without the aid of any dictionary," was written "only with the resources of his overexcited memory" (187).

The difficulty for the doctor was not so much to show how a manic and delirious patient in an asylum could write a thorough and readable historical narrative, but to explain how a tailor with little education could do so:

> When one rereads carefully his inflamed prose, one finds there the clichés dear to journalists. The patient who, like every good Parisian, reads each day his newspaper, collected these expressions despite himself. He rediscovers them under the rule of his exaltation, and . . . his sewing as a talented tailor the costume of the harlequin

> from everyday expressions is by itself a pretty proof of the exaltation of his memory. Let us not forget above all that we are speaking here of a man who received an insufficient education. (188)

Memory, not intelligence or education, enables the *pauvre fou* to sew together a historical narrative. But Guillon also wanted his reader to see that the memories for the tailor are overwhelming, that he does not quite know what he is recording when he writes them down. In other words, the faculty of memory is out of balance with the rest of the tailor's faculties, and the "disharmony" among them is a principal reason why he is in the asylum in the first place. The healthy memory of a true Parisian would allow for more forgetting of the details of those daily papers. And the healthy memory of a normal Parisian tailor would not have led him to confuse himself with a true historian.

Hypermnesia is characterized by both the intensity and the rapidity of memories. As a result of the "overexcitement" of this faculty, the past rules over the present; ideas and sentiments are recalled, and perceptions or what we might call reality testing is diminished. Moreover, the exaltation of memory can negatively affect other features of one's life, throwing them out of balance. If hypermnesia could "permit an ignorant *malade* to become a writer" (215), it could also lead one, as in the case of Monsieur X, to concentrate one's reason and emotions on "useless" tasks at the expense of others.

The tailor's capacity to make sense of the disharmony of the war and the Commune evinces his incapacity to lead a *vie sensé*. As is clear from the diagnosis of *délire ambitieux*, the artisan does not understand how properly to balance his past and his present, his experience and his expectations.[26] The clinician who makes the diagnosis and the doctor who writes up the case sew the *pauvre fou* back into his proper costume. Only just enough of his exalted memory—and his historical narrative—are recalled in order to show just how unbalanced the tailor is. With this balanced, medical approach to his life and writing, he can now be recollected as a *fou* without being exalted as a historian or poet. Just as Ribot's shoemaker was not responsible for his actions that took place without memory and, hence, without *conscience*, Guillon's tailor was not responsible for a history that was the product of hypermnesia. The memory dysfunctions shatter the expected connections between the pasts and presents of the individuals concerned, and these connections are restored through the narratives of the two case studies.

Guillon recognized how deceptive hypermnesia could be. After all, he noted, when a sanity hearing is held a judge might be impressed by prodigious feats of memory that have nothing to do with the health of an individual. Experienced specialists are needed to ensure that the disease is not taken as a sign of health (209, 217).[27] Normally, memory brings order to the present by linking it to the past and signaling possible futures. With hypermnesia, however, memory becomes an agent of disorder, overwhelming the present. In the case of the would-be historian of the Commune, a professional who understands the subtle dynamics of memory and forgetting is needed to restore "harmony" to the narrative of the tailor's life. In this case, we can be assured, the gift of a prodigious memory turned out to be the symptom of a grave illness. This was not a case of yet another member of the popular classes aiming above his peers. Memory here was deceptive, but it could be unmasked as clearly dysfunctional. When understood within the context of disease the memory disorder, and the tailor, are domesticated. The *aliéniste* knows how to read the signs of memory for what they really are. Guillon quotes the psychiatrist Benjamin Ball:

> When a mother tells you that her son is not crazy, that he is more intelligent than ever, that he remembers everything, that his memory is extraordinary, there is only one response to make: "It is precisely because your son has too much memory that he is insane." (216)

Too Many: Dédoublement de la Mémoire

One of the most famous "cases" of the late nineteenth century was the story of Félida X, first recounted by Dr. Eugène Azam of Bordeaux. After 1875, when "split personality" became a popular diagnostic phenomenon, the story of Félida was retold again and again by psychologists, philosophers, and physicians. By the time Pierre Janet lectured at Harvard in 1906, he could say that this story "has gone round the world, and today there is a whole library written about this poor woman."[28] At the end of the century, this case study was important as a weapon against those who wanted to claim the necessity of a transcendental self behind our sensations and experience. Félida's multiple personality was used as "proof" that the self is a construction (and thus can fall apart), not a given.[29] The story is important for our purposes because Félida's split personality is conceptualized as a *maladie de la mémoire*. As Azam put it, she suffered not only from a "*dédoublement de la vie*" but from periodic amnesia.

Azam was an adjunct physician at the *Asile public des femmes aliénées de Bordeaux* when he first met the fifteen-year-old Félida in 1858. Her parents thought her crazy, and Azam saw quickly that she was a hysteric and suffered from a strange "lesion of memory." The "principal phenomenon that shocked her family and entourage" was the following:

> Almost every day, without apparent cause, or under the rule of the least emotion, she is overcome by what she calls "her crisis." In fact, she enters in her second state in the following way: she is seated, some needlework in her hands. Suddenly, after pain in the temples, she falls into a profound sleep from which nothing can awaken her, and which lasts two to three minutes. Then, she awakens. But she is different from what she was before: she is gay, *rieuse*, continues the work begun while humming, makes jokes with those around her. Her intelligence is more active, and she does not suffer from the many neuralgic pains of her ordinary state. In this state, which I have named her *condition seconde*, Félida has perfect knowledge of all her life, remembering not only her ordinary existence but states similar to the one in which she is found. In 1858, this second condition lasted one to three hours each day, sometimes less. After this time, new loss of consciousness, and Félida awakes in her ordinary state. But she is somber, morose, and she is aware of her disease; what saddens her most is her complete ignorance of everything that occurred during the preceding period, whatever its duration. I will recall only one example of this lacuna of memory:
>
> Being in second condition, she surrendered herself to a young man who should be her husband, and one day, in her normal state, she consulted me on the singular phenomena that she was feeling in her stomach. Pregnancy was obvious, but I refrained from telling her. A moment later, the second condition having arrived, Félida said to me while laughing. "I told you just now all sorts of stories. I know very well that I am pregnant."[30]

Whichever personality she was in at the time seemed to Félida to be her normal state. Her doctor knew better, insisting that the *condition seconde* remained "other." As the years went on, Félida's second condition became prevalent. She would spend weeks, and then months, in personality two. During the few days when she returned to the condition that Azam still called "normal," the existence of the poor "*fille du peuple*" was intolerable "because she was absolutely unaware of almost all her life."[31]

Azam waxes poetic in order to convey the gravity of this memory of dysfunction.

> In order to understand this situation, I beg the reader to imagine (it is difficult) that, in his past life, there were from time to time lacunae of two to three months occurring suddenly by chance and erasing the memory of more or less important acts of his existence. He will understand then what is the importance of memory. Is this not what makes of our existence a complete whole? Without it the personality knows not how to understand itself. The existence of Félida has been, for thirty-two years . . . similar to a book from which one would have [here and there] torn out the pages, whether one, twenty, or thirty. What an extraordinary reading! If it is missing only a page, the sense can still be grasped; if it is missing twenty, this is impossible.

The pages from Félida's book are only missing, then, while she is in her "normal" personality. In her second condition (which by the late 1870s and early 1880s dominated most of her life), she could read straight through her experiences and even find them amusing. In his report of 1890, however, Azam noted that forty-seven-year-old Félida had only brief episodes each month of the *condition seconde*. Her "normal" personality had returned, but the pages seemed gone for good.

It was his encounter with Félida that led Dr. Azam to an investigation of hypnotism,[32] where alterations of personality could be provoked and controlled, eventually hoping that hypnotic trances would facilitate a form of painless surgery. He hypnotized the young woman, who already seemed to drift on her own into prolonged trancelike states, and showed her to many colleagues to illustrate both the memory loss and the loss of sensitivity that comes in the hypnotic trance or somnambulism. Indeed, one of the explanations Azam gave of Félida's condition (he tried many) was that she was in a *total somnambulism*, one in which all her senses appeared to be operating normally despite the trance. In other words, Félida's *condition seconde* is a kind of dream. How to know that it is not real? As we do with most of our dreams, Félida forgets her second state. For Azam this is the key element in deciding that the impulsive *rieuse* is not as real as the depressed, hysterical wife. "The absence of memory," Azam writes, "remains the criterion of difference between an ordinary state and somnambulism."[33] The person returning from a hypnotic trance remembers nothing of what she or he did therein.

The "originality" of the story of Félida, according to its first teller, is the patient's limited amnesia.[34] Her total memory in the *condition seconde* resembles a hypermnesia. Forgetting, Azam insisted, is normal. The patient expressed this herself, when after trying to hang herself in her second personality because she believed her husband had a mistress, she exclaimed: "How happy I would be if I had one of my crises. At least I would not be aware of my unhappiness."[35]

The place of the story of Félida's amnesia, her hypermnesia, her double memory, her doubled personality and hysteria in the constellation of ideas in late-nineteenth-century France is discussed in the third chapter of this book. Here we can see that the tale puts in play questions about how much remembering and how much forgetting are necessary to make a normal personality. For Azam, remembering Félida became important for his own career as a physician and scientist. By the end of his life, he had published fifteen versions of the case (including republications). He even thought the case instructive for the burgeoning field of legal psychiatry: Was Félida responsible in her normal state for actions committed in her second condition? Can one be punished, for example, for acts of which one has no memory? For Ribot and Taine, the case offered further proof of the fallacy of the idea of a unified self apart from our memories and sensations. Moreover, the case underlined the importance of the continuity established by normal memory. Without the construction of a stable, continuous identity, pathology would result, but the unity cannot be assumed a priori.[36] The case also situated remembering as a potential illness. Memory by itself is not sufficient for the establishment of a healthy personality; a certain amount of forgetting is the sign that we are in fact really living and not only dreaming.

One of the crucial components of the human sciences in nineteenth-century France was the effort to define the normal. This had to do not only with a consideration of appropriate behavior but with a conceptualization of the healthy connection of past and present. The studies of amnesia, hypermnesia, and periodic amnesia were important in this regard because they provided clinicians and philosophers with pathological extremes between which the normal functioning of memory and forgetting could be situated. Moreover, they allowed one to show how the continuous or harmonious relation of present and past could be organized as a scientific/medical problem.

Neither Ribot, Guillon, nor Azam placed much emphasis on the potential significance of what was forgotten for the amnesic. For the most part, they tried to limit their studies to the mechanisms of memory dysfunctions. Charcot, Janet, and other later investigators of hysteria would ignore the significance of the memories for the person who suffers from forgetting and focus on the neurological potency of what is not recalled. This would change for Freud, of course, who would come to think of memories as not only having a location and "charge," but as possessing a semantic force. "The memory which forms the content of a hysterical attack is not any chance one," he wrote in 1892. "It is the return of the event which caused the outbreak of the hysteria—the psychical trauma."[37] In the psychoanalyst's view, amnesia could be the sign of the disassociation of painful memories; the memories are conserved, but cannot be reproduced by the subject—that is, they are unconscious. On the other hand, Freud and Breuer wrote in *Studies on Hysteria* (1893) that hysterics suffer mainly from reminiscences—memories that *intrude* into consciousness and daily life disguised in form.[38] In his early work, Freud would attempt to provoke amnesia through hypnosis to remove the pathogenic impression of the past.[39] With his development of psychoanalysis, however, the goal was not the erasure of the past but the emplotment of it into a history with which one could live.[40] Throughout his mature work, memory and forgetting for Freud had to do not so much with the location of the past but with the meanings it could have for the subject in the present. Whereas in Ribot's wedding example the woman's memories are destroyed by a cerebral commotion, in Freud's studies it would be the affect-charged memories that caused the ruckus.

In the last third of the nineteenth century, *maladies de la mémoire* are a popular subject for reflection in French scientific culture.[41] The dangers and the excitement of too much forgetting and too much remembering resonate deeply and widely in a culture that was already beginning to experience what Pierre Nora has called the "acceleration of history." In other words, this was already a "turning point where consciousness of a break with the past is bound up with the sense that memory has been torn—*but torn in such a way as to pose the problem of the embodiment of memory*."[42] The past and where to keep it were being formed into a new problematic by doctors and philosophers ready to claim expertise about how much of a connection to the past was good for us. As historians struggled to professionalize their discipline and make the study of the national past more scientific, the new profession of psychiatry joined with philosophy to provide mutual legitimation through a shared commitment to a rational, scientific, or positivist view of the brain as the organ of the mind. This alliance included many who were eager to show how the dysfunctions of individual memory revealed the proper function of the past in a healthy life. And whereas the professionalization of history may have been a sign of the disappearance of a milieu of memory, the investigation of memory dysfunctions contributed to the psychologization and hence privatization of our relationship to our past.

Maladies of memory take place on a borderline between the somatic and the psychological, and part of what is at stake in defining them had to do (and probably still has to do) with efforts to redraw or erase the lines dividing body and mind, matter and spirit, and nature and culture. In this essay we have recalled three scientific efforts in this regard, but they are only a small part of a story. A full treatment of the significance of amnesia, hypermnesia, and periodic amnesia in nineteenth-century France would include, among other things, consideration of nostalgia as a *maladie de la mémoire*, the literary uses of amnesia as a plot device, the connections made between gender and memory disorders, the links between hypnosis and forgetting, the significance of the disorder in the conceptualization and treatment of hysteria and split personality, and the efforts to read the social and political significance of these memory disorders by the early years of the twentieth century.

One of the presuppositions shared by most late-nineteenth-century writers on memory was that, despite the fact that we have limited recall of the past, nothing is permanently lost to our memories. As Ludovic Dugas emphasized, "There is no absolute forgetting: every mental state, no matter how weak, how unperceived it was, can always be reborn, and reborn with an intensity that at first it did not have."[43] Where was this past when it was not in our consciousness? This question, which had its terrifying implications for Baudelaire, extended a promise, or at least a possibility, to Michelet and to Proust. The scientific examination of *maladies de la mémoire* not only provided specific answers to this question, it aimed to limit its significance as part of an effort to *fix* our connection to the past that we carry within us. Any analysis of the place and problematic of the past in modern France must include discussion of the displacement of the past that was observed, categorized, and acted upon by those who used amnesia, hypermnesia, and periodic amnesia to rethink normality and memory in relation to one another.

2. Dying of the Past

Medical Studies of Nostalgia in Nineteenth-Century France

Indiscreet consolations only embitter violent suffering.

JEAN-JACQUES ROUSSEAU

He knows that the more he thinks of his country, and of the objects which are dear to him, the more he will suffer. It makes no difference! It is sweeter for him to suffer.

JOSE·FELICIANO CASTILHO

Case 1

*Eugène L***, born in Paris, was sent to a wet nurse in the Amiens area and brought back to his family when he was two years old. The strength of his limbs, the firmness of his flesh, his coloring, the vivacity and gaiety of his character, everything indicated that he had been well cared for and that he was a vigorous child. During the fifteen days that his nurse remained at his side, Eugène continued to enjoy the most robust health; but as soon as she left he became pale, sad and morose. He was unresponsive to the caresses of his parents and refused all the food that had pleased him the most just a few days before.*

Struck by this sudden change, Eugène's mother and father summoned Hippolyte Petit who, recognizing the first symptoms of nostalgia, recommended frequent walks and all the childish distractions that abound in Paris. These techniques, ordinarily so effective in such cases, failed completely, and the unhappy little boy, who was becoming weaker all the time, remained for whole hours sadly immobile, his eyes turned toward the door through which he had seen departing the woman who had acted as his mother. Called again by the family, the practitioner declared that the only way to save the child was to have his nurse return immediately and take the boy away with her again. When she arrived, Eugène erupted with cries of joy; the melancholy imprinted on his face was soon replaced by the radiation of ecstasy and, to use one of his father's expressions, from that moment he began to revive. Brought to Picardy the following week, he stayed there about a year, enjoying the best of health. During his second return to Paris, Dr. Petit progressively separated the nurse from the child, first for a few hours, then for a whole day, then for a week, until he was used to being without her. This tactic was crowned with complete success.

Case 2

For a great many years there lived in Rue de la Harpe one of those men of stay-at-home habits for whom the only distraction consisted in occasional visits to the flower market and who, on returning home, would rediscover with ever-renewed pleasure his modest lodgings where order and cleanliness reigned everywhere. One day, as he hurried home, his landlord stopped him in the stairway and told him that the house had to be demolished because of some street repairs and that he would have to find another place to live for the next trimester. On hearing this news the poor lodger remained paralyzed with surprise and chagrin. Returning to his apartment, he immediately took to his bed and stayed there several months, the victim of a profound sadness accompanied by a raging fever. In vain his landlord tried to console him, promising him a more comfortable lodging in the new house that was going to be built on the land of the old one: "It will no longer be my lodging," he responded with bitterness, "the one I loved so much, that I embellished with my own hands, where, for thirty years, I had all my habits and where I cherished the hope of finishing my life!"

The eve of the day fixed for the demolition, he was warned that he must absolutely give back his keys the following day by noon at the latest. "I will not return them," he responded coldly. "If I leave here, it will only be feet first." Two days later, the commissaire was required to force open the door of the stubborn lodger. He found the poor man dead; he had suffocated from the despair of having to leave the abode he cherished too much.

These two cases are from Jean-Baptiste-Félix Descuret's 1841 book *La Médecine des passions*.[1] They describe a disease which had received extensive medical attention in the 1820s and 1830s and which would remain a subject of scientific debate through the 1870s. The disease was nostalgia, an affliction that doctors regarded as potentially fatal, contagious, and somehow deeply connected to French life in the middle of the nineteenth century. It had first entered the medical lexicon in the seventeenth century, and it had been used as a diagnostic category throughout the eighteenth.[2] During the early decades of the nineteenth century, and especially in the 1820s and 1830s, there was an important increase in medical writings on nostalgia, and the disease attracted considerable medical attention, discussion, and intervention. By the 1850s interest in the phenomenon *as a disease* had waned significantly and, except for a debate about its medical status in the 1870s, it would never again receive the sustained attention of the scientific world.[3] Of course, the phenomenon of nostalgia did not disappear when the doctors ceased inquiring into it. Indeed, if its demedicalization resulted in the abandonment of the quest for a cure for nostalgia, we are now all potential experts on the condition. Nostalgia is no longer an *exceptional* condition to be studied by medical experts or to be experienced only by the diseased.

Descuret called little Eugène's disturbance "nostalgia from affection." With this label the author emphasized the psychological, or what he would have termed the moral, etiology of the disease. Other physicians placed a greater emphasis on the physical aspects of such maladies. Eugène's first impressions had been in Picardy; it was not only his affection for his nurse but his attachment to the environment around Amiens that had made the return to Paris a threat to his health. In this case, what Descuret called the child's "memory of the heart" was too faithful to its first object.[4]

Separation was experienced as violent deprivation. Was there a point, however, when separation was desirable or necessary? When did it become pathological to experience deprivation as violently oppressive? Moreover, how did physicians (or anyone else) know when they were confronted with a medical problem? In order to judge pathology, some standard of normalcy was necessary; physicians had to determine what was the normal connection to one's past in the nineteenth century if they were to speak about it with expertise. In late-nineteenth-century France, psychiatrists, neurologists, and philosophers joined in the task of constructing the image of a normal *memory* via a conceptualization of memory disorders such as nostalgia, hypermnesia, and split personality. Through the classification of *maladies de la mémoire* they were forming the "proper" connection between present and past.[5]

However, the connection between past and present is never only a problem of memory, but also a problem of history and of desire. Desire for objects in the past or for the past itself may be a necessary ingredient for many forms of recollection, just as it can be the crucial component of a pathological way of being in the present. In early-nineteenth-century France, medical doctors wrote numerous studies of nostalgia as a pathology resulting from an excess of desire for the past, from the longing to return to a specific and crucial place in one's past.

Eugène had been sent to a wet nurse in the countryside, a custom not unusual for a middle-class child in the early nineteenth century, although this does not mean that sending a child away to nurse was uncontroversial during this period. At least since the Enlightenment mothers had been urged to nurse their own children, yet it seems that at least 40 percent of children born in Paris in the mid-1800s were placed with rural wet nurses.[6] In the case of Eugène, the child seemed to suffer no ill effects from his two years in the countryside. On the contrary, he was a vigorous two-year-old, a fact that must have made his decline into lethargy even more frightening to his parents.

It is not surprising that Dr. Petit quickly made the diagnosis of nostalgia in the little boy. Early in the century doctors had already warned that children who were sent out to nurse would be especially vulnerable to the disease. In his medical thesis of 1803, for example, Denis-Francois-Noél Guerbois warned that the child sent out to nurse would confront the pain of the world when still most vulnerable to it:

> It is not the idea of the future that torments him [the child]; he does not have it at all, he cannot have it yet. It is therefore only the memory of the past. It is the first pain that he suffers; nothing can soothe it [*l'adoucir*].[7]

Happily, nature softens the rude confrontation with the world. Most babies forget their nurses and their first pain of separation. Still, Guerbois urged mothers to breastfeed their own children: "[You] give them more than life, since you assure at least for their tender years a happiness which will be unclouded."[8] If mother's milk preserved children from early sorrow, one may, however, wonder whether it made them vulnerable to psychological disorders later on. Most children do not, of course, forget their mothers, who remain the traditional home of nostalgic affection. Indeed, Guerbois himself suffered from the disease of nostalgia during his difficult tenure as an army doctor during the wars of the revolutionary period: "Sweet memory [of his mother], you were my only consolation and yet you tormented me without end!"[9]

Although not many medical writings concentrated on nostalgia as a childhood illness, almost all identified the origins of the disease in the first affective connections to people and places in the child's world. The doctors believed that attachment to one's earliest memories was so frequently the core of this disorder because the first impressions on the brain were permanent. Since they were never erased, they could become the object of attachment at almost any time. Even those writers generally suspicious of physicalist explanations agreed that the first impressions made on the child's brain conditioned his or her later affective life.[10] The desire to return to the scene of those impressions, the desire to experience again the affections of home and native soil were overpowering factors in impeding the nostalgic person from living in the present.

Little Eugène's attachment to his lost nurse rendered him morose, pale, and unresponsive to any pleasures his parents could provide. These signs, we might say, were of depression, or what in the nineteenth century was called melancholy. Although the question whether nostalgia was a discrete illness was the subject of much debate in the medical literature of the period, the disease was usually differentiated from melancholy because of the specificity of the object.[11] Nostalgia was also thought to have a rapid pathogenesis: if left untreated, the disease would soon affect major bodily organs (lungs, digestive system, and the brain were mentioned frequently) and be fatal. Therefore, the nostalgic person suffered not only from a sentiment, but from an affective disorder that destroyed the body:

> Thus, this chagrin becomes a morbid tendency, entering the domain of pathology, since it can terminate in death caused by a series of latent inflammations, and, in as little as a month's time, attacks various organs and weakens all the [body's] functions, above all those of the nervous system, the immediate seat [*siège*] of nostalgia.[12]

Forgetting could be a protection against nostalgia, but no doctor thought it wise to forget one's origins completely. How could physicians understand this disease, which seemed to be the result of "our finest natural sentiments," but which could spread to others and be fatal?[13] The question was not simply academic: they were faced with the task of saving individuals from the slow, steady debilitation brought on by nostalgia:

> Everything one tells him to do he does mechanically; he obeys without murmuring, without complaining; he is the most docile of all

> creatures, but it is a docility with indolence, and he does what he is told without ever going beyond the orders one gives him. Why? It is because he has abandoned his life and reserves for himself only his bitter thoughts, which keep him always distanced from the present and from dreaming of a happier future. Cold, impassible, he proffers not a single word of reproach against those who make his life miserable; everything is indifferent to him; always alone, he does not look for a friend to whom he could open his soul. Yet, if the unfortunate one could find within himself the consolations he needs! Far from it, it is by burrowing into his solitude that he can augment his sorrow. Little by little his features become drawn, his face is creased with wrinkles, his hair falls out, his body is emaciated, his legs tremble under him; a slow fever saps his strength; his stomach refuses nourishment; a dry cough fatigues him; soon the decline of energy does not permit him to leave his bed. Then he wraps himself in his sheets, refusing to respond to the questions he is asked; his lips contract with force if one tries to make him swallow some liquid. He speaks to himself, his discourse is incoherent; the fever becomes even greater, and soon he succumbs.[14]

There were various theories about the causes of nostalgia and even some possible cures, and by the 1830s a consensus existed concerning some basic aspects of the disease. The major symptom was seen as an excessive attachment to something in the past, usually, but not necessarily, one's native soil or one's family. The disease could strike both men and women, and it was found in various age groups.[15] However, young men between twenty and thirty seemed to be the most vulnerable. A multitude of widely varying circumstances could become "predisposing causes" of nostalgia. A dissertation of 1831 lists the following as the principal ones: a melancholic or nervous temperament; too lenient an education followed by a strict regime; no education at all, so that the individual was deprived of the consolations of study and philosophy; strong and sad passions, love (especially happy love), and disappointed ambition; the tribulations of prisoners and emigrants; "ignorance of language"; origins in mountainous regions; "abuse of women" (i.e., womanizing); masturbation; a change in way of life; unusual food; the existence in a new country of native, contagious diseases; premature ossification of bone sutures of the skull and of arteries of the brain; changes in climate (especially high pressure systems). Autumn seemed to be an especially dangerous time, and soldiering a particularly vulnerable profession.[16] Indeed, virtually anything could trigger the onset of the disease. The same thesis lists the following "occasional causes": a love letter, a picture, a conversation, a song, hearing the accent of one's native country, a sudden change in social position or habits.[17]

In the case of little Eugène, the onset of the disease seems simple enough. His attachment to his nurse appeared remarkable only when she was absent; only then was it clear that this connection inhibited other relationships and could even result in serious physical complications. Dr. Petit's advice was standard for the time: create new loves for the person suffering from love sickness; find new joys to erase the domination of the old. Paris offered the small boy a host of distractions from his obsessive desire: the key was to find a new passion. In his medical dissertation of 1866 Sava Petrowitch (with bigger boys in mind) specifically warned that "only *satisfied lave* can perfectly cure nostomania"; platonic love was insufficient.[18]

By what means could the physician direct the patient away from the past and toward the possibility of new passions or distractions? How could he enter the nostalgic person's imagination in order to bring it back to the world of the present? This was especially difficult because the patient wanted nothing so much as to be left to dream of the past, often lacking the energy even to express the desire to return to it. In other words, the satisfactions available to the nostalgic adult came only through the illness; patients did not want to give up the gratification of their symptoms. Several theses and articles emphasize that the doctor should enter into what we would today describe as a transference relationship with the nostalgic. In order to gain his or her confidence, in order to have a role in the patient's imagination, the doctor should participate in the illness. A thesis of 1846 notes that the doctor must become a new father to the nostalgic person.[19] Delmais-Eugène Pilet goes a step further when he writes: "By penetrating into the recesses of a person's heart to read there the desires, passions, solicitudes, the chagrins that react on his organism, you create the ways to remedy the disorders produced, and you elevate your profession to the heights of a true priesthood." Pilet is clearly thinking of an adult patient, and here the emphasis is on redirecting, not merely distracting, him or her. Moreover, the doctor must become a part of the illness, not just an antidote to it: "Joy is not the remedy for pain, nor love for hatred. In order to calm strong passions, one must first appear to share them: in sharing them one weakens them, and in weakening them one can succeed in extinguishing them."[20]

If the cure of a nostalgic adult often depends on a doctor's complex transference relationship with the patient, Eugène's illness allowed for a much more direct therapeutic intervention: send the boy back to the place of his longing. Dr. Petit satisfied the child's yearning to return in order slowly, progressively to detach him from this first relationship at a later stage. Although the physicians were aware that the patient can never actually return to the past, the literature is full of examples that demonstrate the possibility of going home again.[21] Thus, nostalgia is often conceptualized in spatial, rather than temporal, terms: the patient desires to return to the *scene* of his or her memory, and sometimes—as in the case of little Eugène—the doctor can oblige. Even if the scene has changed, the strategy usually works. Reestablishing the connection with the lost object of desire is the surest cure of the dreaded disease.

Of course sometimes it was impossible to send the patient home. Much of the medical writing on nostalgia was done by military doctors who could not return soldiers to their *pays*. Furthermore, soldiers who wanted to avoid combat were tempted to fake nostalgia, claiming to their commanders and doctors that they suffered from being so far away from home. However, these malingerers were betrayed by their complaints: true nostalgics would conceal their disease, withdrawing into lethargy without disclosing the origin of their suffering. True nostalgics derived their only satisfaction from the symptoms of their disease and therefore strove to protect their longing, to concentrate all their energies on it:

> To the extent that this physical deterioration progresses, the brain concentrates its forces with ever-increasing perseverance on an exclusive series of ideas. The sick person seeks solitude, during which he can caress his favorite chimera without any obstacle and feed his pain; and later, when the debility of organic actions makes all movement painful to him, he isolates himself, absorbed by his fatal thinking in a repose that further accentuates the total power of this thinking and the progress of organic degradation that it has already provoked.[22]

The nostalgic, like the masochist, wants to protect his or her desire, wants to preserve the longing.[23] Attachment to a lost object usually connects a person to the world because that attachment is the kernel of the desire to refind the object. One weaves connections with the world because it offers so many imitations of the desired object. In the case of the nostalgic, however, attachment leads the sufferer to renounce the world as an illusory place made up of mere simulacra of the objects desired. As Susan Stewart has noted, "Nostalgia is the repetition that mourns the inauthenticity of all repetition and denies the repetition's capacity to form identity."[24] The task of the physician, then, is to detach the patient from this longing either by granting the wish to return home or by creating new possibilities for satisfying this passion. Dr. Petit's treatment combined these two elements. Eugène was sent back to the scene of his satisfaction so that later he would have the strength to be detached from it. He had not only to be weaned from his nurse but also to be introduced to the world beyond Picardy as a place where he could seek substitutions for the satisfactions that had gradually been left behind.

Nostalgia is the refusal to consider any but a world lost to the past as the habitable world. Our second case describes a man whose world is being rendered obsolete, who finds the scene of his life being *made into the past*. The unhappy lodger cannot imagine being alive in any place other than the one that he is told will no longer exist.[25] It is not the passage of time, necessary psychological separation from origins, or the longing for return that causes his nostalgia. His disease is caused by progress.

The medical literature on nostalgia is permeated by the idea that the disease derives from the very instinct that makes a person attached to his or her native soil, and that without it peoples from all over the globe would flock to the most fertile areas.[26] It is this instinct that ties people to their roots and preserves their fidelity to family, home, and *pays*. Some writers emphasize the links between nostalgia and patriotism, whether to celebrate the French desire for freedom or to explain that the French make poor colonizers because they miss their homeland so much.[27] Pierre-Urbain Briet thought that the 1830 revolution was motivated by political nostalgia, which he describes in the following terms: "the first person who was aware of what he had lost and who in his despair pronounced the word 'tyrant,' this man became nostalgic for freedom."[28] Political nostalgia was an expression of the refusal to feel at home in an unjust political regime. Unlike more typical cases of the disease, this type of nostalgia could lead to action.

Many of the medical writings consider the links between nostalgia and progress. In his article on music in the *Encyclopédie*, Rousseau had already noted that primitive people are more vulnerable to the disease than civilized people.[29] There was a strong consensus that as a country became more civilized, and as people became more cosmopolitan, the incidence of nostalgia diminished. Louis-Alexandre-Hippolyte Leroy-Dupré celebrated this progress in 1846: "Cerebral nostalgia becomes more rare each day thanks to rapid communications which modern industry is beginning to establish among peoples who will soon be nothing more than one big family."[30] Pilet, however, was concerned that the disappearance of nostalgia signaled the development, not of a healthier society, but of one that was no longer able to feel the absence of some of its essential ingredients:

> One has to say it, nostalgia is a disease that is tending to disappear and that is observed less frequently each day: the establishment of rapid communications, the inundation of a ceaselessly invasive civilization, erases one by one the moral colors that so often created the disease in other times. General cosmopolitanism results in one becoming attached to anything . . . everywhere materialist egoism is substituted for the noble instincts of the heart, everywhere the positive kills the imagination and its divine creations . . . the further we move away from a state of simplicity, the less we cling to the tombs of our ancestors and to the soil on which we were born.[31]

For Leroy-Dupré the man who could not leave his apartment was, like his building, almost an anachronism. For Pilet, he was expressing a positive sentiment that was unfortunately being erased in a world bent on modernization.

Most cases of nostalgia were not caused by the destruction of a person's home, but by the longing to return to a home one had left. Doctors noticed that if a person's original home was radically different from the place where he or she now lived, the chances of affliction by nostalgia were increased. Thus, people from mountainous or primitive regions (Auvergne, Brittany) were at great risk when they joined the army or went to work in Paris. Some doctors claimed that women were less susceptible to nostalgia because "they took their home with them" when they moved from their parents' house. As Allard noted, women "ordinarily leave their home [*demeure*] only to establish connections which give birth to an attachment so strong that they easily forget their former habits."[32] Although some physicalist explanations were offered, it was the sedentary mode of life of most women that was said to protect them from nostalgia.

One group of women, however, was especially vulnerable to the disease. Domestic servants sent far from their villages to earn a living were targets for many kinds of abuse. Taking refuge in their memory of home often led to the development of nostalgia. Hyacinthe Musset recounts a dramatic case in 1830:

> Françoise Cottineau, 25 years old, poor but honest, had just had her beloved mother buried. Her father, already old and infirm, found in her a friend who, with the gentleness of her character, her delicate and cheerful attentions and the sweet fruit of her work, charmed his last years. In a region ungrateful by nature, Françoise soon saw that her own work would no longer suffice to keep her father alive, since his suffering increased his needs. She became a domestic in a chateau half a league from her paternal home. Love is so powerful! And when crime, covered with gold, comes knocking at the door of indigence, it is very difficult not to open up to it. Françoise, perhaps in an excess of filial piety, was weak enough to consent to the passion of the young farmer on whom good fortune had been pleased to smile. The cad swore to marry her and to take care of her father. Françoise became pregnant; and, as the proverb says: "Misery is always wrong" [*Le malheur a toujours tort*]. The ungrateful farmer did not keep his promise.

Françoise confessed all to her father, but nonetheless he threw her out of the house. Eventually she was well cared for and had a "happy delivery" in Nantes. "But," Musset tells us, "Françoise had resolved to die."

> Nothing was neglected, she was provided with everything that could please her taste and her senses. The virtuous woman who had taken her under her wing promised to adopt her child and did in fact adopt him. For all the affection she was shown Françoise gave her thanks with burning tears. She had regrets for only one thing; it was not life (she asked for death), but the cottage in which her unhappy father lay. My colleague, M. Aubinais, who came from her region and had had her mother as wet nurse and her as his first housekeeper, came to see her very often and made every effort to heal the wounds of a broken heart . . . one could plant no flower on the tomb of this unfortunate girl. She abstained from all food and died in the midst of the most horrible convulsions, weeping for her *pays* and begging my colleague to ask her father's pardon.

For Musset this was an ideal case of nostalgia because it showed how even our finest impulses can lead to fatal illness. Françoise was a loyal daughter whose sentiments for her father were strong, even noble. But she lived in a harsh, ungrateful land and found a harsh, ungrateful lover. Musset does not say this, but she also suffered from an ungrateful father. Even so, her loyalty to her father remained strong, and there was no sign of nostalgia as long as she could return home. When cut off from her father and *pays*, however, the strength of her noble sentiments made it impossible for her to live. There seemed to be no place worth living in. The shelter and good care she found in Nantes made no difference to her; they only fostered the yearning she felt. Dr. Aubinais followed the standard treatment. As a compatriot he shared her sentiments, tried to distract her, to offer her other attachments, most importantly her child and her new home. For Françoise, however, without hope of return there was no reason to live.

At the end of his essay Musset considers how others might be prevented from falling victim to the disease that had claimed Françoise. "Should one try to smother," he asks, "this sweet sentiment which makes us cherish with such tenderness our family, our friends, and the places where we have been born?"

> Pleasure, joy, agreeable sensations, sweet and constant impressions constitute the happiness of a person, make him the most perfect and fulfilled of beings. One must only try to arm people against the evils sometimes born from a delicate sensibility. There is an immense difference between too much sensibility and cold apathy. A good and sensitive heart may indeed cause suffering, it is true; but it is also the source of the sweetest pleasures and the most beautiful virtues.[33]

Here Musset expresses the same concern as Pilet: the disease of nostalgia is rooted in facets of our humanity whose "cure" would leave us deeply impoverished, even horribly mutilated.

Thus, the investigation of nostalgia led some physicians to reflect on how our ties to the past functioned both to provide meaning in our lives and to make us vulnerable to pathology. As long as Rue de la Harpe was not scheduled for modernization, the habits of the lodger in case 2 were benign, even quaint. However, as soon as those habits were broken, as soon as he was denied the possibility of maintaining them in the present, they became malignant. Françoise's affection for her father was not excessive. On the contrary, it added not only sweetness but also nobility to her difficult existence. However, once she was forced out of her home and *pays* by her father's hardheartedness, these affections proved poisonous.

We have seen that doctors noticed an inverse relationship between "civilization" and nostalgia. Both Pilet and Musset worried that in the course of our becoming civilized we would lose the capacity to be attached to anything over time. By the 1850s, however, this would change, and the triumph over nostalgia would be seen as a victory of historical progress. As France became more modern, the disease would disappear:

> Happily, nostalgia diminishes day by day; by descending little by little among the masses, instruction will develop the intelligence of people, making them more and more capable of struggling against this disease. Everything that touches civilization, in perfecting the human species, makes man understand his role as an individual, his part in the common work, and, in enlightening his spirit, submits the impulses of his heart to reason.[34]

The point here is not merely that with progress everything improves, but rather that with steam engines, regular mail, and telegraph lines we are linked to the "*mère pays*." An 1874 dissertation did warn that if a major cataclysm destroyed these modern networks of communication, there would be a resurgence of nostalgia.[35] By the end of the decade, the entry in the *Dictionnaire encyclopédique des sciences médicales* would be even more confident: "*Le mal du pays*, already rare in our time, is destined to disappear before the progress of hygiene and civilization."[36] A dissenting voice can be found in an anonymous entry for the Lefèvre Prize for essays on nostalgia offered by the Academy of Medicine in 1872. The author noted the decline of nostalgia in society but, like Pilet and Musset decades before, he lamented the loss of the feelings that once gave rise to the illness. Significantly, there were only three entries to this strange competition—and only the one expressing nostalgia for nostalgia received no mark of distinction.[37]

The essay awarded the highest distinction was a detailed account of current thinking on nostalgia written by August Haspel, who was well placed to assume a magisterial tone after forty years as a doctor in military hospitals. Haspel argued that the disease could arise from organic causes or from a "disposition of the soul." He called nostalgia a "hypochondria of the heart," wanting to allow for both moral and organic causes. The other essay to receive a *mention* from the Academy was written by a naval doctor who had intimately experienced nostalgia during long sea voyages. For Auguste Benoist de la Grandière, no one completely escapes the "melancholic influence of his memories," but the nostalgic's memories of his native soil become overpowering. Grandière argued that nostalgia was indeed a disease, although he recognized that it often left no physical trace of its existence. More than any other disease, it showed the influence of the psychological on the somatic, and to deny its existence as a disease would be to deny the importance of the soul, "the seat of our passions."[38]

In 1875 the *Archives générales de médecine* published a blistering attack on Haspel's prize-winning essay, an attack to which Grandière's essay was just as vulnerable. For Charles Lasègue, to speak of a disease without a physical base or clear boundaries in etiology and evolution was a "danger to science," an exercise in sentimentality, not reasoning.[39] Nostalgia had never signified a "pathological unity," he claimed, so it was impossible to say whether there was a decline in the incidence of the disease. The disease was perhaps only a medical fantasy.

Lasègue argued that the army doctors responsible for much of the writing on nostalgia were not real experts on "*troubles intellectuels*." Had they had the proper training and tried to link nostalgia with other recognized psychological disturbances, they would have seen that the "*mal du pays* has more to do with poetic elegies than with medical descriptions."[40] With reference to contemporary efforts to classify the range of mental disturbances, he emphasized that experts in psychological disorders should have made a proper taxonomy of nostalgia and shown where it was situated on the nosological map. His attack on the category of nostalgia was clearly a defense of the recent gains made by the young profession of psychiatry. "The asylums of convalescents, this admirable creation of our time," he wrote, "are a homeland [*patrie*] for no one, and yet how many sick people have found a cure there?"[41]

Nostalgia was disappearing as an illness, whether one believed that it had never really constituted a disease or whether one believed that historical progress was eliminating the malady. Writing at the end of the 1870s, V. Widal attempted a kind of synthesis of the various views on nostalgia. He criticized Haspel for seeing the disease almost everywhere and remarked that too often doctors writing about the illness had "sacrificed their scientific research to the pleasure of riddling their writings with poetic citations."[42] Nonetheless, he considered that Lasègue had gone too far in claiming that the disease had never existed. He noted that the illness was no longer seen because progress had eliminated its chief predisposing agents. In a land where centralization and communication were advanced, people were able to return to the scenes of their earlier happiness.

Recognizing nostalgia as a disease, but a disease of the past, allowed Widal to celebrate historical progress and also to acknowledge the positive evolution of medicine. Lasègue's violent criticism of the literature on nostalgia was too threatening, since it suggested that many doctors were ignorant and unscientific. Widal pointed out some of their errors but underlined instead the fact that medicine had grown more sophisticated in its capacities for differential diagnosis, just as French society had grown more sophisticated in providing people with more possibilities for happiness. Doctors should turn their attention away from nostalgia not because it had merely been an imaginary disease, but because technology and public education were making people less vulnerable to the poisonous claims of the past.[43]

As nostalgia was being eliminated as a medical concern in the 1870s, psychiatrists were directing their attention to another disorder that would become central to those claiming expertise on *troubles intellectuels*. Lasègue had also complained that hysteria was the "waste paper basket of medicine where one throws otherwise unemployed symptoms," and he concentrated on developing a systematic account of the pathological unity of the disorder.[44] It was, however, the work in this area of his colleague (and rival) Jean-Martin Charcot that would be fundamental for French psychiatry from the 1870s. As medical writings on nostalgia diminished by the end of the decade, hysteria became the focus of professional French psychiatry.[45]

The nostalgic person expressed an "excessive" attachment to the past through a retreat from the world of the living. The retreat was such that patients did not even call attention to their malady but quietly pursued their desire to return to the past until death. The unhappy lodger became obsolete along with his apartment. He rejected change. By the 1870s doctors agreed that the rejection of change, the attachment to the past, could now be considered at best a historical phenomenon. They agreed that an excessive attachment to the past was no longer manifested in a disease called nostalgia. The history of medical writings on nostalgia in nineteenth-century France thus shows how physicians developed a narrative to explain not only how the normal, modern individual left the past behind while growing to maturity, but how the country had struck a healthy balance between present and past through hygiene and civilization.

This is not to say that doctors stopped recognizing casualties of progress. If nostalgia was erased by the developments of industrialization and centralization, these same aspects of historical change were said to be responsible for the exhaustion of the nerves defined as neurasthenia. Hysteria and neurasthenia earned their places on the professional map of psychiatry (through neurology) because their psychological dimensions were not given priority over their physical dimensions. In Charcot's terms, the physical "stigmata" of the diseases could be described as necessary moments in their development. The *place* of the diseases was in the body, even if suggestion, hypnotism, and social factors were seen to play roles in their evolution. The *place* of nostalgia, on the other hand, was never successfully localized in neurological terms, nor could it be. The *place* of nostalgia, even when the disease erupted in physical forms, was in the past. How could neurology cure a person of the past? The narrative that made nostalgia a medical anachronism attempted to do that.

The flamboyant hysterics examined and displayed by Charcot in the Salpêtrière seem very far indeed from the nostalgics who wanted to disappear, who desired only to be removed from the present. In the grand gestures and convulsive attacks of the hysterics we may find yet another form taken by maladies of memory in the nineteenth century. After all, Freud, following Charcot, would claim that hysterics suffered from reminiscences, from memories laden with forbidden affect which intrude into consciousness in disguised form. If hysterics, however, suffer from memory, there is no sense in which they suffer from nostalgia: they have nothing to which they long to return. Or perhaps I should say that they do not suffer from the desire to recapture the past any more than other people do. For Freud, the very structure of human desire was nostalgic: "the finding of an object is in fact a refinding of it." Or, as he says later in regard to the death instinct:

> It would be in contradiction with the conservative nature of the instincts if the goal of life were a state of things which had never yet been attained. On the contrary, it must be an *old* state of things, an initial state from which the living entity has at one time or other departed and to which it is striving to return by the circuitous path along which its development leads.[46]

For psychoanalysis, desire is, in a sense, nothing but nostalgic. Thus, if by the end of the nineteenth century nostalgia becomes almost invisible as a medical pathology, it soon reappears as an essential aspect of normal desire. Nineteenth-century French medicine came to see historical progress as the cure for nostalgia and the conditions giving rise to it. Ironically enough, psychoanalysis would come to regard progress itself as a symptom of nostalgic desire.

3. Hysterical Remembering

Our moral health depends on the limitation of these two psychological activities, one by the other, on this equilibrium between the automatic force of the past, and the conscious and voluntary effort of the present.

PIERRE JANET[1]

Everything comes back to phenomena of immobilization, of psychical forgetting. A hysteric who seems paraplegic behaves as if he has forgotten that he has legs; he has lost the mental representation of a part of his body.

JULES DEREJINE[2]

Hysteria was surely the most prominent and memorable *maladie de la mémoire* of the nineteenth century: it served as an intersection for many points of cultural contestation, becoming a marker for positions on issues of gender, sex, mind/body, professionalization, and secularization, to name only a few. And hysteria has remained a privileged site for discussing these issues in critical and historical writing over at least the last twenty-five years. Just as the conceptualization of memory and forgetting were at the core of writings on hysteria in the late nineteenth century, so recent writings continue to debate the ways we are to remember hysteria, those who supposedly suffered from it, and those who supposedly tried to understand or alleviate that suffering. The focus on maladies of memory forced nineteenth-century physicians to consider what it meant to have a healthy memory and a normal relation to the past.[3] What does it mean to suffer from the past, to be pained by memory? How is it that some people manage not to suffer from the past, to orient themselves properly in relation to the loss of the present? How does attention to the past develop from being a choice, a matter of taste, to being a duty, a matter of obligation, to being an obsession, a matter of mental illness? These questions remain crucial for us, with memory disorders continuing to be a major vehicle for their discussion.[4]

The fascination with hysteria and the investigation of it have, of course, a very long history, about which there is now an enormous and high quality body of critical writing.[5] I focus on the moment of this history when the study of hysteria comes together with the study of hypnosis, both tied to a concern with the question of how one recalls and manages to live with the past. Hypnosis becomes an important subject of medical investigation in France after Eugène Azam brings the famous case of Félida X's *dédoublement* (doubling of the personality, or the early form of what is now called multiple personality) to the attention of Paul Broca and the Academy of Sciences in 1859.[6] Hypnosis was a technique that seemed to show that radical disturbances of memory could be created in normal people, that our faculty of memory could be manipulated in ways that deeply compromised its function as the core of personal identity. Hypnosis and hysteria work together to create a crisis in thinking about memory and normality. Who is vulnerable to hypnotic suggestion and why? Who can claim expertise about such matters, when hypnosis in various forms had been part of popular culture long before the birth of psychology? The neurologist Jean-Martin Charcot linked hypnosis to his investigations of psychopathology, ultimately concluding that hypnosis was a form of hysteria. And Charcot's authority in regard to hysteria was second to none. But other investigators inside and outside the medical profession claimed that we were all more or less susceptible to hypnotic suggestion. They did not mean to imply that we were all vulnerable hysterics, but they left it unclear how we discriminated among these phenomena and among the classes of people with whom they should be associated. In the 1880s, the alienist Legrand de Saulle claimed that there were fifty thousand hysterics in Paris, ten thousand having attacks.[7] Did that not mean that there were forty thousand invisible hysterics in the city, radically disturbed people without the major symptoms of the disturbance? How, in this case, to tell the normal from the abnormal?

The effort to define normality and to set firm limits to health was of great importance in late-nineteenth-century France, a period in which the Third Republic was establishing itself as a secular polity of reason, of enlightenment. The new order should have the capacity to define the abnormal, to explain what had been regarded as mysterious or had remained within the realm of religion and magic. The famously deceptive disease of hysteria posed a great challenge to this regime, and the investigation of equally puzzling hypnotic phenomena led even the most scientific observers into areas where they were no longer at home. Doctors knew that hypnosis allowed individuals to have access to different sets of memories, or to forget (to not experience?)

painful events. In medical amphitheaters they showed colleagues women under hypnotic trances with no reactions to or memory of the needles stuck in their arms. But in other showplaces, there were demonstrations that were more difficult to integrate into the domain of science. Spiritists and mediums claimed that hypnotic trances gave them access to different temporal dimensions, that they could in fact speak with the dead. Conventional memory, they claimed, could be supplemented through hypnosis with a cosmic memory. Psychologists, psychiatrists, and neurologists joined hands with the mediums and tried to ascertain whether they were on the road to a revolutionary discovery about the nature of time and memory, or whether they were dupes. Often they arrived in séances with the latest photographic equipment so as to capture ephemeral events in a permanent form. Photography, they thought, was the perfect vehicle for remembering the *materialization* of the spiritual/mental: in medicine and spiritism. Was not photography the proper model for an ideal connection to the past?

In late-nineteenth-century France, hypnosis was a bridge between the normal and the abnormal. Hysterics lived on the bridge and were represented as either revealing to us the otherness of serious illness or the true possibilities that lay hidden within ourselves. Some writers on hypnosis attempted to normalize it as a transition between states that could be described (if not yet fully explained) in the language of science.[8] For them, hypnosis was very much like sleep, and hypnotic phenomena like dreams. The spiritists pulled in the opposite direction, pointing to hypnosis as the link to a realm that could not be accounted for in materialist terms. Thus, for diverse writers concerned with these sorts of issues, there was much at stake in the link between hysteria and hypnosis, and in the question of whether everyone was vulnerable to hypnotic suggestion. Does our faculty of memory contain within it the secrets that allow us to escape from the confines of conventional corporeal (and temporal) existence? Or is our faculty of memory so vulnerable to suggestion that it reveals the fragility of personal identity? Who has the capacity to cross into and return from the abnormal; who has the authority to claim to understand this crossing; and how can they represent what they have found there to the rest of us?

In order for hysteria to become conceptualized as a disorder of memory, the disease had to be separated from its traditional gynecological etiology, a task for which Pierre Briquet's *Traité clinique et thérapeutique de l'hystérie* (1859) was a decisive intellectual step.[9] Briquet's treatise assumes importance in large part because it can be viewed retrospectively as leading toward

Charcot's elevation of hysteria in the 1870s and 1880s to the center of French cultural life. Charcot established a clinical inventory of the disease, reducing its florid variety of symptoms to an orderly series of stages. Although he was convinced that degenerate heredity played a crucial role in the neurological predisposition to the disease, Charcot paid increasing attention to the psychological aspects of the illness throughout his career.[10]

It is crucial to see that in much of the medical writing on hysteria at the end of the nineteenth century the disease was seen as a radical dysfunction of memory. The link between memory and hysteria was the concept of trauma. The term "trauma" had been used regularly in Western medicine to refer to a bodily wound. Charcot developed the category of traumatic hysteria to understand those instances of the disease (especially among men) that could be traced to some "shock" to the nervous system. As Mark Micale has pointed out, Charcot's writing in this regard was part of a general European and American concern with the diverse long-term effects of injuries to the head and spine.[11] In the 1880s and 1890s in Britain and France these injuries were frequently linked to railway accidents, and the term "railway spine" designated an array of posttraumatic pathological effects.[12] But this approach did not result in finding hard anatomical evidence of a wound. To what, then, was the nervous system reacting, when it began to malfunction some time after the original accident (or shock) had taken place? How to understand a wound that refused to heal yet remained invisible?

For Charcot the many lawsuits brought against railway lines by passengers and workers who claimed to have suffered from some traumatic shock as a result of train travel were often based merely "on hysteria and only hysteria."[13] In saying this, Charcot was partly noting the hereditary antecedents of those who suffered from railway spine.[14] But he was also underscoring the disjunction between the pathogenic event (a train accident, a fight, a brush with danger) and the onset of symptoms, a disjunction both temporal and causal. Symptoms might not begin immediately after the original shock, and the symptoms that did arise could often not be reconnected to the original event through some plausible causal chain. The troubles of the young male hysteric might be linked in his mind to the time when he was frightened by a falling object, but it was impossible for the physician to discover how the trauma produced a wound which led to a wide range of hysterical symptoms.

The memory of some occurrence, and not the original experience itself, was seen as the pathogenic factor, and often at the center of the constellation of hysterical symptoms was an event that disrupted subsequent memory. The strange case of Mme. D.'s hysterical amnesia was discussed by Charcot, Janet, and other physicians of the 1880s.[15] Mme. D., thirty-four years old and the wife of an honest workman, was calmly sitting at her sewing machine in the small city of M., when she was told by a man she did not recognize: "Prepare a bed, we are bringing you your husband who is dead." She did not move but began to cry. The strange man told her to stop crying and to prepare the bed. Then, he left as suddenly as he had come. After the neighbors heard her cries, they returned with her husband, who was in good health and knew nothing of this. Upon seeing him, Mme. D. fell into convulsions. She cried out for her husband, and seemed to have hallucinations.

After this attack, Mme. D. awoke without any memory of what had transpired. Indeed, she had lost all memories dating back to the previous July 14, about six weeks prior to the false report of her husband's death. Moreover, and this is what attracted the interest of writers at the time, she seemed incapable of having any new memories. The trauma, when combined with a predisposition to hysteria, led to hysterical "retro-anterograde" amnesia. Charcot used the word "elaboration" to describe the process through which an idea or remembered event acquired hysterical potency over time. Through elaboration or autosuggestion the trauma accumulated force and became the root of the hysterical symptoms. Like hypnotic suggestion, elaboration was a process that took place in the brain, but not one that involved any conscious awareness. In the case of Mme. D., the shock of hearing of her husband's death and then seeing him continued to block her capacity to remember (and thus to experience) any new events.[16]

The concept of elaboration depended on a new and complex notion of the brain and of memory, one presupposing that an original event is remembered by the subject in ways that are independent of consciousness. The subject, or perhaps we can say "part of the subject," registers the event neurologically, storing its representation in the brain. The stored event continues to have effects on the workings of the nervous system, even if the event itself cannot be recalled consciously by the subject. This process, of course, is very familiar to us, but in the late nineteenth century the idea of memories having effects independently of consciousness was new and disturbing. Curiously, Charcot paid almost no attention to the significance of the stored event. The initial experience was treated like an electrical charge that continued to have consequences on the nervous system, not as an event that was cognitively or emotionally unbearable for the conscious subject. The shock of this experience could even divide the faculty of memory or "double" it. A doubled memory led to split personality, faculties of memory working in isolation from one another—the same phenomena that Azam saw in Félida X, a case that also fascinated Charcot because it put memory at the center of hysteria and split personality.

But Charcot did not pursue an investigation of doubling as a separate pathological entity. He saw the phenomenon under what he imagined as controlled conditions in hypnosis. Under hypnotism, subjects are given access to a set of memories different from those that they would recall in their normal personalities. This access can often be remembered, with the proper hypnotic suggestion, so as to integrate the different faculties of memory. In other words, once a forgotten event is remembered under hypnosis, it can often be opened to the normal faculties of recollection. Alternatively, that which happens during the hypnotic trance can, through suggestion, be closed off from remembrance in the normal state. "You will remember nothing of what has happened here after I awaken you."

These techniques were long familiar to mesmerists and more mainstream scientific investigators by the time Charcot announced his serious interest in hypnosis in 1882.[17] But when Charcot lent his prestige to the study of hypnosis and related states, it seemed to make new phenomena visible and old explanations suddenly worth taking seriously. Charcot took a narrow view of his subject, one that legitimated his own expertise. There was nothing mysterious about the phenomena, no invisible fluids or forces from the beyond. Hypnotism was a series of several "nervous states," which, like the stages of hysteria, could be isolated and described in detail. As Anne Harrington notes, "Charcot manages, in one fell swoop, both to give an aura of medical respectability to a formerly shunned and suspect subject, and simultaneously to stake a clear claim to the medical profession's exclusive competency to deal with this subject."[18] For him, hypnotism was an artificially created hysteria, and thus could be used to investigate cases of the spontaneously generated disease. One of the ways the master did this was by hypnotizing female hysterics and suggesting to them that they mimic the symptoms of male hysterics. His best patients performed splendidly.

In the case of Mme. D., hypnosis proved very valuable indeed. First, it allowed Charcot to determine that the woman was indeed registering her experiences, even though she could not recall them. "This woman," the doctor wrote, "whom we have been able to hypnotize, rediscovers in her hypnotic sleep the memory of all the facts that have transpired until the present."[19] Hypnosis thus revealed a "second self" which did not suffer the effects of the trauma that afflicted her conscious self. The traumatic idea, the false report of her husband's death, had acted as a form of suggestion, cutting off a faculty of memory as did hypnotic sleep. For Charcot, the nervous system of the traumatized subject functioned much like the nervous system of the hypnotized subject. They were hysterical. The task for Charcot in the case of Mme. D. was to use hypnotism to overcome the disjunction between the first and second selves. Hypnosis functioned both as the sign of the pathology and the possibility of curing it. If the patient was willing to follow the hypnotic suggestion to remember, then the wound of the trauma could be healed.

But remembering for Charcot did not have any of the connotations of integrating the self or facing one's desires that it would come to have in the twentieth century. Remembering was a behavior that Charcot wanted to promote, a behavior currently inhibited by a (probably degenerate) nervous system that had not recovered from a shock (a trauma) it had received. Marcel Gauchet has emphasized Charcot's indebtedness to the neurophysiologists who by 1870 had established that "the totality of the nervous system can and should be analyzed in terms of unities similar in structure and function; that is to say, in terms of sensori-motor connections and reflex processes."[20] The reflexive reactions of a degenerate nervous system following a trauma leave it vulnerable to suggestion—that is one of the key reasons for the production of symptoms. Suggestion can also be used to get the system back on track.

It is instructive here to examine how Pierre Janet made sense of this same case. Janet had a very different intellectual itinerary than Charcot, although their interests crossed over the field of hysteria and hypnotism. Whereas the latter came to this area from roots in neurology and clinical diagnosis, the former's intellectual formation began in philosophy, and he wrote his doctoral dissertation on psychological automatism on the basis of his experiments with hysterics in Le Havre.[21] Pursuing a second degree in medicine, he was invited by Charcot to direct a laboratory of psychological research at the Salpêtrière in 1889, where he especially studied the operations of memory in hysteria and hypnotism. For Janet, abnormal memory was at the core of hysteria: "I am convinced that amnesia is very important in hysteria," he wrote, "and that it is even one of the cardinal symptoms of this affliction . . . the principal fact which affects more or less all the others, [is] disturbance of memory."[22] Hysterics often seemed to live without past or future. Their amnesia, however, stemmed from their inability to connect to the memories that they did in fact have. The hysterics remembered, but they did not know that they remembered. The investigator could determine this through hypnosis.

> An amnesia of a hysterical nature . . . is not due to the destruction itself of traces left by sensations. In other words, in all hysterical amnesias the conservation of memories still continues . . . this forgetting is only an appearance, an illusion; it suffices to put her to sleep again, through suggestion, or better still through an automatic habit, to put her into a moral state analogous to that from which she has just emerged in order for her to rediscover her memories.[23]

Doctors first became aware that Mme. D. was conserving traces of events when she referred to them while talking in her sleep, crying out about the dog that had bitten her in the street.[24] While awake, she had no conscious recollection of the dog or her cauterization treatment for rabies (with Dr. Pasteur!). As noted above, when hypnotized Mme. D. did show that she recalled all the events since the practical joke. Janet also showed that Mme. D. could retain hypnotic suggestions and carry them out after she had been awakened from her somnambulistic state. There was memory in Mme. D. But where was it, and why was she unable to access it?

This last question is not one that seemed to interest Charcot. He wrote about the patient on the level of the nervous system, not on the level of consciousness. For Janet, on the other hand, Mme. D.'s dilemma was further evidence of unconscious or subconscious memory.[25] Psychologists (Janet was probably thinking especially of Ribot) had written extensively on two facets of memory: the conservation of memories and the reproduction of images. The third ingredient that Janet underlined was the "*perception personnelle des souvenirs*" (the personal perception of memories) or the "*assimilation des images*" (the assimilation of the [stored] images).

> It is necessary that the personal perception seizes this image and reattaches it to the other memories, to sensations either clear or confused, exterior or interior, the totality of which constitutes our personality.[26]

One can see Janet here as translating Charcot's neurological holism back into psychological terms. One of the major accomplishments of neurophysiology in the late nineteenth century was to use neurological response mechanisms to provide an explanation of human behavior without a dependence on the murky area of consciousness. These mechanisms operated independently of consciousness. Janet was, of course, well aware of these processes, having cut his intellectual teeth on the philosophical problem of automatic actions.

At least in regard to memory, however, he made their independence of consciousness an aspect of their abnormality as memory. Thus, in the case of Mme. D. her amnesia resulted from her inability to attach the registration of experience to the other memories which constituted her personality.

> It is as if these patients had become incapable of having a personal perception of their memories, of assimilating to their present personalities the images which continue to be conserved and automatically reproduced in their minds; as if their personalities, definitively blocked at a certain point, can no longer grow through the addition, the assimilation of new elements.[27]

The lack of a "personal perception of one's memories" not only restricts one's personality, it is linked with one's openness to imitate the personalities of others or to follow their hypnotic suggestions. Janet confronted the difficulty of using this tendency to imitation, to accept suggestions, as a weapon against the disintegrated self. Patients could be led to imitate an integrated personality. But did this make them well or merely continue (even deepen) the illness?

Janet's concern with the powers and dangers of hysterical imitation are particularly evident in his discussion of his treatment of Marceline.[28] Marceline entered the hospital in 1887 and was in a severely anoretic state. Refusing almost all food and water, unable to urinate, with severe visual and auditory impairments, and insensible across the surface of her body, she seemed only to have left a "last breath of life." Janet was alerted to the case by his brother Jules, and they attempted to hypnotize the patient in the hope of getting some food into her.

Marceline was easily hypnotizable, and the brothers were shocked by the "singular state" which the hypnotic trance brought on. She ate and drank without difficulty, was able to urinate on her own, and showed sensibility and unimpaired hearing and sight. The vivacity of the hypnotized Marceline was striking, but since the Janets regarded this state as "artificial," they felt obliged to "awaken" her. As soon as the hypnotic state was lifted, Marceline fell back into her prior condition, although she now also had a gap in her memory. She had no recollection of anything that had transpired while she had been hypnotized. Pierre Janet noted:

> Nevertheless, thanks to these artificial somnambulisms, we were able to nourish her and cause her to recover her strength. But it was always impossible to make her eat in the period considered normal,

> which we always brought back by awakening her. So that, tired of thus putting her to sleep at each meal, which was very long, we left her for whole days in the artificial state. The only result was apparently a great advantage, since all day she ate well, urinated completely, and presented more sensibility, memory, and activity. One day her parents, finding her in this fine artificial state, considered her cured, and took her out of the hospital.[29]

The "artificial state," however, did not last. With her first menstrual period, Marceline relapsed into her "normal" state, but this time she had forgotten the weeks since leaving the hospital. All the symptoms returned, and her parents brought her back to the hospital. "In the presence of all these disturbances," Janet reports, "I could do nothing else but put her to sleep again, or rather bring her back to her artificial state" (*MSH*, 88). He continues:

> Incredibly enough, this situation continued for fifteen years. Marceline would come to me in order to be put to sleep, enter into her alert state, and then go away very happy, with complete activity, sensibility, and memory. She would remain thus for a few weeks; then, either slowly or suddenly, in consequence of some emotion, fall back into her numbness, return to the state we had considered primitive and natural, with the same visceral disturbances. The forgetfulness now extended over whole years, and disturbed her existence completely. She would hasten to come to me to get herself transformed again. Things continued thus for years together, till the death of the poor girl, who succumbed to pulmonary tuberculosis. (*MSH*, 88–89)

Marceline's is an important case because it underlines how the study of hysteria became a study of what is normal. Which is the normal woman? How do we measure progress? One clear measure of her progress is that she is eating, that she is not near death. But she must be hypnotized in order to be "normal," and the cost of this progress is her increasing dependence on hypnotism and on the doctor. For Janet, "the provoked somnambulism became for this patient a second existence more complete than the first and was entirely substituted for it."[30] Do we read this as the loss of self or as the acquisition of a reasonable self, given to her by the physician?

Janet came to understand his patient as having lived in a normal state before puberty. Her problem was not that she had more than one personality.

Jules Janet had stressed that everyone has two personalities, but most people have their first at least as strong as the second. Thus, the second personality, the unconscious one, only erupts in dreams, when drunk, and "very occasionally."[31] Pierre came to believe that when they found Marceline in her anoretic state, she had already lost her normal self, and one of the chief signs of this loss was her amnesia. Hypnosis restored her memory and thus her first personality. By reconnecting her to the past the physician returned her to normality. Her second, disordered, destructive personality could be kept at bay through the forces of memory.

But the forces of memory relied on the power of hypnosis wielded by the physician. The success of the treatment depended on the patient's vulnerability to suggestion, but this vulnerability itself was a sign of the illness: "The very power of our suggestions, which seems to us positive, is a mark of the profound disaggregation of the mind, and the more the recovery appears to be easy, the more the mind is, in reality, sick" (*NIF*, 193). Those patients who were apparently healed through suggestion developed a need for more suggestion, a "surprisingly violent" need to confess, to be directed. Suggestion cannot set the patient free from the illness, because in hysteria "*la passion somnambulique*" (the hypnotic passion) is at the center of the illness (*NIP*, 211). The physician will naturally think his treatment is working well, as he sees the patient, eager to please him, returning for more treatments and apparently improving steadily as a result of the suggestions, the "moral guidance" he provides. But the physician should not be fooled:

> The true sign of the recovery of the patient is the departure of the physician, who one sends away with pleasure; unhappily, this sign does not exist among the patients with whom we work. They are always incapable of dismissing their doctor. This influence exercised by the physician on the patients appears crucial to us in these mental disturbances. (*NIF*, 208)

In cases like Marceline's Janet was inclined to attribute the need for suggestion to an extremely weak hereditary constitution. The hysteria is not fixed on a certain idea or a particular memory; it is a global condition which justifies pessimism about any long-lasting therapeutic outcome.

Mme. D.'s amnesia was specific and limited. Although there was some questionable nervousness in her family's past, she had been basically healthy until the "lugubrious joke" that the stranger had played on her. For Janet the case was crucial, because it pointed to what he saw as the root of traumatic hysteria: dissociation of the personality provoked by an intense emotion (*NIF*, 143). How was one to provide the hysteric with renewed capacities for psychological synthesis? One of the chief obstacles was the now elaborated memory of the trauma, which Janet described as an *idée fixe*. But whereas Charcot's neuro-hypnotic approach to Mme. D. was to find an efficacious suggestion to remember, Janet explored how forgetting might be essential to cure: "One of the most precious discoveries of pathological psychology would be that which would give us the certain means to provoke the forgetting of a specific psychological phenomenon" (*NIF*, 404).

After months of failing to get Mme. D. to make the false report a conscious memory, he attempted "to suppress it" ("*la supprimer*") or at least "to modify it" ("*la modifier*") so as to make it less frightening. While hypnotized, Mme. D. heard a knock at the door—but instead of the stranger entering the house, it was the psychologist himself! And instead of announcing the terrifying news, Janet's image said only: "Mme. D., prepare a bed because I would like to sleep at your house in M." (*NIF*, 146). Now when Mme. D. had the recurrent dream about the incident, it aroused much less emotion, thus allowing her personality to integrate the various segments of the past into her personal memory. Janet deelaborates the memory and thus removes its potency. In Charcot's terms, by manipulating the image he destroys its ability to continue to affect the nervous system. The past is in the way. By changing the past, the psychologist opens the possibilities of new memory for Mme. D.

Janet's interest in real trauma has made him an important figure for recent feminist critiques of Freud, and his emphasis on dissociation rather than repression has drawn the attention of many who work with people victimized by violence or traumatic accidents.[32] The Freudian concept of repression always involves the question of desire; how does the person's ambivalence interact with memory to disturb the present? Janet was usually uninterested in this sort of question, concentrating instead on eliminating the potency of the link to the past. Although he departed from Charcot's neurological model in very significant ways, Janet also regarded memory as a potentially pathogenic element, but one that could be diffused through certain techniques in the present. The potency of the past for both men was extremely dangerous, and Janet emphasized how forgetting was essential to any healthy existence. "[I]t is more difficult than one generally believes to forget something. To know how to forget something is often as important as to know how to learn, because forgetting is the condition of forward movement, of progress, of life itself"

(*NIF*, 404). An element from the past which disturbed the possibilities for psychological synthesis (a trauma) could be removed, or at least recomposed. "In a word, after the disappearance of the *idée fixe*, the unity of the spirit is reconstituted" (*NIF*, 405). The hygienic attributes of forgetting led the psychologist to reach beyond psychopathology for a general social law: "Forgetting is very often a virtue of individuals and peoples. 'It is necessary to know how to forget,' said Taine" (*EMH*, 422).

Janet struggled to find techniques that would give his traumatized patients the capacity to forget. Escaping from the grip of the past did not involve returning to it, or coming to understand its significance for one's present. The doctor could remove one's memory of the past, or at least change the past that one remembered. Nietzsche wrote that the will's "gnashing of teeth" and its "secret melancholy" was that it could not will backward, it could not change the past.[33] With hypnosis, Janet (and many of those around him) thought he had found a treatment that could.

Janet used hypnosis as a technology of forgetting in a variety of circumstances. In their somnambulistic states, hysterics had their traumatic memories or *idées fixes* removed like malignant tumors; or, perhaps more accurately, the growths were rendered benign. Of course, in these conditions, it is not the patient's will which is "willing backward." It is the physician's will (in the form of suggestion) which enters into the psyche of the patient when her or his own will is suspended through hypnosis. Janet regarded suggestion as an important psychological phenomenon, but (and here he remained linked with Charcot's school against the claims of Bernheim and the school of Nancy) he also regarded it as pathological. The more vulnerable one was to suggestion, the less stable was one's own psychological synthesis. Traumatic events were those that disrupted this synthesis, allowing unhealthy suggestions to develop into generally pathological behavior. Janet did not classify the types of events that might become traumatic. Everything depended on the overall health of one's psychological constitution—analogous to Charcot's neurological predisposition. If there were degenerate hereditary factors at work, the hysteric would only imitate psychological synthesis to satisfy his or her desire for suggestion. In cases where symptoms were caused by an isolated traumatic event, Janet believed that a healthy personal psychological synthesis could be restored by removing the experiences that had disrupted it.

Another case of Janet's provides an example of restoration through a transformation of the past. "Achille" thought he was possessed by the devil, but the psychologist discovered that it was the past that had taken control of his life.

In "A Case of Possession," Janet exorcises the past with the powerful tools of the new science. After making Achille's internal devil obey his commands under hypnosis, Janet was able to discover the precipitating cause, the *idée fixe* behind his patient's ornate "medieval delusions." Achille had been sexually unfaithful to his wife, was consumed by fear and guilt, and was possessed by a subconscious emotion of remorse (*EMH*, 403). How to remove the remorse? Remove the sin, and the remorse and the delusions around it would also vanish. "An idea, a memory, can be considered as a system of images that one can destroy in separating its elements, in altering them separately, in substituting in the compound one or another partial image for those which exist" (*EMH*, 404). In the case of Achille, a hallucination of his wife could be integrated through hypnotic suggestion into his reconfigured memory of adultery "*au moment convenable*" (*EMH*, 404). Thus, in rearranging the past, the psychologist grants a full pardon. Achille, we are told, returned home and remained in good health.

In this case of what he called *l'exorcisme moderne*, Janet participates in the Salpêtrière school's effort to use the tools of modern science to redescribe phenomena that had been thought to belong either to the world of religion or to the realm of the paranormal. In the *Bibliothèque Diabolique* series and in a variety of other publications, Charcot and his disciples used the language of psychopathology to demystify religious experience. Not only did they argue that witches were hysterics and not criminals, they also rewrote the biographies of saints to show that they, too, were hysterical. As they did with hypnosis, the doctors were attempting to show the power of their new techniques over material once thought to lie beyond the borders of science. By bringing this material into the scientific domain, the doctors were claiming new territory for the empire of rational investigation and thereby increasing their own power within the contest of competing scientific disciplines.[34]

But if hypnosis and suggestion offered a language that could be used to redescribe religious and paranormal phenomena, it also confronted some investigators with occurrences that deeply shook their scientific presuppositions. The experts in hypnosis at the end of the century were not only to be found at the Salpêtrière and other hospitals, but were also scattered around the country in carnivals, séance halls, and even the living rooms of the bourgeoisie. Despite Charcot's stern warnings about the danger of these unprofessional practitioners of hypnosis, in fin-de-siècle France they remained enormously popular.[35] And some of their most faithful auditors were men of science who sought not so much to bring the hypnotists or mediums within the territory of science, but to use their work to destroy its borders.[36]

Perhaps the most important and interesting of these figures is Charles Richet.[37] Richet's interest in hypnotism and in the mesmerists preceded Charcot's by several years, but since he did not medicalize the phenomena his work at first had little impact on the scientific community. A professor of physiology at the Sorbonne, Richet emphasized that the self was comprised of memory, and investigated hypnotism's capacity to erase one's personal memories and substitute for them another set of images, another self.[38] In cases of "artificial somnambulism," the new collection of images were the suggestions given by the hypnotist. Hysterics and those who suffered from a *dédoublement de la personnalité* (doubling of the personality) were often cases of spontaneous or natural somnambulism. How did suggestion work for them? Richet, like Janet, was fascinated by memories which seemed to work outside of consciousness. These memories functioned as suggestions, creating alternate personalities.

For Richet, memory was the "prolongation of an excitation" (*la prolongation d'une excitation*).[39] After some event was registered, the registration remained a permanent trace of the event. Conscious memory was just that bit of the past that we could recall at any given time. In fact, memory was much broader, since nothing was ever lost to it.

> As one has said for a long time, no fact disappears from memory: everything is fixed in it. Everything acts on us and leaves an indelible trace. Our intellectual existence at a moment is the result of all the impressions received in our past existence. How few, in this immense number, are perceived by consciousness.[40]

In order to investigate this broader memory, one had to make use of subjects who had access to the world beyond consciousness, and for Richet, like many of his colleagues, this meant work on psychopathologies. In addition, however, Richet was drawn to people on the margins of conventional society who claimed to have access not only to other states of consciousness but also to other worlds. The truth was revealed at the margins, whether these were in hospital wards or spiritist séances. As Joseph Maxwell, a colleague of Azam's in Bordeaux's hospitals and an assiduous participant in séances of the paranormal with Richet, said: "From the beginning of my experiments . . . I understood that one could study certain apparently supernormal manifestations only with the aid of mental and nervous pathology."[41]

Many of Charcot's colleagues (including Janet) were interested in paranormal phenomena. In the work for his doctoral dissertation Janet researched the claims of a medium, and Charcot's last publication dealt with faith healing.[42] But as we have seen, this sort of work was usually in the mode of demystification, the mode of showing how the extraordinary claims made for paranormal phenomena were either fraudulent or easily explained through the conventional categories of science (often of medicine). Richet thought of himself as a much more open-minded researcher than his counterparts at the Salpêtrière because he was ready to accept the possible occurrence of some phenomena that the doctors would never consider. Thus, he was one of the most enthusiastic researchers into that which could not be explained through our conventional understanding of the natural world. He wed a conventional belief in scientific progress (plus real scientific achievement) with an enormous appetite for the occult and the abnormal.

For example, Richet stressed the reasonableness of research into the appearance of ghosts. Now that we can communicate across space (through the telegraph and the telephone), the next task is to communicate over time. To communicate over time meant ultimately to eliminate the border of death. We do not expect to talk to our dearly departed grandparents, he assured his readers. But we do expect our great-grandchildren to contact us. That is what scientific progress is all about.[43] There would be nothing about this that violated the laws of nature.[44] On the contrary, Richet emphasized, our increased understanding and control of nature would allow us to overcome the temporal and spatial constraints that currently governed our lives. This was, after all, what science and technology had been doing throughout the second half of the nineteenth century. He was, he kept reminding his readers, a very reasonable man.[45]

As a biologist interested in memory, it seemed plausible to Richet to move from the rational investigation of hypnotism and memory into scientific research on life after death. The physiological basis of memory was the "prolongation of an excitation," a trace left somewhere independently of one's awareness. Hypnotism showed that human memory was far more extensive than human consciousness. Richet began with the nineteenth-century scientific truism that nothing disappeared from memory and then wondered whether traces of the past continued to exist independently of the normal human capacity to recall them. If the material basis of memory was simply the "prolongation of an excitation," then perhaps there were media other than the brain in which this prolongation continued. Perhaps normal recall was only one way to access past time, and there were other possibilities unreasonably excluded by mere prejudice.

> This does not mean that what is occult today will be occult tomorrow. Three hundred years ago, electricity was an occult force. Before Schelle and Lavoisier, chemistry was an occult science and was called alchemy; and it is only scarcely twenty years ago that animal magnetism ceased to be an occult science.[46]

Elsewhere, Richet wrote, "It is the first time that one dares to study *scientifically* that which follows death. Who, then, will dare to say, without having cast an eye on this work, that it is a folly?"[47] He wanted only to collect evidence for further scientific work, and he defended his work on telepathy and on spiritism with a straightforward appeal to empiricism. We must have the facts before we can try to make sense of these extraordinary claims!

Photography was the privileged medium for presenting these facts in the late nineteenth century, as it was considered by many as the technology that perfectly copied the world even while prolonging, in a real sense, its excitations. Richet used photography not to define and hence limit what counts as real, but instead to change the way we understood the nature of reality and our connection to it. The photographic plate could record aspects of the world that our eyes (at least the eyes of most people) were not sensitive enough to register. For those who believed that our unaided senses offered us only the most superficial connection to reality, photography provided a tool to investigate the possibility of other realms, other modes of existence (e.g., the supernatural, the abnormal). It also was used to provide evidence of the appearance of these other realms in our reality. Nothing, after all, escapes the camera. In this regard, the camera was imagined to be like memory, for which nothing was ever lost. The photograph *materialized* an event, fixing movement in a concrete, physical process. The abnormal could be made available for all to see.

Thus, many photographers were not only seeking the banal, the everyday, but they were on the hunt for the abnormal and the extreme. Reality contained more than most people ever saw, and the camera could expand the normal range of the visible by bringing the abnormal into it. Photographers went into the hospitals to photograph the sick, into the asylums to photograph the insane, into the jails to capture the prisoners (forever), into the séances to record how hypnosis was used to communicate with the beyond of the unconscious and the beyond of the *après mort*. The transmission of something like the *fluide vitale*, long appealed to by mesmerists, magnetizers, mediums, and hypnotists, would be *seen* through photographic inscription. In late-nineteenth-century France, these "extreme photographs" were used to expand the domain of the real, or at least to alter the conception of reality and its representation that had come to be accepted in the fin-de-siècle.

Photographs of ghosts were used as evidence of the existence of an afterlife, or at least of some world beyond the one visible to us in space and time. These pictures should be seen as part of a more general effort to find a place for the nonmaterial in a culture increasingly dominated by technological change and scientific legitimation. In the age of positivism the search for some evidence of the existence of an afterlife took on new forms. The acceleration of secularization in official culture in the last decades of the nineteenth century reconfigured the organization of interest in the "spiritual" or "nonmaterial" world. The increasing pace of technological change and scientific advance both explained more about the natural world and opened more mysteries in it. The development of electric power, the invention of the recording phonograph, and the discovery of Xrays are only a few of the markers of what was taken to be both signs of scientific power and indices of the profound mysteriousness of nature. For many, photography offered the possibility of recording this mysteriousness with one of the most powerful and accessible products of scientific progress. As Gabriel Delanne put it in 1893:

> We see how much importance critics attach to photographic proof: it establishes, in fact, irresistibly, the certainty that one has really witnessed an objective phenomenon, and that there is no question of hallucination in the Sight of the materialized spirit. . . . Well, we spirits, we have just told the positivists: we have become your disciples, we have adopted your method, and we accept as true only the truths demonstrated by analysis, the senses, and observation.[48]

The disciples of positivism would bring one of its favorite tools into the dark cabinets of spiritism. There the camera would ratify the reality of phenomena that otherwise would lie beyond the limits of the scientific imagination. Séance-goers were no more the dupes of fake mediums than were physicians falling for the malingering of false hysterics. Photography would substantiate the reality of the phenomena. One of the key words here is materialization: the process through which the spiritual or mental world, and especially the world of the past, is made manifest to us. Photography is the medium that can give this process a permanent, concrete form.

Photography was a powerful example of how an increased understanding of natural processes allowed us to have deeper insight into and control over the real. Already in the 1870s, attempts to photograph ghosts were in full swing. Photography could stop time (although, through the 1870s, it still took some time to get a proper exposure), thus making a permanent trace of reality. Thus photography could be used to satisfy—or at least address—the desire to remain in contact with the dead. Photographic portraits of the dead rapidly became a commonplace in late-nineteenth-century bourgeois France, with many of the big Parisian studios advertising portraits *d'après decés* (after death) as part of their repertoire of services for the consumer. These portraits were usually taken in the hours just after death, when the pain of loss was most acute and the possibilities of photographic preservation most apparent. In the 1870s, however, an enterprising Parisian photographer, Buguet, had the idea of using the medium to photograph the deceased even after they had been long buried. He brought mournful clients to his studio at 5 Boulevard Montparnasse where they would be kept waiting with another "client" who in reality was an associate of the photographer and who acquired information about the physical characteristics of the deceased. When the real client entered the studio proper, he or she was asked to concentrate on the dearly departed. Buguet explained that through a very special process the photographic plate could capture the connection that was established between the intense memory of the client and the deceased. After finishing the supposed exposure, the photographer withdrew into a second studio where he sketched on the plate an impression of a head to "satisfy all tastes."[49] Buguet's studio became well known, and it was even doing a mail order business ("concentrate on the photographer and the deceased, and our special camera can record the image . . . distance is no obstacle"). Satisfaction was guaranteed. If the picture does not look at all like your loved one, send it back and we'll try again. Eventually, the police took an interest in the studio, and when Buguet produced a picture of what was supposed to be the commissaire's deceased wife, he was promptly arrested. The commissaire had never married.

The photographic con artist became notorious after his 1875 trial, and the photography of spirits fell into general disrepute by the late 1870s. But with the increased scientific importance given to hypnotism and hysteria in the 1880s and 1890s, photographers were once again enlisted to make the abnormal real and concrete. Hysteria was said by many to be the somatization of desires and of traumatic memory; this process could be revealed by hypnosis. Hysterical symptoms were the materialization of the past, of the hysteric's wounded memory. Physicians, psychologists, and philosophers worked extensively with mediums who could reproduce hysterical symptoms when in hypnotic trance. The hypnotic trance allowed the hysteria to take a material form. The trance could also allow the spirit to take material form. Photography could record this *materialization* of the beyond just as it had recorded the somatization of the hysterical desire in a symptom.

One of the prominent theories of hypnosis in the last two decades of the century linked the trance to "the doubling of personality." The person (usually a woman) in the hypnotic trance was said to enter into (or create) another personality. According to Aleksandr Aksakof, the photographic plate was able to register the form of this other personality—as distinct from the body of the person in trance. For Aksakof, the photograph reveals something that is not visible to the human eye. The light-sensitive plate can capture things that elude us. Aksakof here goes beyond using the camera to make permanent astonishing but ephemeral things we have seen. He thinks of photography as offering us a new tool for recording the invisible so as to expand what we can see.[50]

Hyppolite Baraduc was one of photography's most ardent explorers of the invisible. Unlike the scientists who went to séances armed with a camera in case a ghost appeared, Baraduc was using the light-sensitive plate to record what we never could see, attempting to create an "iconography of the invisible."[51] In this realm, "nothing is lost . . . everything is transformed; and if we now rediscover the earthly dust of worlds or of beings that have existed, we should also be able to rediscover *vécues potentialities* [lived potentialities], the shadows of those who have passed."[52] Photography is not limited to the body, but can register the vital forces that continue to emanate from our spirit. Thus, photography is our chief weapon against time, not because it can freeze the moment in which action takes place, but because it can show us that *nothing is lost* in our world. Death is only transformation and photography can give us evidence of the results of this process.

The publication of photographs that claimed to show the mysterious forces at work in our universe quickly resulted in essays that challenged the interpretations of the images. For the brothers Lumière, writing in the 1890s, the halo effect that so captivated Baraduc was only a technical problem of certain cameras or plates, and it could be alleviated through the choice of particular lenses.[53]

If photographs of the invisible were dismissed as illusions generated in the darkroom, how was one to explain the photographs that recorded the very strange phenomena that were occurring in séances at the end of the century? Verbal reports from even the most distinguished observers could be dismissed or attributed to *tromperie* (fraud), but who could "deny the reality of the photograph"? With the advent of fairly rapid exposure times and of flash photography, cameras joined scientific observers to document how the hypnotic trance (variously figured as access to an unconscious, a second personality, or a different dimension of temporality) allowed another world to become visible in ours. One of the great products of this effort to document the reality of the spirit world through photography is Julliete Alexandre-Bisson's *Les Phénomènes dits de matérialisation: étude experimentale*, published in 1914, based on her experiments in the late nineteenth and the early twentieth centuries with Dr. Schrenk-Notzing and the medium Eva. These experiments produced "ectoplasm," the substance that emerges from the medium as a sign of the beyond (this, after all her orifices had been checked before the séance by Schrenk-Notzing and other observers to guard against trickery), and ideoplasms. Ideoplasms were images that appeared above or behind the medium's head—faces of a spirit called from the beyond. The photographer could capture that ephemeral image in a permanent form.

The ectoplasm that emerges from the medium's mouth or other bodily cavities was evidence of contact with the beyond, and the ideal photograph would show the medium in the throes of putting forth this mysterious substance (figs. 1–2). With ideoplasms, the best example is when the ghostly image seems to emerge out of the ectoplasm—so we have a double dose of evidence from another world grasped by the photographic apparatus (figs. 3–4).

If it was difficult to doubt the veracity of the photographic recording (*something* was in front of the camera and the witnesses), it was very possible to question what was being recorded. Skeptical critics pointed out that the ideoplasms resembled photographs of famous people that had appeared in popular magazines; the medium had cut these out, attached them to a stick and a black sheet, and in the dark room someone had waved them about in front of the gullible séance participants. The photo of the so-called ideoplasm, the critics claimed, was really a photo of a photo! Schrenk-Notzing replied that the ideoplasm was a materialization of the medium's hypnotized memory of a photograph. First there is the photo of a famous person. The image becomes part of the medium's extraordinary memory, and these mnemonic powers cause a materialization of the image, which is then photographed by the

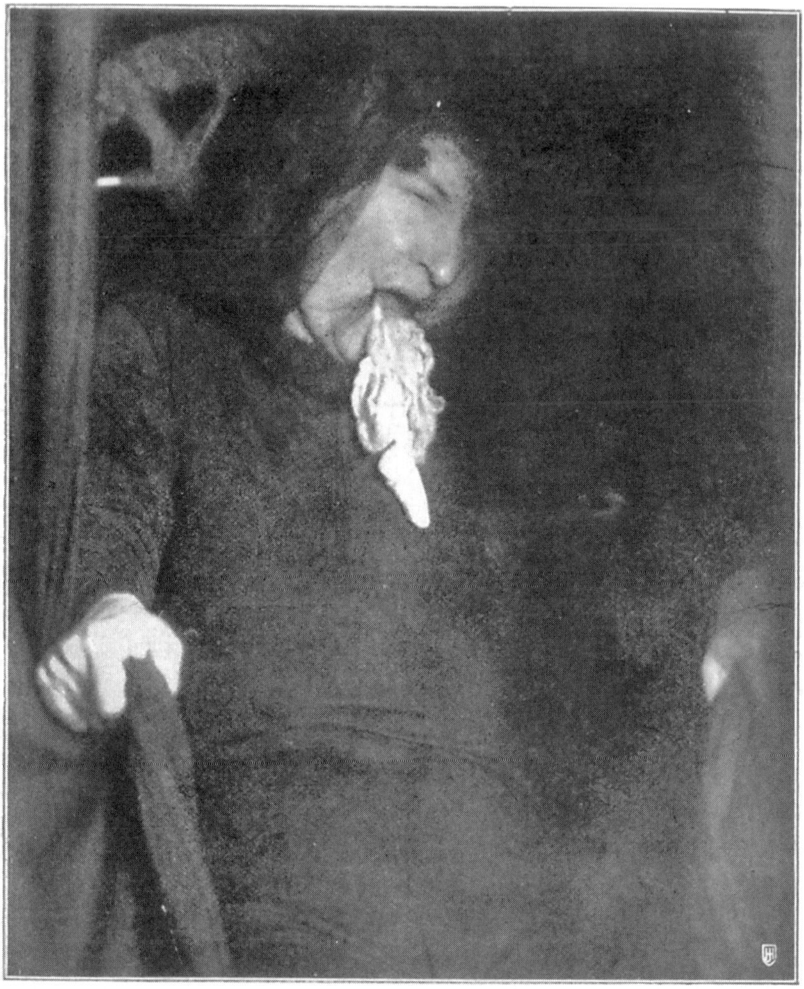

FIGURE 1. Anonymous, photograph of "ectoplasm," a substance that emerges from the medium. From Julliete Alexandre-Bisson, *Les Phénomènes dits de la matérialisation: étude experimentale* (Paris: Félix Alcan, 1914).

FIGURE 2. Anonymous, photograph of "ectoplasm," a substance that emerges from the medium. From Alexandre-Bisson, *Les Phénomènes dits de la matérialisation.*

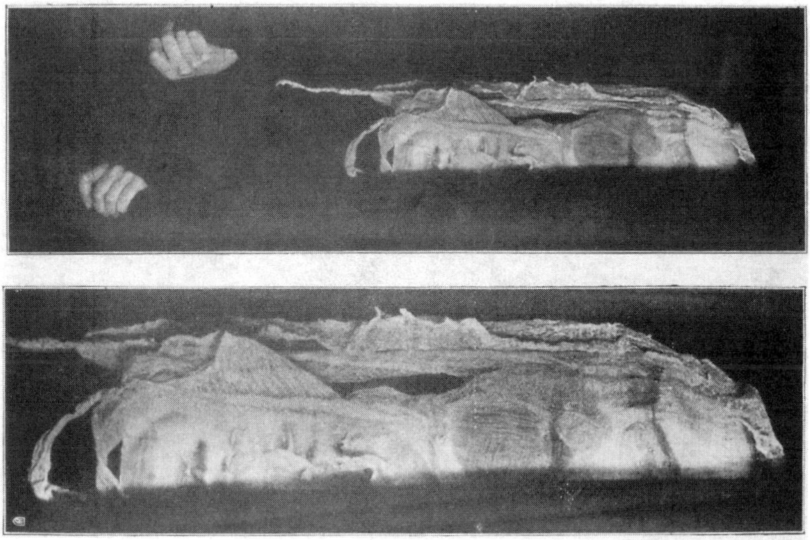

FIGURE 3. Anonymous, photograph of "ideoplasm," an image that appeared above or behind the head of a medium. From Alexandre-Bisson, *Phénomènes dits de la matérialisation.*

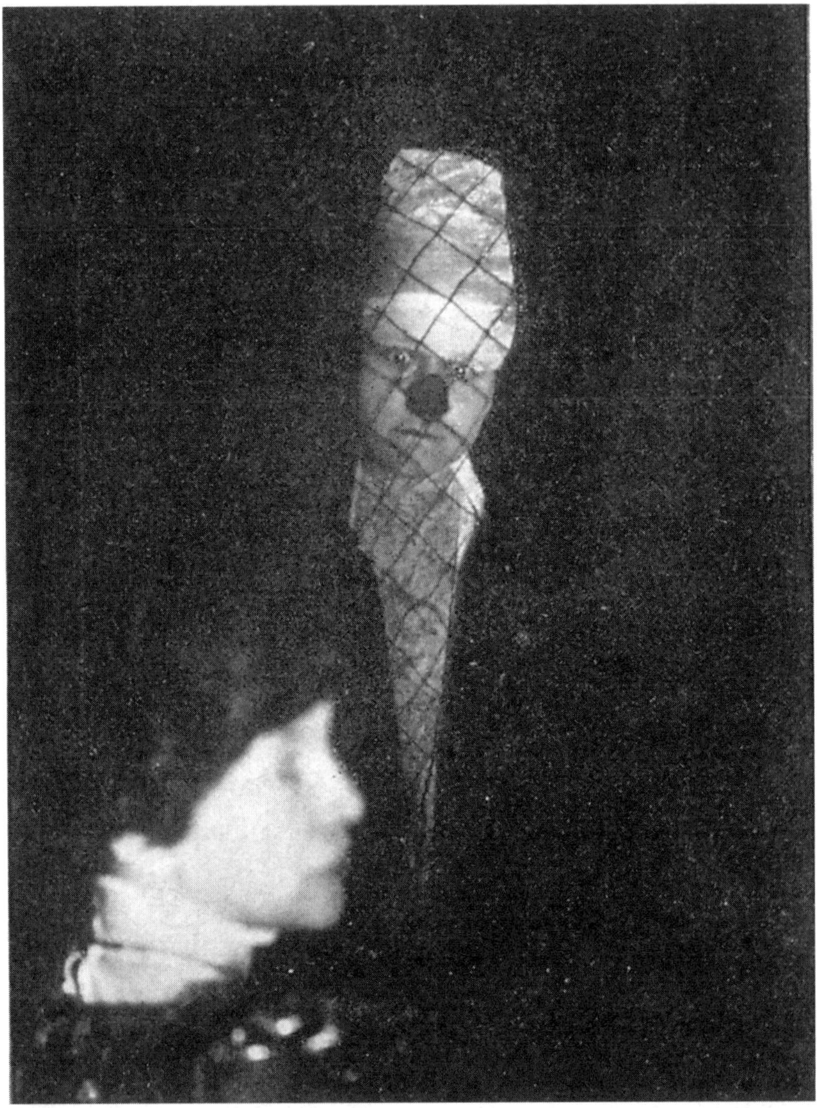

FIGURE 4. Anonymous, photograph of "ideoplasm," an image that appeared above or behind the head of a medium. From Alexandre-Bisson, *Les Phénomènes dits de la matérialisation*.

investigator. Thus, the ideoplasm is not a fraud, it is the return of the image to the concrete through a powerful projection of memory. The photographer in the séance records this projection and the image produced should count as evidence of the reality of the powers of the medium's memory. The medium's powers were real, even if they led only to the imitation of an image. And photography's powers to document remained substantial, even if they led only to copies of other photographs in the effort to realize the fervent desire to see beyond the visible and to live beyond the limits of mortality.

We saw above that doctors working with hysterics considered their symptoms as materializations of the past. In the hospitals, too, photography became a privileged medium for representing these materializations.[54] And these doctors so concerned with the fragility and the malleability of memory sought to register their own work with permanence. In 1875 Bourneville and Regnard set up a photographic service in Charcot's wing of the Salpêtrière, and soon after they began publishing pictures alongside their case studies, This was six years after the establishment of the Photographic Revue of the Hospitals of Paris, a publishing venture in which Bourneville became an editor in 1870. Photography gave direct access to the Truth, and the directors of the journal hoped to have as much success with their medium as did clinical photographers of skin disease who had been at work already for some time. Charcot considered himself not a theorist of hysteria, but someone who was able to see it more clearly than anyone else. Seeing things cleanly, grasping them with the eye and without theory was an attempt to see them outside of time. The perfect instrument for that (the perfect weapon, as Didi-Huberman has said) was photography. It was photography that helped the celebrated doctor respond to the charge that the hysterics in the Salpêtrière were merely imitating the disease that Charcot and his famous patients had prescribed for them. In 1887 the doctor wrote: "It would be something truly miraculous if I could thus create these diseases according to my caprice and my fantasy. But the truth is that I am there absolutely only the photographer; I inscribe what I see."[55] The doctor is a light-sensitive plate, he merely receives and records the symptoms.

The difficulty with this analogy, however, is that the doctor himself is both discursive (the images must be translated into words) and transitory (when he is no longer there to see, what he has seen disappears). The photographic study is the perfect complement to the vision of the doctor. The photograph dispenses with the need for words; nothing can be lost in the translation. The photograph is permanent, an absolute memory which will be fresh long after the doctor is gone. But *what* is seen?

In one photograph (fig. 5), published in 1878, we see Augustine in her normal state. Where in this picture is the hysteria? Where is the recording or the inscription of a disease? A photograph like "Tetanisme" (fig. 6) is to reveal the core of the illness, or perhaps the signs of the illness. Or is it that in hysteria the signs are the core of the disease? By now the series of images known as *Attitudes Passionnelles* (hysterical postures) are quite familiar (figs. 7–9).[56] There are many more photographs of Augustine in the various positions that had come to be famous as the positions of hysteria.[57] The camera, like Doctor Charcot, is presented as inventing nothing, suggesting nothing. The photographic imperative will see all, will demand revelation from *the patient*. The photographic imperative must see into the disease. The model seems to have been the photographs which were eventually housed in the museum of dermatological disorders. These images are able to enclose the disease as they record its signs. The diseased organ, the skin, is there before us in these pictures; but where is Augustine's disease? Where is it *located*?

The photographic imperative will record what is revealed. But with the hysteric, the camera's desire to reveal is itself recorded in the look (even when the eyes are closed) of Augustine. The hysteric is the subject who will be revealed, and although in this period male hysteria is recognized (with some pride) as a possibility, it is the woman who is revealed by the male doctor and his camera. Knowing the desire for revelation, acknowledging this desire in her own look, in the positions of her body, becomes a part of hysterical desire, and perhaps of hysterical suffering. We see revealed by the photographs the desire for revelation of the photographer, of the psychiatrist whose fantasy of passively recording the desire of these women becomes part of their desire, becomes part of their hysteria. And, of course, the mise-en-scène of these pictures, their artfulness, discloses the futility and the denials of this dream of passive recording. In the Archives de l'Assistance Publique one can consult what seems to be some of the original photographs eventually published in the *Iconographie*. On the back of a few of them, written lightly in pencil, there are instructions to the photographer for publication-ready copies: "Lighten a little the bottom of the clothes and the hands; accentuate the eyes in the sentiment of the gaze [*sentiment du regard*]; put a few creases in the blouse."[58]

This was frustrating work for the physician and his photographer. The hysteric's illness, according to many, was in her deception, her *appearance* of illness. This did not mean she was faking, or that she was not ill. As the

FIGURE 5. Anonymous, photograph of Augustine in her normal state. From *Iconographie de la Salpêtrière,* vol. 2 (Paris: P. Regnard, 1879–1800).

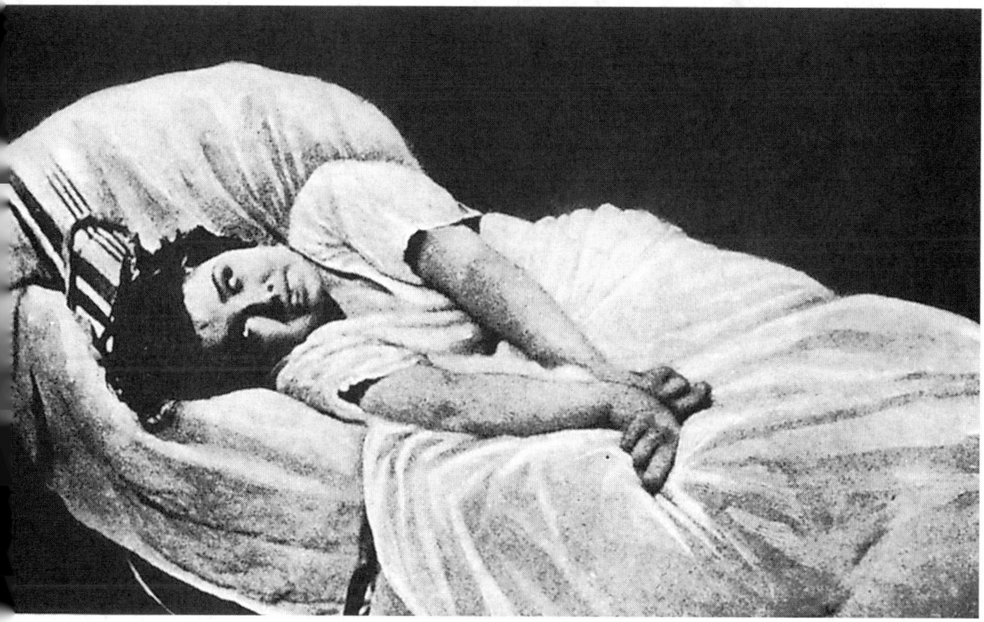

FIGURE 6. Anonymous, photograph of patient with "tetanism," a symptom of hysteria. From *Iconographie de la Salpêtrière*.

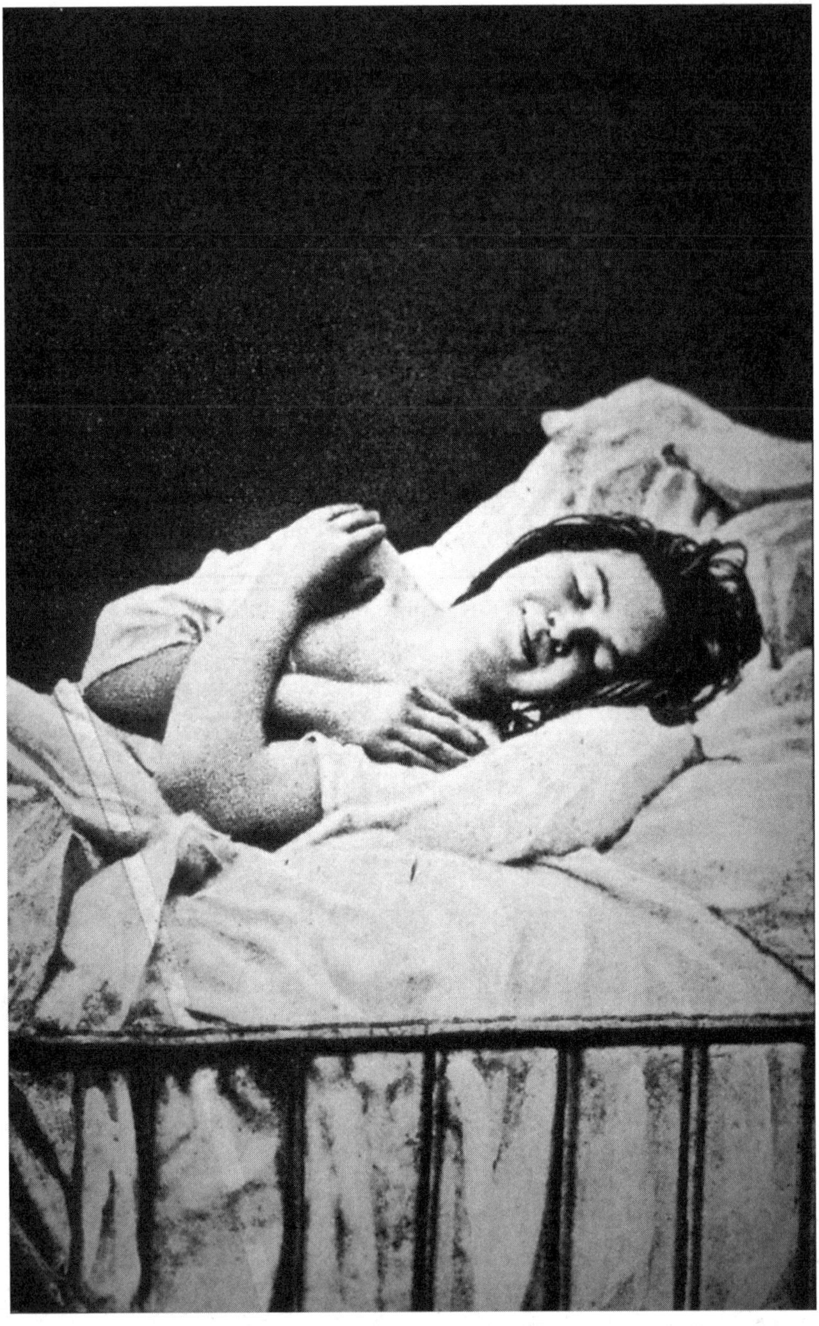

FIGURE 7. Anonymous, photograph of patient in one of the "attitudes passionnelles," or hysterical poses. From *Iconographie de la Salpêtrière*.

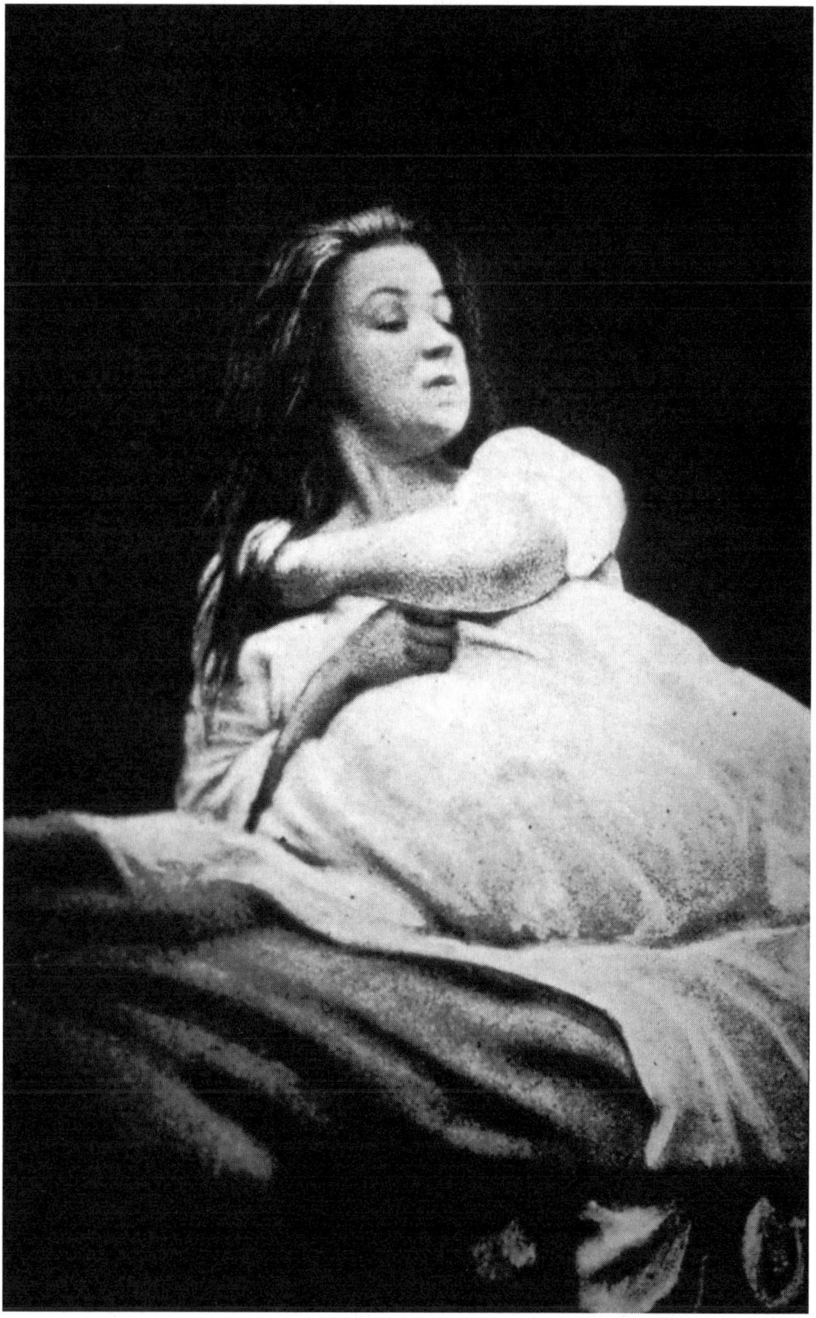

FIGURE 8. Anonymous, photograph of patient in one of the "attitudes passionnelles," or hysterical poses. From *Iconographie de la Salpêtrière.*

FIGURE 9. Anonymous, photograph of patient in one of the "attitudes passionnelles," or hysterical poses. From *Iconographie de la Salpêtrière*.

psychiatrist Lasègue noted, not anybody who pleases can be a hypochondriac; the symptoms of hysteria could be lies, but they were still symptoms of a real illness.[59] (Remember the photograph of the ghost/photograph.) How does the hysteric force her body to lie? How could photography, in recording that lie, capture the truth? What if the hysteric's production of symptoms is stimulated, aroused by the photographer's sensitive recording of appearance? The attempt of the physician to record the hysteric, to commit her through images to a memory which knew no forgetting, placed the photographic imperative within the dialectics of hysterical desire, by which I mean a desire for recognition combined with a radical denial of the possibilities for satisfying this desire. The physician/photographer was in the position to reward the hysteric by seeing (and preserving) her as a model of the disease. The hysteric was in the position of rewarding the physician/photographer by giving him the model of hysteria. The pictures were immediately criticized for being modeled, that is, for picturing merely imitations of symptoms. The models were too good. The women, the critics said, were only responding to suggestion, not from some trauma in the past, but from the doctors or other patients. The photographs only recorded the product of the suggestion. But was susceptibility to suggestion a real disease, and, if so, how was it to be recorded?

After leaving the Salpêtrière, Dr. Bourneville became the director of the service of hysteria, epilepsy, and idiocy at Bicêtre, a men's hospital outside of Paris. At his new post, the doctor continued to make use of photography. He wanted to commit the physicians' work on disease to memory in forms that escaped the problems of the interdependence of the hysteric and her photographer. Bourneville is an exceptionally interesting character. An accomplished physician, he was a radically anticlerical deputy to the National Assembly. Not content with chasing the church from hospitals and positions of pedagogic power, Bourneville edited the *Bibliothèque Diabolique*, which published retrospective diagnoses of saints and miracle workers as hysterics *avant la lettre*. In 1885 Bourneville established the *musée pathologique* (pathological museum) at Bicêtre. The museum collected human skeletons, bones of animals, and fetuses in various stages of development. Mme. Forino, a midwife from the suburb of Gentilly, considerably enriched the museum's collection with her own private holdings in 1886. The museum also contained portraits of physicians at the hospital, and photographs of patients in various stages of their illness, including portraits of the dead and of cadavers during autopsies. Bourneville seemed to worry that the public would think of the museum as a collection of curiosities, and in the *Bulletins* of 1887, and also

1888, 1889, and 1890, he repeated that he had not collected objects for the merely curious, but materials to be used in serious research. Not only should physicians be able to use the museum for further study, the general public should find there the evidence of medicine's steady progress against the ravages of disease.

In 1887 Parisian newspapers reported the visit of the Minister of the Interior to the pathological museum at Bicêtre. The museum was made up of one room that stored specimens meant to shed light on various diseases: epilepsy, idiocy, hysteria. A favorite technique for preserving the signs of disease were wax models of bodies twisted by illness. But photography remained a privileged form. One paper noted that the minister stopped for some time before photographs of children under the care of Bourneville. "It was easy to follow the phases of the disease. To the extent that the patient entered the path of healing, the structure of the face is modified, the brutal impression of characteristics is attenuated, pupils are dilated, the eyes become clear and lively and the cheeks are colored and take on a shade of freshness and health."[60] Progress for the patient. Progress for the doctor. Progress for the minister.

But these are not the photographs I have seen. What remains of the *musée pathologique* are not signs of progress but signs of the inexorable degradation that disease brings. We see children standing next to a measuring stick when admitted to the unit; we see them next in various stages of their stay in the hospital. In one series, a young girl, Blaise, is shown looking scared, small but almost precious next to the measuring rod. Like all the other children in these pictures, she is clothed in warm, winter greys. Then we see her some months later and the illness has overwhelmed the person. We then see her dead, photographed on the cold metal table. But this is not the end of the story: the insistence on taking the camera to the core of the disease ends up with a photograph of a brain, which the inscription beneath tells us was once hers.

In other photographs (figs. 10–14) we see the death masks—or should I call them death skulls?—made before autopsy. They are among the many found tucked away on the shelves in the basement of the Museum of Public Assistance of the City of Paris. Some of the skulls show extraordinary deformations. Others are striking for their expression, the wisps of hair which still cling to eyelashes and scalp after a hundred years. The skulls—and remember the claim that these were not objects of curiosity, but tools for serious research—were kept in cabinets to be seen by hospital visitors, doctors, and those who would in the future admire the work done to understand illness and heal the sick.

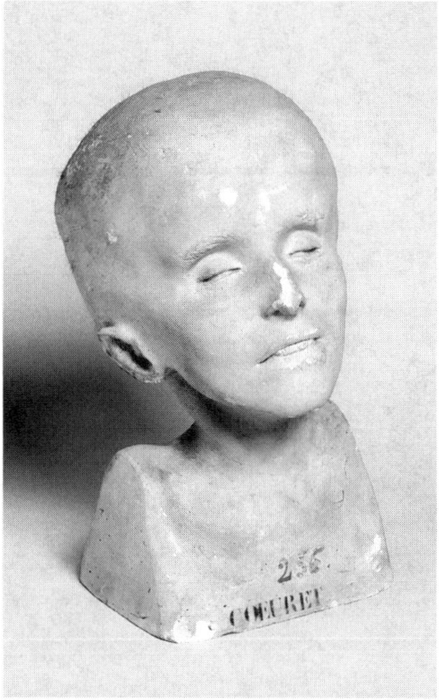

FIGURE 10. Plaster cast taken from a young patient of Dr. Bourneville, ca. 1885. From the Musée de l'Assistance Publique de Paris.

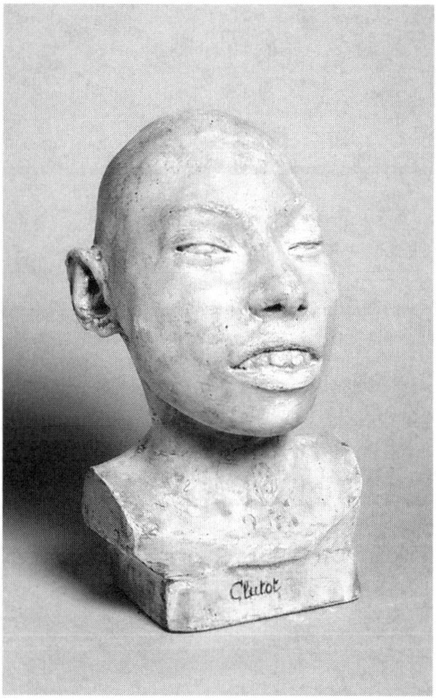

FIGURE 11. Plaster cast taken from a young patient of Dr. Bourneville, ca. 1885. From the Musée de l'Assistance Publique de Paris.

FIGURE 12. Plaster casts taken from a young patient of Dr. Bourneville, ca. 1885. From the Musée de l'Assistance Publique de Paris.

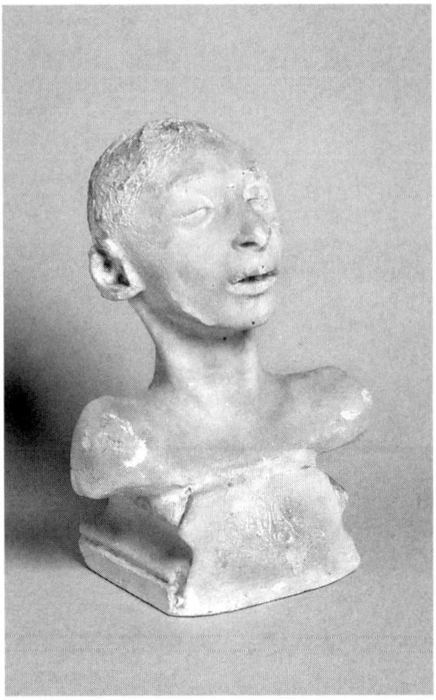

FIGURE 13. Plaster cast taken from a young patient of Dr. Bourneville, ca. 1885. From the Musée de l'Assistance Publique de Paris.

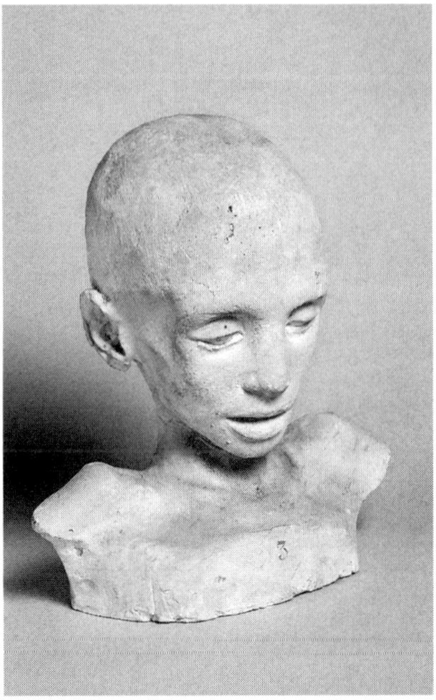

FIGURE 14. Plaster cast taken from a young patient of Dr. Bourneville, ca. 1885. From the Musée de l'Assistance Publique de Paris.

Charcot had told the doctors in his department that they should think of the extraordinary number and diversity of ailments available to them at the Salpêtrière as a vast *musée pathologique vivant* (living museum of pathology). Later, like Bourneville, he aimed at something more permanent, and more public: a museum that would house the challenges and triumphs of the new school of psychiatry. Bourneville, in his pathological museum at Bicêtre, wanted to inscribe his work in permanent forms: photography, wax figures, plaster skulls. A living museum, a museum of the living, would die, its figures disappear. With photographs and sculpture, the terror of illness and the capacities of medicine to overcome that terror could be rendered permanent. Memory, these doctors knew, had to be embodied. But bodies, they also knew, degraded, vanished. The *musée pathologique* would overcome forgetting in a permanent tribute to scientific progress and the powerful physicians who made it possible.

But as I said, the skulls are in the basement of a museum, and not one known for attracting long lines of people. There is almost nothing left of

Charcot's museum at the Salpêtrière. Soon after these doctors died, their memorials were unfunded, their treasures unclaimed or dispersed. The museum's traces, its remains, have been almost forgotten. What do these photographs and plaster figures still express of the doctors' hopes for recognition, for permanent progress; what do they express of the patients' agony in the final degradation of disease?

Following Charcot, Freud wrote of hysterical symptoms as residues and mnemonic symbols of particular experiences. He compared the signs of disease to monuments and other symbols of memory.[61] In late-nineteenth-century French psychiatry, Freud learned to think of hysteria as the failure to overcome trauma. A fixed idea is elaborated into a symptom or into a sign, the past remains in the present. The doctors, too, tried to keep the past in full view of the present. Of course, they did not embody past traumas, they tried to memorialize past triumphs. French doctors at the end of the nineteenth century seized new technologies of representation to immortalize patients whose pasts continued to wound them. In so doing, it would be too much to say they behaved like their hysterical patients. But we can see how the pathological museums came to resemble the hysterics in their display of temporal disorder; the painful disruptions of hysteria and the cool display of disease and death in the museum are inverted metaphors for one another. Both embodied signs (of achievement, of trauma) which were never to be forgotten. And both exemplify that desire which can become pathological: the desire to overcome memory and forgetting, to overcome the passage of time by representing and collecting the ephemeral in permanent form.

PART 2

HISTORY AND THE PSYCHE

4. Trauma, Representation, and Historical Consciousness

Trauma is a problem both for psychoanalysis and for historical consciousness. At the core of the problem are the links among trauma, repetition, and the dilemmas of representation (particularly narrative representation). Those dilemmas and the demand for acknowledgment through some form of representation are crucial for understanding contemporary debates about memory and its putative recovery, and for coming to terms with some of the most pressing issues with reference to the construction of historical meaning. A useful place to begin discussion of these matters is with models of trauma against which psychoanalysis originally defined itself, particularly those of Jean-Martin Charcot and Pierre Janet. Psychologists of the late nineteenth century in France were intensely concerned with dramatic failures to live with the past, hysteria being perhaps their prime example. But they worked in a milieu in which the more general concern was with how people, and countries, came to live successfully with their pasts while dealing with rapid change and the cult of the future. The pathologies of memory that concerned these psychologists were often connected with social pathologies that commentators saw plaguing their societies. This was among the important contexts, of course, in which Freud came to formulate his own ideas about how to make sense of the past in order to live with it in a less painful way. What does one do with a painful past that cannot be simply willed to disappear yet is a source of enormous difficulties in the present? This was as much a question for the nineteenth-century doctor working with hysterics as it is for the contemporary historian of traumatic events. The dilemma of living with one's personal past may be quite different from that of living with others with whom one shares only certain aspects of a past—there is no perfect isomorphism between the psychological and the historical—but skepticism is in order about claims that there is an obvious chasm between these realms of memory.

When Freud began his work in neurology, the concept of trauma had only recently been imported into that field and into the new discipline of psychology. He encountered the neuropsychiatric understanding of trauma in his studies in Paris with Charcot, whose work on hysteria at the Salpêtrière in the 1870s and 1880s placed the disease at the center of French cultural life.[1] Although the famous neurologist saw trauma at the heart of the etiology of hysteria, Charcot himself gave almost no attention to the *meaning* of the traumatic event. An extraordinary experience is treated as if it were an electrical charge that continues to have consequences for the nervous system (as opposed to an event that is cognitively or emotionally unbearable for the conscious subject). The shock of this kind of experience may divide the faculty of memory, or "double" it. A doubled memory is held to lead to split personality, to faculties of memory working in isolation from one another. This phenomenon (termed a "hypnoid state" by Josef Breuer in his work with Freud) had been described by Eugène Azam in regard to his famous patient, Félida X.[2] Félida X fascinated Charcot because her case placed memory at the center of hysteria and split personality. But Charcot did not investigate doubling as a discrete pathological phenomenon; he observed it, under what he imagined to be controlled conditions, through hypnosis. In a hypnotic trance, subjects are given access to a different set of memories than they would otherwise recall, and once a "forgotten" event is remembered under hypnosis and thus opened to the normal faculties of recollection, the different faculties can be integrated. On the other hand, what transpires during the hypnotic trance can, through suggestion, be closed off from recollection in the normal state. Hypnotism was, according to Charcot, an artificially created hysteria, and thus could be used to investigate cases of the spontaneously generated disease. One of the ways Charcot accomplished this was by hypnotizing female hysterics and suggesting to them that they mimic the symptoms of male hysterics.

As discussed in chapter 3 Charcot found hypnosis very valuable in the case of Mme. D., the unfortunate woman whose hysteria seemed to have been instigated by a practical joke played on her. Although in her "normal" state she did not seem to register any events in her memory, under hypnosis she had normal recall. Hypnosis thus revealed a second self that did not suffer the effects of the trauma that afflicted her conscious self. For Charcot, the nervous system of the traumatized subject functioned much like the nervous system of the hypnotized subject; both were hysterical. The traumatic idea, in Mme. D's case the false report of her husband's death, acted as a form of suggestion that cut off one faculty of memory, much as hypnotic sleep would do. The task for Charcot was to use hypnotism to overcome the disjunction between the first and second selves. Hypnosis functioned both as the sign of the pathology and as the possibility for curing it. If the patient was willing to follow the hypnotic suggestion (that is, to remember), then the wound of the trauma could be healed. But remembering did not have for Charcot any of the connotations of integrating the self or facing one's desires that it would come to have in the twentieth century. Remembering was a behavior that Charcot wanted to promote, a behavior inhibited in the cases he studied by what he thought of as a degenerate nervous system that had not recovered from a shock (a trauma) that it had suffered. Remembering was for him part of the ecology of a healthy individual. A balance between present and past seemed as necessary for the individual as for the *patrie*. Progress appeared to depend on some sense of the past: not so strong as to distract one from normal development toward the future but strong enough to orient that development in a hygienic direction.

Recall how differently Pierre Janet, who worked in Charcot's section of the Salpêtrière, made sense of Mme. D's case. After using hypnosis to show that there was indeed memory in Mme. D, he wanted to discover why she was unable to access it. This question seems not to have interested Charcot. He wrote about the patient on the level of the nervous system not on the level of consciousness. For Janet, Mme. D's amnesia was comprised exactly of her inability to attach the registration of her day-to-day experiences to the other memories from prior to the hysterical attack that constituted her personality. It was not enough to preserve the traumatic past in some isolated neurological archive or storage system for it to be benign, it had to be integrated with the rest of one's life.

The lack of integration—what Janet called a personal perception of one's memories—is debilitating in many ways, and it is importantly linked with an openness to imitate the personalities of others or to follow their hypnotic suggestions. Janet confronted the difficulty of using imitation and suggestion as weapons against the disintegrated self: patients might obey a suggestion to imitate an integrated personality, but did this make them well or merely continue (even deepen) their illness?

These concerns have their parallels in the discussion of historical trauma in late-nineteenth-century France.[3] There were intense debates about how the national culture should be tied to its sources and traditions in order to be more successfully modern or more essentially French: how was the nation to be brought back to tradition, if tradition was an automatic and natural practice? At the same time there were strident voices calling for France to become truly modern so as to compete with her European rivals. But did becoming modern mean imitating those rivals, and, if so, was it possible to prevail yet still retain one's identity? These familiar questions were radicalized and more closely tied to the language of psychology after World War I. Recovering from shell shock became a metaphor for national difficulties of reconstruction. Since World War II, historical trauma has often been discussed as an event in the past that is repressed, or at least insufficiently attended to, and thus not properly part of historical consciousness. The problem is not that the past event has been forgotten—many events are forgotten—but that the event has not been left behind successfully. It continues to have effects in the present.

One of the effects and signs of an "elaborated" (to use Charcot's term) or potent historical trauma is the vulnerability of the traumatized group to suggestion, its propensity to imitation. Having lost its own orientation because a part of its history is inaccessible, the group mimics or appropriates the behavior of more successful, "healthier" groups. The discussion of national imitation as a response to collective trauma has been an important feature of recent debates about World War II in both Europe and Asia. As the dynamics of imitation (and more dysfunctional symptoms) have become a point of focus, debates are reengaged about what to do with a past that is both known and not known. Some argue that it has to be more completely remembered, attended to, worked through. Others claim that, since the event is already an obsessive concern in the present, the task is to return the event to its proper place in the historical scheme of things (as only one event among many in the nation's history). The former response calls for more powerful recollection; the latter for more powerful forgetting. We might say that both presuppose the kind of psychological holism that was the framework for Janet's work, and that, like Janet, neither response pays much attention to how remembering and forgetting serve particular desires or interests in the present.

How did Janet arrive at his solution to the problem of memory, identity, and imitation, and what relevance might his solution have to the dilemmas of national memory? He regarded the memory of the report of M. D's death as Mme. D's *idée fixe*; after some months of failing to help her make it a conscious memory, he concentrated his efforts on "suppressing" it, or at least reducing its potency. The strength of the memory was such that it could not be removed, so Janet "modified it," using hypnosis to "transform" the idea to make it less frightening. Now, when Mme. D had her recurrent dream about the incident, she only thought of a pleasant visit to her house by her doctor, the kindly Janet. This, he tells the reader, aroused much less emotion, thus allowing her to integrate the various segments of her past. Janet deelaborated the memory—lessened its potency so as to restore the possibility of psychological balance—or, in Charcot's terms, Janet disabled its continuing effect on the nervous system. The past had been obstructing the present and future. By changing the past, the psychologist could open the possibility of new memories for Mme. D.

Janet's emphasis on dissociation rather than repression has drawn the attention of many who work with people victimized by violence or traumatic accidents.[4] The Freudian concept of repression is troubling in such cases because it always involves the question of desire, of how the victim's own ambivalent desires interact with memory to disturb the present. This is often perceived to be an offensive question since it can imply that the violence or accident instigated desires that then have to be dealt with. Janet was usually uninterested in this sort of issue, concentrating instead on lessening the potency of the trauma, reducing the disturbance from the past, since, "after the disappearance of the *idée fixe*, the unity of the spirit is reconstituted" (*NIF*, 405). Escaping from the grip of the past did not involve revisiting it or coming to understand its significance for one's present. The doctor had found techniques to enable traumatized patients to forget, or at least to alter the past that they remembered. Nietzsche wrote of the will's great gnashing of teeth that it could not will backward, that it could not change the past. But Janet (and many in his circle) thought that he had found in hypnosis a treatment that could do so.

The difference between the views of Freud and those of Janet and Charcot on memory and pathology provides an important perspective on the contemporary theory of history. Freud, like Charcot, was intensely concerned with the process through which a memory could become a psychological wound. In the early writings (those that precede, roughly, *The Interpretation of Dreams*) Freud strove to lessen the potency of memories, not in Janet's way (by the patient's forgetting), but by a discharge of energy that resulted from a special form of historical recollection. The talking cure demands that one situate oneself (or one's desires) in relation to the past, not that one reconstruct the *actual* past in the present. Freud developed a hermeneutics of memory rather than a tool for an unmediated expression of the past that would pretend to get free of it. He developed, that is, a way of using the past rather than of revolting against it. But the historical wound of the First World War forced Freud to reexamine the role of psychological trauma in the construction of the past. Shell-shocked soldiers returned to the source of their pain in dreams and fantasies. As Freud noted: "It is as though these patients had not yet finished with the traumatic situation, as though they were still faced by it as an immediate task which has not been dealt with."[5] It is the unfinished quality of the relationship to the event that reveals it as traumatic, that reveals the presence of an unhealed wound. While Charcot and Janet used hypnosis as a technique for finishing with the event and for achieving psychic balance, Freud thought that there was no possibility of ending the conflicts that drive the psyche. Moreover, desire is, he argued, a product of those conflicts. His questions, then, were first, how does the unfinished quality of one's relationship to an event serve particular desires in the present? And second, how does serving *those* desires make it impossible to serve others?

These questions are internal to psychoanalysis as a theoretical and clinical enterprise, and also central to the construction of history as a theoretical and practical enterprise. Trauma as an unfinished relationship with the past is a problem for historical consciousness because the traumatic event draws one to it even as it demands acknowledgment that one can never comprehend what happened at that time in that place. The models of Charcot and Janet are alien to modern historical consciousness in that they are unconcerned with the investment that one has in the past. Each employs technologies of memory or forgetting but neither has conceptual space for the desire that one has for the past, a desire that can result in an effort to link present and past through narrative. A trauma appears to demand inclusion in any narrative of the development of the present yet makes any narrative seem painfully inadequate. As Bessel van der Kolk and Onno van der Hart make the point: "Traumatic memories are the unassimilated scraps of overwhelming experiences, which need to be integrated with existing mental schemes, and be transformed into narrative language."[6] The "need" for integration stems from the claims that the traumatic past can still make on one in the present: flashbacks, reenactments, severe anxiety. But integration is also a threat—it is possible, after all, that the horrific past may be distilled through "existing mental schemes." Successful integration would necessarily relativize this part of the past with reference to the rest of one's life, and the process is as difficult in a historical as in a psychological context. The *Historikerstreit* made this clear, as have recent controversies about commemorating the end of World War II.

Telling the story of the traumatic past makes it part of ordinary life: the trauma is robbed of its uniqueness, its aura destroyed. Narrative memory is threatening because it can be forgotten—unlike hallucinations, automatic memories, and acting out, in which the past takes over, and the "pastness" of what one is conscious of evaporates.[7] Conventional narrative history poses a similar threat. Banalization of a trauma through narrative pleasure, through what Martin Broszat called *die Lust am geschichtlichen Erzählen*, threatens recovery, normality. Once we recognize that historical representation is taken as a sign of forgetting, we can appreciate the nature and degree of the threat, but, as historians, critics, or psychoanalysts, we must ask the awkward and painful question of what desires (or interests) are served by the need to return repeatedly to the origins of pain. What desires are satisfied by keeping the traumatic past as unfinished business? Specific answers to these questions vary from the political interests of groups aiming to alter foreign policy to the narcissistic needs of individuals trying to shore up a component of their own identities by maintaining solidarity with others they perceive as victims. But, in general terms, the need to return to the past as wound emerges from the recognition that to narrate the past, whether personal or historical, is to bring it into confrontation with the forces of forgetting. If a trauma is unforgettable, this is, paradoxically, because it cannot be remembered, cannot be recounted.

Narrative memory and history integrate specific events into existing mental and rhetorical schemes. The emplotment of the historical past, as Carl Schorske has noted, "reconstitute[s] the past by relativizing the particulars to the concepts and the concepts to the particulars, doing full justice to neither, yet binding them into an integrated life as an account under the ordinance of time."[8] Sometimes "doing full justice to neither" can be accepted as a fact of life (or, at least, of looking back at life). However, the explanatory or domesticating power of historical discourse (its medicinal effect, as psychiatrists see it) hides what Hans Kellner has called the "primitive terror" behind us, "obscuring the possibility that a 'non-sense' lurks behind all 'sense.'"[9] This primitive terror explodes in trauma and is at the heart of trauma's relation to historical representation. Insofar as that representation is tied to narrative, the quality that makes an experience traumatic (that we cannot take it in through the mental schemes available to us) is lost in the telling. This loss can be felt as a cure; and it can be felt as a betrayal, a sacrilege, or a renewed act of violence.[10]

Modern artists, writers, filmmakers, and to some extent historians have explored the question of how historical consciousness can acknowledge the powers of forgetting, the possibility of the sublime, the potency of the traumatic past to remain an open wound. These are the powers and possibilities that Hegel defended against (in the *Phenomenology*) in writing that "the wounds of spirit heal and leave no scars behind"; they are also what

Hayden White has argued professional historiography defined itself against as the discipline was being formed in the nineteenth century.[11] But in the contemporary context, following the debates around psychological and historical trauma since the Second World War, the writing of history itself is also a sign of the process of forgetting, of the loss of past. From the perspective of one postmodern reading of Nietzsche, one might conclude that the fear of forgetting is a false, perhaps even a sentimental, issue. There could be no *problem*, from this perspective, of losing the past unless one started from the naïve assumption that the past needs to be retained as a basis for action (or inspiration) in the present. Although coherent and powerful on more than one level, such arguments deny that parts of one's past can remain unassimilated to one's present, can resist representation, and yet can restrict one's capacity to act in the present—and this denial of the existence of trauma is so obviously untenable in the postwar context that it has led to its opposite number, the extreme claim that all history is somehow traumatic. Whether made under the sign of Lacan or of deconstruction, the claim is vacuous. Such claims do not permit us to make distinctions in order to understand particular kinds of responses to particular kinds of memories and the emotional states to which they are linked.

In facing a genuine historical trauma, only silence appears, at least to some, an honorable response because it does not trivialize the event.[12] On the other hand, silence always raises the problem of forgetting, for the event seems to demand representation, commemoration: how can I come to terms with my past and leave *this* out? Dominick LaCapra has noted that there are "two complementary ways of responding to trauma that may mistakenly be seen as alternatives" (*RH*, 192). The first is through a redemptive narrative that either marginalizes the traumatic event or folds it into a story in which the progressive realization of some goal evacuates (or makes up for) all negative elements. The second is the insistence that the traumatic event reveals the so-called truth of all experience, namely, that traumatic violence is the key to history. This second response poses as the sophisticated, hard-edged alternative to the naïve optimism of the first. Among American academics, the second is often termed "radical" and the first "liberal." LaCapra points out how both reactions avoid working through the relationship to the traumatic past by repression and repetition, respectively.

There is, however, no easy formula for arriving at a representation of the traumatic past by working through one's relation to it. LaCapra poses no answer to the question of whether a constructive form of historical knowledge can be created from our connection to the Holocaust, and that is to his credit. He offers suggestions instead as to how one might consider the question without falling into either of the twin traps of redemptive teleology and nihilism. His interest is in the construction of historical representations that aim at empathic understanding while showing the impossibility of ever knowing "how it really was." "In other words," he writes, "one would attempt to put oneself in the other's position without taking the other's place" (*RH*, 198). Such complex representations would allow for connections to the past combined with acknowledgment of irredeemable losses: they would allow for forms of mourning that communicate their own incompleteness. I am very much in sympathy with LaCapra's call for historical narratives that reflexively challenge their own formations of meaning, especially in the case of narratives that deal with extreme events that disrupt our very capacity to make sense of the past. Still, there is no way to defeat the forgetting that comes with the recovery from trauma, and the most powerful and subtle forms of forgetting are narrative memory and history. Narrative memory, which is at the core of historical representation on paper or on film, *transforms* the past as a condition of retaining it.

That transformation may recall Janet's manipulation of Mme. D's memory, but with a crucial difference: Janet was aiming to restore harmony in the mind by eliminating an individual's connection to a specific part of her past, while narrative memory (in this, like psychoanalysis) aims to preserve a connection to the past but in so doing necessarily changes the past that is preserved. Freud's concept of transference, like contemporary neurological theories of memory, implies that preservation of the past is always already a reworking of it. The recognition of this transformation through representation need not lead to a general antinarrative or antihistorical stance, but instead can stimulate the development of forms of historical writing that acknowledge this process as they engage in it—that convey that historical consciousness is always unfinished business, and that balance is not necessarily the goal of recollection or representation.

The acknowledgment of the past in the present is a necessary ingredient of modern historical consciousness and hence, I would suggest, of modern freedom. The acknowledgment of trauma and forgetting (even within the process of recollection) is also a condition of piety, of the caring attention one can provide to parts of one's past. Whether history is written on behalf of accuracy or expressiveness, it is perhaps always written ultimately in the service of either freedom or piety. We construct histories for critique and for inspiration.

That's what I mean by writing in the service of freedom. We also construct histories to acknowledge something as a past worthy of recollection, so that our histories can be forms of testimony or witnessing. That's what I mean by writing in the service of piety. In either case, to write against forgetting while recognizing the implication of that writing *in* forgetting is the burden and possibility of posttraumatic historical representation today.

5. Trauma

A Dystopia of the Spirit

This chapter examines how the terrain demarcated by the concept of trauma has become a crucial form of negative utopia of the late twentieth and early twenty-first century. Utopia has come to designate a place that cannot be designated, a nowhere of perfection in which order reigns. A utopia points away from the messy, complicated world in which we are condemned to live toward a harmonious world in which everything is balanced in working simplicity. Dystopias have a negative perfection in which some form of working simplicity nonetheless still squashes what we hold most dear.

The word "dystopia" is cited in the Oxford English Dictionary as first being used in 1868 by John Stuart Mill. Like Bentham before him, Mill was searching for a word that would describe a situation or a government that would be the "worst imaginable." Bentham had used the word "Cacotopia" for this pathological state. It seemed important to be able to designate the political environment that would be beyond the border of the acceptable, perhaps even the imaginable, but that would still be recognizable as a political world. In core traditions of political philosophy, this environment might be designated by "chaos," "war," even tyranny. But when Mill wrote that his enemies appeared to favor what was "too bad to be practicable," I think he was joining in the modern discourse around utopia. In this discourse the negative of utopia is not pointing toward a state of affairs that we would all strive mightily to avoid but rather to a state of affairs that we might intensely desire. Dystopia is the utopia you must be careful not to wish for.

Since the French Revolution, many thinkers have explored the borderline between utopia and dystopia. When Robespierre spoke of Terror and Virtue in the same breath, he was opening a new page in the possibilities of engineering political perfection in such a way as to create a genuine nightmare. This is the utopia in which you awaken to fulfillment and find that fulfillment is the greatest disappointment. With the advent of the liberal democracies and the acceptance of the sovereignty of the people, the capacity to create the world in our image inspired individualists and communitarians alike. Without a notion of natural or divine limits, and with a strong dose of the ideology of progress, utopianism was not just for dreamers but for planners. This could be done through a low-key trickle-down economic strategy, or through more radical means. Regulate your way to the Promised Land with industrialists or with the Saint-Simonians; or give birth to it through violent revolution with the radical right or the communists—but we were all marching in the same direction. Of course, it wasn't too long before some would claim that a successful march was the worst trajectory of at all. That is the true meaning of modern dystopia: the desired goal is what must be avoided.

By the end of the nineteenth century the question was common in discourse around Europe and North America: was the realization of our liberal democratic dreams the beginning of a well-ordered, balanced world, or, as Max Weber famously put it, the iron cage of "specialists without spirit and sensualists without heart"? Even if one found Marxism the Autobahn to the Himmelreich, did that mean to each according to his abilities and from each according to his needs, or rather, as Nietzsche saw it, the triumph of the last man who had nothing to look forward to but boredom in a universal state?

We can find many examples of thinkers who argued the utopia-dystopia issue, especially around the fate of communist regimes after the Russian Revolution. One of the more instructive debates is that between the French Hegelian philosopher Alexander Kojève and the American political philosopher Leo Strauss. It is certainly relevant to the history of dystopia to note that Kojève could also be described as a Russian philosopher and Strauss as a German. Be that as it may.

Strauss and Kojève knew one another in the Weimar period. Kojève (at that time called Kojevnikoff) had fled the revolution and civil wars in Russia and continued his philosophical studies in Germany. From his early writings we can see a theme that would animate all of his later work: How does an absolute come to have significance, fulfillment, or verification in the historical world? How, in other words, is the ideal realized? Strauss, too, was deeply concerned with this question, but the two men came out eventually on opposite sides of the fence. For Kojève, the ideal could not truly be ideal unless it was tested by, incarnated in, reality. Otherwise, he emphasized, the ideal was merely utopian. History was the realization of the ideal—making utopia somewhere, everywhere. For Strauss, the ideal could only remain ideal if it were radically removed from the historical world. It was that according to which—against which—the historical world could be judged.

Kojève argued that a transhistorical standard could only be validated by being incarnated in time. History was the actualization of the standard, and, as he famously added, this had already occurred. With a certain rhetorical flourish, he maintained that history "ended" in 1806 with Napoleon's victory over Prussia in the battle of Jena, a victory which opened the rest of Europe and, in the long run, the rest of the world to the principles of the French Revolution.

> What has happened since then has been nothing but an extension in space of the universal revolutionary force actualized in France by Robespierre-Napoleon. From the genuinely historical perspective, the two World Wars with their train of small and large revolutions have only had the effect of bringing the backward civilizations of the outlying provinces into line with the (really or virtually) most advanced European historical stages. If the sovietization of Russia and the communization of China are anything more and other than the democratization of Imperial Germany (by way of Hitlerism) or of the accession of Togo to independence, or even of the self-determination of the Papuans, they are so only because the Sino-Soviet actualization of Robespierran Bonapartism compels post-Napoleonic Europe to accelerate the elimination of the numerous more or less anachronistic remainders of its pre-revolutionary past. This process of elimination is already more advanced in the North-American extensions of Europe than it is in Europe itself. It might even be said that, from a certain point of view, the United States has already reached the final stage of Marxist "communism," since all the members of a "classless society" can, for all practical purposes, acquire whatever they please, whenever they please, without having to work for it any more than they are inclined to do.[1]

Strauss rejects out of hand the proposition that people can or should be satisfied in Kojève's "universal and homogeneous state." The basis of this realized utopia was mutual recognition, and even if there was recognition of everyone's equal freedom of opportunity and dignity, Strauss did not find that this would satisfy what was best in human beings (or satisfy the best human beings). Indeed, Strauss frequently leaves the distinct impression that, in his view, freedom and equality are not so much goals as they are concessions to weakness and passion. He challenges Kojève to show how the citizens of his universal and homogeneous end-state differ from Nietzsche's "last men."[2]

The last men are self-absorbed and self-satisfied. They know neither wonder nor awe, neither fear nor shame. Their souls are atrophied. They are utterly repugnant. The mere fact that we cannot help recoiling from them clearly shows that we aspire to more than the satisfaction of being recognized as free and equal. In particular, a political society that does not allow adequate scope for the soul's aspiration to greatness might succeed in destroying or subjugating man's humanity for a time, but it is most likely to lead to its own destruction in the long run. When souls driven by great ambition are denied scope to seek what is noble and beautiful, they will become bent on destruction. If they cannot be heroes, they will become villains. With these few terse references to the soul, Strauss returns to the problem of nature, and most specifically to the problem of human nature: any adequate ethics and politics has to take the nature of the soul into account. Kojève grants that if there is a human nature, Strauss is right. But he rejects human nature as a standard, and he most particularly rejects it as the standard for morals or politics.[3]

Both Kojève and Strauss rejected utopian thinking. The former because he thought it was merely intellectual chatter without effects in the world, and the latter because he thought that the aspiration to reconcile philosophical ideals and practical politics was wrongheaded and dangerous. When the reconciliation brought by the end of history began to look increasingly bleak, Kojève took an ironic stance toward it. Rather than seeing the final state as part of the triumphant ascension of humanity, he came to picture a final decadence in which humans are distinguished from other animals only by their snobbism. We, the last men, may be repugnant (as Strauss noted), but we cannot step outside that condition to judge it from a philosophically safe place. Instead, Kojève seemed to indicate, we can be ironically self-conscious about it. We can show that we know where we are. This can be called, as I have argued elsewhere, the "ironist's cage"—a discursive constraint in which much postmodern thought has found itself since the late 1960s.[4]

The Kojève-Strauss debate was typical of the negative-positive utopia paradigm linking the nineteenth and twentieth centuries. With the dissipation of utopian energies in the last twenty years, what has become of thinking utopia for us? I would like to suggest that the concept of trauma has come to perform some of the same functions that negative utopia or dystopia once did. Trauma, like utopia, designates phenomena that cannot be properly represented, but one characterized by radical intensity. A widespread longing for intensity has come to magnetize the concept of trauma, giving it a cultural currency far beyond the borders of psychology and psychoanalysis. Trauma has become the dystopia of the spirit, showing us much about our own preoccupations with catastrophe, memory, and the grave difficulties we seem to have in negotiating between the internal and external worlds.

Trauma as Nowhere

The modern concept of trauma points to an occurrence that both demands representation and refuses to be represented. The intensity of the occurrence seems to make it impossible to remember or to forget. The traumatic event, Freud wrote, is "unfinished," it appears to the individual as "an immediate task which has not been dealt with."[5] Contemporary psychiatry tends to define trauma as an event that overwhelms one's perceptual-cognitive faculties, creating a situation in which the individual does not really experience the event as it happens. This may be why victims often describe themselves as spectators of their own trauma. In any case, the traumatic occurrence is not remembered normally because it was not registered through the standard neurochemical networks. The lack of a reliable memory of the trauma is felt by many as a gaping absence, sometimes filled by flashbacks or other symptoms. Yet the occurrence was too intense to be forgotten; it requires some form of re-presentation.

The intensity which makes forgetting impossible also makes any specific form of recollection seem inadequate. The traumatic event is too terrible for words, too horrifying to be integrated into our schemes for making sense of the world. Yet any representation of the trauma may have to rely on words and will be limited by the very schemes that were initially overwhelmed. I have argued elsewhere that a "successful" representation (a representation that others understand) of trauma will necessarily seem like trivialization, or worse, like betrayal.[6] The intensity of a trauma is what defies understanding, and so a representation that someone else understands seems to indicate that the event wasn't as intense as it seemed to be. A trauma—much like a utopia—is supposed to be beyond a representation that would fix it firmly in the conventions we have for taking in the world.

Being beyond the borders of representation is a status that protects the distinctiveness—even sacredness—of the phenomenon to which one gestures. The very intensity of the phenomenon should convey that it cannot be described or used in the standard ways. It has become a commonplace of theoretical work on history to note the constructedness of historical representations, and to underline that historical representations tend to be appropriations of the past for the sake of an agenda in the present. Instead of reflecting on how close a representation gets to the past *wie es eigentlich gewesen*, one has tended to ask how we *use* the past for a variety of purposes in the present. The traumatic past has a peculiar status in this context. One might say that in looking at trauma, one is looking at a past that in a fundamental sense is *immune to use* since by definition the traumatic defies sense making. This is part of what Freud meant by his phrase "unfinished business"—traumatized people still have the "immediate task" of processing an occurrence that has overwhelmed their faculties. This must be quickly qualified, however, since this immunity can itself be put to work. The claim that nobody can understand my history except someone who has also suffered my traumas has become all too familiar. One can use the isolation of the trauma from integration into broader patterns of meaning as a way of isolating oneself or one's group. Although nothing can be made out of the trauma, one can use *this* very fact about it as identity defining.[7] The island of trauma is a negative utopia to which one can point but from which no coherent set of mediations can be traced.

Another way to talk about the trauma's immunity to use is its historical singularity. To treat something as historical means *at least* to connect it via chronology to events before or after. Historical meaning, as Carl E. Schorske has noted, "reconstitutes the past by relativizing the particulars to the concepts and the concepts to the particulars, doing full justice to neither, yet binding them into an integrated life as an account under the ordinance of time."[8] Trauma denies the possibility of an "integrated life." It is a particular that refuses relativizing because its intensity makes the lack of "full justice" untenable. Can the singular *be* historical, or does entrance into the historical record require a kind of contextualization that is a denial of singularity? When we try to historicize a traumatic event, we necessarily reduce its singularity. Making something "history" means making it part of something else, or placing it in relation to something else. That is why there can be no unique historical events—except in a trivial sense (in which everything is unique). There has been an effort to adopt a religious or sacralizing attitude vis-à-vis certain extreme events, which is in part an effort to keep a distance between them and the run-of-the-mill occurrences that we remember or write about as history. We can understand these efforts as aiming to prevent the trauma from becoming "merely historical," something that fits easily into the narratives we tell about the past. This is in many ways parallel to the discourse about utopia and its realization.

Trauma violates our conventions when it happens, and we may want it to violate our conventions when we retell it. We want to avoid its domestication, and yet we want to understand it. Does understanding entail domestication? These are the issues that Hayden White has pointed to with his notion of a "modernist event." For more than thirty years, White has been showing how the conventions of historical realism established in the nineteenth century function to normalize the events they are used to describe.[9] More recently, he has underlined that key events in the twentieth century render inadequate the conventions of realistic representation developed in the nineteenth-century historical novel and historiography. "After modernism," he writes, "when it comes to the task of storytelling, whether in historical or literary writing, the traditional techniques of narration become unusable—except in parody."[10] Events no longer serve as indices of fate; they no longer reveal the meaning of that which led up to them or point to the essential direction of what is to follow.

There is some slippage in White's account between the literary form and the quality of events. That is, it is unclear whether modernism as a formal innovation makes it impossible for us to believe in straightforward narratives of events, or whether the terrible events of our century have made it impossible for us to believe in straightforward narratives. Even White, the most powerful constructionist in regard to historical discourse, seems to think that the *events themselves* in the twentieth century require new forms of representation. This slippage serves White well, since he continues to call our attention to the vexed intersection of facts and meaning, events and narratives. The Holocaust is White's paradigm for a modernist event, an occurrence that cannot be left alone and yet cannot be recounted through conventional realistic techniques. But is this because of the intensity of the events or because of our modernist suspicion of such techniques? For White, the issue must be fundamentally undecidable; for that reason the literary techniques that call attention to their own inadequate referential powers seem most appropriate. "Modernist techniques of representation," White writes, "provide the possibility of defetishizing both events and fantasy accounts of them which deny the threat they pose in the very process of pretending to represent them realistically."[11] This call to find other forms to represent the extreme events of our century has echoes among historians trying to avoid narrative simplification, fictionalization, and myth making.[12] I am very much in sympathy with this call. However, it is important to note (following the spirit of White's work) not only that the terrible events of the twentieth century may demand new aesthetic forms, but that those who are invested in these forms may be attracted to the very extremity of modern traumatic events. In other words, there are features of modernist and postmodernist discourse that are drawn into the attractive field of trauma. Whereas once utopia thinking drew together the political dimension of the arts, trauma has become a magnet for the privileged aesthetic forms of our time.

The affinity of modernist strategies of representation with extreme events has led to a problem concerning the truthfulness of representations of trauma. The truth-as-correspondence promised by realism is undercut by modernist innovations. These innovations often call attention to the processes of representation so as to emphasize that we never have unmediated access to the occurrence to which we are trying to refer. The lack of unmediated access has led to skepticism for some, relativism for others. These general epistemological positions are superficially linked: if we cannot know what really happened, then one interpretation is as good as another. But who really holds this position in regard to either an extreme historical event or a personal trauma? To do so would mean that one would have no way of apprehending events *as* extreme but only understanding interpretations that render them extreme. Surely, one can acknowledge that people perceive the intensity of events differently without making the bizarre claim that there are no differences in the intensity of events.

Cultural Trends Reinforcing Trauma Talk

In very general ways, the occurrence of modernist events on the historical scale together with the vagaries of the theories of memory and truth on the personal scale have contributed to the currency of trauma talk in the humanities. In the remainder of this essay, I shall discuss three key specific cultural trends that have helped shape the use of "trauma" in the last fifteen years: Holocaust studies, feminism and identity politics, and gallery culture and literary theory. These three cultural trends all aim to escape the ironist's cage that I described in relation to the Strauss-Kojève debate above. The field of Holocaust studies has been developing as a cultural force both on university campuses and within the general public since the late 1960s, but in recent years much intellectual energy has been devoted to tracing the less tangible effects of the Shoah on survivors and their descendents. The notion of trauma has been used to make sense of these effects. The identity of the "survivor," once closely associated with those who went through the Holocaust, has come to stand for someone who has gone through any form of trauma. Incest survival and rape survival in particular have become important subjects of academic, autobiographical, and self-help books. Holocaust survival has become a paradigm of an identity-making trauma.[13]

Another key word that has become linked with the notion of trauma and the Holocaust is "testimony." This is surely related to the vast efforts in recent decades made at video documentation of remembrances by victims. "Testimony" has both juridical and theological connotations and derives considerable force from this combination. One gives testimony in a court of law, but one also is moved to testify by the spirit in a religious context. Testimony is given both to address a debt to the past, to witness the past for the purposes of the present, and for the therapeutic purposes for the person who gives the testimony.[14] Of course, the issue of truth in regard to these imperatives is a vexed one. For many, the empirical veridicality of testimony takes a back seat to its potential healing power, pragmatic concerns winning out over some "big T" notion of Historical Truth.

The temporal dynamic of Holocaust remembrance has been derived from a vaguely psychoanalytic notion of trauma. The terms are probably familiar: "denial," "repression," "flooding," and "working through." A period of relative silence about the Holocaust immediately followed its occurrence. By the 1970s, when the generation of survivors was nearing the end of life, there was a flooding of memory and abundant discussion, sometimes prompted by subsequent generations. Most recently, there has been the possibility of more critical, self-conscious reflection on the events and their representation. This has included a critique of the trauma model for understanding Holocaust remembrance. The historian Peter Novick, for example, has argued that the memory of the holocaust for Americans has been constructed for particular political and sociological purposes, and that the notion of trauma has merely served that construction.[15]

A second cultural trend shaping the concept of trauma in the humanities has been feminism and identity politics. Western culture since the Enlightenment has viewed memory as the core of individual identity, and since the nineteenth century romanticism has placed memory at the core of collective identity. Feminism, being a critical heir to both these movements, has insisted on the notion that women are made, not born. The identity of women is created and maintained in memory, and, since women live within patriarchy, that memory is laced through and through with traces of occurrences that cannot be successfully recalled or forgotten. One of the features of patriarchy is the "conspiracy of silence" about such occurrences, and modern feminism has fought against this conspiracy as a struggle against a "secondary wound." Finding the ability to tell one's story of trauma thus becomes not only a potentially personally healing act, but also a political act. By the mid-1980s, giving voice to traumatic memory had become an important feature of feminism and contributed much to the debate around the putative recovery of memories of childhood abuse.[16]

Rather than rehearse the debates about recovered memory here, I simply want to note that this notion of giving voice to traumatic memories has gained wide currency among groups that perceive themselves to be oppressed. Holocaust testimonies come to mind here, but the phenomenon of defining one's identity through articulating the traces of one's traumas has become a much more general phenomenon. This articulation may be a privileged form of discourse in the sense that giving testimony about one's own traumas is not subject to the same regime of truth as giving testimony about an event one has witnessed. These days, in voicing one's own traumas, one assumes a moral authority vis-à-vis the past that trumps questions both of factual truthfulness and practical efficacy.[17] Speaking becomes its own truth.

Trauma has replaced utopia in providing overriding legitimation. What is the origin of trauma's moral authority? How does an appeal to the traumatic override empirical and pragmatic issues? One can speak here of the "aura" of the traumatic, its capacity to keep our normal modes of intellection at a distance. Since the trauma violates our very structures of experience, so the argument goes, an empirically faithful representation of it is impossible. Since the trauma cannot be integrated into broad historical or biographical contexts, it cannot be put to pragmatic use. The empirical and pragmatic are two of the principal sources for our approaches to history and memory. The third is piety, and it is from this source that the aura of the traumatic draws its power. Piety is what draws some to the past *just because it has been*—not to get it right or to make use of it. We usually associate piety with obligation, duty, reverence—not obvious attitudes to take vis-à-vis the traumatic. But the object of piety is also associated with power, something awesome that commands our reverence and imposes duties. The power of trauma is evinced in the way that it commands our attention, as sufferers or as witnesses. It may be an exaggeration to say, as the critic Mark Seltzer has said, that trauma is the site of our public life today, the place where contemporary communities gather, but it is important to note how traumas seem to urge us not to look away.[18] To be sure, there are many horrendous things that we would prefer not to see, horrors from which we want to avert our gaze. But paying attention to trauma has come to be regarded as a virtue, as character building, and even as morally uplifting.[19] This is the case even when no explicit lessons are drawn from the event. The intensity of trauma commands our respect, imposes obligations of remembrance or commemoration; the suffering involved in trauma provokes our compassion, that mixture of pleasure and pain that some distance (but not total remove) from an awful event can inspire.

In the United States, we have seen in recent years a variety of attempts to claim ownership over some communal trauma. We who have suffered these events, or who share identity markers with others who have suffered them, have some deep understanding of and investment in what happened. You who have not suffered or do not share these identity markers will never understand our connection to this pain, but *you should not look away*. Thus is piety used as an exclusionary device, as a way of demarcating one community from another by virtue of a link to a collective trauma. Identity here is grounded in what is unrepresentable to others, in what is automatically understood by members of the "we-group." But this is an attention-demanding exclusionary device. We who are separate demand your recognition of our separateness based on trauma. Our separateness must be recognized by you who do not share in it. One doesn't have to be Kojève to see this as a farcical repetition of the master/slave dialectic.

The first two cultural trends contributing to the popularity of the concept of trauma among humanists and social scientists are clearly linked. Holocaust studies on the one hand, feminism and identity politics on the other, intersect on questions of traumatic memory, and certainly research and commemoration of the Shoah have been used as an instrument to strengthen Jewish identity. The final elements I shall discuss contributing to trauma talk in the last decade come from a rather different cultural sector, the more rarified domains of gallery culture and of academic literary theory. Hal Foster has traced some of the ways in which contemporary art has veered toward the abject and the traumatic.[20] For Foster, the fascination with repetition in contemporary art (he begins with Warhol's *Death in America* work) is key to the emergence of what he calls "traumatic realism." This is a realism that rejects the illusionist traditions of representation that led to both surrealism and expressionism. Instead, traumatic realism uses a depiction of wounds or the abject to evoke the real. The trace of the real (or at least of our encounter with it) returns as the traumatic in artists like Kiki Smith, Cindy Sherman, Robert Gober, and Zoe Leonard.

Foster notes how the move away from the text, from minimalism, and from illusionism has driven artists to the real as trauma. So have persistent social crises ranging from the AIDS epidemic to urban violence. The traumatized subject is empty, incapable of authorship or even experience. Yet Foster notes how this same subject can become an icon of survival, or an unchallengeable witness:

> Here is indeed a traumatic subject, and it has absolute authority, for one cannot challenge the trauma of another: one can only believe it, even identify with it, or not. *In trauma discourse, then, the subject is evacuated and elevated at once.* And in this way trauma discourse magically resolves two contradictory imperatives in culture today: deconstructive analyses and identity politics.[21]

The intersection of identity politics and deconstruction has been an important force in contemporary art and in theoretical academic work. And at this intersection we find the concept of trauma. In recent years, several thinkers who have been deeply marked by deconstruction in the United States have turned to trauma as a subject for their inquiries into representation.[22] This turn was surely overdetermined, but it can be understood as a response to critiques of French literary theory (as it was often labeled in America) in the wake of scandal concerning the early journalistic writings of Paul de Man. The discovery of de Man's anti-Semitic articles, and the rhetorical acrobatics used to evade them, seemed to lend more force to the notion that deconstruction was a way of thinking compatible with just about any politics. Given the fact that many influenced by this way of thinking considered themselves "radical" in some way, the charge of political promiscuity or base nihilism cut deep. Was theory's continued insistence on unmasking truth claims, realism, and intentionality merely a screen to conceal its own inability to engage the world? How were practitioners of theory going to show that theory mattered, *that it made a difference*?[23]

Part of the issue here was surely due to the success of literary theory in making scholars in the humanities more aware of the vicissitudes of representation. When the critique of the subject and of representation burst on the scene, there was an *effet du scandal*: the things we held dear or felt sure of were being undermined by a sophisticated critique steeped in close reading. And there was a strong ironic component to theory's critique. Rather than suggesting alternative perspectives in aesthetics, politics, or ethics, those inspired by deconstruction were able to show that our habitual perspectives were without foundation, that they deconstructed themselves when looked at intently. As this mode of reading and thinking became more and more established in American universities, its ironic techniques of unmasking seemed less radical, less amusing, and less relevant. For those now *trained* in this area, the question became how to connect a critique of representation and subjectivity with things that happen in the world. How to make it real?

The cultural trends discussed above, feminism and identity politics, intersect with theory here. Theorists inspired by deconstruction and by Lacan were very useful for a critique of patriarchy and of the white power establishment. The pretensions of power and of hegemonic truth claims were tempting targets for those entering the academy in the beginnings of a more aggressive multiculturalism. And "theory" provided some of the tools for radical critique. Insofar as this theory was skeptical about all modes of representation and all claims for stable subjectivity, however, it eventually got in the way of groups wanting to build their own communities, identities, canons. The radical critique of representation could not be embraced if one was trying to build forms of political representation grounded in the experience of oppression. If theory prevented this construction of identity, was it merely complicit in maintaining the status quo?

The traumatized subject, the victim of overwhelming intensity, was something that theory could connect to. The paradox at the heart of trauma, that the most intense occurrences may be those we are unable to represent or even experience, is perfectly compatible with the view that we are not fully present to ourselves and that we represent all our experiences to ourselves in highly mediated forms. More simply put, the notion that we are never at home with our experiences or with ourselves was good soil for the seed of concern with the posttraumatic. This self-estrangement is given a temporal form in theories of trauma as belatedness and repetition. We are too late to take in the intensity of an event as it occurs, and we reenact the event in a futile attempt to finally arrive on time. To use what is by now a quaint old phrase: we are *always-already* too late. We can rephrase this in Lacanian terms of a "missed encounter with the Real," but the point remains essentially the same: these pictures of subjectivity in general are perfectly compatible with the view of traumatized subjectivity. Contemporary theory is traumatophilic. Mark Seltzer puts it this way:

> No doubt the "traumatic" shifting of interest from the event to its self-representation or theorization makes up at least in part the general

> gravitation of modernist/postmodernist discourse to the categories of shock/trauma. For if the trauma is marked by the disruption or reversal of causal interpretation (an effect in search of a cause), there is, on this level at least, an exact fit between such a definition of trauma and the "deconstructive" notion of the subject as that which breaks with linear causality and determination and the notion of the subject as that which unremittingly "puts itself in question."[24]

Seltzer's account of the fit between the subject according to deconstruction and according to contemporary trauma theory is important and compelling.[25] On the basis of this fit some contemporary theorists have gone on to talk about ethics, and it is the link between ethics and trauma that is the final aspect of the confluence between literary theory and trauma talk.

Cathy Caruth has been exploring issues concerning trauma, history, experience, and representation in a number of important essays. She, along with Shoshana Felman and Dominick LaCapra, are attending to trauma as a way of connecting their critical interest in representation and psychoanalysis with some form of ethical engagement. The idea of "belatedness" and of Lacan's "missed encounter" are at the core of Caruth's writings on trauma:

> For history to be a history of trauma means that it is referential precisely to the extent that it is not fully perceived as it occurs; or to put it somewhat differently, that a history can be grasped only in the very inaccessibility of its occurrence.[26]

> Traumatic experience . . . suggests a certain paradox: that the most direct seeing of a violent event may occur as an absolute inability to know it; that immediacy, paradoxically, may take the form of belatedness.[27]

The phenomenological or epistemological feature of belatedness and inaccessibility has been remarked on by most of the disciplines working on trauma. But Caruth wants to use this feature to develop an ethical stance. The paradoxes of perception and retelling should lead to another way of treating one another. Thus, in the paragraphs that follow each of the passages cited above, Caruth writes that "events are only historical to the extent that they implicate others," and that "the shock of traumatic sight reveals at the heart of human subjectivity not so much an epistemological, but rather what can be defined as an *ethical* relation to the real."[28] Caruth wants belatedness ("the failure to have seen in time") to be "transformed into the imperative of a speaking that awakens others."[29] Trauma should give rise to new forms of listening and new responsibilities for transmission. This seems to be what she means by an "ethical relation to the real."

But why should trauma work this way? Why wouldn't we simply ignore our belatedness or enjoy it? There seems to be nothing in the phenomenology or epistemology of trauma that would justify a particular ethical stance. Indeed, trauma may simply dramatize a variety of possible stances, some of which we might want to label "ethical." Caruth, being herself mindful of ethics, wanting theory to lead to ethics via trauma, finds that it does. But only her hope—not argument or even narrative—gets us there.

Dominick LaCapra has himself written on the "ethical turn" in conjunction with his work on memory and trauma. LaCapra distinguishes between structural and historical trauma. The former may be described in the psychoanalytic terms of the temporality of human sexuality or even as a missed encounter with the Real. The latter are particular events with more or less contingent historical causes. LaCapra wants to make this distinction so as to allow the possibility of understanding our basic responses to intense experiences of whatever kind, while also preserving a space for the detailed exploration of specific causes and effects. In other words, LaCapra leaves a place for theoretical reflection on the significance of trauma for understanding desire and perception while retaining empirical questions concerning why particular extreme events happened as they did. This strategy is emblematic of LaCapra's approach to trauma-talk more generally. He is skeptical about overreaching claims yet critical of a narrow-minded empiricism that refuses to acknowledge its own theoretical assumptions.[30]

In his work on trauma, LaCapra uses the notion of "working through" that he had already developed in his writings on transference and history.[31] A history that is "worked through" avoids the pitfalls of repetition and of acting out. It remains obscure how one can determine whether one has successfully avoided the pitfalls. We are supposed to prefer "working through" to "acting out," but what if the former is just a label we give to examples of history writing we prefer? LaCapra is aware of this difficulty, but he is loath to set out firm criteria for demarcating one kind of approach to the past from another. Instead, he issues warnings about what to look out for: repetition of tropes, bizarre appropriations of events for dangerous political purposes, excessive empirical defensiveness. LaCapra's theoretical work does not provide answers about how to judge history but, instead, suggestions on how to grasp the ways that historical discourse uses the past (or is used by it) for a variety of purposes in the present.

After work inspired by Bakhtin, deconstruction, and psychoanalysis, why has trauma come to be LaCapra's subject for reflecting on history? The distinction between structural and historical trauma allows him to develop broad transhistorical speculation (like the possible necessity of scapegoating or questions about the negative sublime), while consistently returning to issues about specific historical events and actors (like the Holocaust). He does not see anything intrinsically ethical about what we get from attending to trauma, but he does emphasize some of the more vexed ethical and political issues that arise from this attention. Trauma is the terrain that connects the theoretical and the empirical, providing a dramatic ground for the theoretical prudence that LaCapra has (quite rightly in my view) come to adopt.

The "ethical turn" in either Caruth's or LaCapra's hands is quite far from the concerns about utopia-dystopia that were at the heart of the Kojève-Strauss debate. The philosophers arguing over politics and philosophy in the period that bridged the Second World War were worried about whether a theoretical ideal could become real. Kojève thought that if it could not become real then it was false (false meant *merely* utopian). Strauss, on the other hand was certain that the attempt to make the ideal real was at the heart of modernity's problems. Contemplation of the ideal and exploring it through fundamental questions was not "merely utopian," it was genuinely philosophical. In a passage in Strauss's *Thoughts on Machiavelli*—underlined in Kojève's own copy of the book—the author summarizes his view of modern philosophy:

> The new philosophy lives from the outset in the hope which approaches or equals certainty, of future conquest or conquest of the future—in the anticipation of an epoch in which the truth will reign, if not in the minds of all men, at any rate in the institutions which mold them. Propaganda can guarantee the coincidence of philosophy and political power. Philosophy is to fulfill the function of both philosophy and religion. . . . The domination of necessity remains the indispensable condition of every great achievement and in particular his [Machiavelli's] own: the transition from the realm of necessity into the realm of freedom will be the inglorious death of the very possibility of human excellence.[32]

If philosophers participate in the struggle against nature at the expense of the contemplation of the natural, they forget the basis of philosophy; in accepting the realm of freedom as the realm of the comfortable, they deny the possibilities of excellence. If the goal of all human effort is the triumph over nature, victory removes the very ground of the human. Here we see the Enlightenment dilemma of positive-negative utopia clearly: the realization of our dreams is the greatest nightmare.

Kojève came to believe we did indeed live in this nightmare, and irony seemed to be his only theoretical recourse. In recent years the idea of trauma has been used to break out of this ironist's cage. Trauma is the black hole of dystopia, revealing the borders of representation and experience through its intensity and through its command to pay attention to suffering. We may not know how to build the world, and we may not even have any confidence in knowing the fundamental questions, but we do *feel* the intensity of suffering connected to trauma. This is the dystopia of the spirit that is supposed to make us more ethical, or at least to make us more attentive to the most dangerous aspects of feeling and thinking in the world.

6. Falling into History

Freud's Case of "Frau Emmy von N."

I made it impossible for her to see any of these melancholy things again, not only by wiping out her memories of them in the plastic form but by removing her whole recollection of them, as though they had never been present in her mind.

SIGMUND FREUD[1]

Studies on Hysteria is a curiously hybrid text. It belongs to the prehistory of psychoanalysis, and one of the interests it has for us is that in it we can see Freud in the process of breaking away from, even as he is nourished by, a variety of influences: Meynert, Charcot, Breuer, and Bernheim, to name just a few. We can also see Freud staking out a terrain for psycho-analysis: the effects of the remembered past, mediated through desire, on the present.

The "effects of the past" that concern Freud and Breuer are, of course, the symptoms of hysteria. Hysteric patients suffer mainly from reminiscences, they wrote, and their investigations in the 1890s were aimed at removing the potency of the past. Breuer and Freud were committed to the view that the reminiscences that caused hysterical suffering were historical in the sense that they were linked to actual past traumas in the patient's life. The affect associated with the past trauma cannot be acknowledged, and the amnesia (or paramnesia) which results means that the force of that affect is dammed up. "The injured person's reaction to the trauma only exercises a completely cathartic effect if it is an *adequate* reaction," they wrote (8). The past which continues to wound is the past which originally found no outlet. Denied an "appropriate" response, the ghost of past experience continues to haunt the hysteric:

> The ideas which have become pathological have persisted with such freshness and affective strength because they have been denied the

> normal wearing-away process by means of abreaction and reproduction in states of uninhibited association. (11, italics in original)

In the whiggish histories usually written by partisans of psychoanalysis, *Studies on Hysteria* is read as Freud's recognition of the value of "uninhibited association" for coming to terms with the past, and especially of the role of sexuality in that past and our present relation to it. The uninhibited Freud, the conquistador as he liked to say, was ready to go where no one had gone before—or at least where very few doctors were willing to linger. Where abreaction was, there association would come to be. In the demonic accounts of Freud's nefarious effects on our century, *Studies on Hysteria* is read as the tale of the psychoanalyst's first learning to listen to his female patients, but of his coming to ignore the realities of what they were telling him. The patriarchal, authoritarian Freud was about to lose his nerve when confronted with the testimonies of women who were often the victims of male sexual violence.

The whiggish and demonic emplotments of the history of psychoanalysis neglect Freud's precursors in this terrain of release/understanding through association, as they simplify Freud's own reluctance to move into what was for him frighteningly uncertain ground. Conquistadors are not supposed to be dragged into the new territory by the natives. But in Freud's case, the natives of neurosis were the ones who best knew the terrain of dammed desire, and he had to learn to follow them. But like his patients, Freud was full of resistances: doctors were not supposed to learn from their patients, they were supposed to *make them better*. The doctor was the scientist, the man of reason, and his neurotic patient had to be brought onto *his* terrain: and it should be firm ground in contrast to the swamp of (feminine) hysterical desire. But who would conquer whom?

The case of Emmy von N. presents a complex Freud, neither hero nor villain, a theorist undecided about the relation of memory to real events, and a doctor not yet convinced that the "normal wearing-away process" is best achieved through a talking cure that allowed the patient to acknowledge the past as a way to escape its domination. When Freud began treating Fanny Moser (Emmy von N.'s real name) in 1889, he was intrigued by the possibility of simply removing the reminiscence that caused the hysterical suffering. Hypnosis, Freud had learned in France, could be used as an *amnesic technique*, a tool for removing the past from patients so that they could get on with their lives. Amnesic techniques gave the doctor enormous authority, the possibility of remaking the identity of the patient. But in order to become a real Freudian, Freud would have to dispense with the dream of removing the past in favor of a model of recollection, of constructing a past with which one could live.

In this chapter I will discuss the school of forgetting against which Freud would define psychoanalysis. This school is most familiar to us as the group of researchers and clinicians around Charcot. Although Charcot and his colleagues at the Salpêtrière were locked in an intense rivalry with Bernheim and his students in the city of Nancy, for Freud their use of hypnotism and suggestion linked them as a common temptation and as an other against whom he would define himself. In the case of Emmy von N., Freud was still trying out his French lessons as he attempted to assume the authority of suggestion and to wield the power of erasing the past. In this case study we see him working through the French forgetters, as he began to make the problem of suggestion an issue for any attempt to make sense of the past—not just as a tool for erasing it. This issue—how can we actively recover the past for the present without simply inventing the past—would remain at the core of psychoanalysis and of modern historical consciousness generally. It is not an issue that can be driven away through suggestion nor through the attack on suggestion.

As discussed in chapters 3 and 4, for Charcot and his school, hysteria could often be traced back to a shock to the nervous system that disrupted subsequent memory. An original trauma continued to produce a psychical piercing, or a dynamic lesion of the nervous system, and could be healed through forgetting. In treating Mme. D's hysterical amnesia (she seemed unable to recall any new memories) Charcot turned to hypnotism to overcome the disjunction between the first and second selves (only the second having normal recall). The trauma accumulates power through autosuggestion and association as it becomes the root of the hysterical symptoms, and hypnosis was to combat autosuggestion with suggestion from the doctor. From Pierre Janet's perspective, *elaboration* led to what he saw as the root of hysteria: the dissociation—the breaking apart into isolated fragments—of the personality. Janet set about to modify the memory of the past, if it could not be entirely erased.

The problem with hysterics, it seems, was that they neither remembered nor forgot. That is, they could not bring to mind consciously (by an act of will) the element in their past which disturbed them, or when they did so it was without any of the affect that seemed to have been linked to the memory.

But the therapeutic task was not simply to help the patient forget or ignore the pathogenic past. Hypnotism was thought to be a way of giving the hysteric access to this past; but whatever happens during the hypnosis is often forgotten upon awakening. Thus, only during hypnotism did some of Janet's patients feel connected with the past which otherwise haunted the present. As a result, a dependence on hypnotism and on the hypnotist often develops. Janet's patient Marceline would need to be hypnotized every two to three weeks (in secret, since her employers knew nothing about this) in order to avoid a relapse into a catatonic, anorectic state. Blanche Witt, a severely hysteric patient from the Salpêtrière, grew even more dependent on her physician, Jules Janet.

> Blanche will now speak only to me, will only be touched by me. She does not pay any attention to the words addressed to her by the other people present.[2]

The hypno-psychologist may complain about dependence (or *electivité*, as Jules Janet called the attraction to the doctor), but this did not stop him from remaking the personality of his patient. In Blanche's case, he even named his new creation!

> If I asked her what she thought of this new state [of hypnosis], she would tell me that she still feels herself to be Blanche Witt; but, on the other hand, she discovers a personality, inclinations and properties so different that she has difficulty believing that she is still the same. She accepts, therefore, very willingly the name "Louise" which I propose that she take.[3]

Finding the right balance between memory and forgetting was very difficult. Who would define what the balance should be? In the case of the hysteric patient Irene, she remembers the *fact* of her mother's death, but displays none of the affect "appropriate" to the event. But in this age of mediums and spiritist reconnections with the dead, what *should* she have felt? How can the memory be brought into relation with the emotions "proper" to it? In the end, when Pierre Janet considers the great body of his own and his colleagues' cases, he chooses another solution. The final sentence of his weighty, *L'État mental des hystériques* runs as follows: "In conclusion, the biggest favor that the doctor can do for his patient is to direct his mind."[4]

If some form of autosuggestion or hypnoid state is at the root of hysteria, then a cure would be to replace the poisonous claim of the traumatic past with the hygienic claim of the benign physician. But this replacement would not cure hysterics of their vulnerability to suggestion. Indeed, the need for, demand for, suggestion was one of the by-products of the treatment. Janet called this the *passion somnambulique*:

> The hysteric who awaits somnambulism resembles in many ways the morphine addict who awaits his shot, even though his anxiety has perhaps a more moral and less physical character.[5]

Although Janet seemed uneasy at times with the power these patients were willing to give him, as he wondered what it said about "the dependence which exists naturally among people,"[6] he did not think through what it would mean to "cure" the hysteric of his or her need for suggestion, direction, or authority. After all, hysteria was an ancient illness perhaps always triggered by the power of suggestion, and hypnosis seemed to put this power into the (well-scrubbed) hands of the physician. The authority was immense, but in the hands of a truly scientific doctor it need not be infallible only self-correcting. Pontalis quotes Charcot as saying: "What one does one can always undo."[7] Suggestion from the past was malignant; suggestion from the doctor as the voice of Progress and Reason was benign. Janet put the well-worn appeal to the weak predisposition of the patient in a new form: "some minds more than others, have the need for perpetual imitation."[8] The problem was a technical one. How could the physician be present enough for the hysteric in constant need of direction?

> "The true treatment of hysteria," Briquait said, "is happiness." I have tried to understand what was this happiness which is proper to hysterics; it is, in my view, simplicity, almost the monotony of a simple existence which reduces the effort at adaptation.[9]

The monotony of a simple existence would mean that hysterics would have less need for suggestion; little variety would mean they could continue imitating the tried and true models provided by the physician. Reason, when imitated, created normality.

In addition to Bernheim's hypnotic techniques, Charcot's and Janet's views on suggestion and hysteria had a decisive impact on Freud's understanding of the etiology of hysteria and of the possibilities for cure. Freud, like Charcot, was intensely concerned with the process through which a memory could be a psychological wound; that is, a trauma. In his early work (writings that precede, roughly, *The Interpretation of Dreams* [1900]) Freud strove to remove the memory's potency, not through forgetting like Janet but through the discharge of energy that came through a particular form of recollection. Freud came to develop psychoanalysis as a mode of interpretation that would create a past with which one could live. Psychoanalysis emerged out of mourning, out of the work that enables a person to detach him or herself from the past even while retaining some (narrative) connection to it. The talking cure demands that one situate oneself (or one's desires) in relation to the past, not that one reconstruct *the* actual past in the present. The role of trauma has been of decisive significance in the history of psychoanalysis, and as Freud emerged from mourning for his father he also radically altered the place of childhood trauma in the theory of hysteria. This has led some writers to claim that Freud was either fleeing from an insight into the persecution of (especially female) children, that he was covering over his and his friend Fliess's gross incompetence, or that he was protecting his own abusive father. I shall not discuss these claims here, but want to emphasize that Freud created psychoanalysis as a mode for connecting with and representing the past that has important affinities to mourning, in contradistinction to neurosis. He developed a hermeneutics of memory rather than a tool for some unmediated expression of the past (whatever that might be) which would pretend to get free of it. That is, Freud developed psychoanalysis as a way of using the past rather than revolting against it.[10]

But in *Studies on Hysteria* psychoanalysis had yet to emerge, or rather its early modes of inquiry and application were in competition with other approaches to dynamic psychology. One of the most fascinating aspects of Freud's treatment of Emmy von N. is his attempt to play the role of the powerful physician wielding the latest tool of science, hypnosis, to direct the mind of his patient, who happened to be one of the richest women in Europe. And when hypnosis didn't work, he reverted to overt command: *If you don't accept my explanation for your stomach pains by tomorrow, I will ask you to leave. You'll be on your own and in need of another doctor.* The normally independent woman returned "docile and submissive" (82), we are told. Freud is clearly pleased with what he seems able to do (for a change), but he is also uncomfortable with the feeling, the illusion of power and authority. He is at best awkward in making his patient forget too much, and at worst irresponsible as he gives her a suggestion as a joke. Freud, who has great ambition for but little confidence in what he is doing, always feels about to be judged, perhaps dismissed by this "normally independent" and abnormally powerful woman. His authority, when he has it, is hysterical, a symptom of the patient's inability to live with the powers of the past. How to use this authority without merely producing new symptoms or acting out his own and the patient's fantasies?

Under hypnosis, Emmy described scenes from her past, and after she had done so, Freud would remove the fear of the visions associated with them. "My therapy," he writes, "consists in wiping away these pictures [of frightening episodes from the past], so that she is no longer able to see them before her. To give support to my suggestion I stroked her several times over the eyes" (53). The therapy goes well as the patient "unburdens herself without being asked to. It is as though she had adopted my procedure and was making use of our conversation, apparently unconstrained and guided by chance, as a supplement to her hypnosis" (56). While in hypnotic sleep, she would punctuate her stories of frightening memories with the "protective formula": "Keep still!—Don't say anything!—Don't touch me!" (56). Emmy is afraid, she later explains, that if her reminiscence is interrupted, then "everything would get confused and things would be even worse" (56).

Freud listened to these stories, and tried to piece together their significance. At the same time, he used the power of hypnotic suggestion to change the content of the memories that had given rise to the stories in the first place. Thus, there is a deep tension in the case between Freud's aggressive use of his authority through hypnosis to change his patient's relation to her past, and his recognition that before the memory of the past could be successfully altered it had to be constructed in a conscious, possibly narrative form. "I cannot," Freud complained, "evade listening to her stories in every detail to the very end" (61). This tension is most evident when Emmy complains about Freud's eagerness to erase her memories before she has had the chance to recount them for him.

> Her answer, which she gave rather grudgingly, was that she did not know. I requested her to remember by tomorrow. She then said in a definitely grumbling tone that I was not to keep on asking her where this and that came from, but to let her tell me what she had to say. I fell in with this, and she went on. (63)

In this passage we can see the conquistador stopped (at least for a moment) in his tracks. It is the patient who sets a limit, or at least a context, for his authority.

Let me speak these memories before you try to explain them or wipe them away with the tool of hypnotic suggestion. Fall in with me before you use that authority to which I am supposedly so susceptible. Freud eventually describes himself not as giving definitive explanations nor as wiping away the past with the tool of hypnotic suggestion but as "falling in" with the patient's chosen procedure (*Ich gehe daruf ein*). Like Anna O. (at least in the stories told about her), Emmy teaches her doctor to listen.

By "falling in" with Emmy's stories, Freud was falling into psychoanalysis and falling away from Charcot, Bernheim, and the road taken from them by Janet. What is the significance of this fall, for psychoanalysis and for thinking about history generally?

The significance for psychoanalysis is well known, if still controversial. By falling in with the patient's stories, the analyst becomes part of a relationship, a component in a process in which he or she has only limited (albeit important) control. Freud certainly recognized the phenomenon that so impressed the Janets: patients make an enormous, sometimes bottomless, investment in the relationship with the doctor; they reproduce their illnesses in this relationship. But whereas this phenomenon contributed to therapeutic pessimism about the capacities of the hysteric to lead a normal life, it also became a therapeutic opportunity for the psychoanalyst. That is, the "need for suggestion" and the "perpetual imitation" evinced by patients within the therapeutic process was an exposure of the history of the illness, a revelation of the etiology of its symptoms, if only the analyst was prepared to read it properly. Freud would later understand this exposure through the concept of transference, and the psychoanalytic investigation of the therapeutic relationship itself became one of the defining theoretical and clinical elements of this new approach to the mind and to mental illness.

The concept of the transference also describes the power of the analyst in treatment. This empowerment is a function of the unconsciously repetitive elements of the transference itself. How to use this power without sinking the patients further into the dynamic that was itself at the root of their problems? How to use one's authority to expose one's authority as neurotic? These questions were already apparent in *Studies on Hysteria*, and would remain crucial for the criticism and defense of psychoanalysis as a clinical enterprise. By falling into Emmy's stories, Freud was falling into the domain demarcated by these questions.

Since Freud's time, psychiatrists and therapists have tried to escape this domain in two very general ways: (1) by denying they really have authority;

(2) by denying that the basis of their authority is neurotic. Those who favor the first option often underline the *relational* aspects of the psychotherapeutic situation (as if these were not always present in Freud's work), apparently with the happy thought that by telling clients they are in an equal relationship they suddenly acquire equality. The power of suggestion obviously remains strong. The second option assumes that the legitimacy of the therapeutic practice (whether analytic, psychopharmacological, or both) somehow naturalizes and neutralizes the dependence that the client comes to have on the doctor (after all, so this reasoning goes, patients *should* be dependent!). This was the route Janet himself took when he defined the kind of happiness needed by the hysteric and attempted to provide that kind of happiness. Since the dependence is on a reasonable person—a source of Reason and Progress—it is suddenly no longer supposed to be a symptom.

The route taken by Janet has been very well traveled by contemporary psychiatry, in which dependence on the authority of the scientific physician is routinely taken for granted. The acceptance of the authority of the doctor goes hand in hand with an indifference to the meaning of the patient's history. Peter Kramer's case of "Lucy" represents a post-Freudian (and posthistorical) approach to the self and it pathologies.[11] Lucy is a college student who finds herself taking too many risks in seeking men primed to hurt her. Once in a relationship, Kramer tells us, she invents countless ways to feel rejected. For example, she tests her boyfriend's affections in ways that are bound to show that he is about to leave her. The psychiatrist reveals that Lucy's youth was marked by tragedy and trauma: her mother was murdered by a trusted member of the household, and her subsequent relation to her father was marked by persistent, complex difficulties. But Kramer's treatment protocol ignores this history, and he charts a course of treatment for Lucy that treats her present symptoms at what he calls their "face value." For him this means treating the symptoms not in relation to a history that she might still carry in the present, but as discrete products of an "autonomous syndrome." Kramer is well aware that one could weave together a narrative that would connect Lucy's trauma to what he comes to regard as her "oversensitivity." But he believes that his patient's symptoms, although they may indeed have initially been triggered by early events, now have causes that must be dealt with in the present. "If Lucy can be spared the pain that rejection causes her," he writes, "she will not need to behave in a dependent or self-injurious way." Medication can spare her the pain. In this case "the examination of history, even so evocative a history as Lucy's will be superfluous" (70).

Kramer's discussion of the treatment that renders the examination of history superfluous draws on the psychiatrist Donald Klein's notion of "functional autonomy."[12] Klein introduced this idea to describe how a symptom becomes unmoored from its original cause. A trauma might give rise to what is in that original situation an adaptive response (such as panic or anxiety), but this response persists (now as a symptom) long after that trauma. The original cause (the trauma) is no longer "relevant" to the symptom, which persists as a neuro-chemical holdover originally called for in specific conditions (like the presence of danger or confrontation with loss). Rather than delving into a person's history to discover the patient's original trauma or subsequent feelings about it, the physician can, through medication, alter the current neuro-chemical context that is provoking the symptom. For example, by chemically raising the threshold at which anxiety occurs, the physician can control (or even eliminate) the symptom. This is not, Klein emphasizes, to treat *merely* the symptom. It is to treat the cause that is now producing the symptom *in the present*.[13]

In Kramer's account of Lucy, medication could raise her threshold of responsiveness toward others (making her "less sensitive"), even as it may have made some of her own feelings more available to her. This leads him to consider that the "set point for sensitivity should be biologically regulated" (96). He does not say by whom, or according to which criteria. How does the doctor (or is it now the insurance company?) determine what is proper or appropriate sensitivity? In making the patient less sensitive, what else is the doctor eliminating from the patient's life? To his credit, these are not questions Kramer ignores, but they are ones he is willing to bracket in the service of alleviating symptoms causing suffering in the present.

We can see the trajectory from the Janets' hypnotic treatments of pathogenic memories to psychopharmacology today. For them, it was crucial to reduce the potency of the past; if this could be done by providing the patient with an alternate past, so be it. The doctor provided new memories for the patient, a benign past that would not give rise to painful symptoms. In Kramer's treatment of Lucy, medication renders the past, even one with dramatic trauma, superfluous. Lucy's present symptoms are not seen as dependent (any longer) on her history. They have contemporary neuro-chemical causes that can be treated with medication. The Janets and Kramer are intent on removing symptoms, on bringing the patient back to normality. The former thought they could do this through hypnotic suggestion that allowed them to give their patients a benign past. Kramer thinks he can bring his patients back into the normal by chemically adjusting things like their "set point for sensitivity." By helping patients into the normal, the doctors want to make it possible for their charges to live more fully in the present—whatever their histories.

In these paradigms of medical intervention, transference, like history, is irrelevant. The authority of the doctor is assumed; his or her ability to know the normal and to know what is "superfluous" is taken for granted. The doctor has both feet planted firmly in the world of science, rationality, normality. How different this medical paradigm is from the transference model of interaction that we can see emerging in Freud's case of Emmy von N.! The domain demarcated by the transference is tricky ground on which to stand because it is always in danger of shifting under one's feet. As critics of psychotherapy regularly remind us, there is no firm (epistemologically clean) place to stand in this domain. The analysand makes multiple investments in the possibilities for insight through the analytic relationship, and doing so is part of the conflicted history which leads the person to desire change; yet doing so is also part of that history which in the present makes any change extremely difficult. The conflicted history of the person *is* the present, and any change that can occur must occur *through* that history. The French theorists of *amnesics* who Freud was still trying to follow in the case of Emmy von N. were developing techniques that would remove the troublesome parts of the patient's history, or that would transform the reminiscences causing suffering in the present. They wanted to act on the person's contaminated past *from outside that past*, thereby protecting their intervention (and themselves) from contamination. The same is very much the case of psychopharmacology today. By contrast, in falling into Emmy's stories, Freud was falling into her history; there was no longer an intervention possible from a point outside it.

Of course, the transference itself can be abused, and there are plenty of examples of the analyst mistreating patients all the while blaming the patients for their desires. The term "counter-transference" is used to describe the analyst's projection back onto the patient, and it is a concept that has been used to cover many sins. Freud infamously fell into some of this behavior himself, and my descriptions of the Freudian model of self-consciousness through understanding how history comes alive in transference might be said to be an aspirational model or an ideal type. Freud himself didn't consistently follow it, as we know from several biographers. Since I cast Kramer's treatment of Lucy in a negative light, perhaps it is best to cite his critical and thoughtful account of Freud's abusive treatment of some patients, and his use of the transference concept to explain away that abuse, especially in the Dora Case.[14]

Be that as it may, Freud's fall into history has been suggestive, if I can use that word, for theorists of history trying to understand the stories that are left to us from the past. Since the professionalization of history writing in the mid-nineteenth century, there has been an effort to ensure that historians stand outside of—or at a distance from—the events that they are attempting to explain or interpret. The standpoint of objectivity was to ensure that the authority of the historian was derived from established scientific criteria in the present, not from some personal, biased connection to the material from the past being described.

Recent theorists of history have called into question the picture of the neutral, disconnected historian relating past events from the outside. The point of this questioning is not that all interpretations of the past are equally valid, but that it is important to interpret the complex ways historians establish connections between their own present and the past they are bringing to it. Some of these connections can, as Dominck LaCapra has stressed, be usefully described as transferential since they facilitate the unconscious repetition of past patterns in the present. Historians re-present the past, and often in doing so also act out their unconscious or hidden investments in the objects of their research, which are often objects of complex longing and loathing. An acknowledgment of the transferential relations between historians and the pasts we construct enables us to attend to the processes of mediation and unconscious repetition that contribute to any historical representation.

By falling in with Emmy's stories, Freud was beginning to develop psychoanalysis as a form of historical consciousness that focused on the role of desire vis à vis the past. How does our relationship to a remembered past, or to the past which we imagine is inaccessible to us, serve particular desires in the present? And how does serving *those* desires make it impossible to serve others? These are questions Freud was already beginning to pose in *Studies on Hysteria*, and they would become crucial to the domain of psychoanalysis as a theoretical and clinical enterprise. I have argued that they are also central to the construction of history as a theoretical and practical enterprise. Historical representations attempt to satisfy or stimulate certain desires, and it is usually impossible for them to do so without denying others. Recent controversies surrounding the commemorations of World War II provide many examples in this regard. But the retreat from the transferential, attempts to have uncontroversial museum exhibits, cool detached histories, or neat little positive therapeutic experiences are merely denials of, not solutions to, the problem. One can hope to make the workings of transference in historical representation more apparent, but one cannot avoid this dynamic through some properly hygienic stance toward the past.

How does the remembered or imagined past draw one to it? How does the traumatic past compel our attention, care, or obsession even as it seems to demand acknowledgment that one can never comprehend what happened there? These questions are as important for psychoanalysts as they are for historians. The models of Charcot, Janet, and Kramer point in a different direction. They are alien to modern historical discourse and to psychoanalysis because they are unconcerned with the investment that one has in the past. Charcot, Janet, and Kramer employ technologies of memory or forgetting, but neither has conceptual space for the desire that one has for the past, a desire that results in an effort to link present and past through narrative.

This conceptual space is what Fanny Moser opened up for Freud in the case of Emmy von N. It is the space of modern historical consciousness, which understands freedom as the result of acknowledging one's past in a present containing possibilities for change. It is the space into which Freud is beginning to fall in *Studies on Hysteria*.

7. Why Freud Haunts Us

There's an old man we go to see when we are feeling bad, or just confused. He doesn't say much. He sits behind us when we lie down on the couch. We can hear him breathing, and we know that it's cigar smoke we smell. The old man doesn't really tell stories, but we start telling stories when he is around. It seems he makes us talk, if only because he refuses to say much. We know what he wants. Not just any old stories will do. He wants to hear about our secrets, about our longings. We can start talking about the latest disappointments, the most recent crises. But we know that's not enough. *He* wants to hear about things we won't tell anybody else. He is there, waiting for us to open up some cave in ourselves to wake that hibernating animal. That's the story he wants, isn't it? That's the story we want to tell him, isn't it? Why do we come here? What do we need?

Freud won't go away. We know he was wrong, really we do. Medication is so much more effective, and then there is all that embarrassing stuff about sex and penises, about inescapable aggression and guilt. And mothers. All of it is from another time, isn't it? After all, now we know that women are equal to men, so we don't try too hard to explain how patriarchy gets reproduced generation after generation despite our professed ethics. Now we know that sex can be healthy, that it can even be so safe as to be less than desirable. Yet Freud haunts us. He keeps popping up in places he has no business being. Just when we succeed in pushing him out of medicine because it is inconvenient for the profits of drug and insurance companies, he appears in the university humanities programs, novels, *television*. A generation ago he animated Woody Allen's jokes; more recently we could sense his presence when Brian, the thoughtful canine on *The Family Guy*, wondered with the therapist if his wetting the floor was an act of aggression. Freud was in the room when Tony Soprano and his therapist, Dr. Melfi, tried to understand what it meant to be abandoned by your sister and have to inherit your mother. And when it seems that we can dismiss Dr. Freud (with a laugh) from overly theoretical work by our jargon-laden literary scholars, then there are nostalgic noises from psychiatry complaining about meds without baseline evaluations, about insurance-driven mental health treatment, and about the need for patients to make meaning. There he sits, behind us.

When we begin to tell our stories, to give an account of ourselves, we use narrative to construct a picture of our identity in relation to other people and in relation to change over time. No matter what story we tell, there is a basic, disturbing Freudian question that can be posed to shake up the tale: *What are you getting out of this?* This is often meant as "What are you *really* getting out of this?" As Freud himself noted in the *Psychopathology of Everyday Life*:

> When a member of my family complains to me of having bitten his tongue, pinched a finger, or the like, he does not get the sympathy he hopes for, but instead the question: "Why did you do that?" I myself once gave my thumb a most painful pinch when a youthful patient told me during the hour of his treatment of his intention . . . to marry my eldest daughter. (180)

Freud pinched himself, and we bite our tongues looking for sympathy. In a story about being picked on by a friend, a wife, or a sibling, for example, to be asked "What are you really getting out of this?"—"What are you getting out of being picked on?"—is an offensive query. What desire is expressed by your injury, or in telling the story of the injury? What desire is the war against terrorism *really* satisfying? Why does little Malcolm drive that Hummer? Why are some straight people really so angry about some gay people embracing monogamy? These questions merely assume that the apparent answers—the reasons of which we are aware—will not get at the motivating factors. When asked Freudian questions, we know that the answers are supposed to uncover motivating factors that are connected with desires of which we are not only unaware but about which we are likely to feel ashamed. The origin of this genre of question can be found in Freud's theory of dream interpretation, in which he famously declared that every dream is the expression of a disguised wish. Intense wishes are always disguised (the best disguises can be apparent straightforwardness) because they are never simple; desires are always, according to Freud, bound up in (articulated through) conflict.

One of the reasons Freud haunts us is that we have grown to expect this genre of question: what are you getting out of X? And we have grown to expect that the answer to this question will always describe a kind of *ambivalence*. Ambivalence began as a technical term in psychiatry, and it came to connote a quality of all strong emotions: they give rise to and may be the product of conflict. The strongest love, for example, will always be mixed with aggression. When Janice asked Tony Soprano, "Where does your hate for me come from?" the old man knows that it comes from the same place as his love for her. Love cannot be satisfied without aggression, and intense antipathy is always bound up with desire. These elements can no more be separated from one another than nourishment can be separated from digestion. The Oedipal triangles, in which recognizable sexual behavior is molded into form, are fueled by ambivalent desires. There is no possibility of full, sustained satisfaction in the Freudian model because the desires one aims to gratify are contradictory. You can't kill the father you love . . . or is it that you can't love the father you kill? Satisfying some desires will always mean the denial of others. Moreover, satisfaction breeds guilt, and guilt breeds still new desires. What *are* you getting out of X? Lots more than you bargained for, and that makes for complex, interesting stories. We want to hear them, but more importantly, we seem to want to tell them and be in them.

But Freud, of course, gives us a detailed account of why it is so difficult to tell these stories, even why it is so difficult to gain access to them ourselves. *Repression* was certainly one of Freud's key concepts (he famously called it the cornerstone of his whole enterprise) and it has led to the staying power of the Freudian genre of questioning. In this genre, no matter how much we question, we will never get to the bottom of our own motivations, let alone those of other people. As much as we might want to know what stories to tell when we are lying on the couch, there are other desires aimed at keeping us from knowing what stories to tell. Since we "get something" (some satisfaction) out of not knowing, there will always be a basic inhibition against knowing ourselves. We are motivated to obscurity even as we strive for understanding. Freud's concept of repression helps him to continue to haunt us because it stands for our willful refusal at self-understanding; it is a psychical mechanism preventing us from claiming our own desires. Freud's presence reminds us that our actions and our narratives may be motivated by a desire not to see who we really are. No story we could possibly tell would count as fully overcoming repression because repression is a necessary psychical mechanism, according to Freud. This is more than a full-employment program for therapists. It is a dogmatic insistence on our incapacity for transparency even as it expresses our desire for it. If Freud were no longer haunting us, we might worry that we were repressing him or his message. Such a worry would be a form of haunting. Heads he wins, tails we lose.

The smell of cigar smoke that reminds us someone is listening, the "uh huh . . ." and the pauses which we can't help hearing mark the presence of an other who waits for us to keep talking, to make an association, to make a connection. . . . These have been the passive signs that the psychoanalytic ghost is in the room. Ghosts can be most frightening, most real, when they do the least: a few noises here and there, missing items, gusts of wind when the windows are closed. Similarly, Freud seems to have the most interest not when he is forcing an explanation of psychopathology, but when he is asking questions, or when his mere presence (the kind of thing he *could* be thinking) inspires *us* to ask more questions. When the psychoanalyst finally lets loose with a full interpretation, the effect is somewhat like the ectoplasm becoming visible as someone screams "Aaack, a ghost!" We are disappointed in the vulgarity, the obviousness of the apparition. Freud's interpretations may not always strike readers as they struck Nabokov ("greek myths crudely applied to our private parts"), but they are hardly the most memorable elements in his oeuvre. Did the infant Wolfman really see his parents having sex with his father behind his mother? Did Dora really want the awful Herr K? How close were little Hans's fears of horses and his inclination to play with his widdler? No, it is the *search* that is interesting in Freud not the so-called discovery. That our mental houses *might* be haunted by the past turns out to be much more interesting than what the ghosts of the past would actually *do* were they around.

Freudian interpretation remains most interesting as a threat, as a possible avenue of inquiry, that would tie together associations and uncover motivating factors that had been invisible from surface reading or listening. Many have asked how we could ever know whether a particular interpretation was true, or even how we might go about choosing among competing interpretations. Freud recognized the difficulty of this issue, and he speaks most coherently about the pragmatic value of interpretations. A good interpretation is one that should help us move along, enable us to get to a narrative about the past in relation to the present with which we can live. There is, I know, something unsatisfying about this. Many have asked whether such a story is *really true*. Freud did say that a story would only help us get along if it "tallied with what is real in the patient." Adolf Grünbaum, among others, has claimed that this was Freud's "tally argument," which means that the old man really was looking for a match between his interpretations and the facts of the real world. If this were true, we could then devise tests to determine whether there was such a match. I don't think that the Freud who developed testable hypotheses is the old man who haunts us with his questions and stories. When this ghostly Freud talked about an interpretation tallying with what is real in the patient, he was talking about how an interpretation speaks to something within us, how a story gets to what is real in us.

What makes a good story, or what makes a story good for us? In Freud's case, the good stories are the ones that give rise to more stories, more narratives that combine complexity of meaning with a basic human intensity. Freudian stories deal with anxiety and pleasure; they are concerned with the limits of memory and expression while exploring our fascination with pleasure and dissolution. Freud's tales are about prohibition and desire, about love and death. How *could* they go away?

When we are haunted by the Freud of these stories, we are haunted by the presence of intensity. This means that we are haunted by a lurking drive or instinct, and this we usually understand as being haunted by sex, or possibly aggression. The intensity is part of us, but it is not a part of us we can easily recognize as our own. How do we live with this intensity without losing its capacity to generate significance in our lives? The intensity and ambivalence of our desires have given rise to massive attempts to control them, and these controls have in turn fueled these very desires. What satisfactions are we getting out of the prohibitions against certain satisfactions? The delights and ravages of guilt are central themes in psychoanalysis. Freud suggested that there isn't more satisfaction, let alone happiness, in the world because we make ourselves so miserable, and because we have created a society that is very good at making us even more miserable. Recognizing the ways that we contribute to our own misery is a pleasure (one of the reasons we keep coming back to the old man, I suppose), and it also gives us some possibility of changing the cycle of our self-punishment.

Self-inflicted misery isn't going away, even as we vigorously try to protect ourselves against harm from others. In the Freudian world, as in the political world, homeland security, putting fences around what is precious to us, is a threat as well as a promise. The issues Freud explored have remained vital for us even as his findings and methodology have come under increasing critical pressure. Our notions of identity, memory, childhood, sexuality, aggression, and, most generally, of meaning have been shaped in relation to—and often in opposition to—Freud's work. Though always contested, Freudian thinking informs the ways we perceive ourselves and our society, and it remains relevant to how some of our most pressing concerns (from drug abuse and aggression to gender and sexuality) are addressed. Our vernacular psychology is Freudian in some fundamental sense. For no matter how critical we are of the old man's influence on our culture, there seems to be no good way of making him disappear. Freud, unlike Marx and Nietzsche, the so-called masters of suspicion with whom he is often compared, has retained a capacity to haunt us not because of his explanations of psychopathology, or even because of his model of therapy as a talking cure. He continues to haunt our culture because of the threatening and the comical possibilities opened up by his genre of questioning. As a theorist, I have argued, Freud was most concerned with making meaning out of memory, with constructing histories with which we could live. As a ghost, Freud continues to have some presence in our culture because that presence undermines the conventional ways we use to make sense of the world.

Think, if you will, of Freud as a certain kind of action figure, or, I should say *in*action figure. By now I have received three of these as gifts from different friends and colleagues. At the last occasion at which I was presented with one, my then five-year-old daughter (fed up with her daddy receiving toys) wanted to play with the toy. After moving the old man around a bit, my Sophie asked with some exasperation, What does he *do*? The makers of this toy are ingenious. They know that Freud is most present when he does the least. So, Freud, the *in*action figure, moves just a bit, his cigar rising. If the makers of this toy were aiming at a higher price point, they would have allowed us to pull a string on the back of the doll just so that you could hear the toy say . . . nothing.

In everyday life, knowing that the old man (or one of his followers) is around has been troubling and interesting because it has suggested that someone is asking the question "What are you really getting out of this?" or "What does this gesture, this sign, this way of living, really mean?" As Freud wrote in 1905: "He who has eyes to see and ears to hear becomes convinced that mortals can keep no secret. If their lips are silent, they gossip with their fingertips; betrayal forces itself through every pore." The secrets that the patient betrays are signs that the stories we've told ourselves about how we've gotten from past to present may only be symptomatic of another way of making sense of ourselves and our past. Some have argued that we have moved into an epoch when "making sense of ourselves and our past" has as little relevance to reality as privacy on the web, psychosomatic erectile dysfunction, or depression as a sensible response to the ways of the world. They have argued, in other words, that history and the narratives through which it is constituted are products

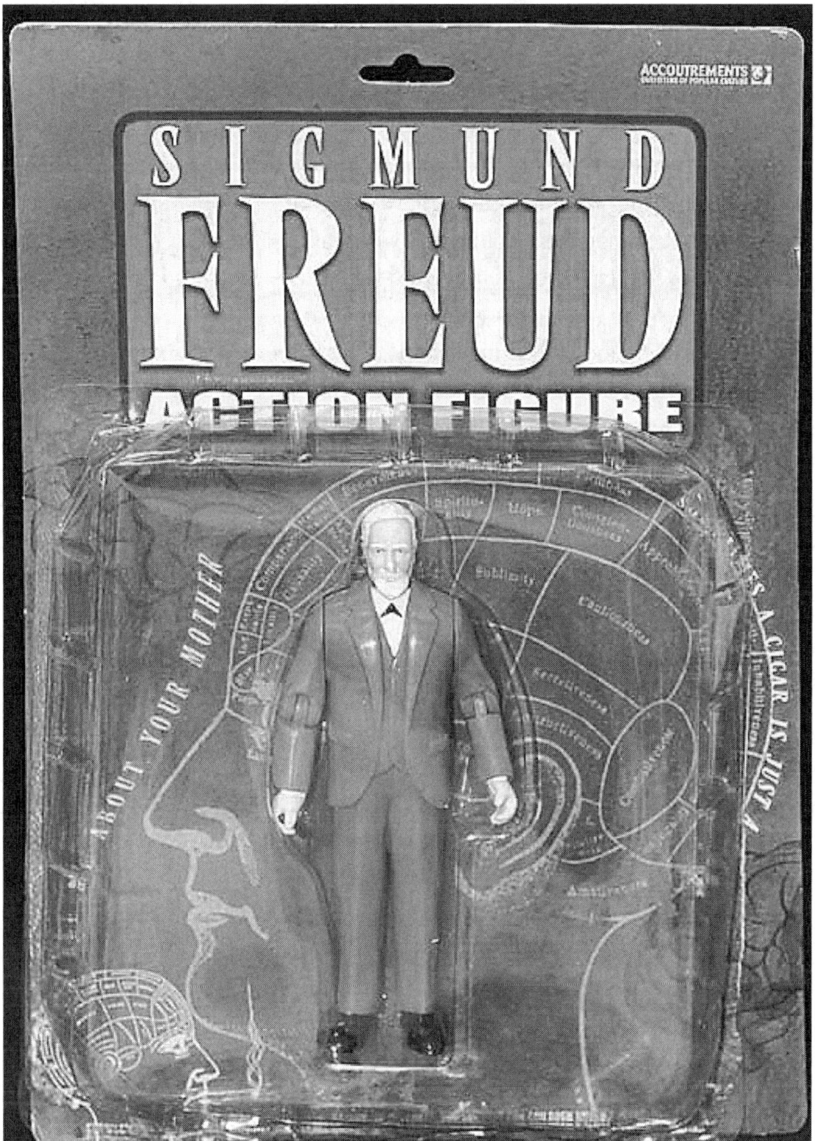

FIGURE 15. Freud action figure. Archie McPhee, www.mcphee.com.

of a bourgeois, or modern, or patriarchal mode of thinking from which we can liberate ourselves. In *The Possibility of an Island*, a trashy science fiction sex farce by the French novelist Michel Houellebecq, a scientist explains that long ago people thought they had to understand their pasts in order to change their lives. The scientist explains that neurologists have discovered that remembering the past only enslaves you (at the biochemical level) to it. Houellebecq imagines neohumans who have no need to revisit the past, but even they secretly keep diaries. And, of course, they (and we) have their novelist.

If we *are* ever liberated from history, if history ever becomes superfluous to how we live in the future, Freud would no longer haunt us, because his threat, his inaction, would no longer be relevant. In that case, psychoanalysis (and much else) would certainly disappear. Maybe then we would truly be neohumans. But if we continue to consider the past important for giving meaning and direction to our lives, then it's a good bet that we will hear faint noises from the old man, as we are moved again to find a way to tell our stories to better understand who we are and what we want.

PART 3

POSTMODERNISM AND CULTURAL POLITICS

8. Why Warburg Now?

Now that we have come at least full circle in the humanities concerning the nature of interdisciplinarity and the value of apprenticeship and training, we may be able to examine more coherently the nature of disciplinary authority. Some of those who attacked this authority in the past have come to defend their version of it as they have grown older and more established in their chosen fields. What a surprise! Interdisciplinary programs now defend their own turf with the same zeal as the old departments against which they once rebelled.[1] When I first gave this chapter as a lecture at the College Art Association in 2000, I was an Associate Director of the Getty Research Institute for the History of Art (GRI). When I had first come to the Getty as a visiting scholar and then as an administrator, the name of our unit was Getty Research Institute for the History of Art and the Humanities. The words "and the Humanities" were sandblasted off the stone that sat in front of the serpentine Richard Meier building in Los Angeles. There may be no better symbol of the decline of interdisciplinary work in American art history, unless it's the journal *October*'s defense of medium specific art and the profession's efforts to marginalize visual studies.

To say that this is a question of power is to say almost nothing, except that one is evoking Foucault and the world of texts around him. Evoking "Foucault" can be a good strategy in showing one has some—but not too much—theoretical sophistication. In the humanities and arts, this use of names is an essential aspect of the rhetoric used to exercise disciplinary authority. For example, the name "Walter Benjamin" can serve as a header for almost anything in the humanities, although the backlash against overuse has been underway for some time. In the historiography of art history (like other fields) certain authors are legitimated as providing the sponsorship under which diverse (even contradictory) moves in the field can be made. The name "Baxandall" was for years a good example in this regard. Almost anything having to do with the context of a work will benefit from an association with "Baxandall." The name "Fried" has been a more risky sponsor, even in the modern and contemporary fields, unless, that is, one is trying to pick a fight. "Krauss" may have lost some its contemporary cachet, but how long can a name be expected to stay new? We will likely find out the answer to that question through the exchange of the name "Rancière." Suddenly we are awash in "Rancière," probably because the name legitimates a discussion of aesthetics while maintaining some vague politically progressive connotations. The word or brand "Elkins" is now so ubiquitous that it has lost its identity.

In part, this is how a discipline maintains order by creating a pragmatic canon: essential words with which members of the trade need to be acquainted (at least so as to be able to write the knowing footnote or make the appropriate citation) as partial proof of their own disciplinary literacy. This literacy is supposed to guarantee membership in the trade. Membership in the trade has always been of particular importance to art historians, perhaps because they are so sensitive to the value of inclusion in a canon (or an auction).

Names, I would suggest, play a particularly important role in the rhetoric of a scholarly field at times when dominant paradigms are obscure, unstable, or incoherent. Rather than marshalling *arguments* for a particular mode of analysis, interpretation, or description, research and argumentation take place under the *name* of a figure who stands for a variety of ways of seeing, remembering, writing, describing, arguing. Aby Warburg is such a name and this is such a time. In the last twenty-five years, Warburg's writings have become a locus for more than just a small coterie of faithful followers, and by now the writings have become distinct from the research institute and library that bear his name. His texts can be used to legitimate conceptions of art and visual studies, understandings of history, and practices of interpretation. The texts are also viewed as a symptom of the massive social and political pressures that have been brought to bear on intellectual and personal life in the twentieth century, pressures which have not entirely disappeared in our own time. In this chapter, I want to briefly examine what work the name "Warburg" does: why is "Warburg" a banner for scholarship now?

On the occasion of the publication of a translation of Warburg's writings in Italian in 1966, Carlo Ginzburg wrote: "But 'discovering,' at this late date the importance of the teachings of Warburg and of his friends and followers, as the latest intellectual fashion, seems at first to be a little ridiculous."[2] More than thirty years later, the Getty Research Institute published an English translation of *The Renewal of Pagan Antiquity*, a decisive work from the

1920s that resonated powerfully with the agenda of the Institute in the 1990s.[3] The Getty was hardly alone in celebrating a return to Warburg as a vehicle for stimulating deeper reflection on how art history can contribute to the study of the history of culture. And this was what connected the disparate scholars interested in the Weimar-era researcher: the possibility that art history could contribute to a general understanding of the history of a culture without losing its distinctive abilities to increase our comprehension of art objects. The discipline of art history in the United States has long had real ambivalence about this ambition because "a general understanding of the history of a culture" might not in the end privilege art objects for their own sake.

Anthony Grafton, writing in the informal mode of the "Diary" page of the *London Review of Books*, discussed the revival of interest in Warburg in Germany as part of a generational shift toward intellectuals eager to retrieve their own prewar intellectual heritage. For Grafton, the recovery of Warburg by German academics and journalists who came of age in the late 1960s was a liberation from the hidebound university establishment, a liberation that opened the way to creative, eccentric but erudite pan-disciplinary perspectives. Grafton's article incited a spirited letter from the historian Norman Cantor. Cantor saw Warburg as confining himself to "iconology," and, along with Panofsky, as responsible for locking art history into the "cautious" and "increasingly sterile" picture-to-text approach. In the next issue of the *London Review* David Freedberg objected strenuously to what he called Cantor's "confusions." Warburg was no Panofskian, and the narrow versions of iconography that came to dominate parts of Anglo-American art history were betrayals, not continuations of Warburg's legacy. If Cantor had even the most superficial acquaintance with the field and its issues, Freedberg growled, he might begin to understand these things.[4]

In this brief exchange in the *London Review* we can see a key dimension of what work the name "Warburg" can be made to do now: to satisfy the mainstream disciplinary desire to dispense with any method of establishing *the* meaning of a visual representation. Warburg can be used to sponsor the notion that the work of art presents beholders with a *problem*, but not a problem that anybody really wants to see *solved*. This effort at what we would now call "problematizing a representation" appears regularly in the history of art history. Iconography itself was thought of as offering a more complex view of the work of art than the narrow formalism against which it pitted itself. The development of the social history of art was seen by many of its practitioners as a vehicle for decentering the methodological certainties of both iconography and formalism. And semiotic theories of the visual have often taken as their targets the empirical or metaphysical pieties of historical accounts of the social dimensions of art. Each of these trends in the history of art, although in deep conflict with one another, can find some support in Warburg's oeuvre. The revival of interest in his work is due in part to the fact that his fragmentary and often cryptic writings can be used for almost any intellectual movement proceeding under the perfectly innocuous banner of "the work of art is more complicated that that!" Or, to put it in the more sympathetic (but, alas, equally fuzzy) terms used by Kurt Forster in his introduction to the translation of *The Renewal of Pagan Antiquity*: "Warburg emerges as the historian of those areas of human culture that resist hard and fast classification and interpretation."[5]

We don't like "hard and fast classification and interpretation" just now, and perhaps this is the most general reason for Warburg's current appeal. Cantor's negative remarks about Warburg stem from this same rejection of any method (formalist, iconographical, historical, semiological) that would promise hard and fast knowledge about a work of art. But if our own time is uncomfortable with what we too comfortably call positivist approaches to works of art, we aren't too keen on aestheticizing approaches either. And Warburg can easily be invoked as a scholar who took postage stamps as seriously as paintings, who didn't confuse his love of particular artists and objects with his desire to understand cultural change and human expression. His early-twentieth-century rejection of both scientism and aestheticism has encouraged scholars to embrace him as our contemporary.

In order for Warburg's name to evoke the appropriate antiscientistic and antiaesthetic intellectual mood, there has been one important difficulty to overcome. We saw it in Cantor's letter, and we can find it in many of the commentaries developed in recent years. This is the problem of iconography (sometimes lumped together with iconology). The decoding of pictorial elements into verbal formulae was important to the professionalization of art history in academic institutions in the United States. Iconography aimed to put erudition in the service of problem solving rather than in league with the refinement of taste. However, the teaching of iconography as a dependable method often resulted in the reduction of pictorial content to discrete messages that were either less interesting than the images themselves or that seemed only tangentially connected to the maker of the image. Iconographic reading, doubtless a useful tool to have in one's kit, seemed to become a crutch for dealing with complex visual experience, or even a prison to keep one from thinking about it. How to separate Warburg's name from these reductive developments?

Although he certainly used iconography, Warburg was scarcely systematic about it. Here the name "Panofsky" has been extremely useful. For many involved in the Warburg revival, Panofsky represents the bad side of the tradition. He can be blamed for reifying iconography and then for wrongly attaching the name of Warburg to that reification. Margaret Iverson's essay "Retrieving Warburg's Tradition" (1993) offers a good example in this regard. Under the guise of a feminism that usually thumbs its nose at such "binary oppositions," Iverson sees a good, decentered, divided, feminine, overdetermined tradition versus a bad, transcendental, masculine, rational tradition. Warburg represents the former and Panofsky, she says, the latter. With the name "Panofsky" around to represent the things we love to hate about art history, we can safely use the name "Warburg" to sponsor the things we really want to do. I confess to some confusion about why feminist art history would want to find a good-enough mother in a founding father.

With the name "Warburg" cleansed of its iconographical associations, the task has been to give it some new ones. This has developed by linking it with contemporary trends in history, anthropology, and theory. Warburg had a creative, nuanced perspective on the work of art as a historical artifact. The German art historian began where Jacob Burckhardt left off, and he took great pains to situate artists and the pictorial problems they faced in relation to social and psychological forces. Only documentary evidence could provide the leads that would allow the art historian to understand how an object was a response to specific conditions and expectations, and how it in turn created new conditions for those who encountered it in specific settings. If archival research was the basis for enwebbing the work of art in a hermeneutic of understanding, there were no a priori constraints on what *kinds* of documents might be most relevant. Astrology, poetry, science, technology . . . anything might provide clues for understanding the interaction of individuals and the contexts that provided them with the vocabulary and motivation for making and encountering works of art. Warburg's combined good old historical *Sitzfleisch* with the license to try to make anything relevant to the understanding of a painting, and today this combination has enormous appeal. Rather than being seen as the originator of a method for the exclusive use of those studying visual materials, Warburg can now be embraced as a forerunner of cultural studies. Since the culture he chose to study was the Renaissance, and since the aspect of that culture on which he focused was the revival of antiquity, *his* cultural studies approach is less threatening than it might otherwise be to traditional art-historical inquiry. But as Edgar Wind noted almost seventy years ago:

> It was one of Warburg's basic convictions that any attempt to detach the image from its relation to religion and poetry, to cult and drama, is like cutting off its lifeblood. . . . It is not just a manner of training the eye to follow and enjoy the formal ramifications of an unfamiliar linear style, but of resurrecting the original conceptions implied in a particular mode of vision from the obscurity into which they have fallen.[6]

The "resurrection of conceptions *implied* in a particular mode of vision" would allow one to understand the "historical situation" of a work of art. So much rides on the word "implied." For Kurt Forster, Warburg's subject was the individual in what he calls the "playground of history." Choose the swing you want, climb on the jungle jim, or take the slide—there is no logic to these choices, either for the art maker or the art historian. And, of course, nothing outside of your particular playground will be affected by the choices you make. History is the field for making meaning; not to worry if the meaning is correct, as long as the associations are rich and tied to documentary sources.[7] This picture of history as a reservoir or meaning but *not* as a source of explanations seems to be part of Warburg's current appeal.

Warburg's name now connotes not only a hermeneutic historical playground, it also has some anthropological associations that resonate with important trends in the history of art. There seem to be two major sources for these associations in Warburg's work: his emphasis on *Nachleben*, "recycling," "reuse," or "rebirth"; and his essay on the snake dance ritual among the Hopi. Running throughout Warburg's essays and fragments is the problem of how an object, idea, or gesture can reappear and signify in different cultural contexts. Warburg, of course, was especially interested in the reappearance of antiquity, but he pluralized this into the notion that every age has the antiquity it deserves.[8] His famous 1923 lecture on the snake dance among the Pueblo Indians (the publication of which in 1988 helped jump start the Warburg revival in Germany) pursues this theme in searching for the native antiquity that is reborn in contemporary North American Indian cultural practices.[9]

Warburg's problem was thus to understand the reappearance and reuse of the past in different cultural contexts. This can be given an anthropological research dimension, and it can also be used as a theoretical weapon against any simple-minded, linear historicism. He was interested both in how the past can inform a present and how it can haunt it like a menacing shadow. Georges Didi-Huberman has been drawn to Warburg, for example, because of the way his notion of *revenance*, of haunting, breaks through any simple notion of historical time.[10] The anthropologist Carlo Severi is drawing on Warburg in his research group devoted to the study of how objects retain the past in ways that can be activated by contemporary rituals.[11] The archaeologist and art historian Salvatore Settis takes seriously Warburg's efforts to create a psychology of human expression and a natural history of art. For Settis, these efforts are an invitation to the researcher to search for cross-cultural affinities as well as differences in the ways that artifacts are used to connect to or escape from past traditions.[12] All of these projects refer back to Warburg as an intellectual sponsor and resource.

The historical and anthropological associations with Warburg intersect in the theme of cultural memory, a topic currently attracting much interesting theoretical and empirical work. Cultural memory, for Warburg, was the conduit for the reuse or revival of past experience and emotion—both in the objects he studied and in his conception of the reason for studying them. As Wind noted, Warburg thought the scholar was both a "trustee of a repository of human experience" and an analyst of the way that repository worked.[13] Memory and empathy were closely linked together by Warburg as features of historical work and cultural creation, and exploring their connection, as Juliet Koss has done, is likely to be one of the most vital dimensions of the Warburg *Nachleben*.[14] The revival of interest in his work has coincided with the resurgence of interest in cultural memory and in the connections between memory and history. The extraordinary exfoliation of publications on memory over the last twenty years has been stimulated by the effort to understand how people retain the possibility of connecting to the past even as their communal traditions grow weaker and their official historical accounts more remote from their experience. Warburg's vague notion of a "repository of human experience"—depending on no particular archival structure or narrative practice—comes in handy here because it allows one to think that an artist is retrieving the past without having to show the paths of mediation and communication through which he or she comes into contact with the past or its representations. Some commentators might fall back on quasi-biological or natural accounts to explain how cultural memory can reappear after what seemed to be generations of radical amnesia, others can use constructionist, morphological, or semiotic accounts. But the idea that there is a living past that can (or must) be tapped into by culture makers seems to have appeal today, as it did in Warburg's time. We get to have a connection to the past without being bound to any particular narrative recounting of it.

Of course, Warburg was not merely nostalgic. He recognized that the past that could be tapped into was also violent, dangerous, and potentially overwhelming. Being connected to cultural memory wasn't just staying in touch with beloved and friendly ancestors who might inspire one's creativity in history's playground. It was also being vulnerable to forces that one had with great effort tried to leave behind. As Matthew Rampley noted in a 1997 essay on the philosophical import of Warburg's work, social memory "serves both as a tool of redemption and as a focus of regression."[15] Redemption is never final, since regression is always an open possibility.

The subject of ambivalent cultural memory and the potential danger of forces anchored in the past leads me to the final section of my considerations of why Warburg is now such an attractive figure for art history today. This concerns his dramatic biography. There are two features of that biography that are prominent in contemporary appropriations of his work. The first concerns his mental illness and the second his Jewishness. It is difficult to detach the mental illness entirely from the work because of the art historian's own view that he was investigating the dark, atavistic powers that occasionally rise out of the past to overwhelm the forces of harmony and enlightenment. Like Nietzsche and Freud, Warburg was convinced that no age could divorce itself from these dark powers, and that their return was an open, dreadful possibility. The fact that he emerged from almost six years of institutionalization in 1923 and gave evidence of his mental stability by lecturing on Native American ritual and pottery making, ties his research and his personal struggles together in a particularly poignant way. Warburg was not one of those detached, aloof scholars who manage a neat separation of work and life. He not only saw his historical research as an empathic engagement of personal and cultural memory, it was also part of the cultural battle against the vicious close-minded intolerance of his contemporary world. The dialectic of respect for historical otherness and passionate personal engagement has attracted scholars as diverse as Margaret Iverson and Kurt Forster, Carlo Ginzburg, and Charlotte Schoell-Glass. All seem to agree that Ernst Gombrich's attempt to construct Warburg as an Enlightenment rationalist misses the mark because it evades this dimension of his life and work.

There is far less agreement about whether Gombrich erred in seeing Warburg's Jewish heritage as having had a relatively minor impact on his mature historical work. Some (like Michael Steinberg and Charlotte Schoell-Glass) are convinced that there is a red thread running through Warburg's work leading back to his early interest in solving the Jewish question in Europe. One can see this in his interest in the renaissance of ancient, violent rituals in general, and in his collection of reports of contemporary anti-Semitic violence in particular. Other scholars (like Forster and Settis), however, are persuaded that he saw himself as far more German than Jewish, and that Gombrich was absolutely correct in framing the young Warburg as making a decisive break with his Jewish history. This second group of scholars sees those who emphasize Warburg's Jewishness as either projecting contemporary concerns about identity and ethnicity onto another historical moment, or, even worse, as unwittingly contributing to dangerous racialist discourse. Does Warburg represent the persistence of Judaism as resource and motivation in the modern world, or the all-too-brief moment of cosmopolitan, assimilationist potential? Can scholarship about him avoid only mirroring contemporary debates about the general role of identity in shaping intellectual engagement, and the particular place of Jewishness in forming secular versions of that engagement? The fact that there is no developing consensus about these questions indicates that Warburg's dramatic biography will continue to be a subject for debate as art historians seek to come to terms with his intellectual legacy and with the place of their field in contemporary discussions of identity and culture.

The name "Warburg" has long been present in art history through the Library and Institute that bear his name, and through the small band of distinguished scholars who have been inspired by the historical, anthropological, and theoretical challenges posed by his research and writings. As his publications and notes have become increasingly well known in recent years, Warburg's name has become a sign under which investigations into historical recycling, the afterlife of forms and gestures, and the intersection of memory and empathy can take place. As Salvatore Settis and I developed an international scholars program anchored by a working seminar at the Getty Research Institute, we thought our problems-oriented approach to the visual arts in cultural history placed us within some broad Warburgian tradition. I have come to think that the most fruitful research developed in the afterlife of Warburg's contributions will be research that explores specific intersections of memory and empathy in the visual domain, research that tries to understand the past as part of the history of the present. This is to be distinguished from simply projecting the present back onto the past—an exercise in narcissism, not empathy. Making Warburg part of the vital history of art will mean not just stuffing his name into our footnotes or appending his words as epigrams to our essays. It will mean trying to understand the problems that faced Warburg in his own personal and historical moment in relation to those that face us now.

9. Classic Postmodernism

Keith Jenkins

Keith Jenkins has been beating the postmodern drum for some time now.[1] He is, please forgive the phrase, an old-school postmodernist. He continues to sample some of the best beats from those cherished vinyls: Hayden White on literary form and relativism, Jacques Derrida on undecidability. Jenkins even goes way down in the alley to remind us of Jean Baudrillard's "illusion of the end." Jenkins's brief text is meant to be heard over the din of the pop music assaulting the ears of history students from the corporate radio stations of the discipline: its golden oldies from E. H. Carr to Natalie Z. Davis, from E. P. Thompson to Joyce Appleby. Part of his dilemma is that Jenkins himself, along with by now a chorus of postmodern critics, is often programmed as part of the background music with which students of the discipline are expected to be familiar. Yet, Jenkins thinks that the (his) postmodern challenge to history-as-a-discipline is a radical one, and so he resists what Peter Novick some years ago nicely called "rejection through partial incorporation."[2] On the other hand, Jenkins wants the discipline to acknowledge the (his) postmodern challenge, to take it seriously and legitimate his radicalism. That's why the radical is so proud to tell readers of this book that his earlier assault on the profession's values, *Rethinking History*, is about to be reissued as a Routledge Classic (6)! The writer of classics wants to demolish a discipline's convention; the postmodern critic of historicism is sure that we are in a totally new historical epoch; the champion of the radical uncertainty and density of language has chosen to publish this volume in a most accessible and conversational rhetoric. These are just a few of the paradoxes of Keith Jenkins's latest book.

Little in the sermon Jenkins offers in *Refiguring History* will be new to those who've been singing in or listening to the postmodern choir. His is basically an antiepistemological position. Jenkins doesn't believe that history as a discipline can be grounded in a theory of knowledge because he doesn't think that any discipline can be grounded in a theory of knowledge. In other words, he is persuaded by the French poststructuralist critique of modernism and of modern science. The postmodern canon that he dips into really has little to say about history specifically. Hayden White is the exception in this regard, and Jenkins uses him to connect the relativism of the linguistic turn with the particular rhetorics on which history has come to depend. Rather than epistemology, aesthetics is the arena that Jenkins thinks is proper to historical discourse. Here he depends on Ankersmit's recent attempts to think through how history pictures the past rather than representing it.[3] Finally, Jenkins repeatedly asserts that the reconfiguring of history has powerful ethical and political ramifications. That is, he thinks that moving away from epistemology and embracing aesthetics, that abandoning modernist striving for truth and purity in favor of postmodernist reveling in the intensity of commitment without foundations—that these theoretical turns would pave the way for a radical democratic practice open to otherness and egalitarianism. This final gesture to ethics and politics is meant to give the volume its *raison d'être*. Alas, it is this gesture that is the most feeble part of the book. Although Derrida and Jenkins may share certain political affections, or (more likely) hostilities, there is nothing theoretical to link their critiques of epistemology to their radical democratic proclivities. The fact that there may be an interesting history to tell about this link between skepticism and engagement, between deconstruction and democracy, is a sign that history as a form of writing (and thinking) may have qualities to which this postmodern critic has turned a deaf ear.

The three chapters of Jenkins's thin volume operate on two levels: epistemological critique and political moralism. Both are fairly straightforward. His critique grows out of a skepticism born of the linguistic turn in philosophy as it was appropriated by deconstruction. In its most simple form, it amounts to this: we can never know anything for certain because the language we use for knowing never can convey or contain stable meaning. Since language is essential for knowing, and language is a slippery instrument, there is no stable knowing. In the all-or-nothing universe of deconstruction that Jenkins enjoys, a lack of totally stable knowing means radical uncertainty. Without absolute knowledge there is only skepticism. If you can never be fully certain that people mean exactly what you (or they) think they mean, then, in Jenkins's view, you are radically uncertain. Jenkins will go on to say that this radical uncertainty is a good thing, or is at least a happy condition.

How is this by now conventional linguistic skepticism relevant to historical studies? Alongside his embrace of deconstruction on epistemological grounds rooted in a view of language, Jenkins has a metaphysical skepticism about the status of the past. There is nothing in the past to be found, and the "things held by most historians to be intrinsic (historical facts, structures, periods and meanings) are actually only extrinsic ascriptions. . . . For there really is nothing *in* the past to prevent the exercise of endless interpretive freedom by historians" (10). Here Jenkins is drawing on the work of the constructionist philosophers of history who have emphasized that we bring meaning to the interpretations of the past, or that we impose structures upon it from our own situations:

> Nobody has a patent on "the past"; it can be used or ignored by everyone. And why is this? Because the so-called past (the before now) doesn't exist "meaningfully" prior to the efforts of historians to impose upon it a structure or form; the "before now" is utterly shapeless and knows of no significance of its own either in terms of its whole or its parts before it is "figured out" by us. (11)

That the present imposes meaning on the past is something about which recent philosophers of history from Collingwood to White have agreed. Jenkins wants to make this point a dramatic postmodern one by insisting that, since we impose meaning, the result is both slippery and uncertain (because of language) and arbitrary (because there are no "logical or proper" rules for imposing meaning). This leads him to say some imprudent and even wrongheaded things: "No historian or anyone else acting as if they were a historian ever returns from his or her trip to 'the past' without precisely the historicisation they wanted to get; no one ever comes back surprised or empty-handed from that destination" (11).

Of course, the fact that historians bring their own values or preconceptions to their study of the past does not prevent them from being surprised. No more than the fact that physicists use a certain methodology or paradigm prevents them from finding disconfirming evidence. Or, no more than the fact that we speak our own language prevents us from communicating with someone else. Jenkins might want to say that scientists, like historians, are never *totally* surprised because their categories for taking in the world prevent them from seeing certain things (which would surprise them). Scientists may find disconfirming evidence at the micro level, but they are blind to *really* disconfirming evidence that would undermine the paradigm of judgment and knowledge. Scientists, like historians because of the assumptions they bring to the evidence, cannot even perceive the phenomena that would surprise them.

Evidence that disconfirms a hypothesis just doesn't count as a real surprise for Jenkins because the researcher was able to make enough sense of the material to process it as a disconfirmation. But this is merely a trivialization on Jenkins's part. He is claiming that historians fail to be surprised when they turn to the past because he has imagined a world in which there is no such thing as a (real) surprise.

The energy for Jenkins's prose seems to come from how he imagines the responses of his (impossibly naïve) adversaries: "How can you celebrate radical uncertainty?" "Without logical or proper rules for historical explanations and narratives, anything goes . . . any history is as good as any other?" "What about the Nazis?" Jenkins imagines the "kick the stone" realist as his only adversary. And he is in his Nietzschean "bring 'em on" mode in this book: he is willing to concede—no, celebrate—a condition in which you can never know (really know) if your story is the right one, or even whether it is a pretty good one. He imagines a naïve empiricist and angry response to his relativism, and he sees himself as a forceful critic of the disciplinary status quo defended by this empiricism. For Jenkins, the theoretical arguments have been made, and the discipline must no longer remain locked in pretheoretical naïveté. He does not consider the positions of authors who avoid positivism without embracing either deconstruction or constructivism. David Carr's argument that the world is experienced in narrative form is not considered here, nor is Hans Kellner's notion of a sublime "outside" of history.[4] Although Ankersmit's work on aesthetics is used, there is no mention of his views concerning mortality, the past, and the sublime. In this book Jenkins is looking back on what he sees as theoretical battles already won but not acknowledged by the discipline in practice, and he refuses to be distracted by any nuanced views that might not fall neatly into the silly old empiricist box: "For we are now fully aware that we have to live with an intellectual outlook where truth and objectivity, neutrality and disinterest, are simply agreements produced in conversations which are always between interested parties and within and against which we do have to make ultimately groundless decisions" (13). Here Jenkins rather typically overplays his hand. Why "ultimately groundless decisions"? Is this simply to annoy the imagined positivist out there? Why wouldn't the disciplinary conversations (and other practices) themselves produce all the grounds we (ultimately) ever need?

Jenkins wants to reject the pragmatist and postmodern position that the lack of a deep foundation need not destroy the conventional practices that never required a foundation in the first place. He wants to reject this position because it does not entail the ethical or political posture he would like to encourage. In other words, Jenkins is troubled by the possibility that historians might embrace a thoroughgoing pluralism that he feels would be a poor substitute for authentic, radical, earthshaking postmodernism. Under the guise of pluralism, even under the guise of accepting interpretive openness and the lack of certainty about the past, Jenkins observes that historians are able to continue to write and think in pretty much the same ways as before. Is it possible that postmodernism can really amount to so little, when interpretive pluralism and undecidability are more or less accepted by senior members of the department or by the presidents of the American Historical Association? Jenkins energetically rejects this possibility, claiming that most historians remain committed to the form of empiricism even if they claim to be pluralists about the content (15). In other words, the form of history remains stable because historians have never really accepted the radical implications of the uncertainty they claim to be able to live with.

Here Jenkins's own postmodernism returns to undermine his argument. He desperately wants experimentation with literary and political forms to follow from the postmodern critique of epistemology. Although I have some sympathy with his aims in regard to both aesthetics and politics, postmodernism should have taught Jenkins that *nothing* follows from the critique of epistemology, since this epistemology did no real work to begin with. Hayden White has for years delighted in showing that you cannot justify the literary form of historical discourse by appeal to the historical record since that record cannot be represented or accessed independently of a literary form. But it is also the case that no theory of the knowability of the past will necessarily lead to any particular literary representation of it. Experimentation in literary form may be desirable for those who read or write history, but it does not follow from any theory of the past. In other words, realist literary forms can survive the demise of theoretical empiricism. Postmodernists shouldn't be surprised.

If Jenkins wants his epistemological critique to have practical consequences for how historians think and write, this is because he believes that there is some connection between this critique and the development of a more open, democratic, and tolerant society. Somehow, the lack of definitive knowledge is supposed to facilitate a more just, experimental, and free polity. In the postmodern context, historical writing should become more reflexive and "explicitly emancipatory" (13). "Unending interpretive flux . . . is an integral part of political freedom" (53). Here, Jenkins makes use of Derrida, Baudrillard, and Alain Badiou to plant political crops in the ground cleared by the critical power of linguistic skepticism. Derrida "yokes together" his personal belief in emancipation with the ironic results of his theory. Baudrillard exposes the reproduction of complicity, and Badiou celebrates an ethics of intensity even after all certainties have been demolished. None of these gestures, however, has much to do with the theory of history or the practice of historians. Nor do they have anything to do with the theoretical apparatus that is part of postmodernity. Indeed, for all the talk about undecidability and the imposition of meaning on the past, Derrida underscores the ways that we cannot avoid our inheritance, and the ways that we are haunted (like it or not) by the past. Although Jenkins is attracted to Derrida's insistence that we make the meaning out of the inheritance, the deconstructionist's talk of the pressure of inheritance and of unavoidable haunting cannot be easily integrated into Jenkins's constructionist view of the historian's retrospection. For Jenkins, there is nothing in the past until we get there with our categories, our schemes—the meanings we will project onto the "before now." This would make impossible the kind of haunting that interested Derrida in the last decades of his life.[5]

Jenkins seems to believe that a person paying attention to the theoretical arguments must become a postmodernist because of the successful critique of epistemology. But he also believes that the antifoundationalism that is at the core of postmodernism will lead someone to be more experimental in literary form, more just to "the other," and more democratic. As Stanley Fish has shown, this is merely wishful thinking:

> But if antifoundationalism leads to none of the bad consequences often attributed to it, neither does it lead to any of the good consequences sometimes claimed for it. Holding antifoundationalist views does not make you more generous and less absolutist (generosity and absolutism are possible modes of engagement within local contexts . . .). Holding antifoundationalist views will not make you less judgmental (you will be judgmental, if you are, in relation to the local norms and standards to which you are attached). Holding antifoundationalist views will not make you more open; you will be more or less open to the extent that your opinions on some specific matter of concern or debate are or are not settled; there is no *general* stance of openness.[6]

Just as fidelity to the past demanded no specific literary form or politics, the higher infidelity that Jenkins preaches demands no specific kind of discourse or political context. Jenkins insists that "one ought to try to be as free from one's inheritance as circumstances permit so that the least *violent* decision is enacted upon the other who is on the receiving end of it" (24). More freedom from the past and less violence against others are certainly nice enough goals to advocate, and of course they have been part of the Enlightenment project for a long time. But they have nothing to do with the supposed triumph of postmodernism.

Alas, Jenkins is not satisfied with the slim pickins of pragmatist postmodernism. He wants something full and important to emerge from the dismantling of foundations. For this he turns to aesthetics, with the notion, following Ankersmit, that histories are not representations but *things* that act in the world as proposals (54–55). Still, for this refiguring of histories to be meaningful, it would have to help us understand why we are engaged by some proposals (historical accounts) rather than others. Here, Jenkins's approach offers no help: "All I can say is that something in one's life, something in one's experiences, something ultimately undecidable to do with one's mood(s), disposition(s), dream(s), imagination, makes one like this rather than that; decide this way rather than that way" (57).

This is, evidently, Jenkins's view of aesthetics: sometimes this, sometimes that. He notes that if you visit the museum with your new lover, not only won't you notice some of the other spectators, but even the pictures will look different (57–58). Sure. It seems that without an empiricist bogeyman to attack, Jenkins can't think of anything interesting to say about how we come to judgment (provisional or not, with a new lover or not) about works of art, or about meaningful actions in the past. How *do* we change our mind about the past, and why do we come to accept these changes without having any foundation at all? Jenkins is right, I think, to note that these changes are without an ultimate ground, that they are made without absolute certainty. He is wrong, however, to think that therefore these changes are arbitrary, or that there is no historical (and, perhaps, poetic) account to be given of them. Without foundations to destroy, this postmodernist hasn't much to say about the conversations we continue to have, the histories we continue to write, and the art we continue to make.

There are, of course, interesting experiments in history as a form of writing in the juridical arena, in the novel, in academic history, and in anthropology. Sophisticated debates about the legitimate parameters of legal argumentation cast a powerful light back onto questions of history, nature, intention, and consensus.[7] Questions about history and memory circulate between historical writing and fiction, as does the problematic status of the anecdote or powerful detail.[8] The International History Initiative accepted as given the theoretical antifoundationalism that animates Jenkins's prose. But under the direction of Elazar Barkan, this Initiative worked to develop negotiated histories that would be "good enough" so that parties to intense social conflict would be able to find ways of living with the past without that past inspiring continued violence.[9] "Truth and Reconciliation" commissions don't pretend to get at some absolute truth; they make no pretense to certainty. Yet rather than reveling in their inability to know, they try to use histories to deal with trauma and its legacies of violence.[10] It would be so interesting to consider how these experiments in writing and living with history might be related to both theoretical postmodernism and to experiments with the forms (and matter) of historical representation.

The theory wars are over. Jenkins's *Rethinking History* is a Routledge classic, Hayden White is required reading, and subalterns speak from tenured positions. But Jenkins refuses to believe that postmodernity might have snuck up on us:

> [I]t is no good thinking that postmodernist insights . . . can be somehow grafted onto modernist histories which might allow them to overcome postmodern "critiques" and thus survive intact. For this is not possible; the break between modernity and postmodernity is as epochal, I think, as that between the medieval and the modern, and it is inconceivable to think that modernists will be able to survive in postmodernity any more than medievalists might be expected to survive in modernity; these are just different worlds. (69)

We might ask what is postmodern about the view of epochs offered in these sentences; indeed, they seem curiously naïve from even a modern perspective. In any case, Jenkins does not *feel* that the radically new epoch of postmodernity has arrived. The theoretical battles have been won, but is that all there is? He is still surrounded by modernists; he is still awaiting the "new births" of a radically different epoch. Jenkins has forgotten that according to his own theories, he could not be surprised, could not even recognize radically new births. "I have to be loyal to the new," writes Jenkins (64), apparently not remembering that this was one of the key oaths of modernism. The new has grown old. It's time to write the history of postmodernism.

10. Ebb Tide

Frank Ankersmit

This is what I find so absolutely suffocating about contemporary culture: it has become utterly incapable of any authentic and immediate contact with the world.[1]

For the last decade or so recognition has been spreading that the linguistic turn that had motivated much advanced work in the humanities is over. The massive tide of language has receded that connected analytic philosophy with pragmatism, anthropology with social history, philosophy of science with deconstruction; we are now able to look across the sand to see what might be worth salvaging before the next waves of theory and research begin to pound the shore. As language recedes there is much of talk of ethics, but also about intensity; of post colonialism but also about empire; of the sacred but also of cosmopolitanism; of trauma but also about animals. Much of the work in these areas shares with F. R. Ankersmit's latest book a desire to be free of the prison house of language. Even in the heyday of pantextualism there was a sense for many that beyond the borders of language lay the sublime. Discourse about the sublime, however, was contained or limited by the notion that you shouldn't try to say too much about something that was supposed to lie beyond the borders of language. In *Sublime Historical Experience*, the author has thrown off this reticence famously characterized by Wittgenstein in the *Tractatus*: "Whereof one cannot speak, thereof one must be silent." Ankersmit wants to find a way to write about the unrepresentable. As himself a mighty contributor to postmodern history and theory, he engages in this enterprise fully aware of its paradoxical features.

Ankersmit addresses the question of why we want to represent the past in the first place. He is asking why we are moved by the past, why the past becomes a problem for people (or collectivities) at particular times. Before language, he argues, there is experience, and now that the delight in language's prison house has worn thin, he aims to articulate how the experience of the past (or, the feeling that the experience of the past has been lost) first becomes a problem—perhaps a subject—for the historian who then attempts to represent the past (tell a history) in a text.

Ankersmit informs the reader early in the book that his is a "supremely impractical" study (xv). He is not offering anything that would help practicing historians do their job more effectively, although he will offer advice as to how the paradoxes in our relation to the past should work their way into writing history. He is not interested in the cognitive dimensions of historical representation, nor is he concerned with why some modes of history writing are superior to others. He is interested in why we are aware of there having been a past at all (xv); he wants to explore the "state of mind" of someone who is led to or drawn to the past. His notion of a "sublime historical experience" is meant to describe how the past becomes a felt issue, thus showing the origin of historical consciousness itself. Although there may not be any practical scholarly consequences in the concept of the origin of our interest in the past, Ankersmit does believe that he will be showing that once a culture enters into historical consciousness, living without the past would mean committing an act of the deepest violence against itself (xv).

In order to clear the ground for his investigation of an experience of the past that gives rise to representation itself, Ankersmit presents chapter-length criticisms of Richard Rorty and Hans-Georg Gadamer. In both cases he has enormous intellectual affinities with the philosopher he is taking on. Ankersmit finds heroic Rorty's use of history against his colleagues in analytic philosophy. This is the Rorty who gave up on epistemology, and who powerfully deconstructed the ideal of the philosopher as a cultural referee. His story of the history of philosophy punctured the myths of timelessness and the quest for an ultimate truth; he ironically deflated the cognitive claims of his fellow philosophers and ultimately concluded that edification—not objectivity—was the payoff of the genre of writing they practiced. Ankersmit applauds this ironic storytelling, but he is affronted by Rorty's "failure" to spare a notion of experience from his deflationary gaze. It's not that Rorty denies that we have experiences, but just as language "goes all the way down" to color any kind of knowledge claims, language also is there to block access to the "immediacy of experience." Ankersmit wants that immediacy; he seems to think it important that there be a realm immune from the contamination of language. More problematically, he wants to write about it.

Ankersmit is right to underscore that Rorty would have none of this. The author of *Philosophy and the Mirror of Nature* thinks that this notion of "immediacy" makes little sense, and that in any case we don't need it to do any work. Ankersmit doesn't argue against Rorty here; instead he makes the odd claim that if you care about history, then you can't stay on the path that Rorty has cleared.[2] Your care about history should trump Rorty's critique, and you must hold onto your care, your faith in the importance of the past, against all reason.

Ankersmit writes in the mode of a disappointed colleague or follower: *You came so close to seeing the truth, yet you did not arrive at the notion of sublime historical experience.* Ankersmit likes italics. He actually writes that Rorty "must strangely remind us of Moses, who was not allowed to enter the land that he himself had promised to the people of Israel" (66). The Promised Land flows with the milk and honey of experience, and Rorty just can't get there because, according to Ankersmit, he is sidetracked by the antihistoricism of Donald Davidson. It may be true that Rorty's "thin descriptions" make him less useful to historians than some other writers, but this can't be allowed to excuse Ankersmit's crude contextualization of the pragmatist as yet another Anglo-Saxon who hasn't had to open himself up to the tragic dimensions of real history:

> Rorty's oeuvre is an illustration of the general rule that however much an American scholar may have read Hegel, Nietzsche, Heidegger, Gadamer or Foucault, when you scratch the surface sooner or later an Enlightened and anti-historicist Jeffersonian liberal will appear who is largely insensitive to the drama and the tragedy that is so much the essence of the past. (64)

Ankersmit even goes on to write that "a sensitivity of the full weight of history [has], in fact, always remained an affair of the European continent"(64). This "affair" evidently allows the historical theorist from Gottingen to seize the essence of the past. What Ankersmit calls the "Anglo-Saxon mind" just hasn't experienced enough tragedy, evidently. As usual in this kind of argument, where the rest of the world fits just doesn't matter.

Why does Ankersmit suddenly lose his theoretical sophistication and engage in crude stereotyping? He wants to use Rorty (and also Gadamer) to argue for a mode of interpretation that undermines what is often called a positivist approach to knowledge. But he also wants to talk about a romantic, quasi-mystical feeling for the past for which these thinkers are less useful. Indeed, not much thinking at all is necessary for this mushy, self-serving philosophy:

> Historians should learn to trust their most private and most intimate feelings on those rare occasions when what Huizinga called "the grace of historical experience" is given to them. They should realize that the best, the most sophisticated, and the most finely tuned instrument that they have at their disposal for understanding the past is themselves and their own experience. (67)

Who knew?

As in almost all philosophical appeals to experience, in the end only some forms of experience will do. The effort to champion immediacy conceals a judgment that rejects as inappropriate anything that might be "tainted" by mediation. So, just after Ankersmit tells historians to trust their experience, he adds the caveat that they should do so only if their experience hadn't been "infected by the disciplinary historiographical epidemics . . . infecting a majority of their colleagues" (67). This is precisely the kind of move that Rorty exposed in his critical work. Philosophers (like politicians and clergyman) who appeal to experience in general will usually introduce some distinctions that allow them to champion the kind of experiences they find most useful. Under the rubric of the value of immediacy, of untainted experience, normative judgments reappear.

After showing that neither Rorty nor Gadamer provide the philosophic path that continues into the Promised Land of experience, Ankersmit turns to Huizinga's practice of history to illuminate what it means to eliminate transcendentalism and all its traces (105). The problems of transcendentalism can be avoided if one eschews talk of the representation of the past in favor of the experience of the past. In order to do this, Ankersmit posits that "the past *itself*" has survived in certain objects, and that the practice of the historian leads to the experience of this past. It's not that one has transcended time through language or mysticism, but that "the past can properly said to be present in the artifacts that it has left to us" (115). He wants this presence to be no less reasonable than the "presence" of observation to an astronomer, but he is led to a language very different from that found in the physical sciences:

> All spatial and temporal demarcations have momentarily been lifted; it is as if the temporal trajectory between past and present, instead of separating the two, has become the locus of their encounter. Historical experience pulls the faces of the past and present together in a short but ecstatic kiss. Historical experience is, in this way, a "surface"

> phenomenon: It takes place on the surface or interface where the historian and the past meet each other. (121)

Huizinga's *ekstasis* is light years from Rorty's ironic presentism, but Ankersmit follows the sentences just quoted with the defensive reassurance: "But this certainly does not imply that we have now entered the domain of mysticism and irrationality" (121). It seems to this reader that this is precisely the domain that Ankersmit has been forced to enter, for this is the only alternative he has left himself after rejecting pragmatism, hermeneutics, and the problematics of representation.[3]

Ankersmit is drawn to Huizinga's discussion of how an encounter with history can change one's perspective on both present and past. Normally, this encounter is framed or mediated by many factors, including the contexts of scholarship and popular culture. But Ankersmit is interested in those moments of revolutionary rupture when "the historian momentarily 'forgets' the historiographical context within which he normally operates" (125):

> For a moment there is only the past itself, revealing to him its quasi-noumenal nakedness with an unusual directness and immediacy. And the same can be said for the past, the object of historical experience: It hurries toward the historian with the same eagerness to rupture its ties with what surrounds it, as is the case of the historian. (125)

There follows an embarrassing quotation of the most famous lines of Juliet's balcony speech. Wherefore art thou, history? Ankersmit is asking, but I found myself asking how we might escape from this attempt to bring mystical romanticism to the rescue of theory in the name of authentic experience.

Ankersmit is attracted to Huizinga's "call of the past" because this call is supposed to be direct and immediate. That's why the former spends so much energy arguing against contextualization as a feature of historical experience. For him, authentic experience is ecstatic, and it must be both fragmentary yet forceful. He calls it a kiss, but he says it's a "short kiss." Paying attention to context (either one's own, or the context of a moment in the past) means being open to mediation. You won't be able to hear the call of the past if you are distracted by the music (or noise) of the discourse surrounding you and it. Ankersmit makes much use of Baudelaire and Benjamin, two writers who knew one had to "undo" knowledge in order to prepare for experience. Of course, Ankersmit doesn't want to "undo" the knowledge he gains from *them*, nor the inspiration he receives from Huizinga, Rousseau, and Hölderlin. These are thinkers who appeal to him, and so he claims what they say resonates with what was already inside us. They haven't contaminated readers with mediation, they have mirrored what was in "the depths of our souls." When we have our "most authentic experiences," Ankersmit writes, these will appear to us as "something that had been inscribed in our minds a long time ago already" (188, 371). Can this usually astute critical writer have so lost his bearings to think that his encounter (and ours) with the past is not mediated by the very writers from whom he wants to learn the lessons of immediacy? Does the feeling of immediacy trump all critical questioning?

Ankersmit realizes that his notion of historical experience is at odds with the professional writing of history, even though he says that the former only makes sense against the background of the latter (173). It is crucial for his argument that this connection in no way affects the radically unmediated quality of the experience. I cannot see how this is possible, and perhaps this impossibility is what Ankersmit wants to point to with his concept of *sublime* historical experience. For the word "sublime" here is meant to gesture at a region that cannot be made sense of through our normal epistemological categories. By definition the sublime (as idea or as practice) resists theorization, even though he spends roughly the second half of his book trying to evoke what this sublimity amounts to in relation to the past. Ankersmit counsels the historian to build the mutual exclusion of ecstatic experience and professional research practice into his or her writing (174). To whom is he addressing this counsel? How could one tell whether it was followed?

Ankersmit describes himself as being well aware of the "painful irony" of writing a theory against theory in this book. He has convinced himself, although he makes no attempt to convince the reader, that such a book is necessary for the liberation of historical practice. As noted above, he initially acknowledged that his was an impractical enterprise, but in later chapters he seems to believe that writers about the past can be set free from the constraints of mediation or of professional practice by his arguments or exhortations. To whom is the argument addressed, and what should be its effect? It is clear that Ankersmit wants to romanticize our relation to the past, and he emphatically recommends that historians trust *themselves* rather than *theory* (283, his italics). Trusting oneself, for him, means being open to our capacity to experience the past as lost, to experience the tragic, mournful connection to history. "Historical experience is the resonance that the 'music of the past,' its moods and feelings, may have in the historian whose mind happens to have been written in the same key" (309). Ankersmit wants to show that experiencing the past is like experiencing a work of art. But, as he surely knows, sometimes our aesthetic education is made more profound not by finding ourselves confirmed in a work of art but in finding works of art produced in keys that we didn't know even existed.

As Martin Jay has recently shown in *Songs of Experience*, the modern philosophical project can be understood by charting how its different movements have dealt with the concept of experience.[4] Jay's critical explication of the major positions on how to understand the ways embodied consciousness interacts with the world is helpful for situating Ankersmit's attempt to invigorate the notions of experience and the sublime vis à vis the encounter with the past. In the last section of his book, Jay discusses how three major intellectual movements of the last century have reconsidered the concept of experience in relation to the changes brought by modernity: pragmatism, critical theory (the Frankfurt School version), poststructuralism. Ankersmit draws on all three movements in developing his notion of sublime experience.

Among the pragmatists, James and Dewey were inspired by Emerson to develop a robust concept of experience that would not depend on a powerful self or homogeneous subject having the experience. The pragmatists emphasized experience as a kind of never-ending experiment, a way of trying things without being committed to how it should all turn out in the end. Jay is attracted to their vision, but, like Ankersmit, he is also critical of Rorty's contemporary appropriation of it. Rorty deromanticizes the pragmatist quest when he emphasizes the mediated nature of all supposed encounters with otherness. Of course there is otherness out there, Rorty argues. But when we have experiences, we bring that otherness "in here"—that is, into our linguistic or conceptual schemes. Rorty challenges our celebration of otherness by emphasizing how we must make things our own. This is where Ankersmit sees the corrupting influence of Donald Davidson; for the Dutch historian, this is where Rorty (remember, his Moses figure) falls for the golden calf of linguistic mediation. For the American philosopher, no doubt hampered by what Ankersmit called the Anglo-Saxon failure to appreciate tragedy, we just don't have to worry about the purity of experience. Impure experience, whether mixed up with language, concepts, the influence of others . . . impure experience is good enough.

Like Ankersmit, Jay prefers the pathos and politics of German critical theory to the ironic nominalism of Rorty's version of pragmatism. Benjamin longed for a notion of experience in its unity, a unity that has been lost in the fracturing of modernity. But even if he struggled toward a redemptive perspective, Benjamin knew that there was no possibility of simply recovering an imagined wholeness from the past. Instead, he wanted to find *through* the shocks and traumas of modernity a path to a new form of experience that would acknowledge both passive and active dimensions of encountering the fullness of the world. Ankersmit notes approvingly that Benjamin understood that an experience of the past "can come into being only as a figure of loss" (189). Both Jay and Ankersmit are also attracted to Adorno's idea that our aesthetic experience can remind us both of this loss, and of what our lives might yet be. Art can keep our hopes alive through a radical openness to the unexpected (146).[5] But Adorno furiously resisted the wholeness, the consoling kiss, to which Ankersmit always returns, and for that reason our author thinks he must go beyond Adorno's "openly Hegelian" view (146).

Adorno refused immediacy and consolation, and to go "beyond" him Ankersmit develops the idea of experience without a subject. This is a notion of experience that picks up on some of the themes in contemporary trauma studies, a field that has (at least in the humanities) developed in the wake of poststructuralism's critique of subjectivity. During the decline of grand theory in the early 1990s, deconstruction and its derivative forms were repeatedly charged with nihilism and political impotence. In response, thinkers interested in "theory" attempted to move from a skeptical critique of representation to an engagement with the real. In this regard the concept of trauma was very useful, because it seemed to connect one to the real without either the filters of consciousness or the mediation of culture. Trauma seemed to trump mediation.[6] Eelco Runia has recently called trauma the "busiest and liveliest speak-easy" in an era when there was otherwise a ban on speculative philosophy of history aimed at meaning making. "Exploring trauma," Runia concludes, "is the substantive philosophy of history of modern days."[7] This is an exploration that for Ankersmit dovetails with the sublime.

In his chapter on "the post-structuralist reconstitution of experience," Jay noted the similarities between Roland Barthes's idea of a photograph's *punctum* and the productive shock that Ankersmit sees at the core of sublime historical experience.[8] Many critics have connected the immediate, precognitive prick of the *punctum* with the meaning they can make out of the traumatic. Moreover, we can see the connection between Ankersmit's longing for immediacy (his "naked noumenal") with the desire for an ecstatic limit experience that was powerfully magnetic for Maurice Blanchot, Georges Bataille, and Michel Foucault. For all these authors, according to Jay, experience can only be rehabilitated if it is preserved from context, language, and all the mediations (read contaminations) of contemporary culture. They want their experience to be beyond the ordinary, to be beyond language. For Ankersmit, this is where trauma and the sublime can enter: "In sum, trauma can be seen as the psychological counterpart of the sublime, and the sublime can be seen as the philosophical counterpart of trauma" (338). Trauma and the sublime serve as reminders of an immediacy we have lost, of a world that can be more or less awkwardly represented, but that cannot be fully reflected in writing about the past.

It is important to acknowledge, as Ankersmit does, that historical representation always involves some loss, always is at some distance from the reality it aims to remember. Indeed, I have argued that all historical representation is a form of forgetting, and that trauma represents an occurrence that will not be forgotten precisely because it cannot be remembered through the conventional channels of recall.[9] This is why traumatic flashbacks are not a form of recollection, not a part of historical consciousness. "Modern historical consciousness arises," Ankersmit correctly points out, "from the experience of the discrepancy between the perspective of the past and that of the present" (357).[10] But he dreams of going beyond modern historical consciousness, beyond historical language; he seems to think that by acknowledging a sublime experience one can erase or overcome the discrepancy between present and past. When this unity is felt, he really believes that one is discovering "something that had been inscribed in our minds a long time ago already" (188, 371). Ankersmit here substitutes the mirror of the soul for the mirror of nature that Rorty deconstructed.

The last pages of *Sublime Historical Experience* offer the author's own translation of passages from Hölderlin's *Hyperion* because he thinks the poem transcends the dichotomies of modernity through a love that both acknowledges difference and overwhelms it. The dream of a beautiful trauma, of an immediate fluidity with the world, is much older than modernity. Ankersmit self-consciously offers a romanticized version of this mystical dream in an effort to leave self-consciousness behind. Recently, in an autobiographical essay for *Rethinking History*, he expressed his frustration with a culture that cites names of theorists and writers but never has an urgent connection to the world itself. "We are a generation of epigones . . . because for some perverse reason truly original work has become impossible."[11] Perhaps this book is his attempt to break out of the realm of the epigone, and Ankersmit has produced a brave, excessive volume. However, it is in the end an awkward and tedious exhortation to become unmediated. I cannot imagine how one might successfully respond to this plea, since any response would be by definition mediated by the plea. Ankersmit is too smart not to realize this, and I suppose he pursued the project in any case as an example of the paradoxical impossibility of the sublime.

As the tide of language recedes, we may find many things, but I can't see that purity and a direct connection to the world through something deep and authentic in our souls is among them. For there is no recuperation of the immediate, and trauma is not a foundation for historical theory. The theorist's footnotes do not inspire the mystical embrace for which he seems to write, and for which he seems genuinely to long. Instead, *Sublime Historical Experience* is a reminder of how difficult it is to evoke what we have lost without diluting it, and how challenging it is to try to tell a memorable story of what we have chosen to recollect.

11. The Art of Losing Oneself

Anne Carson and Decreation

The creative self is the central figure of the romantic wing of modernity, and its roots can be found at least as far back as the Book of Genesis. In her recent volume of poems and essays Anne Carson pursues decreation, a less familiar figure, but one whose ancestry is just as deep as our cultural memory. Simone Weil, the twentieth-century French philosopher, mystic, and activist, defined decreation as a program for getting the self out of the way while making something new. Sometimes this program is imposed on the self by violent outside forces, leaving the person traumatized, without a clearly constituted self that can even have an experience. Sometimes this program emerges as the practice of an artist, a viewer, a beholder. Carson is interested in the tension that arises when an artist wants to tell the story of this process: "To tell is a function of self," as she says (172). So how can one tell that one has lost it, lost the self? It is characteristic of Carson's poetics to mine the ambiguity of sentences (like this last one) by rearranging words and making new combinations to release unexpected meaning. Getting the self out of the way allows one to lose one's hold on meaning so as to open up other paths of significance.

The first section of *Decreation* is titled "Stops," and the poems in it gravitate around the poet's aging mother.

> In the ancient struggle of breath against death, one more sleep given.
> We took an offer on the house.
> In the sum of the parts
> where are the parts? (7)

Carson weaves personal anguish together with the simple mournfulness of witnessing her mother ("love of my life") die. In a cold snowscape, she writes,

before the gliding emptiness of the night coming on us,
our lanterns throw
shapes of old companions
and
a cold pause after. (13)

Typically, Carson reaches beyond the personal without leaving its embrace. She can abide with the ordinary as well as the ecstatic. The section ends with two poems, "Beckett's Theory of Tragedy" and "Beckett's Theory of Comedy," that move from Hegel to picking gooseberries. But the latter poem's penultimate line, "Goes back up the path, no sign of you," also returns us to the mother and to loss.

Tell one has lost it, how?

Throughout the rest of the volume, Carson returns to states of mind, and of body, in which the self seems to dissolve, but from which the poet is able to retrieve something precious: Sleep, for instance, offers her entry into "something incognito," a glimpse that is presented to a self that is not there. Sleep can be a kind of decreation, a realm whose effects "may cross over from night to day and change the life of the sleeper" (22). Carson brings together Asclepiadic priests, Jacques Lacan, Elizabeth Bishop, and Virginia Woolf into her chorus of praise for sleep—for that state of dissolution in which we have the opportunity to receive things "that come from somewhere else."

There are some famous good sleepers: Penelope is one, and so is Socrates. They can sleep deeply and return with things from elsewhere. Getting the self out of the way opens them up to different possibilities, different visions. Others are more easily disturbed by distractions from the here and now. Kant, Carson shows us, was disturbed by the singing of prisoners, and was able to convince the authorities to have them lower their voices. Can this be the origin of Stendhal's description of the bourgeois jailer Monsieur Valenod in *The Red and the Black*, who was able to have his prisoners banned from singing? There are many things troubled sleepers do to set themselves up for the restful dissolution of the self. One can reduce attention and distraction, but can we ever really *try* to sleep well, to put ourselves in position to receive these gifts from elsewhere? Or does the very fact of trying make us unworthy, or at least unlikely recipients?

Can one tell how one has lost it?

Decreation can happen through the soft landing of sleep, but it can also take the more intense path of an experience of the sublime, the joy of "spilling" with an artist, of losing oneself as one joins the work of art. But falling in with an artist can also be dangerous. A "sublime soul is threatened not only from without but from within," Carson notes, "for this soul's own nature is too big for itself" (48). Size matters.

> The Sublime is big. . . . Its bigness is always threatening to go out of control, to submerge and vanquish the soul that seeks to enjoy it. Threat provides the Sublime with its essential structure, an alternation of danger and salvation, which other aesthetic experiences (e.g., beauty) do not seem to share. Threat also furnishes the Sublime with its necessary content—dire things . . . within which the sublime soul is *all but lost*. (48)

Magnitude becomes menacing, but it is in the menace that the necessary content, and the displacement of the self, can be revealed. One can feel here the intersection of Christian and romantic patterns, but with Carson nothing is promised, nothing born again.

One has lost it—tell!

Carson's idea of the sublime soul moving toward decreation extends beyond the romantic notion of a creative self who is the author and the recipient of experience. The idea of "experience" has once again become a concept attracting attention in the academy, especially when one can "get the self out of the way." Martin Jay's *Songs of Experience* and Frank Ankersmit's *Sublime Historical Experience*, for example, are both interested in rehabilitating a notion of experience now that the theoretical linguistic turn has run out of steam. They are not all that concerned with the concept of experience at the root of empiricism; nor are they particularly focused on the epistemological issues that a reliance on experience has generated (although Jay gives a reasonable account of the most important of these). Like Carson, both historians are drawn to a concept of experience that can be linked to intensity, and that can be uncoupled from an idea of a continuous self or a homogeneous subject. In other words, these historians take seriously the displacement of the self while maintaining their interest in the self's connection to the real. Their exploration of experience self-consciously comes after postmodernism's celebration of promiscuous mediation and after deconstruction's language-based skepticism. Whereas playful postmodernism took pleasure in layers of mediation that made any sense of origin or authenticity seem futile, Ankersmit wants to resurrect the possibility of an uncontaminated connection to the real and to the past. And whereas deconstruction undermined empirical appeals to knowledge, Jay explores how our experience may indeed do the work of grounding what we know, and how we in fact act on this knowledge. But how can we tell if we have achieved this grounding, or if we are uncontaminated by experience? *How to tell?*

Having apparently exhausted epistemological efforts to purify the foundation of experience, several twentieth-century thinkers focused on reevaluating what had been considered contamination. Many of the philosophical problems that arise from relying on a concept of experience stem from the unstable, even incoherent, features of the self—the very subject that is supposed to be having (feeling, remembering) the experience. Rather than try to protect the notion of the self from this instability, why not focus on it as emblematic of our uneasy relation to the world? Instead of trying to defend the integrity of the self, perhaps one could explore the forces that get the self out of the way. It is this interest in the dissolved self that has stimulated work on trauma in the last several years. Contemporary trauma studies became an empirical field safe for humanities theorists emerging from the wake of poststructuralism's critique of stable subjectivity. During the decline of grand theory in the early 1990s, deconstruction and its derivative forms were repeatedly charged with nihilism and political impotence. In response, thinkers interested in "theory" attempted to move from a skeptical critique of representation to an engagement with the real. And what could support one's inquiry into reality better than a focus on pain? As the art historian Norman Bryson remarked in an essay on the photographer Cindy Sherman:

> When meaning is identified with cultural convention . . . paradoxically the body returns with an urgency it never before possessed. For pain marks the threshold at which the signifying contract and the language games that compose social reality come up against some kind of absolute limit: there is no *sign* that I can exchange for my pain, it cannot be channeled into words (only cries), it exists beyond my powers to represent it before others. . . . At the very moment when the claim is eventually staked that the body is built exclusively in and as representations, instead of the body's becoming weightless, translucent . . . the body instead establishes itself as discourse's unpassable limit.

In this regard the concept of trauma was very useful, because it seemed to connect one to the real without either the filters of consciousness or the mediation of culture. Despite their sharp theoretical differences, literary critic Cathy Caruth and historian Ruth Leys both explored how the dissolution of the self under the pressure of trauma illuminated the human encounter with the real more generally. The self of the traumatized subject is fractured, lost in the painful incoherence produced by an overwhelming occurrence. Does this self have something to teach us about how we take in the world in less extreme circumstances? A traumatic event trumps mediation because it can be defined as an event that overwhelms the conventions we have for taking in (for mediating) experience. The event invades us with its awful rawness, and the effort to remember or work through the event means finding a way to get the self's conventions back around what happened. Trauma gets the self out of the way, it de-creates.

But could one tell it?

Discussions of trauma and aesthetics almost invariably invoke Roland Barthes's notion of the *punctum*. For the Barthes of *Camera Lucida*, there was an element within the photographic image that could connect one to the original object in the past without the mediation of a code. The trace of the object can strike the beholder regardless of the intention of the photographer or the culture of the viewer. Countless writers have by now connected the precognitive prick of Barthes's *punctum* with the meaning that reverberates from the intense disorientation of psychological trauma. In both cases the intensity of immediacy is overwhelming, and the conventions through which one filters ordinary experience are dissolved. For artists and theorists emerging from the linguistic turn in which all expression is "always already" mediated, the desire for an ecstatic limit experience was powerfully magnetic. Experience, it seemed, could only be rehabilitated if it is preserved from context, language, and all the contaminations of contemporary culture. The desire is for an experience beyond the ordinary, beyond language.

Lost the self, now tell!

In his exhortation to historians to cultivate the sublime, Ankersmit, for example, wants contact with the past to be ecstatic; but for that to happen the historian has to dissolve his or her connections with the present. This is where trauma and the sublime can enter because they mark the violent break from the ordinary present. "In sum," Ankersmit writes, "trauma can be seen as the psychological counterpart of the sublime, and the sublime can be seen as the philosophical counterpart of trauma" (338). Trauma and the sublime serve as reminders of the immediacy we have lost in our convention-bound ordinary lives. There is a great contrast here with Carson, whose pursuit of decreation, of getting the self out of the way, is not at the expense of the embrace of the everyday. Ankersmit wants to defend theoretically the possibility of direct experience, and to inspire the sublime effort to grasp or recall it. But can the idea of trauma be effectively used as an incitement, a lure toward more direct experience? Through the voice of Simone Weil, Carson seems to warn against this:

> Is it permissible to seek out affliction?
> No it is not.
> Affliction is defined by
> necessity. I was afraid this might not
> happen to me.

The self is unmoored in Carson's work not through the cultivation of pain, but as the poet threads her readers into a conversation among writers in which we finally lose the distinction between commentary and original. Toward the end of *Decreation* the reader finds her essay and opera libretto both bearing the volume's title. In these two sections she brings Weil into relation with the ancient poet Sappho and the thirteenth-century mystic Marguerite Porete—"women who wanted to tell God." They all wrote of divine love and they all wondered how they could describe the nature of this love so intense, so sublime that its bigness is annihilating. "What is it that love dares the self to do?" Carson asks. She answers in italics: "*Love dares the self to leave itself behind, to enter into poverty*" (162). All three of Carson's women were willing to enter this poverty for the sake of divine love, but, as Carson puts it, how could any of them "get herself out of the way so as to arrive at God"? Or as Weil put it, "God allows me to exist outside himself. It is for me to refuse this authorization." (167).

One has lost it. Can one tell?

It is difficult to experience this love when the self that does the experiencing has been unmoored. Rather than evoke the dramatic trope of the traumatic, Carson settles for sleep, for dreams. Her three writer-mystics create a "dream of distance in which the self is displaced from the centre of the work" (173). Rather than celebrating pain or the traumatic, Carson attempts to preserve this dream by writing her poems and essays in dialogue with their work, getting herself out of the way so that we can hear their voices. She is only partially successful because she is such a very fine writer. Her own language, her own sensibility, is powerfully evident on every page. And we are grateful for that—mediation not as corruption or exhortation, but as a gift.

In Carson's opera "Decreation," with music by Guillermo Galindo, her themes of longing, of the sublime, of the desire to refuse the authorization of individual existence are all made vivid. "What would the singing of the real world sound like," she asks, if the self were not in the way of us hearing the songs? (24). Carson's language returns us to the poetic worlds she has been creating now for decades. She goes beyond the explications of a historian, but she never preaches the power of the sublime. She rearranges the words of others and her own to tease out new sounds and senses, new ideas and emotions from successive combinations. In spilling into her poetics we are able to acknowledge, to tell, we have lost it.

Carson's own capacity to connect disparate figures (the Greek philosopher Longinus and director Michelangelo Antonioni, Kant and actress Monica Vitti) across cultures and centuries can't help but signal her extraordinary spirit even as it opens these figures up to new possibilities of understanding. Decreation marries creation in these poems, essays, and now, opera, and we are fortunate to hear the world's singing through this writer's distinctive yet generous voice.

12. Inquiry as Hope

Richard Rorty

> *My sense of the holy, insofar as I have one, is bound up with the hope that someday, any millennium now, my remote descendants will live in a global civilization in which love is pretty much the only law. In such a society, communication would be domination-free, class and caste would be unknown, hierarchy would be a matter of temporary pragmatic convenience, and power would be entirely at the disposal of the free agreement of a literate and well-educated electorate.*[1]

Philosophy as Cultural Politics appeared early in 2007, just a few months before its author succumbed to pancreatic cancer.[2] Richard Rorty, the most widely read and influential American philosopher of the last fifty years, brought together in this collection essays on topics ranging from atheism to the linguistic turn, from justice to romanticism. Although readers familiar with Rorty's work will find little new in these articles written over the last ten years (as he himself acknowledges in the preface), they do illuminate how what he called "conversational philosophy" draws on historical thinking to redescribe political and social issues in ways that make it more likely that we can successfully address them. As has been the case for the last thirty years, he draws on this history of philosophy to accomplish what his hero, Dewey, strove for: "to modify people's sense of who they are, what matters to them, what is most important" (ix).

Rorty's unique place in American philosophy stems from his having been in the center of language-oriented analytic philosophy, and then "redescribing" this intellectual enterprise as a mistaken stage in the history of the discipline. Unlike critics who came from the continental traditions, Rorty understood *from the inside* what analytic thinkers were up to, and then he rejected both their agenda and their self-image. He was an apostate, and some of the vitriolic attacks on his work can best be understood as defensive operations of a sect. Although he bemoaned the parochialism of Anglo-American departments, he continued to engage in debates within analytic philosophy. Indeed, the last section of *Philosophy as Cultural Criticism* is entitled "Problems in Analytic Philosophy." Readers should take this as a signal that Rorty's critical perspective did not prevent him from continuing to be an interlocutor in the analytic conversation.[3]

Rorty's critique of modern philosophy has been so thoroughly discussed that it is unnecessary to recapitulate it here in detail. His *Philosophy and the Mirror of Nature* (1979) offered an historical account of how the very idea of representation had led thinkers astray by suggesting to them that philosophy could become an arbiter of accuracy, methodology, or "realness." Which sentences are closer to reality? Which modes of thought are really scientific? Which beliefs are rational? Who really loves Truth? Rorty thought that all these questions grew out of a misunderstanding of language, of thinking: namely, that some forms of language and some forms of thinking were more closely tied to the world than others. If this were the case, then we would need an intellectual discipline (like epistemology) to help us do the measuring of this closeness, or the refereeing of who was working on something "really real." Analytic philosophy itself (especially as practiced by Quine, Sellars, and Davidson) helped one to see that these questions were unhelpful. In the wake of that perception, Rorty adopted a conception of language as a tool, and he suggested that we consider how the tool worked in various contexts. Rather than think of sentences as being "closer" to real (i.e., nonlinguistic) stuff, he urged us to think of language (like other human attributes) as being *caused* by real stuff, or as being a response to reality. If we could lose the picture of language as representation and think of it as a tool, then much of what had preoccupied philosophers would simply disappear.

Rorty's critique can be described as a rejection of the paradigm of skepticism that has animated much of philosophy since Descartes. Rather than try to carve out an arena safe from the challenges of the skeptic, Rorty wanted to show that the whole model of skeptical doubt was based on a pseudoproblem. If you didn't think of the mind as a theater in which images of the world were being projected, then you wouldn't have to wonder whether these images were close to reality. If you didn't create the notion of perceptions as distinct from the natural world, then you wouldn't have to worry about how "real" they were. If you just thought of perceptions as having causes, then your naturalism wouldn't give rise to questions of the "how real" sort. If you considered mind and language as part of the world instead of representing or mirroring it, your holism would keep you from taking seriously questions concerning ontology. Naturalism and holism do not give rise to skeptical doubt because they do not demand a distancing of humans from the world. "We shall fear that the world is on the verge of absconding," Rorty wrote in response to John McDowell, "as long as we think that causal connection with the world is not a tight enough way of bonding with it."[4] He thought causality was a tight enough bond.

Sometimes Rorty suggested that with the demise of epistemology, philosophy itself would disappear. No wonder his former colleagues responded so vigorously. Rorty laconically admitted that universities would still need people who were good at interpreting old texts in the field, just as it needed literature professors who were good at talking about the nineteenth-century novel in England, or medieval poetry in France. But many philosophers thought they were doing more than finding new ways to talk about old texts. They thought they were solving problems and making progress. Rorty pointed out that the so-called problems had become of no interest to anyone in the wider culture, and that the discipline-focused philosopher's notion of progress was akin a scholastic thinker claiming that now he really knew how many angels fit on the head of a pin. Increasingly technical analytic philosophy was pretty useless; it made no difference to anybody else in the university what went on in the philosophy department. That's why Rorty started to talk about philosophy as cultural politics. He wanted a kind of philosophy that would offer something of import to the wider culture. If it couldn't solve problems, at least it could tell stories that could "modify our sense of who we are."

Rorty came to view philosophy as a form of writing, and interpretation as the art of telling stories or as redescription. In the introduction to this collection he writes: "Hegelian historicism and a Wittgensteinian "social practice" approach to language complement and reinforce one another" (ix). By the "Wittgensteinian 'social practice' approach to language," Rorty means an understanding of communication as being fully context dependent. Conversations are part of a culture, and accuracy "is a matter of what a community will let you get away with" (11). Understanding a language is learning how to play a game—not knowing that this is the best or the real game. What happens to "Truth" with this emphasis on social practice? The ideal of truth is replaced by the ideal of inquiry. For the Rorty of *Philosophy as Cultural Politics*, it is important to find ways to keep talking, to discover moves that keep the discursive game interesting. There should be no final terminus of the game, no ultimate Truth after which inquiry and conversation would be pointless. Indeed, just when one thinks that "nothing new can be said," it may turn out that a great new player emerges to reinvigorate the enterprise. If not, players will start noticing the new games in town and try to learn those moves, to join those conversations.

How does Hegelian historicism complement this notion of language games? For Rorty, Hegel came to stand for philosophical narrative construction on the grand scale. Hegel's *Phenomenology of Spirit* created the paradigm for weaving together an account of how ideas emerge over time to engage specific social and political problems. Rorty likes to quote Hegel's notion that philosophy is "its time seized in thought," because this emphasizes context dependence as historical dependence. In Hegelian terms historical dependence is also presentistic, because in Hegel's account the present is understood as containing a multitude of pasts:

> The life of the ever present Spirit is a circle of progressive embodiments, which looked at in one aspect still exist beside each other, and only looked at from another point of view appear as past. The grades which Spirit seems to have left behind it, it still possesses in the depths of its present.[5]

Over the years, Rorty found Hegel's emphasis on a narrative of historical progress increasingly compelling. After all, Hegel defined history as "progress in the consciousness of freedom,"[6] and for the American philosopher this meant that narratives of the past should be created to inspire works that aimed to enhance progress. Rorty wanted philosophical narratives to inspire social hope, and he understood Hegelian narratives to do just that.

Rorty is well aware that Hegel did more than just write narrative. What does the pragmatist make of the philosopher of the System? Not much. Rorty has no use for the Hegel's *Encyclopedia of the Philosophical Sciences* because it is shot through with the "ambition for transcendence" that he wants to leave behind. He sees Hegel as having made an unfortunate mistake in trying to grab for an ultimate truth beyond history, and instead emphasizes the Hegel that remained grounded in context, in narrative, and in philosophy as making sense of the history-of-the-present.[7]

There is a basic historical structure that provides a skeleton for the essays in *Philosophy as Cultural Politics*. Rorty accepts the Nietzschean critique showing how Plato distracted us from the world around us by encouraging us to get to the "really real," the forms behind appearances. Nietzsche's "god is dead" meant, among other things, that we no longer have any need of the "really real." In regard to post-Greek philosophy, Rorty describes the following stages:

> [T]he intellectuals of the West have, since the Renaissance, progressed through three stages: they have hoped for redemption first from God, then from philosophy, and now from literature. (91)

These three stages of development are steps toward increasing self-reliance. Instead of thinking that redemption could come from an external, divine source, philosophers promised redemption through Truth or self-understanding. But in literary culture "the question 'Is it true?' has yielded to the question 'What's new?'" (92). Rorty sees this as a "sensible" turn to asking if anybody has any new ideas about "what we might make of ourselves" (93). There is no real version of ourselves that we should try to discover, or to which we should correspond. We create ourselves, and in our literary culture the philosopher might contribute stories that stimulate that creativity.

I have been quoting from the essay that is at the center of *Philosophy as Cultural Politics*, "Philosophy as a Transitional Genre." According to this essay, philosophical argument was helpful in liberating us from religion's dependence on redemption from elsewhere, but it got bogged down in trying to replace God with Truth. The pragmatists taught us to substitute inquiry for Truth, conversation for conclusions. This meant that we prized the process of discovery, the expansion of horizons, the development of increased self-reliance:

> The sort of person I am calling a "literary intellectual" thinks that a life that is not lived close to the present limits of the human imagination is not worth living. For the Socratic idea of self-examination and self-knowledge, the literary intellectual substitutes the idea of enlarging the self by becoming acquainted with still more ways of being human. (94)

There is no one *true or authentic* way of being human. It is not something *out there* to be discovered. Sure, Rorty prefers humans who cherish self-reliance and inquiry, and he weaves a story of how this preference emerges from our culture. Someone who prefers humans who cherish service to a god, or obedience to a set of rules, or who are racially pure will have another story. Rorty does not think there is a neutral argument or appeal to reality that will allow someone to decide which story is true. The literary intellectual, unlike the traditional philosopher, doesn't seek this neutrality. Rorty does think that we can compare the stories and explore the benefits that come from living in accord with one or the other narrative. That's an important part of what he calls "cultural politics."

What's the place of science in the literary culture that Rorty describes? For Rorty, who was much influenced by Thomas Kuhn, science is a powerfully rule-governed, problem-solving activity. Its constraining disciplinary norms are extraordinarily good at answering questions that are agreed upon in advance. Rorty just wants to strip away the metaphysical pretensions in which some philosophers still clothe scientific research. Solving problems does not mean you are substituting Reality (the really real) for Appearance.

> Modern science is a gloriously imaginative way of describing things, brilliantly successful for the purpose for which it was developed—namely, predicting and controlling phenomena. But it should not have the sort of redemptive power claimed by its defeated rival, idealist metaphysics. (100)

"You can have expert culture if you agree on what you want to get," Rorty writes, and science is a very powerful expert culture. But it doesn't do much in telling us *how* to live, or what purposes to strive for. Only stories (and poems and art) help us in this regard because they offer suggestions for redefining our purposes, our lives.

In various places in *Philosophy as Cultural Politics* and throughout his oeuvre, Rorty makes the case for intersubjectivity as the realm of objectivity or of truths. Some philosophers who share his views in this regard, most notably Habermas, want to go beyond stories about human purpose to ground politics and morality in the very nature of intersubjectivity. In other words, they want to find principles where Rorty sees only narratives or social practice. Rorty thinks that our politics or morality is always steeped in our historical context. We can try to expand that context through persuasion, but that doesn't mean that there are neutral principles that ensure that people will in fact be persuaded (or that it is rational that they be so persuaded). We are loyal to our communities, and we can explain (tell a story about) that loyalty. There is no deeper foundation to loyalty in "communicative reason," or in nature, or in God's choosing us.

This is where critics will often raise the Nazi question. Are you saying, they ask, that the Nazis just have another story, that there is no way to prove them wrong? Rorty's response is that there is no "neutral" proof that would be acceptable to a Nazi and a liberal American. There are no nonlocal (or context-independent) modes of justification. All justification, all storytelling and argument, take place within the norms of a culture (within the game), and Rorty's account of the literary intellectual is as dependent on the culture of the American Left as the Nazi's is on the German Right. Rorty just expresses gratitude that he belongs to his own culture, which is like being thankful for being oneself:

> But I am well aware that my barbarous ancestors thought themselves lucky to have been raised within their culture, that my cousins in Germany thought themselves lucky to be able to enroll in Hitler Youth, and that my descendents in a hypothetical fascist culture would have a similarly warm sense of gratitude for their own upbringing.[8]

Rorty is ready to admit that "a bigot and I can say the same Foucauldian/Nietzschean thing: that the only real question is one of power."[9] If you can't agree with your opponent about what counts as a person, a community, or a "competent audience," there is no philosophy to be done, because there is no possibility of conversation. In such cases, "we may both have to reach for our guns."[10]

Rorty's antiuniversalism, which at first glance had appeal to critics of an imperious philosophical foundationalism, is also a self-conscious parochialism, or avowed ethnocentrism. He made this clear several years ago in a sharp, illuminating exchange with the anthropologist Clifford Geertz.[11] In *Philosophy as Cultural Politics*, he revisits this issue in "Justice as a Larger Loyalty." Following Sellars and Brandom and connecting to contemporary discussions by Michael Walzer and Annette Baier, Rorty articulates a non-Kantian (that is, nonprincipled) conception of justice as based on identification, in the view that another person is "one of us." Rorty wants to historicize Rawls, to admit that our notions of justice are a product of "the tradition of liberal thought and the larger community of political culture of democratic societies."[12] There are no transcultural standards, and so Rorty advocates "that the rhetoric we Westerners use in trying to get everyone to be more like us would be improved if we were more frankly ethnocentric, and less professedly universalistic" (55).

> If we Westerners could get rid of the notion of universal moral obligations created by membership in the species, and substitute the idea of building a community of trust between ourselves and others, we might be in a better position to persuade non-Westerners of the advantages of joining in that community. (55)

The West has "an instructive story to tell," not a discovery about essential human rationality to share. The liberal legacy of the Enlightenment does not depend on its rationalist legacy. Why Rorty thought that the story would remain compelling without the rationalist underpinnings remains very unclear. In our contemporary situation, one in which a political discourse that increasingly relies on the conversation stopper of belief in God, this hope for a discourse of community building without foundations may be difficult to sustain.

Rorty wrote that "we can work toward intersubjective agreement without being lured by the promise of universal validity" (85). In his recent essays he didn't display a strong belief that in the United States this was at all likely. On the one hand, there was resurgent fundamentalism and the powerful erosion of the separation of religion and public life on which the philosopher's own liberalism was built. On the other hand, the politics that had developed on the "postmodern Left" was anathema to Rorty. Although he shared with this intellectual current an aversion to universalism and to foundations, he found its theoretically sophisticated cynicism to have falsely substituted knowledge (or "critical thinking") for hope.[13] Hope is a key word in Rorty's cultural politics: if philosophy cannot offer knowledge or a path to wisdom, he believes it can help construct narratives that inspire a hopeful solidarity.

The cultural politics often associated with postmodernism compromised solidarity on the basis of theoretical self-satisfaction. Rorty's views in this regard can be seen in his changing appraisal of Michel Foucault. In his early work, Rorty saw Foucault's historicization of philosophy and the human sciences as a useful complement to his own deconstructive efforts. Foucault could also be thought of as using a Wittgensteinian perspective on knowledge and language to undermine foundationalism. But Foucault's Nietzschean anti-Hegelianism prevented him from ever *joining* with a notion of philosophy being its own time grasped in thought. Instead, his antifoundationalism was joined to an ecstatic notion of politics that rejected the construction of solidarity on the basis of shared narratives and hope. The theoretical Left that Rorty came to identify with Foucault has led to a "spectatorial" politics. By contrast, Rorty thought that in order to engage in movements for social change, one must be able to generate a sense of shared future possibility. From the perspective of the "spectatorial Left" this engagement was worse than wrong—it was naïve. "Hopelessness has become fashionable on the Left," Rorty wrote, "principled, theorized, philosophical hopelessness."[14]

Although Rorty's volume is entitled *Philosophy as Cultural Politics*, it is important to underscore that he felt modern philosophical theory had little to offer struggles for political change. Indeed, he wrote that intellectuals who might have once thought it their responsibility to form alliances on behalf of social justice now were content with academic alliances grounded (loosely) in a school of thought.

> The Fouacauldian Left . . . exaggerates the importance of philosophy for politics, and wastes its energy on sophisticated theoretical analyses of the significance of current events. But Foucauldian theoretical sophistication is even more useless for leftist politics than was Engels' dialectical materialism. Engels at least had an eschatology. Foucauldians do not even have that. Because they regard liberal reformist initiatives as symptoms of a discredited liberal "humanism," they have little interest in designing new social experiments.[15]

Rorty sees philosophy as cultural politics not because he thinks critical thinking or "theory" can help keep us from political illusions. He sees philosophy as cultural politics because he wants to encourage a philosophical narrative of progressive action that would encourage active engagement on behalf of freedom, equality, and solidarity.

Of course, there is no philosophical *foundation* for this narrative; there is only potential philosophical inspiration for it. What makes the inspiration philosophical? The family of texts it includes (Wittgenstein, Hegel, Dewey), its critical tools for showing "dead ends" for thinking or living, and its aspiration to weave together a variety of cultural phenomena into an ever-broadening language game. As Rorty puts it at the end of *Achieving our Country*: "it is only those who still read for inspiration who are likely to be of much use in building a cooperative commonwealth."[16] In *Philosophy and the Mirror of Nature* he wrote of "edifying philosophy," and in the current collection he speaks of his kind of philosophy as "willing to give up the goal of getting things right, and to substitute that of enlarging our repertoire of individual and cultural self-descriptions" (124).

> The point of philosophy, on this view, is not to find out what anything is "really" like, but to help us grow up—to make us happier, freer, and more flexible. The maturation of our concepts, and the increasing richness of our conceptual repertoire, constitute cultural progress. (124)

Although he writes in support of this progress, Rorty was not sanguine about its continuation. Indeed, he warned against the development of more radical economic inequality that could readily lead to fascistic governmental action to protect the super wealthy.[17]

Rorty's own work as a teacher and a writer aimed to encourage opposition to the cultural of radical economic inequality by creating narratives that drew on a philosophical and literary "cultural repertoire" to inspire hope for a more just and inclusive democratic polity. "You have to describe the country in terms of what you passionately hope it will become, as well as in terms of what you know it to be now."[18] These redescriptions become historical tales aimed at creating more flexible, engaged citizens.

> Once we give up the idea that rationality is a matter of applying ahistorical criteria. . . . we have nowhere to turn except to such stories. . . . Hegel's solution was to start replacing transcendental arguments with narratives—stories about how we hook up with our past. (89)

Rorty doesn't want us to hook up with the past just so that we are deeper, more cultivated people. As he put it in the essay "Wittgenstein and the Linguistic Turn":

> *C'est magnifique, mais ce n'est pas la guerre.* Admirers of Dewey like myself think that the point of reading philosophy books is not self-transformation but rather cultural change. It is not to find a way of altering one's inner state, but rather to find better ways of helping us overcome the past in order to create a better future." (169)

Throughout the last thirty years, Rorty's work aimed to free us from a "picture that was holding us captive," and then to offer narratives that create new possibilities of solidarity and additional resources for inspiring hope. He would have been skeptical about whether he had made a significant contribution to the task of creating a better future, and he probably would have encouraged us to reread Dewey for such a contribution. His modesty was all the more real because it was bound up with his energy for argument and conversation, whether it was with other stars in the theory world, or with students or activists. Richard Rorty was my teacher, and I have rarely seen the combination of generosity and conviction that was at the core of his pedagogy. Perhaps his teaching was part of his inquiry: "All inquiry . . . is a matter of reweaving our webs of beliefs and desires in such a way as to give ourselves more happiness and richer and freer lives" (188). Readers will be grateful for the reweaving that *Philosophy as Cultural Politics* provokes. Dick Rorty's friends and students are grateful for the gift of his inquiry, and for his devotion to working through philosophy to make a difference in our lives.

PART 4

PHOTOGRAPHY AND PIETY

13. Photographic Ambivalence

Photography maintains the presentness of the world by accepting our absence from it. The reality in a photograph is present to me while I am not present to it; and a world I know, and see, but to which I am nevertheless not present (through no fault of my subjectivity), is a world past.

STANLEY CAVELL[1]

[History] is constituted only if we consider it, only if we look at it—and in order to look at it, we must be excluded from it.

ROLAND BARTHES[2]

In this chapter I focus on three topics that arose at a conference sponsored by the journal *History and Theory* devoted to photography and historical interpretation. These topics concern the capacities and impact of photography as a practice for representing the past:

(1) Photography's incapacity to conceive duration
(2) Photography and the "rim of ontological uncertainty"
(3) Photography's "anthropological revolution"

Each of these can be related to how photography affects our ability to think of being in another place or time than the one we are in now. This problem has a long history. It animated the work of the nineteenth-century artist Nadar as he dreamt of traveling through time, and the work of Roland Barthes, as he struggled with his grief.[3] More generally, "thinking of being in another place or time" can be related to the problematics of empathy, projection, and social context that are themes current in much contemporary writing about photography from historical and theoretical perspectives.

1. Photography's Inability to Conceive Duration

This incapacity is the inability to imagine or recognize extension through time. In other words, one could recognize temporal juxtaposition (this, then that, then that), but not the interconnection of those things that are juxtaposed. Henri Bergson might have said that a symptom of the inability to conceive duration would be our continued spatialization of the temporal—our tendency through technology to imagine the temporal as a series of self-contained units that take up space.

The problem of conceptualizing duration out of the instantaneous has been a topic of philosophical interest at least since classical Greece. To solve this problem Hegel reformulated it within the realm of history via the dialectic. Duration can be apprehended through the density of the now: "The life of the ever present Spirit is a circle of progressive embodiments, which looked at in one aspect still exist beside each other, and only looked at from another point of view appear as past. The grades which Spirit seems to have left behind it, it still possesses in the depths of its present."[4] The dialectical conception of history as embodied duration—the notion that every historical moment contains both layers of the past and seeds of the future—was the field in which photography was inserted in the mid-nineteenth century. However, photography's ability to break a "moment" down into the instantaneous radically disturbs the easy immanence associated with historical narratives that rely on dialectical unfolding.

At first glance, photography might have seemed to be the perfect technology for the era that gave birth to modern historiography. The documentary power of the camera became a powerful metaphor for realism more generally,[5] and the indexical promise of the photographic image seemed to provide a toehold in the real for sweeping dialectical narratives. As shutter times decreased dramatically in the last quarter of the nineteenth century, personal or public occurrences became "true events" because a camera was there to make a record of them. If the dream of the historian was to describe the past *wie es eigentlich gewesen*, then the mechanical operation of photography seemed like a perfect ally.

By the last decades of the century, however, it was becoming clearer that photography's capacity for representation of the instantaneous might very well explode the historicist field that had first seemed so congenial to it. Bergson's use of Marey's chronophotography as part of his critique of the modern conception of time illustrates this nicely. Marey and then Muybridge had devised an instantaneous photographic technique to capture particular segments of animal motion. Most famously, they depicted the stride of a galloping horse in seemingly awkward detail. An automatic camera controlled only by a timing clock "broke down" what had seemed to be a fluid, graceful motion. Bergson thought this invention emblematic of the modern distance from actual experience, a distance that led to an approach to knowledge based on analysis and delusional objectivity:

> Along the whole of this movement we can imagine possible stoppages: these are what we call the positions of the moving body, or the points by which it passes. But with these positions, even with an infinite number of them, we shall never make movement. They are not parts of movement, they are so many snapshots of it, they are, one might say, only supposed stopping places. The moving body is never really *in* any of the points; the most we can say is that it passes through them. But passage, which is movement, has nothing in common with stoppage, which is immobility.[6]

Anson Rabinbach summarizes Bergson's critique of the photographic effort to capture the instantaneous: "Marey thus confirmed Bergson's diagnosis of the crisis of all perceptual systems: objective time was infinitely divisible; moments of experience were organized spatially, that is, the reduction of quality to quantity."[7] Modern time-consciousness for Bergson abandoned duration in favor of a spatialized objectivity. For Bergson, duration is really indivisible, and so no temporal segment can be isolated without distortion: "[S]cience cannot deal with time and motion except on condition of first eliminating the essential and qualitative element—of time, duration, and of motion, mobility."[8] Bergson anticipated how photographic technologies would infect human self-consciousness. In the pursuit of accuracy and precision, we would try to isolate parts of human experience in order to better understand it. But understanding, say, perception in isolation from memory was to begin with a distortion. Perception is always already infected with memory because the isolated moment does not exist in the real world without temporal extension.

> Pure perception, in fact, however rapid we suppose it to be, occupies a certain depth of duration, so that our successive perceptions are never the real moments of things, as we have hitherto supposed

> but are moments of our consciousness. Theoretically, we said, the part played by consciousness in external perception would be to join together, by the continuous thread of memory, instantaneous visions of the real. *But, in fact, there is for us nothing that is instantaneous. In all that goes by that name there is already some work of memory.*[9]

Mary Ann Doane glosses Bergson's claim this way: "Perception 'exists only in theory, because it is continually invaded by memory.' Perception, from this point of view is only 'an occasion for remembering.'"[10]

Photography is the perfect anti-Bergsonian technology because it records through segmentation. No segmentation, no objectivity; what Bergson called distortion *is* the accuracy promised by photographic recording. And insofar as our conception of memory—and even our actual ways of recollecting the past—is conditioned by photography, we lose the ability to perceive duration.

Michel Frizot makes the point that photography's "power to attest" allowed the medium "to completely reorganize the way the world is perceived" because photographic "data" become the standard for judging realistic representation. "The photographic image has defined the concept of an event," he writes.[11] And the event is an instant—a segment of time so small that we could not have grasped it with our own eyes. Photographic power is the power of segmentation. Precision is in part dependent on the rapidity or brevity of exposure. Duration is thereby defeated.

Barthes notes that the "era of Photography is also that of revolutions, contestation, assault and explosion—in short, of different forms of impatience, of all that is opposed to the notion of maturing."[12] The ability to seize the episodic is of a piece with the inability to conceive duration. If everything can be broken down into pulsing moments, into "different forms of impatience," then there would no longer be a sense of the passing of time. When Susan Sontag, almost a century after Bergson, wrote of the ways photography had come to substitute for experience and for memory, she was describing the fulfillment of the Bergsonian nightmare.[13] Thierry de Duve has recently made a similar point: "Whereas the snapshot refers to the fluency of time without conveying it, the time exposure petrifies the time of the referent and denotes it as departed."[14] In either case duration is missed; we lose the ability to attend to it. As our blindness for duration grows, so does our confidence in our ability to represent with ever-greater exactitude the most fleeting aspects of the world around us. We look only to the fleeting.[15] In becoming attuned to the fleeting, our ability to sense events as unfolding one from the next escapes us. Stephen

Bann points this out about the power of lithography in Nadar's time. Nadar recognized that lithography's reproducibility without obvious signs of authorial or artistic mediation gave it a powerful authority as a witness. But it could witness only instants. And so "instants"—intensely revelatory moments—are increasingly sought after as "news," as "facts." Photography would only accelerate this phenomenon. Iterability—repetition and circulation—gave these mechanical techniques an authority to capture the real as episode. When the real is only a collection of reproducible episodes, duration is no longer part of the real.

2. Photography and the "Rim of Ontological Uncertainty"

The "ontological uncertainty" associated with photography is tied to how its indexical nature changes our relations to other images, and to how its temporal or episodic power alters our sense of change over time. Bann notes that lithography introduces many of the elements that will eventually characterize photography's impact on our notions of realism because of its "evidence of rapid registration and the advantage of multiple diffusion."[16] Rapid registration matters because it promises a reduction of mediation between "event" and beholder. As the recording becomes more automatic, it seems to become less interpretive. The "real itself" is offered to the viewer, rather than a version of the real being given by a subject with his or her own desires, prejudices, and so on.[17] A purely automatic process of registering the world seemed to promise to bring the distant real present to the viewer. The "distant real" can be thought about in spatial terms—colonial photography and efforts to "capture" the exotic would be relevant here. But the more profound disturbance brought on by increasingly rapid (unmediated) recording is making the temporally distant present. Photographic images seem to offer the possibility of reexperiencing the past, or of experiencing a past for the first time without a subjective intermediary.

This lure of reexperiencing is disturbing because when entering into the past depicted in the image we also remain aware of what happened after the picture was taken. The time frozen in the image is preserved from death or decay, but it also reminds us of the death and decay outside the image. The by now famous example of this is Barthes's description of the handsome young Lewis Payne shortly before he was executed for his attempt to assassinate the

U.S. Secretary of State. The caption for the image in *Chambre Claire* is "He is dead and he is about to die."[18] Why does the viewing of this image create an "ontological disturbance" differently from, say, reading a newspaper interview that was done with Payne in the hours before his execution? Both might be said to be "evidence" concerning the condemned man. Why does the photographic evidence raise different kinds of questions?

There is a sense in which the quasi-automatic nature of photographic depiction seems to bring us "closer" to the indexical trace of the subject of the image. When coming upon an old newspaper interview with Payne, we are still getting at the past through the apparatus of the newspaper: interviewer, editors, printers. We are at more "removes" from the past than we seem to be with a photograph "taken" from the real. Suppose we compare the photographic image to a handwritten diary entry from Payne instead of the newspaper interview? The two would still be very different because of the sense that the subject's hand created the signs on the paper of the diary entry. (For the same reason the experience of reading the diary entry on a computer is likely to be very different from the experience of reading while holding the old paper in one's hand.)

The photograph seems to function as a trace of the past because it makes a claim of having automatically registered the body of the subject pictured. As Barthes says, the photograph is a "certificate of presence."[19] This is akin to finding letters from a person, written in his or her own hand, or, for example, jottings in the margins of a book in the library of a person long deceased. I remember the thrill I felt when I did research in the study of Alexander Kojève, a philosopher on whom I focused in my dissertation. As I came across notes in books, or letters tucked away between folders, it wasn't just the *content* of the notes that was exciting to me. It was that *this* marking had been made on *this* paper in *this* study by Kojève. The feeling of the presence of Kojève was compelling, though I never thought of it as a substitute for, or even as a trumping of, the published material.[20] Was the allure of this presence, or the fantasy of this presence, akin to the power of the photograph to disrupt one's sense of time?

In recent years there has been a resurgence of interest in "presence" as a category for the philosophy of history. Eelco Runia has offered the following explication: "'Presence,' in my view, is 'being in touch' with people, things, events, and feelings that made you into the person you are. . . . Presence—being in touch with reality—is, I believe, just as basic as meaning."[21] The document, the memorial, reenactment—all seem to offer the experience of getting in touch with one's past. In my case the impulse for archival work, in addition to its empirical payoff, also expressed this desire for presence. Another way to describe the allure of these felt traces of the past (in my case, of a dead philosopher) would be in terms of the fetish. In Dominick LaCapra's memorable 1984 critique of cultural and social history, he made the point with characteristic verve:

> For Freud a fetish is a substitute for a lost object, and it is related to the quest for full identity and narcissistic unity. The archive as fetish is a literal substitute for the "reality" of the past which is "always already" lost for the historian. When it is fetishized, the archive is more than the repository of traces of the past which may be used in its inferential reconstruction. It is a stand-in for the past that brings the mystified experience of the thing itself—an experience that is always open to question when one deals with writing or other inscriptions.[22]

LaCapra polemically described social history's empiricist anti-intellectualism as a fetish, but it is also apt for characterizing the post-postmodern exploration of presence as an antidote to the linguistic cage of "representationalist" philosophy of history.[23] The social historians LaCapra criticized saw the archive as a touchstone of the real in contrast to the abstract theorizing or endless interpretations of intellectual historians and philosophers, just as contemporary writers resurrecting presence want to feel connected to the vast "storehouse" of the past rather than be reminded that linguistic (and social and temporal) mediations always keep history at a distance. The lost object of the past is supposed to be (metonymically) felt in the present as a "being in touch." The past wasn't lost after all! And this is especially worth claiming (even embracing) when the past is traumatic. Frank Ankersmit's recent proselytizing for the sublime under the guise of "historical experience" is the most dramatic example in this regard. Ankersmit is most interested in the moments of rupture when we forget the place from which we are remembering the past: "For a moment there is only the past itself, revealing to him [the historian] its quasi-noumenal nakedness with an unusual directness and immediacy. And the same can be said for the past, the object of historical experience: It hurries toward the historian with the same eagerness to rupture its ties with what surrounds it, as is the case of the historian."[24] Past and present are imagined to meet in ecstatic embrace.

How is the notion of the photograph as a "certificate of presence" related to this attempt to get beyond the mediations of language? Is the image of the would-be assassin Lewis Payne disturbing and attractive because it doesn't only bring forth meaning but, in Runia's words, "transfers presence"? Walter Benn Michaels has brought this issue to the fore in "Photographs and Fossils," pointing out that the hope (or desire) that photography is not merely a picture has become central to contemporary artistic practice.[25] For many writers focused on the photograph's indexical dimensions "the hope is 'about the real world' and the desire is for some kind of access to it, 'a real outside of representation.'"[26] If photography is more fossil than picture, then we have avoided the subjective mediation of the photographer's intentions.[27] Should we locate the "ontological disturbance" of photography in this very (uncanny) ability to give the beholder the impression of touching the past? Or is the notion of "touching the past" just the latest example of an inability to deal with loss? Is it another attempt to reconstitute "narcissistic unity," this time through the effort "to commune with the numinosity of history"?[28]

The problem with conjoining Barthes's notion of the ontological disturbance of the photograph with the recent attempts to bring the world "close to our skin" so as to touch it is that Barthes always underscored the remaining distance between the photographic image and our desires for wholeness. The desire for presence is so strong in the face of loss, of death, and photography conveys *both* this desire *and the fact that it cannot be gratified*. Photography stokes the desire for fullness or presence, but this also means that the photographic image never satisfies this desire. The photograph points to and accentuates this ambivalence.

Cora Diamond's recent discussion of Ted Hughes's poem "Six Young Men" is helpful here.[29] The poem begins with the speaker looking at a photograph of six young men taken forty years before, in 1914:

> The celluloid of a photograph holds them well—
> Six young men, familiar to their friends.
> Four decades that have faded and ochre-tinged
> This photograph have not wrinkled the faces or the hands.
> Though their cocked hats are not now fashionable,
> Their shoes shine. One imparts an intimate smile,
> One chews a grass, one lowers his eyes, bashful,
> One is ridiculous with cocky pride—
> Six months after this picture they were all dead.

The young men, so alive and vibrant in the photograph, held by it, are made present to us in their youthful vitality—a vitality that we know was destroyed. Here is the last stanza of the poem:

> That man's not more alive whom you confront
> And shake by the hand, see hale, hear speak loud,
> Than any of these six celluloid smiles are,
> Nor prehistoric or, fabulous beast more dead;
> No thought so vivid as their smoking-blood:
> To regard this photograph might well dement,
> Such contradictory permanent horrors here
> Smile from the single exposure and shoulder out
> One's own body from its instant and heat.

Diamond focuses on the poem because it evinces "the experience of the mind's not being able to encompass something which it encounters" (44): "It is capable of making one go mad to try, to bring together in thought what cannot be thought: the impossibility of anyone's being more alive than these smiling men, nothing being more dead." She calls this a case of the "difficulty of reality," a difficulty, I would suggest, to which photographs expose us in a distinct way. There are language games, she notes, in which this difficulty can be made to vanish. "They were alive when the picture was taken, and then they died. But the picture persists independently of their lives.—What's the problem?" But Diamond wants to abide with the difficulty, not to dissolve or deflect it, because she thinks that exposure to recalcitrant and paradoxical reality makes us (the viewer of the image, the reader of the poem) more aware of our own entanglement with life and death. "Ted Hughes's poem is about *a single exposure*," she writes, "but the single exposure is *our* exposure, as we find ourselves, or are meant to find, in a shuddering awareness of death and life together" (73). "To regard this photograph might well dement," Hughes wrote, but we need to expose ourselves to this dementia because it is an aspect of the "difficulty of reality."

Hughes is looking back on World War I from the 1950s, but exposures do not only reach backward. The difficulty is not just in trying to understand the life and death of another, but in acknowledging our own prefigured absence. Derrida underscores this point in *Echographies*: "As soon as there is a technology of the image, visibility brings night. . . . Because we know that, once it has been taken, captured, this image will be re-producible in our absence, because we know this *already* we are already haunted by this future, which brings our death. Our disappearance is already here."[30] The technology of the image goes beyond the technology of writing, of the text. Exposure of our person, the taking of our portrait, or the viewing of the portrait of another, is not the same as making (or discovering) a mark on a page that will persist independently of us. We do not make our photographic images in the same way as we write our texts, or mark another's.

Thus the photographs on which Barthes focused had a different status as trace than do the inscriptions in a book, or even a handwritten diary entry. Barthes was interested in portraits, or at least in photographs of the face of a person, in images that might have conveyed something of the person as a whole, or as he or she really was. He sometimes calls this the "air" of the person. Rather than see this in the metonymic terms of "transfer" recently articulated by Runia, Hayden White's rather idiosyncratic use of the term "synecdoche" seems to capture Barthes's efforts to find the *just* image.[31] The photographic image that does justice to its subject is one that conveys him or her essentially. Even though it's only an image (we know), the right picture captures the subject "the way the subject really was." This is akin to the synecdoche that refers to a whole not from just any part, but from some essential (*juste*) attribute. The just picture is a rare picture, indeed. Photographic images, according to Barthes, almost always disappoint, but they also contain something that (unintentionally) pricks one's sensibility, stirs one's heart. This is, of course, the famous *punctum*. The image gives (transfers?) more than "it means to." The stream of photography criticism and theory that flows from Barthes would not label this simply "presence," because what is given is also always absence. No unity, but not merely skepticism about the desire for unity, either.

So, photography "amplifies the rim of ontological uncertainty" by raising questions of presence and temporal disjunction in a mnemonic context of desire and absence. The photographic image calls one to (and perhaps from) the past, while reminding one that the object one beholds is "just an image." The tension between the indexical lure of presence and the representational reminders of absence intensifies the photograph's affective and cognitive value for the beholder.

3. Photography's "Anthropological Revolution"

Many of commentators on photography would accept the notion that the advent of this form of mechanical reproduction introduced decisive changes into our relationship to the past. When Barthes claimed that photography created an "anthropological revolution," he was pointing to how the combination of rapid registration and the widespread distribution of photographic images radically transform what it means to be human.[32] This mechanical process promises access to the real (or at least to its trace) but it does so while unsettling our notions of temporal continuity and stability. As Marianne Hirsch and Leo Spitzer have shown, photography's realism produces "incongruous images" that disrupt linear time lines.[33] And as Mary Ann Doane has noted in another context: "The lure of the indexical is linked to its intimate collusion with what Didi-Huberman calls the 'fantasy of referentiality,' with the inert stability of the real, most fully realized in death."[34] In the remainder of this essay I will discuss Doane's work on the changing notions of time and meaning in the age of photography and cinema, work that has teased out the anthropological/historical ramifications of the ontological uncertainties discussed above. Finally, I will close with a reminder of what Barthes called the "great mutation" brought on by the enormous distribution of photo-based images: pleasure now passes through the image.

For decades now, several cultural historians have shown how the consciousness of time and history underwent a dramatic shift in the late nineteenth century. Carl E. Schorske and Debora Silverman have shown that in fin-de-siècle Vienna and Paris a crisis of historicization affected art, architecture, music, and politics.[35] Both Stephen Kern and Anson Rabinbach have explored the ways that late-nineteenth-century European culture and society were struggling with changing notions of time that deeply affected the worlds of labor, transportation, literature, and science.[36] Jennifer Tucker has made the case that photography in the Victorian period helped shape scientific practices as well as notions of objectivity and truth.[37] In *The Emergence of Cinematic Time*, Mary Ann Doane has zeroed in on how photography and cinema contributed to "the rationalization of time characterizing industrialization and the expansion of capitalism."[38] Key for Doane is how photography's indexical powers gravitate toward an inscription of the contingent or the accidental. The ability of photographers to record the accidental is a sign of their realist credentials. They are not choosing subjects whose significance has been established outside the frame; rather, they are there to record *whatever might happen*. "Contingency introduces the element of life and the concrete, but *too much* contingency threatens the crucial representational concept of totality, wholeness. Description is a capitulation to the vast and uncontrollable, and ultimately meaningless, realm of the contingent."[39]

Siegfried Kracauer had already noted photography's gravitational pull toward the meaningless in the 1920s.[40] The price of its realistic precision and ever-faster exposure times was not only the blindness to duration discussed above, but also the loss of an overall structure of meaning.[41] Robin Kelsey describes chance as a type of "photographic madness" that historians must learn to come to terms with. He has written of how the medium's openness to (and anxieties about) chance have influenced picture-taking since Talbot.[42]

As photographic image making becomes both more powerful and more readily available, the relationship to a past with a shared meaning becomes more tenuous. As Doane notes: "The embarrassment of contingency is that it is everywhere and that it everywhere poses the threat of an evacuation of meaning. The concept of the event provides a limit . . . and reinvests the contingent with significance. The contingent is, in effect, harnessed."[43] Doane sees the concept of the event as "on the cusp between contingency and structure, history and theory."[44] An event may seem a mere occurrence, just something that happened, but it comes to stand for an occurrence important enough *to be put in relation with other things that have happened* to create a meaningful pattern, a significant diachrony. The concept of the event points not only to something that "just happened" but also to something that fits into a causal or narrative structure. This "fit" is an attempt to compensate for the loss of an immediate (traditional or natural) sense of duration. Events have causes, and they have consequences. They may have been torn from what Bergson saw as a primordial duration, but they are open to (indeed, call for) significance.

Thus the notion of an event maintains singularity while warding off meaninglessness. Chance, to borrow Ian Hacking's word, is tamed.[45] "Indexicality is inevitably linked with the singular, the unique, with the imprint of time and all its differentiating force. . . . The project of the cinema in modernity is that of endowing the singular with significance without relinquishing singularity."[46] Photography, too, has taken on the project of "endowing the singular with significance without relinquishing singularity." Indeed, photography's episodic intensity dialectically seems to call forth a variety of framing devices to provide a context of meaning—the book and the archive being two of the most important in the nineteenth century. "The obsession with indexicality in the nineteenth century," Doane writes, "is a desire for revivification, for endowing the 'dead' past with life."[47] Photographers strove to capture the face of death and even to seize images from beyond the grave because they were not just creating representations of the past. They were holding onto, or even resurrecting, traces of what had been thought forever lost.[48] All of these efforts are part of a new dynamic of living with the past—and with the passage of time—while refusing meaninglessness. This dynamic was part of the anthropological revolution precipitated by photography that radically transformed how we connect to our histories.

The "anthropological revolution" stimulated by photography concerns our relationship to our desires as well as to our histories. Toward the end of *Camera Lucida* Barthes wrote that in the aftermath of photography "pleasure passes through the image."[49] And not just pleasure. When commenting on how newspaper images of murdered corpses could be used to incite a thirst for revenge, Nadar already made clear in the mid-nineteenth century that the right pictures could stir public passions in much more powerful ways than even the purple prose of the penny press. "The representation of the corrupted body in this unequivocal form," Bann notes, "creates an irresistible pressure for the death penalty to be exercised on the husband and his accomplices."[50] Images with the authority of the trace create the desire for death as they produce a vision of crime. Of course, easily disseminated images produce other desires as well; their global circulation serves not only to make viewers aware of (and perhaps open to) varieties of pleasure, but also to promote the codes through which any pleasure will be sought. The images teach us how to love and how to hate; they teach us about our bodies and about the bodies we want. Rather than learning about ourselves and the world by struggling with others for recognition, as Hegel had imagined, we now learn about our own desires through images of pleasure, pain, and possibility.

This "progressive acculturation of the senses" might be said to expand the range of pleasures sought, of desires experienced. But Barthes has a different perspective at the end of *Camera Lucida*. As pleasure now passes through the image, even our most private and perhaps idiosyncratic desires pass through the filter of the conventional—of that which can be circulated. Even the porn shop, he notes, is full of *tableaux vivant*, of worn-out stereotypes. This is the paradox of the photograph's realism. By depicting the world so faithfully, photography has given us a world in which we live as-if-we-are-to-be-pictured. No camera, no experience; no image, no idea of how to be in the world. Our memories, which photography initially seemed to support, have now been replaced by photographic images of the past. Just as people who now use their GPS for even minor trips lose the ability to find their way around town, with the triumph of photography's capturing events of the past we can no longer find our way in history—no longer navigate within our own personal memories—without the filter of photo-like images. The triumph of the photographic means the past has become accessible, but only accessible in image-like terms. Even Runia's attempt to get the presence close to the skin, his "storehouse of presence," resembles a photo archive.

We have returned to the theme of the cost of photography with which we began this essay. Initially, we considered the blindness to duration as the result of photographic precision. Now we encounter the blindness to our own desires, which Barthes characterizes as the loss of authenticity, as the price of photographic ubiquity. These forms of blindness, however, are not so much disabilities to be overcome as they are aspects of modern consciousness to be acknowledged. The challenges of perceiving duration or of recognizing one's desires cannot be wished away. Photographs have become part of our reality. The engagement with photography's impact on historical consciousness gives rise to reconsiderations of temporal extension and to the difficulties of acknowledging one's desires in an increasingly open and fractured social field. The medium's indexical stain, its frightening specificity, its staggering reproducibility, and the ease with which it travels give rise to photographic ambivalence. As with other forms of ambivalence, we should be less concerned with diluting its constitutive tensions than with learning to live with its conflicted possibilities.

14. Why Photography Matters to the Theory of History

Il n'y a pas d'irreprésentable comme propriété de l'événement. Il y a seulement des choix.

JACQUES RANCIÈRE[1]

Photography maintains the presentness of the world by accepting our absence from it.

STANLEY CAVELL[2]

Georges Didi-Huberman's *Images in Spite of All: Four Photographs from Auschwitz* and Michael Fried's *Why Photography Matters as Art as Never Before* approach photography with very different theoretical agendas.[3] The former is a short, polemical study concerned with epistemological and ethical questions that arise from visual representations of the Shoah; the latter is a large, richly illustrated tome concerned with the ontological lessons explored by contemporary art photography. Didi-Huberman is focused on small photographic traces of mass murder that can change our relation to history; Fried is focused on large-scale images that can change our relation to art. Nevertheless the books have two things in common: an argument against postmodern skepticism, and an insistence that photography has become a field in which questions of history, truth, and authenticity are being explored with particular acuity. How do photographs work in telling the truth about history? What is the work of photography in illuminating the grounds of truth telling at this moment in the history of art?

I

The first part of *Images in Spite of All* is a reprint of an essay that Didi-Huberman prepared for the catalogue of the exhibition *Mémoires des camps: Photographies des camps de concentration et d'extermination Nazis* (1933–1999). This essay concentrates on four photographs that were taken in Auschwitz and smuggled out of the camp by members of the *Sonderkommando*—the special units of death camp prisoners who were charged with overseeing the work of the crematoria. At least two of the images depict what seem to be the recently gassed bodies as they were being cremated in front of the gas chamber of crematorium V.

Making these pictures involved the risky cooperation of several people. The camera probably was smuggled into the camp by a worker, and then it had to be carefully sneaked into the crematorium while others posted watch. The four pictures had to be taken quickly, and then the piece of film in the camera was removed and rolled into a tube of toothpaste that was spirited out of the camp by an employee from the SS canteen. On September 4, 1944, the film reached the Polish Resistance, with a note written by two prisoners:

> Urgent. Send two metal rolls of film for 6 x 9 as fast as possible. . . . Sending you photographs of Birkenau showing prisoners sent to gas chambers. One photo shows one of the stakes at which bodies were burned when the crematorium could not manage to burn all the bodies. The bodies in the foreground are waiting to be thrown into the fire. . . . Send the photos to Tell—we think enlargements of the photos can be sent further. (17)

The note is evidence of a will to document the mechanized murder that so many had described (and still describe) as "unimaginable." This so-called inability to imagine or represent the annihilation is at the core of Didi-Huberman's study. Some have said that the final offense to the witness/survivor was not to be believed. If the nonwitness could not imagine that "such a thing could happen," then the testimony would literally fall on deaf ears. The blank stares that greeted a witness because the testimony could not be imagined was yet another stage in the process of obliteration.

Photography, Didi-Huberman writes, "shows a particular ability . . . to curb the fiercest will to obliterate" (23). The "bureaucratic narcissism" (24) of the

Nazi regime led it to document everything it did, and this naturally included photographic documentation. Despite Nazi efforts to destroy archives of Auschwitz as the allied forces approached, there remain about forty thousand pictures of the death camp (24), many of which were saved by prisoners desperate to preserve images of what otherwise might be said to be unbelievable. Historians have had access to the images for some time now, though for many of us it is still disconcerting to know that there is a visual record of Auschwitz and other death camps.

One must pause here. Photographs, even thousands of them, do not necessarily make a "visual record."[4] At least since the 1950s, one of the most important streams of thought about the efforts to annihilate the Jews emphasized that these efforts (or the "experiences" of the victims) were "unimaginable," or "unthinkable," or simply "unrepresentable." In the film *Night and Fog*, one of the great early efforts to bring Nazi mass murder into public consciousness, the voice-over declares repeatedly that you can understand nothing of what went on here, even as you are shown heaps of body parts.

> How to discover the reality of these camps, when it was despised by those who made them and eluded those who suffered here? These wooden blocks, these tiny beds where one slept three, these burrows where people hid, where they ate furtively and where even sleep was a threat? No description or shot can restore their true dimension, that of uninterrupted fear. One would have to have the very mattresses where they slept, the blanket which was fought over. Only the husk and shade remain of this brick dormitory.[5]

Resnais's film contained an explicit warning about the limits of representation even as it confronted viewers with images of immense brutality. And this warning would be strongly echoed over the years, even as viewers, readers, and spectators were confronted with ever-more numerous representations of these events. The words "Holocaust" and "Shoah" were introduced to name occurrences that found no place in the normal lexicon of historical events.[6] Scholarly discussions of these events rarely took place without some gesture to indicate one understood the necessary failure of representation in regard to their horrific nature. Often this necessary failure in the face of the enormity of events has been assimilated to notions of the sublime. The field of trauma studies, which has grown so dramatically in recent decades in Western scholarship, has as its central tenet the notion that traditional empirical representation necessarily breaks down in the face of the traumatic.[7]

According to this tenet, no matter how many thousands of photographs one has of the death camps, one cannot have a "visual record" of what went on there. This seems reasonable in the (almost trivial) sense that even a complete series of photographs of any event wouldn't provide a total historical picture. But believers in the doctrine of the intrinsic unrepresentability of the Shoah demand more than this sober view of the limits of visual understanding. Writers stressing the uniqueness of these events have been led to call them beyond *any* representation; the death camps are even said to be "unimaginable." Thus, if historians (or artists) tried to represent them, they would, according to those invested in unrepresentability, be denying the enormity of the trauma.[8] Claude Lanzmann's magnificent film *Shoah* was built on this ideology (or theology) of the unrepresentable. Lanzmann has been quoted as saying that if he had discovered footage of the killing centers, he would have destroyed it.

Jean-Francois Lyotard is one of many philosophers and critics who have articulated this view of the sublime, unrepresentable nature of the Shoah as trauma. He compared the attempt to exterminate the Jews to an earthquake so powerful that it breaks the very tools used to measure its impact. Language is broken after Auschwitz. The "black hole of meaning" of the Shoah is enormously powerful, and for that very reason cannot be captured or contained in representation.[9]

Didi-Huberman takes a strong stand against this view of representation and of history: "To remember, one must imagine" (30). And imagination is deeply linked to, though not reducible to, images. He writes about the four surreptitiously taken photographs of Auschwitz not because they comprise the truth of the extermination camp, but because they can contribute to our ability to make tentative historical sense of some of it. The pictures should stimulate thought—not merge into a total image that keeps us from thinking about the details of what happened. Didi-Huberman quotes Hannah Arendt to make this point: "Lacking the truth, [we] will however find *instants of truth*, and those instants are in fact all we have available to us to give some order to this chaos of horror. These instants arise spontaneously, like oases in the desert" (31).[10] Arendt's metaphor reminds us that an oasis is more than a mirage. The photographs should help us pay attention differently, and that in turn will help us imagine and remember.

Didi-Huberman repeatedly insists on the point that attention to some images is not a substitute for, or even a claim of, historical understanding. He knows that for many French intellectuals the very consideration of Holocaust photographs would be an affront, an obscenity. Hence he turns to Arendt, and also to Walter Benjamin's notion of the "flash"—of the illumination of an instant that should not be confused with a claim of totality, of complete comprehension. But the abdication of totality should not be, Didi-Huberman insists, a rejection of what traces might be able to tell us. We must do the "archaeological work"; we must dig into the images to help us think more precisely, to help us imagine and remember.

II

The critical response to Didi-Huberman was swift and extreme. In an interview in *Le Monde*, Claude Lanzmann reiterated his opposition to any attempt to visually document the genocidal crimes against the Jews. Lanzmann commented that Didi-Huberman's "obscure intentions" led to a fetishizing of the image and a devaluing of accounts by witnesses. In Lanzmann's view, those who desired to find photographic documentation played into the hands of Holocaust deniers who held to a simple-minded notion of factual documentation that likewise discounted the testimony of survivors. Bruno Chaouat offers a helpful gloss on Lanzmann's position:

> [T]he only "good" images are the ones that point to the inherent inability of all images to bear witness to the Holocaust. A photograph, an archive, or a document, for Lanzmann, betray the historical truth, because they purport to represent the past instead of acting it out in the present. By representing the past "bad" images cover it up instead of recovering it. Instead of securing memory, images further oblivion.[11]

Quoting Paul Klee in his 2001 *Le Monde* interview, Lanzmann emphasized that art should not aim to reproduce the visible but to expand visibility. The "cult of the image for the image" as he called it, constructed a new memory based on an adoration of specific photographs, a memory that became a substitute for thinking and imagining what happened.[12]

Les Temps Modernes, a journal edited by Lanzmann, extended this line of criticism in articles by Gerard Wajcman and Elisabeth Pagnoux.[13] Wajcman offered a particularly stern and even uncivil criticism of Didi-Huberman's claim that in spite of the thesis of the Shoah's unrepresentability, there do exist images of the Shoah that help us imagine and remember. Following Lanzmann's comments in *Le Monde,* Wajcman accuses the art historian of "fetishizing" the image, and of giving the spectator the ability to create whatever he or she wants to see:

> It is the viewer who makes the image. The very idea of an exhibition of photographs of the camps that purports to base the originality of its project on historical rigor, on the fact of "documenting" photographs, is quite surprising. Georges Didi-Huberman takes four photographs and says in substance: change your point of view [*regard*] and you will see the gas chambers. (50)

Wajcman accuses Didi-Huberman of loving images more than the historical truth, of caring more about photography than about the Shoah.

The nastiness of this polemic has a tendency to obscure what is theoretically at stake in the question of the representation of extreme events. Wajcman takes the position (often associated with Adorno but also common in French philosophy after its confrontation with Heidegger and Nietzsche) that all representation offers a form of consolation. And consolation is a sign of weakness, or at least of a failure to acknowledge the traumatic and the sublime.

> But the fact is this: the photograph, even the most raw, even the most meticulous as to what happened, every image of horror is a veil over horror; every image, because it is an image, protects us from horror; every image, because it is an image, at the same time that it makes us see something, that it makes us discover something, it covers it over as well; the image turns us away from that which it makes us see. (69)

Images veil, they don't reveal. And those who can't take the truth in its pure form accept the consolation of the veil of images. Finally, Wajcman disputes Didi-Huberman's notion that imagination is necessary for one to remember and for one to grasp some dimensions of historical events. For Wajcman, imagination is a part of identification. Otherness is denied when one imagines the past, and the horror of the traumatic is avoided in favor of the narcissistic consolations of the image.

The critique of the identification and consolation offered by images of atrocity is longstanding, and Didi-Huberman is well aware of the dangers of making a spectacle or a morality tale out of the holocaust: "From the journalistic *coverage* to the media *cult*, from the legitimate construction of an iconography to the improper production of social icons, there is often a single step" (70). But recognizing the problems with the television series *Holocaust* or Stephen Spielberg's *Schindler's List* does not authorize a metaphysical repudiation of all images. The postmodern mainstream's radical skepticism is as cheaply won as Hollywood's sentimentalism.[14]

At stake in this controversy is whether photography (but why only photography?) leads to a "we were there" approach to historical knowledge that denies the otherness of the past. The concerns raised by Lanzmann and Wajcman are warnings against a view of the past that would allow us to appropriate it or assimilate it to agendas in the present. This is, of course, always a danger in historical knowing, but it becomes particularly acute with regard to extreme or traumatic events. How dare you, the historian, ever claim to know what it *really* felt like to be there! The production of a sense of familiarity with the past, conveying its presence, can be offensive. Roland Barthes, in a different context, noted that all photographs offer a certificate of presence. For certain key writers on the Shoah, there is no presence that remains for us to hold onto. There "remains" only the annihilation.

Didi-Huberman offers an alternative to the choice between skepticism and consolation. "To approach does not mean to appropriate," he writes. The "very otherness [of the photographs] demanded that we approach them" (88); but approaching images of the past need not mean fetishizing them as magical keys to unlock the otherwise unknowable. The alternative to postmodern denial of the image must include "attending to one's own absence," a modest approach to both knowing and skepticism (88). Such modesty would mean attending to possibilities rather than achieving certainties:

> It is not a matter of unilaterally positing the unsayable and the unimaginable of this story; rather, it is a matter of working *with* it, yet *against* it: by making the sayable and the imaginable into infinite tasks, necessary yet inevitably lacunary. (155)

Images are not the cure for the lacunae of a traumatic history, but they do change our relationship to those fragments of the past that are left to us. We must not treat images, and other testimony, as communicating the unveiling of the one essential meaning, but neither should we reject them as always already deceptive.

> Images become previous to historical *knowledge* the moment they are put into perspective, in *montages* of intelligibility. The *memory* of the Shoah should continually be reconfigured—and, one hopes, clarified—as new relationships are established, new resemblances are discovered, and new differences underlined. (159)

The historian's responsibility toward the traumatic is complex because this responsibility is never definitive.[15] The historian cannot, though, be limited to being a guardian of silence, or a high priest of unrepresentability.

In the final pages of *Images in Spite of All* Didi-Huberman turns to theories of historical redemption as articulated by a number of Jewish thinkers from Kafka to Rosenzweig, from Scholem to Benjamin and Kracauer. He touches quickly on these writers as "reference points" for a notion of redemption without consolation. The Jewish notion of redemption at work in these thinkers is a response to exile that has no room for the idea of historical progress—no room for simple consolation. Didi-Huberman quotes Benjamin:

> We ask those who will come after us, not gratitude for our victories, but the recollection of our defeats. This is consolation: the sole consolation that is given to those who no longer have any hope of being consoled. (171)

Recollection, in images or words, does not resuscitate anything, but it does save the historical real from indifference, from oblivion.

> We must know how to look into images to see that of which they are survivors. So that history, liberated from the pure past (that absolute, that abstraction) might help us *to open* the present of time.
>
> This saving doesn't promise a particular future, but it does open possibilities. And possibilities, imagined with the help of traces, survivors, are all we can glean from the traumatic past.

III

The notion that any representation of the Shoah, especially any putative image of annihilation, would be a contamination can be said to stem from a fear of theatricalizing the historical event. The moralizing, sentimental, ideological, or religious exploitation of the holocaust—finding a meaning in the events to be deployed for contemporary purposes—is what has happened, of course, in the "Shoah Business," as in "there's no business like the Shoah Business." Theatricalization, indeed. Didi-Huberman's evocation of a recollection "that does not resuscitate anything" aims to recuperate images of the event (but not only this event) as flashes of evidence that do not perforce fall into the degraded world of theater or spectacle. To discuss the image in relation to a resistance against theatricalization puts us squarely in the world of the art historian Michael Fried. For more than forty years Fried has explored the dynamic tension between theatrical display and absorption in the history of art. Recently he has turned to contemporary photography as the field in which this issue can be said to be at the core of ambitious artistic practice.

Fried articulated his idea of the dangers of "theatricalization" in his critique of what he called literalism in contemporary art.[16] That was in 1967, and although his essay has generated much heated discussion over the years, most observers of contemporary art would agree that the literalists (usually called minimalists) won, and that Fried lost. Minimalist art and then installation art very purposively "took account of the spectator." Call this theater, if you will, but the artists and other critics thought it more honest to make work that didn't pretend to create its own universe. From installations to participatory art events, contemporary art rejected the goal of absorption that Fried had identified as the heart and soul of modernism. Fried, of course, is well aware of this, and notes early on, in *Why Photography Matters as Never Before*, that high modernism was "routed" and that by the "early and mid-1970s theatrical, beholder-based art definitely held the field" (43). He attends now to recent photography not because he perceives a simple return to the values of high modernism, but because

> new art photography seeks to come to grips with the issue of beholding in ways that do not succumb to theatricality but which at the same time register the epochality of minimalism/literalism's intervention by an acknowledgment of to-be-seenness, just as ambitious painting after Manet acknowledged painting's facingness (not flatness, as is usually said) while nevertheless reserving an imaginative space for itself that was not wholly given over to soliciting the applause of the Salon-going public. (43)

New art photography, in other words, comes to grips with beholding by acknowledging it without being corrupted (irredeemably) by it.

The reference to Manet in the quotation above signals the art historical current of Fried's work over the last thirty years, namely, his charting of the dialectic of absorption and theatricality identified by Diderot in the eighteenth century. For Fried:

> A central current or tradition in French painting from Jean-Baptiste Greuze . . . to Edouard Manet and his generation around 1860 may be understood in terms of an ongoing effort to make paintings that by one strategy or another appear . . . to deny the presence before them of the beholder, or to put this more affirmatively, to establish the ontological fiction that the beholder does not exist. Only if this was accomplished could the actual beholder be stopped and held before the canvas. (40)

In three major books, Fried has shown how "strong painting" in the years leading up to the advent of modernism was wrestling with the status of the beholder.[17] Modernism would emerge from a "crisis of acknowledging the beholder without caving into her demands—without pandering to her." Fried uses the term "facingness" to describe this acknowledgment of the beholder in Manet's work:

> What took its place in Manet's art was a new acknowledgment that paintings were indeed made to be beheld . . . an attempt to make not just each painting as a whole but every bit of its surface—every brushstroke, so to speak, face the beholder as never before. (151)

Fried's argument in his latest book is that the challenge taken up by modernist painters in the nineteenth century to acknowledge the presence of the beholder without making the work for or about the beholder has been taken up again by some of the most prominent photographers of our time.

Why Photography Matters to Art as Never Before is comprised of a series of readings of some of the major photographic artists of the last two decades, with a look back at some older work, especially by Bernd and Hilla Becher. It also offers a critical reconsideration of Roland Barthes's *Camera Lucida*, a text that has been discussed by just about every major writer on photography in the last twenty-five years. Throughout the richly illustrated book, Fried returns to his critical argument against the postmodern emphasis on the experience of the spectator, and to his historical argument that art has advanced since the eighteenth century by wrestling with issues of absorption, theatricality, and acknowledgment.

> [O]nce it became imaginable that a "world" could be "contaminated" by the mere fact of being beheld, the situation was ripe for the emergence of an esthetic that would accept such "contamination" as the basis of its procedures. Inevitably, the esthetic found its home in photography. (35)

WPMANB represents a confluence of Fried's critical and historical concerns in powerfully compelling ways. His argument and his examples also allow one to understand why photography might matter not only as art, but also to the theory of history as never before.

IV

A key figure for Fried over the last several years is the Canadian photographer Jeff Wall. The artist has been explicit about his philosophical interests for some time, and his reading of post-Kantian aesthetics and the literature of ideas has played a crucial role in his practice.[18] Moreover, Wall has read Fried on the dynamics of theatricality, and, as James Elkins has pointed out, the artist can be said to have been significantly influenced by notions of the beholder, the everyday, and absorption.[19] Fried makes the point himself, saying that "the connection between us is part of the argument of this book" (39).

Wall's portrait *Adrian Walker, Artist, Drawing from a Specimen in a Laboratory in the Dept of Anatomy at the University of British Columbia, Vancouver* (1992) is a key picture for Fried. The work is a transparency in a lightbox, 119 x 164 cm, and depicts a man seated at a table, mechanical drafting pencil in hand, with a sketchpad on his lap. On the table rests a peculiar specimen: a preserved severed human right arm and hand, the skin flayed back to reveal the muscles of the forearm. The young man—jeans, light blue sweater, white collared shirt—sits with legs crossed and stares intently in front of him. Presentation of the image in a large light box, hung on a wall in the manner of a sizeable painting, contributes to its arresting quality. Fried has much to say about this image that is of interest, but here I want only to emphasize what he and the artist call "near documentary." Adrian Walker, like other figures in Wall's oeuvre, appears oblivious to the spectator (in part because he doesn't seem to realize that he is being photographed). He seems to have been captured in his absorptive work. But a moment's reflection tells us that this can't be true at all, that the picture is carefully staged.

> The picture involved a performance in that Adrian was working with me, but he didn't do anything he didn't normally do. . . . The picture is an example of what I call "near documentary." (41)

Wall calls the feeling of absorption the effect of Walker's "performance" for the photographer. For Fried this performance is not a giving in to theatricality but an acknowledgment of "to-be-seenness." Naïve documentary—photographically surprising the world so that it is in a pre-performative state—is no longer possible for us, if it ever was. "Near documentary," or the deliberate construction of a world to be seen but not to be theatricalized, is the best we can do because it acknowledges the dynamics of spectatorship without pandering to those dynamics.

Wall's photographic work, according to Fried, has wrestled with this problem of absorption and acknowledgment by concentrating on the everyday. As Heidegger provides the philosophical concepts about "worldhood" that Fried employs in relation to Wall's portrait of Walker, Wittgenstein gives the conceptual tools Fried uses to tease out the philosophical dimensions in the photographer's concentration on the ordinary. Fried cites a thought experiment that the philosopher described in 1930 in which someone who thinks he is unobserved goes about his everyday business, but the person is really on stage in a theater. "We should be seeing life itself," writes Wittgenstein, and from a point of view that is normally closed to us in our everyday world. It's both banal and uncanny: banal, because the person is going about his or her business without doing anything out of the ordinary; uncanny, because we don't usually get to pay close attention to the ordinary within the framework of a stage, within a framework of a work of art. By paying attention in this close, intense way, are we lifting the actions out of the ordinary, or are we seeing their everydayness for the first time? The artist's task is to enable us to pay attention in this way. As Wittgenstein put it:

> But only the artist can represent the individual thing [das *Einzelne*] so that it appears to us as a work of art. . . . The work of art compels us—as one might say—to see it in the right perspective, but without art the object [*der Gegenstand*] is a piece of nature like any other &

the fact that *we* may exalt it through our enthusiasm does not give anyone the right to display it to us. (76)[20]

Fried notes that the artist must present the everyday in an antitheatrical form in order to maintain the qualities of wonder and attention. Otherwise the everyday appears as inauthentic. This is what "near documentary" aims to do—to bring out the absorptive qualities of daily window washing at a museum, to convey "the historicalness of the everyday" at an archaeological site, without giving the beholder the sense that these things are there only for him or her. The real is imagined, even performed, but it remains real and not only theater.

For Fried, the point of reading Jeff Wall's celebrated photographs in relation to the dynamics of theatricality and absorption is to show that "some of the most important and vital recent initiatives in photography turn out to have been renewing, even while radically revising, the artistic and philosophical stakes of the most ambitious high modernist painting and sculpture of the 1960s and 1970s" (81–82). Those initiatives aim to achieve a presentness and instantaneousness that continues what Fried has called the "war" with theater.[21]

Contemporary photography has taken up the war with theatricality by reanimating the effort to negate (or overcome) "objecthood" by creating "its own" world. One sees this in the German photographer Thomas Demand's "effectively replacing the real-world context with a merely depicted one, every detail and aspect of which is exactly what he has intended it to be" (271). Demand's images are based on scrupulously constructed environments made of paper that look nearly real, uncannily exact but for some tear or fold. "My tyrannical condition," Demand says, "is that I prescribe your vision" (271). Fried nicely ties this view back to Baudelaire and to his own arguments about modernism. "A picture," Baudelaire writes, "is only what it wants to be; there is no way of looking at it [other] than on its own terms" (271).

The "exclusive and absolute" nature of painting for Baudelaire is for Fried now taken up by photography as the key tactic in the war against theater. The artist makes a world photographically, challenging the minimalist, theatrical pandering to the world. This can be done by constructing a world to be photographed, like the near documentaries of Wall, or the artificial realties of Demand, or through choreographed typologies of decayed industrial sites created by the Bechers. For Fried, the Bechers didn't just reject the "objecthood" of a work of art, they created a category of "good objecthood" through a Hegelian process of negation:

> [W]hat is missing from the world of things as it stands—what is to be supplied by the Bechers' typological "tableaus"—is precisely a "showing" of the grounds of its intelligibility, which is also to say of its capacity for individuation *as* a world. Or, as a *world*, one bearing the stamp of a particular stage of history. (327)

The worlds offered by these photographic projects achieve presentness while acknowledging their "to-be-seenness," by accepting that they are to be beheld. But this acknowledgment resists being there merely *for* the beholder; the photographic world is not made for or by the beholder.

V

We can see how Fried's understanding of ambitious art photography of recent decades is relevant to the debates concerning representations of the traumatic events outlined above. In the wake of postmodern critiques of conventional narratives of the past, we now recognize the constructed nature of historical representation. Some ironic skeptics take this constructedness even further, dismissing any possible connection of the representation to "what really happened." Those who want to retain some notion of the unrepresentability of the Shoah hope to bypass this dynamic of irony and skepticism. The guardians of the Shoah's unrepresentability are concerned that any photographic depiction will be contaminated by relations of spectatorship that every image necessarily creates. As has been noted by critics for several decades, photographs make pandering to, playing for, the image a way of life. They undermine our sense of reality apart from the image. Fried shows that the photographers he most admires are acutely aware of this danger, but that they have given up on the dream of surprising reality in a street snapshot, or of digging beneath a false surface to discover the "really real" lying buried beneath it. Wall and Thomas Ruff, Andreas Gursky, Philip-Lorca diCorcia, Thomas Demand, and Candida Hoefer all make the dangers (and possibilities) of beholding the very condition of their artistic practice. Their images ask us to consider what is performance, and what is real, what is documentary depiction, and what is artistic construction. In so doing, they are fulfilling the highest calling for contemporary art, which is not to defeat theatrical inauthenticity, but to acknowledge that possibility without giving in to it.

Didi-Huberman's measured use of historical photographic images complements Fried's work. Didi-Huberman is not seeking the consoling image that helps us understand or imagine the Whole of the Shoah. He wants only to use specific fragments to help us achieve a flash of understanding of events that are never-to-be-present. Of course, by using images one runs the risk of trivializing the past, participating in the Shoah Business. One also runs the risk of thinking that one has gotten closer to the really real—the past in its essence. But Didi-Huberman's readings of the photographs don't fall into those traps. His readings acknowledge that any representation of the past can succumb to theatricality, to playing for the present. But they also provide flashes of insight into the possibilities of what might have been. "The *imaginable* certainly does not make radical evil 'present' and in no way masters it on a practical level: what it does do is bring us closer to its *possibility*, always open in the open [two opens] of some familiar landscape" (155). By bringing us closer to this possibility, we have increased our chances for the flashes of understanding of the traumatic past.

Although Didi-Huberman chooses in *Images in Spite of All* not to engage in a discussion of Barthes's work, probably because of what he calls its "overuse," Fried's discussion of *Camera Lucida* does provide a final opportunity to connect the historical, artistic, and philosophical dimensions of the two books examined here. Barthes notion of the *punctum* is, of course, the most frequently used concept from *Camera Lucida*. The *punctum* is a detail of a photograph that just "happens to be there," a detail that wounds or pricks a beholder. The *studium* of the photograph is its overt content, the actualization of the photographer's intentions. Concentration on the *punctum* by commentators on photography and on Barthes has usually meant a concentration on the personal or subjective aspects of responses to the medium. Regardless of the "Operator's" (as Barthes sometimes says) intentions, I might find something striking or wounding about an image; and you might see the same image and not care at all. It's all about the Beholder. As Walter Benn Michaels has pointed out, the *punctum* is "squarely on the side of minimalism/literalism's emphasis on the indeterminancy of meaning and the primacy of the experiencing subject" (345).[22] What could be more theatrical?

Fried more or less concedes Michaels's point about the *punctum*, but he brilliantly weaves this into what he calls the "antitheatrical animus that runs through [*Camera Lucida*] from first page to last" (345). Fried argues that this antitheatrical animus is why the French critic dismissed photographs of people seemingly unaware of the camera as more or less cheap performances by the photographer. Truly antitheatrical work has to confront the question of theater head on. That's why Barthes was so interested in "the pose," and why he argued that the most interesting frontally posed images succeeded in defeating theatricality, by acknowledging conditions of spectatorship. No matter how constructed the image is, or the portrayed person's "look" is, a photograph can unintentionally contain a detail that defines the emotional core of the image. "[I]n order for a photograph to be truly antitheatrical for Barthes," says Fried, "it must somehow carry within it a kind of ontological guarantee that it was not intended to be so *by the photographer*. . . . The punctum, I am suggesting, functions as that guarantee" (101). Thus, rather than registering the importance of the subjective responses of the beholder, the idea of the *punctum* establishes the photographer's not having been corrupted by a desire to appeal to (or shock or disgust) the beholder. Fried reads Barthes as having called for a photographic exploration of antitheatricality while "acknowledging more fully than any previous writer on the topic the inherently theatrical basis of the photographic artifact" (346).

It is the perception of the "inherently theatrical basis of the photographic artifact" that fuels the outrage expressed toward Didi-Huberman's consideration of the Shoah photographs. Since all photographs risk theatricality, we must, his critics claim, protect the Shoah and other traumatic historical moments from the images' always-already corrupted evidential pretensions and inauthenticity. Didi-Huberman is not at all suggesting that photographs solve the issues of corrupt evidence, but only that they signal the difficulties and the possibilities of apprehending and representing some aspects of the past.

Fried has shown that contemporary photographic work has taken on the ambitions of high modernism by accepting the challenge of "to-be-seenness." Didi-Huberman has shown that we can use photographic images "to see that of which they are survivors." Photography as an art practice does not provide an escape from the dynamic of absorption and theatricality; it acknowledges this dynamic as the condition of its own work. Photography as a "historical practice" does not escape from the difficulties of evidence and of the "constructed" nature of historical understanding; photography functions neither as a pure trace of the past, nor as a mere invitation to spectacle. In spite of all, photographs remind us of what cannot be seen, and that is why they matter to the theory of history.

15. Ordinary Film

Péter Forgács's *The Maelstrom*

Maelstrom: A large, powerful whirlpool, often resulting in unusual reconfigurations of objects in its vicinity.

I

The opening of *The Maelstrom* (1997) presents a silent image of small, seemingly fragile beings tossed on a stormy sea. Silence draws us out—where are we and what are we looking at?—and then the film pushes us back. The remainder of the film, with only a few punctuations, uses sound (music, cries, sound effects) to bring us along. But we start with silence and the sea—drawing us out. Where are we being taken?

When the sound emerges near the beginning of *The Maelstrom,* we see people drawn to the waves that crash ominously against a floodwall. They are attracted to the raging sea, and then they retreat from the waves. They want to feel that power, but they fear being swept away by it. Wanting to be swept away, we approach. And then we run for our lives.

The figures in the grainy footage run up to the floodwall, seem to lean out to look at the churning sea, fascinated by its power. They are alive, and they are looking out into the death-tossing waves. How long can they stand there as the swell approaches? When is it too late to run for it?

The word "maelstrom" originally referred to a whirlpool off the coast of Norway, a whirlpool so powerful that it could draw down boats from miles around. If you could know this whirlpool, would that mean you had felt its pull, that you had been "reconfigured"? Would you want to approach it to be sure it was really pulling you, to feel more? How much pull would you want to feel before you lunged for escape?

Peter Forgács is the magician of the whirlpool. He is our navigator around the maelstrom. His maelstrom is what others have called "the black hole of meaning" in the twentieth century: the Shoah, the Holocaust. It has reconfigured our ability to make sense of what led up to it, and what has happened in its wake. He cannot bring us too close, for then we would close our eyes to what we have to see before us. But if he turns away too quickly from what he has found, we will see nothing that matters to us, for us. How can he navigate in these waters?

Forgács finds films. That's simple. He finds old movies, home movies, movies taken for no good reason except to mark occasions, to create a record, to remember the daily life and the bodies and the people we used to be. Banal. A common joke about home movies is that we usually want to flee from the friend or family member who enthusiastically proposes showing us the movies of the wedding, the children, the last vacation. And yet the friend is oblivious to the boredom he inflicts on us. He, of course, has no reason to be bored because he is looking at himself. But how can the home movies of other people hold any interest for us? How can we feel their pull?

In *The Maelstrom*, Forgács warns us early on. After we see the waves, and after we hear them, we are given the subtitle of the film: *A Family Chronicle*. The family that will be chronicled is the Peerebooms. We are introduced to several solid citizens. Why should we care about them? Good bourgeois. Jews. To label them is already to begin to care, or at least to create a quality of attention. We already frame them in this way because we are given a date, 1934. And then all the signs—the name, the profession, the newspapers they edit, the physiognomy (I know, but I can't help thinking about how Jewish they *look*) . . . all of these signs spell doom. The movies that Forgács finds are silent, but we can hear the maelstrom churning in the distance. Drawing us—or is it just the Peerebooms?—closer.

Forgács finds films from the 1930s. But it's not that simple. He buys them, trades them, negotiates with people who are holding onto their private archives. And, along with his great creator of soundscapes, Tibor Szemzo, he turns these home movies into something else. He takes them out of the home, making them *unheimlich*, uncanny. But that is already to overdramatize, which Forgács consistently refuses to do. He wants to remain with the banal, to draw us into it. He does not bestow on his films the dignity of historical, metaphysical, or even theoretical importance. When we approach a Forgács film, we have to allow ourselves another mode of attention, another rhythm of seeing. Why can't we just ignore these Peerebooms? What have they to offer us that we don't have already, that we don't know already? We know what it means that this is the 1930s in Europe: all that we see will be destroyed. How many stories of murdered Jews do we need? Yet, here they are in front of us: planning marriages, making babies, opening shops, frolicking in the snow. We watch them, shocked not only by their own ordinariness (what, after all, can bring the ordinary to us here, now?) but by their capacity to maintain those everyday lives even as the maelstrom sucks them closer and closer to its murderous turbulence. "*Why don't they pay attention?!*" we say as we watch them. "*Can't they feel themselves sinking?*" Whom are we talking about?

Forgács's challenge as a filmmaker, as a film explorer, and as an archivist is to preserve the ordinariness of his subjects even as he frames them for us in extraordinary times. The Peerebooms are trying to maintain their normal rhythms of family life as Jews in Europe of the 1930s. And when we see them in these pictures, it doesn't look that hard. They have the commerce, the family alliances, the work with the Red Cross, the vacations. Jozeph edits the *Nieuw Israelielisch Weekblad*, eldest son Max finds a happy bride in Annie, while daughter Loes marries the strong-shouldered Nico (where ever did she find him?). We begin ominously enough, in 1933, a year of great significance for the Peerebooms because it is the year that Max and Annie get married. Somebody get the camera to record the momentous event! We viewers bring different criteria of importance: 1933 is the year that Hitler becomes Chancellor in Germany, and, when we hear the weather forecast of the following summer, "sunshine all over," we know there is going to be trouble. We don't really need the frames of the pet black cat, but here is one of the few times that Forgács permits himself to emphasize the tension he more typically just allows to swell up into the viewer's consciousness.

II

Marriage and vacations. Sunshine all over. How to maintain that ordinariness? There is a danger in exposing it. The ordinary can be an embarrassment for those who notice it because to do so is an acknowledgment, maybe even a confession, of one's own banality. Artists, theorists, philosophers, often flee ordinariness, or, as some like to say "try to make the ordinary extraordinary." I prefer Stanley Cavell's project, which he has called, after Wittgenstein, Emerson, and Thoreau, a "quest for the ordinary," the ordinary being that place where "you first encounter yourself." How are we to think about our lives and about the pictures of our lives without separating these images from ourselves, from our ordinary world? Are we prepared to run the risks of skepticism, of melodrama, or of the cage of irony? The skeptic might ask how we could be sure that our experiences of images have any meaning at all. What if they are merely found footage, the dreck of home movies into which we pump significance that we later claim to discover? The seeker of melodrama might demand that we underline the lachrymose history of those pictured. Are these not always already tragic figures, martyrs who cry out to us to act as their witnesses? The ironist might smile at our attempt to take seriously what we might normally glide by, artful images that we should see at a festival lubricated by drink and cryptic conversation. We leave ourselves open to such questions when we pay attention to the everyday. Skepticism, melodrama, and irony are three standard responses to the nonfiction film, responses that may have even more potency in regard to the reframing and rethinking of home movies that is part of Forgács's project. Remaining open to these responses is a key to his project and is (as Cavell has taught now for more than forty years) necessary for any kind of real thinking.

Real thinking about the ordinary is problematic because of the insistence of particularity. The problem of home movies is the problem of particularity; that is, trying to find a way to make sense of something individual, on its own, distinct, without erasing its individuality and distinctness. Such thinking is problematic because in order to make sense of something, to know something, we must first put that thing in relation to something else, or subsume it under some broader conceptual scheme. There is a happy, optimistic side to this feature of understanding: our connection to the individual object of knowledge is enriched, made more complex, and deepened by enwebbing that object in the world that we know. But there is a frightening, sad side to this feature of our understanding, too: we lose the specificity, the particularity of the object as we come to see it as one among many objects that are similar and different from it.

We know all this from our everyday experience. As soon as the home movie is taken out of its native environment, it has the capacity to become either senseless or *unheimlich*. We need to wrap the home movie in something else: film makers like Forgács and Robert Nakamura use music and history to bring the private film—the orphaned film—into the world of sense. Comparison—with other families, groups, histories—is supposed to make some other person's home movie our own. But comparison always involves a loss of meaning as well as a gain, and persistent comparison with others can feel like a mode of erasure. We can see this in private life: think of the lover who tells you how much smarter and neater you are than all of his or her ex's; think of the sibling who is always measured by the brother's or sister's achievements. The problem of particularity is a problem of the home, but it is not limited to the home. Think of the strenuous efforts to have a heinous crime labeled a crime against humanity; think of the contested use of the words "genocide" and "holocaust."

The problem of particularity is also apparent when we consider people or places of extreme beauty. We may be content to just take pleasure in these people and places, and to leave them aside from our understanding. They invite delight more than comparison and knowledge. To engage in the attempt to *know* the beautiful can deepen our delight, but also spoil it—or, what's worse, spoil the delight of others. This issue is visible in the museum world when you ask academically minded interpreters to talk about beloved works of art. Curators and the general public often feel their pleasure being compromised by the savant. To hear the professor describe to you how Monet was really painting the bourgeoisie's sense of triumph over nature might seem like an assault on your own experience of the painting itself. The description is no mere error of pedantry. It is a feature of understanding and of knowledge—but not of wonder. Understanding and knowledge demand that you move away from the intimacy of your relation with any object or event. Understanding may promise a richer experience in the end, but there is risk in the movement-toward-distance that knowledge entails.

Forgács, who has visualized the domestic horror of the process that led to extermination camps, is seduced by beauty. He revels in the joy of his subjects. Home movies are a medium of joy, and he wants us to feel that with his subjects. The movie camera comes out for the vacation, for the new baby, for the first snow of the winter, as if the ephemerality of those moments commanded us to record them, to capture them. Or is it that the sight of the camera triggers a certain glee—a universal commandment to smile and find the Esperanto for "Cheese!" The Peerebooms seem incredibly *happy*, full of a life force. Here they are skipping, even dancing, down the street. (Forgács seems to delight in the sight of large, encumbered bodies leaping through space with joy. His short films around Wittgenstein's *Tractatus* return to this kind of image.) And then we see the clan on the beach leapfrogging one over the other. The comic failures of Mama are a total success as Peerebooms tumble to the sand. It is 1934. For the rest of the decade we see them building families, houses, businesses. The vacation in Paris in 1939 would be the last trip abroad. And watching their ferocious play in the snow makes us feel how alive they were. It is the winter of 1940.

The problem of particularity—although evident in relation to beauty—can be seen in an especially acute way in regard to trauma. The modern concept of trauma points to an occurrence that both demands representation and refuses to be represented. The intensity of the occurrence seems to make it impossible to remember or to forget. The traumatic event, Freud wrote, is "unfinished," it appears to the individual as "an immediate task which has not been dealt with." Contemporary psychiatry tends to define trauma as an event that overwhelms one's perceptual-cognitive faculties, creating a situation in which the individual does not really experience the event as it happens. This may be why victims often describe themselves as spectators of their own trauma. In any case, the traumatic occurrence is not remembered normally because it was not registered through the standard neuro-chemical networks. The lack of a reliable memory of the trauma is felt by many as a gaping absence, sometimes filled by flashbacks or other symptoms. Yet the occurrence was too intense to be forgotten; it requires some form of re-presentation.

The intensity which makes forgetting impossible also makes any specific form of recollection seem inadequate. The traumatic event is too terrible for words, too horrifying to be integrated into our schemes for making sense of the world. Yet any representation of the trauma may have to rely on words and will be limited by the very schemes that were initially overwhelmed. A "successful" representation (a representation that others understand) of trauma will necessarily seem like trivialization, or worse, like betrayal. The intensity of a trauma is what defies understanding, and so a representation that someone else understands seems to indicate that the event wasn't as intense as it seemed to be. No direct speech is possible.

If we ignore the traumatic event (if we try to leave it alone), we seem to have neglected a moral obligation to come to terms with horror and pain. If we understand the traumatic event by putting it in relation to other events (if we try to make it a part of our history), we seem to be forgetting the intensity that engendered the obligation in the first place. This, then, is the problem of particularity: you can't leave it alone, but it does not abide company.

Perhaps it is already clear how particularity is a problem for history in general, and for translating home movies into historical or aesthetic objects in particular. The American historian Robert Dawidoff has talked about this in terms of the resistance we have against seeing something we love become *merely* history because this means it gets swept up with all sorts of things that reduce its distinctness for us. There is a tension between the clarity of vision of the particular artifact and the comprehension that comes through establishing interrelationships. To treat something as historical means at the very least to connect it via chronology to events before or after. *The Maelstrom* is punctuated by dates; the chronicle extends a bridge between private and political history. The singular, disconnected phenomenon cannot be historical because its entrance into the historical record requires a kind of contextualization that denies singularity. Thus, when we try to historicize an event that is dear to us because of its intensity, we necessarily reduce its singularity. As Carl Schorske has noted in his introduction to *Thinking With History*: "thinking with history . . . relativizes the subject, whether personal or collective, self-reflexively to the flow of social time." Making something "history" means making it part of something else, or placing it in relation to something else. That is why there can be no unique historical events (except in a trivial sense in which everything is unique).

There has been an effort to adopt a religious or sacralizing attitude vis à vis certain extreme events, which is in part an effort to keep a distance between them and the run-of-the-mill occurrences that we remember or write about as history. We can understand these efforts as attempts to prevent a catastrophic event from becoming "merely historical," that is, something that fits easily into the narratives we tell about the past. But the efforts can backfire, creating an easy target for those who would confuse our caring about particular events with a refusal to pay attention to others. This, obviously, has been one of the sources of debate about how to understand the holocaust historically. To do so means necessarily to understand it comparatively. Comparison can feel like a mode of erasure; but it can also be a mode of memory and sustained attention.

III

Forgács introduces a mode of comparison into *The Maelstrom* that is both delicate and extreme. The Peerebooms are not the only family pictured in the film. He also takes us—very briefly—into the world of the Seyss-Inquarts. The paterfamilias is the Reich Commissioner for Holland in 1940. Forgács has prepared us to meet this family by showing us earlier clips from amateur film of a Nazi youth group in Holland in 1935, and by voice-overs that announce

Hitler's welcome in Vienna in 1938 and the attack on Western Europe in 1940. In two of the rare instances in the film where sound is synchronized with image, a baby's cry is heard as we see an infant shriek. A carnival booth's target shooting suddenly erupts in an audible shot. We hear the "Sieg Heil!" as we watch a child walk down the street.

The Seyss-Inquart clan has its own home movies. We see them at more restrained forms of play—riding, or tennis with the Himmlers. And when we see the private life of the Reich Commissioner, we hear about new laws affecting Jews: stopping the production of kosher meats (the humanitarian gesture of anesthetizing warm-blooded animals); forcing Jews to put their funds in special accounts; creating a ghetto in Amsterdam for all Dutch Jews. Meanwhile, we all know that time is running out for the Peerebooms. It is so hard to tell from these glimpses into their lives whether they realize it as well. Here the viewer becomes more sharply aware of a tension that has existed from the very beginning of the film: we have knowledge of history (of *their* history) that the families in the film lack. Did they feel the maelstrom pulling them? Did they feel themselves being reconfigured by its force? One reason it is difficult to answer such questions is that home movies have a logic of their own. Their powerful conventions (*Over here, SMILE!*) make the problem all the more acute. Home movies have a strong imperative to show something positive: they are something you will want to look back on; they are meant to be a *nostodisiac*, a stimulant of nostalgia. We see the Seyss-Inquart grandchild playing while she eats; we see the Peerebooms again on vacation—this time just on the roof in the ghetto, no longer at the beach or in Paris. Images of happiness . . . colliding in history.

Forgács introduces another kind of film clip into *The Maelstrom*: chilling, clandestine recordings of Jews being led from their homes. These are not family chronicles but historical documents. We have entered the 1940s and Nazi domination. Family members Louis and Nico have already died in Mauthausen when Jews are forbidden to appear in public in 1941. The home movie cameras continue to record: the Nazi official's grandchild giving a kiss, the new baby born to Max and Annie, named, as an act of resistance or hope, Jacques Franklin. It is late 1941 when they record what would be their last lighting of the Hanukkah candles. The following fall they film themselves preparing to leave for a "workcamp" in Germany. As throughout the film, we know better. We see the pull downward, even as we watch the women sew for the trip. Max, Annie, the children, Flora and Jacques Franklin are going to die in Auschwitz. The home movie records the women sewing as if they were preparing for another vacation, another event to be remembered in the family chronicle. But can there be a family to look back on these events? From where do *we* watch and remember?

The only survivor of the Peereboom family is the youngest of the siblings, Simon. We have seen him throughout the film, playing the role of the baby, the jester, the wise guy. As a youngster, he is trying to look tough, cool, and we laugh as he blows cigarette smoke at the camera. As the film and family near their awful conclusion, in the month after Max, Annie, and the children are deported, Simon, the wise guy, marries—we don't know whether it was in defiance, for survival, or for love. But he does survive, and he returns to Holland. In discussions of the making of *The Maelstrom*, Forgács reported that a postwar chance encounter led Simon to the family films. Walking down the street one day, Simon bumped into Chris, the non-Jew who worked in the family shop. Chris had buried Max's home movies. They, too, survived the war. The most banal images you might imagine had now become a buried time capsule from another world.

Forgács is fond of quoting and responding to Wittgenstein, that great philosopher of the ordinary. In describing why he makes films from found footage, the director cites the *Tractatus*: "Everything we see / could be otherwise. / Everything we can describe at all / could be also otherwise." This resonates nicely with the fragility of Simon's survival, of the film's survival, and of the montage that is *The Maelstrom*. But there is another ingredient in Forgács's work that is not captured in the philosopher's aphorism. When the figures run to the floodwall, they know that the waves will return. They must return. When we watch the Peerebooms go about their lives as Jews in the years of Nazism, *we* know they will confront death in ways *they* could never have conceived. We who live on the other side of that war have passed beyond contingency, beyond "it could be otherwise"; we look back with knowledge of a destiny we can never unlearn.

Forgács's films balance the feeling of contingency and ephemerality with the feeling of fate and necessity. We approach the maelstrom or the floodwall of our recent history wanting to have a closer look but knowing the horror beneath those swells. This was a horror, a history that was never recorded in Max's films of the lusty lives of his family. It may be a horror that Peter Forgács's films can provoke in us, but it was one that, perhaps until near the end, the Peerebooms were spared.

16. Graves of the Insane, Decorated

For Death must be somewhere in a society; if it is no longer (or less intensely) in religion, it must be elsewhere; perhaps in this image which produces Death while trying to preserve life.

ROLAND BARTHES, *Camera Lucida*

Photography allowed the return of what had come before—and with it the prophecy of future returns. Whatever its nominal subject, photography was a visual inscription of the passing of time and therefore also an intimation of every viewer's own inevitable passing.

GEOFFREY BATCHEN, *Each Wild Idea*

Where Do the Mad Go?

Now we see them on the street corners of our cities, on the ramps to our highways, sleeping in the parks. But do they choose to be there? Are they mad? Now we know that the insane make up a significant part of our prison populations. But how do we know when a person in prison is insane? Now we know that mental illnesses are diseases for which we can seek cures. But what do we know about where the mad go? Do we know where madness brings them?[1]

In the early 1960s, when the forces of imagination and fantasy were turning against the triumphs and catastrophes of reason and civilization, there was a resurgence of interest in madness, and in how we treat the insane. It may not be an exaggeration to say that, whenever progress gets called into question in some deep way, the *alternative* of madness receives renewed attention. But for whom is madness an alternative?

Before the onset of modernity, you might have found the madman on the streets of the village; you might have turned to him for special insights or even prophecy. The crazy person was there among us, sometimes shouting, sometimes in his own world; but we could see him, so to speak, up close. As notions of reason and normality become more prominent, as we become more civilized, the madman loses his place among us. He is a threat to normality, and so he now must exist outside of the spaces that we enter and leave freely. He must be confined; perhaps he can be helped. Even when we see the "homeless person" raving on the urban street corner, we often feel we should not look or listen too closely. If we see the madman today, we are no longer merely gazing across the street; we are looking across a border to another world, another way of being. What is our relationship to that world?

In earlier times we were encouraged to look. In the eighteenth and nineteenth centuries visits to view the insane in their confinement could be a nice weekend outing. As Michel Foucault and others have pointed out, to look at the mad in their asylums, and later in their hospitals, was a way of shoring up a sense of normality and of reason. They were not we. We could visit the places of the mad, but they were no longer close to home. We could leave the places of the mad and know that these were not the places to which we belonged. They were in, after all, their own worlds. And we, in ours.

In America in the late nineteenth century, asylums for the insane were being built across the land. As Carla Yanni makes clear in her book *The Architecture of Madness*, the institutions that were conceived in the middle of the nineteenth century were bound up with the ideology of progress prevalent in much of the West.[2] Asylums were to house an effective treatment of insanity, techniques for bringing the "alienated" person back to him or herself. In the 1840s Dr. Thomas Kirkbride became superintendent of the Pennsylvania Hospital for the Insane, and over the next decades influenced the construction of asylums around the country. Kirkbride designed hospitals to be part of the treatment, helping patients find their way back to sanity. This was curative architecture, designed to foster normality inside the walls, and to make a statement of the value of civilization to the outside world.

The modern asylum conceived in the nineteenth century had grown in size and visibility. It seems that with the increased visibility of the asylum came a greater social acceptance of committing a relative to its care. Some historians, like Andrew Scull, have argued that in economies increasingly focused on productivity, there was no longer a place at home for the crazy relative who couldn't pull his or her weight. Others, like Roy Porter, point to the increasing array of services available to deal with marginal cases. In an ever-more civilized society, asylums were there to treat, to correct, those on the margins. They were part of the growing service economy. The nineteenth-century asylum was not just a safe place, as its name implied. Nor was it a warehouse of the ill, as one came to call mental hospitals in the mid-twentieth century. The nineteenth-century asylum was to be a place of cure, a place for what was called the "moral treatment" of the insane. The moral treatment posited that through proper care and proper surroundings a person could return to himself, to his moral, rational self. The key was to provide the patient with vehicles to overcome his mental alienation: exercise, routine, conversation, diet. These were some of the paths to which physicians could steer those in their charge.

In the middle of the nineteenth century, common wisdom among doctors was that the insane person had to be taken away from the family, and that the person had to live in a highly structured environment with access to nature as well as to physicians. Problems became apparent when it became obvious how difficult it was to cure certain patients, now to be called "inmates" when they were "committed" to official care by relatives or by the authorities. Inmates were not just being treated at a hospital; they were forcibly *confined* in an asylum. When they tried to escape, there were officers of the state to bring them back against their will. After all, the will of the insane person was the core of the disease; mad people were incapable of freedom because of their madness, and thus confining them was not really taking away their freedom. Fathers were committed to the care of asylums by sons who wanted control of the property. Wives were committed to the care of asylums by their husbands, or perhaps escaped abusive husbands by becoming mad.

A key term emerges by the 1870s to describe the recalcitrant cases: *incurable*. The incurably insane had to be separated from the less volatile, more socially acceptable mentally ill. The asylum had to house the incurable while it was charged with transforming the merely ill. Thus, it had its sinister as well as benevolent sides. As cultural pessimism becomes more pronounced in many parts of the United States in the mid-1870s, pessimism about the possibilities of an effective moral treatment of the insane also grows. By the turn of the century, insanity seems to have been a very broad category, and many public asylums become places of custodial rather than therapeutic care for people who just couldn't fit in. In other words, once confined within the asylum's walls, it was increasingly difficult to leave.

The Oregon State Insane Asylum opened in 1883 on a hill just east of Salem, not far from the penitentiary. A few hundred men and women would soon be transferred there, "representing almost every known stage or degrees of insanity, idiocy, imbecility or helplessness."[3] At Oregon State, like other large asylums, the physical health of many of the patients was precarious, and within a short time arrangements had to be made in an annex to a nearby cemetery for the burial of deceased patients. Among the first to be interred there was Lizzie Hazelton of Umatilla County, and afterward there would be more than fifteen hundred other burials in what would be called the Asylum Cemetery.

The Asylum would become the Oregon State Hospital in 1913, and expansion plans were in the works. From its inception, the asylum/hospital was to have been as self-sufficient as possible. There was an asylum farm, and an asylum blacksmith, a carpenter, and a gardener. The community needed its own cemetery, but in 1913 the burial land was identified as a site for a new building, and so the state had the bodies exhumed and cremated with unclaimed remains stored in the basement of the hospital. Afterward, cremation seems to have become the rule at the state hospital. The crematorium was on site, within yards of the wards. It may well have been that patients at the asylum helped to staff the facility, and the incinerator was named "Steiner's Chimney" in honor of the superintendent of the asylum who had it built in 1910. Sometimes remains were claimed by family members; sometimes they were stored in the basement in individual copper canisters. The canisters were labeled with ID numbers or names, in case family members did make inquiries. In the 1970s the hospital created an underground memorial vault where the canisters were to be more suitably buried. A plaque was created to mark the site as a memorial. Unfortunately, the vault was repeatedly flooded, and the canisters, ever more corroded but still stubbornly persistent as objects, as reminders, were returned to a storage building on the hospital grounds. This is where David Maisel found them and photographed them.

Where Do the Dead Go?

The Age of Enlightenment, when men of reason attempted to gain a distanced, objective view of madness, was also a period when Western attitudes toward death were undergoing an important transformation. As various historians have noted, a modern practice of caring for the dead, of memorializing them, developed in the late eighteenth and nineteenth centuries. The most succinct description of this change might be to say that the cemetery replaced the churchyard. When the dead were buried in the local churchyard, they were in the center of town. They, like the church, were part of the fabric of daily existence. In the eighteenth century a quasi-scientific discourse emerges that calls this ancient practice into question. How crowded can the crypts become? More importantly, as concerns for public hygiene increasingly become part of Enlightenment scientific and governmental discourse, people begin to ask whether it is sanitary for the living to be so close to the dead.

We should not imagine that scientifically minded people suddenly discovered new facts about death that led them to change burial habits. Instead, as the historian Thomas Laqueur has noted, we should recognize that in the emerging middle-class view of hygiene and order, new modalities of civic community and segregation were developing that would allow for a re-placement of the dead. They would be placed outside of daily life, in the modern cemetery, much like the mad would be placed in the modern asylums. Indeed, Laqueur notes a mid-nineteenth century reference to the cemeteries as "Asylums for the Dead."[4]

For eighteenth-century writers the decaying dead body became an object of fear and fascination. It was thought to give off "putrid exhaltations" that were injurious to those who might come in contact with the smell. Although doctors at the time disputed these tales, the public health discourse of the growing state bureaucracies won out. The dead would have their own cities, and the emphasis there would not be on bodily decay but on living memory. The cemeteries were to be "memorial parks," spaces to recall loved ones without contact with anything that might remind us of their physical remains. Pastoral settings, memorial sculpture, and cemetery professionals would mediate between the dead and those that would come to pay them visits. In increasingly secular societies, in which traditional recourse to religious beliefs in an afterlife had become contentious, cemeteries became vehicles for distancing the physicality of death while promoting a culture of remembrance.

With the development of penitentiaries and asylums, and with the increasing secularization of society, institutional cemeteries become a fact of life in the nineteenth century. Cemeteries are not places of worship but places of remembrance. The people who wind up being buried behind the prison, though, or next to the asylum are people who go "unclaimed." People who are "unremembered." Sometimes the desire to forget someone in a family will lead to a later, more active attempt at recollection. That's what happened with Ben Tabler, who in his retirement moved back to Oregon and traced the destiny of his paternal grandmother, a family member who had remained shrouded in mystery during his childhood. Tabler discovered that she died at the Oregon Asylum in 1903. Learning that her remains were among the copper canisters, he took steps to "bring her home." He's been foiled by the passage of time. Though he has the number that should be on the canister, so far the hospital can't find it.[5]

Remains and Remembrance

We are all, of course, defeated by the passage of time. When bodies were interred in the churchyard, there was no sense that one had a "personal grave." Bodies were treated like compost, and they had to be shoved around to make room as best one could for newly deceased members of the community. In the modern culture of remembrance that grew up in the memorial parks of the nineteenth century, it became important to visit a person's individual grave, or at least to know that the person had her own final resting place. Individualism was supposed to persist even after death, although belief in the afterlife for a personal soul was waning. In the early years of its development, photography was enlisted in this culture of individual remembrance. In the late nineteenth century, photographs of the recently deceased were a commonplace tool to recollect the dead. When the body was laid out, the photographer would be called to create an image of arrested decay. More aggressive photographers claimed to be able to capture the images of departed loved ones from beyond the grave. They claimed to photograph memories of the deceased, or their powerful auras that still glowed around the bereaved. Spirit photography—images of ghosts—attempted to show that photography could not only stop time, but that it could reach into the eternal. These efforts all have in common the faith that photography made the ephemeral material, and that the process of capturing light reflected off a body was a way of preserving that body over time.[6]

The literal connections of photography to death and to ghosts became the seeds for twentieth-century reflections on photography's theoretical (or simply metaphorical) connections to death and memory. From Walter Benjamin's reflections on Eugène Atget's photographs of a disappearing Parisian cityscape to Susan Sontag's claim that every photograph is a *momento mori*, philosophers and critics have focused on the medium's connections with mortality.

Writing in the 1950s, André Bazin noted: "photography does not create eternity, as art does, it embalms time, rescuing it simply from its proper corruption." It is this "proper corruption" that is unavoidable in Maisel's photographs from the Asylum's crematorium. His images are vibrant and alive with color and detail, but they are picturing death. The copper canisters contain cremated remains that are a trace of another time. Copper ages, it corrodes and turns colors. It records, in its own way, the passage of time, what Bazin called "proper corruption." Maisel's images recall the necessity of decay and the fact of death, even as they can be said to "embalm time."

The unclaimed remains at the Oregon State Hospital are an affront to the notions of individualism and remembrance that have developed in the modern age. Most of the labels that were affixed to the canisters are long gone. The copper is stamped with a number, but many of the numbered labels are no longer legible, and some even repeat. We can never know "who" is inside. That's why Ben Tabler can't "bring his grandmother home." The remains can only be distinguished by the corrosion of their containers—the marks of time.

It is tempting to compare the illegibility of these containers to the unreadability of hospital. The Kirkbrade structure was supposed to bespeak rationality and cure, but asylums came to signify incarceration, hopelessness, and the loss of freedom. Indeed, the Oregon Asylum was the site for the filming of *One Flew Over the Cuckoo's Nest* (1975), which took the mental hospital as a metaphor for the imposition of authority on free spirits more generally. No longer a place for visiting the mad from a position of normality, the mental hospital in the second half of the twentieth century became for many a place of fear, the "snake pit" for unfortunates who lost control of reason, of memory, and who hence lost their freedom. For others, the mental hospital became a metaphor for society's frenzy to normalize everyone; one could see the insane as rebels against the tyranny of rationality and the civilizing process (as long as one neglected their all-too-real suffering).

David Maisel's photographs bring us up short because they remind us of the desire for recollecting the individual, for remembering the dead. But the photographs offer this reminder in a context of the obliteration of individuality, in the context of the insane and their asylums. The pictures are strikingly beautiful, and yet we don't want to be seduced by their colors, their biomorphic forms, their arresting clarity. These are, after all, photographs of death, of the failure of remembrance and of the persistence of the unclaimed. But through the dramatic reversal that is at the core of photography's power, these images of the unclaimed provide their own form of recognition, perform their own work of memorialization. We may not be able to recover the destiny of each individual, or find the traces of their descendants. But the photographs make a claim for the importance of remembrance within the context of a community. The persistence of the remains, now recorded, becomes an expression of our desire not to forget even as they remind us of the inevitability of corrosion. Our memories do disappear, but we can recollect that very fact about memory and learn to live with its necessary relation to forgetting. We can reclaim the past without trying to preserve it from inevitable forms of forgetting, from proper corruption.

On June 3, 1886, the *Daily Oregon Statesman* printed the following notice:

> **Graves of the Insane, Decorated**—On decoration day, the little inmates of the orphan's home, under the supervision of their matron, gathered a lot of wild flowers, and decorated the graves of the insane dead, who have been buried in the asylum field adjoining the Lee Mission cemetery. The deed was a worthy one, and to the little ones is due a great deal of credit for doing this act of mercy to the unfriended dead.

Decoration Day, now called Memorial Day, began after the Civil War as a time to honor those who were killed fighting to preserve the Union. "Decoration" in this context meant to confer a distinction, to recognize or acknowledge. The "little ones," who must have known something about being unclaimed, were conferring distinction upon, acknowledging, the insane dead. They were making a claim, even if it was as transitory as wild flowers.

David Maisel's project also makes a claim, reminding us of forgetting, of corrosion and oblivion, while also recollecting the unfriended. His photographs recognize the dead, even though the images cannot resurrect their individuality. His "visual inscription of the passing of time" is an act of decoration and acknowledgment; his deed, a worthy one.

CODA

RISKS AND LIMITS OF LIBERAL EDUCATION

17. On a Certain Blindness in Teaching

Wherever a process of life communicates an eagerness to him who lives it, there the life becomes genuine and significant.

WILLIAM JAMES

"*By Christmas I will be in the hospital.*" Those are the words I remember best. They bespoke a knowledge that was frightening. She said them with certainty and with urgency. "*By Christmas I will be in the hospital. This has happened before. I can feel it coming.*" She stared at me intently. "OK, *what happens now that he* KNOWS. *What changes, what remains the same? What will he do with this knowledge?*" What did I say? I recall some lame questions such as "Are you getting some help?" and "What kind of medication are you taking?" Perhaps they were not so lame as they felt to me at the time. Perhaps they allowed her to continue speaking what she knew and confessing what she did not. In any case, she went on in some detail about her experience with manic-depression (was it yet labeled bipolar syndrome?). The mental hospitals, the recovery, and the fall back into normality . . . the slipping away of that recovery and the excitement and terrifying qualities of that slipping away.

Her name was Eve. Eve was very ill when I encountered her in my first year of teaching, though it took me quite some time before I realized this. Her aggression in the classroom was, I imagined, like that which one might find among some intelligent people somewhat bored by school, and very frustrated with the decorum of the seminar situation. I had known lots of students like this, so I thought, in my own undergraduate years. She acted out a lot; she disrupted class and then made up for it with incisive or witty remarks. One week she would not complete assignments, and then in another class she would overwhelm the seminar with the quality and depth of her work. She also changed appearance radically during the course of the semester, gaining formidable amounts of weight and then losing much more than she had put on. Eve made her presence felt, but it was very unclear to any of us in the class how we were to acknowledge that presence.

How did I cope with this provocative participation? Rather typically, I think: I rewarded her contributions and punished (with grades, with cutting remarks) her disruptions. It was a serious seminar on "History and Fiction in the Nineteenth Century," and I was a very young professor (still in my twenties). We tried to wrestle with questions about how one represents the truth, and with how some decisive nineteenth-century texts developed strategies for responding to historical changes through new ideas about truth and its representation. What counts as true in different contexts? How do we respond to different modes of truth telling and how are these responses mediated by our own histories? How is the attempt to recount the truth mediated by history, and how is our understanding of history mediated by our notions of truth?

By Christmas I will be in the hospital. What counts as true in this context? How was I to respond to this unusually frank and fearfully confident mode of truth telling? I suppose I could have changed the mode in which I had been responding to this student. Like many of my colleagues seem to do when undergraduates express the desire to no longer be a student, I might have adopted the role of counselor, friend, or confidant. These roles might have been helpful to Eve, and they might have established the kind of relationship she was looking for. But I did not move in these directions; I remained the teacher. But what knowledge could we explore that would be able to stand up to her own certainty and fear? What subject could we discuss that would have something to do with what was clearly the most pressing issue for Eve: *By Christmas I will be in the hospital.*

By the time Eve had started the seminar, she had already developed an enthusiastic interest in Nietzsche. His writings drew her like a magnet, and she hungered for more time with his texts and more guidance in reading them. Our seminar was already planning to read *The Genealogy of Morals*, and I suggested that we meet weekly for a supplementary discussion of *Thus Spoke Zarathustra*. We read slowly and puzzled out some of the important issues together; or, rather, I should say that she fought her way to clarity about some particularly powerful passages. Zarathustra has to descend very far before he can return and before he understands what it means to overcome. Overcoming is never separated from repetition in Nietzsche's work, and perhaps this was part of what attracted Eve to his philosophy. She wrote a splendid paper at the end of term and was really pleased with herself, full of pride and achievement. I still vividly remember her gleeful shouts when she received her grade and comments. She did not return the next semester. She was in the hospital by Christmas.

Carol never said much in class, and when she did nobody quite knew what to make of her remarks. She seemed not all that interested in the material for the seminar, a course called "History, Memory, and Desire" in which we read texts from Jean-Jacques Rousseau to Toni Morrison on questions of recollection, truth, narrative, and loss. We were reading Roland Barthes's book *Camera Lucida*, an essay on photography, on representing the past, and on living on after the death of his mother. This is a text, I thought, that twenty-year-old students would have a lot of trouble with. Barthes meditates on how we use photography to cope with loss in life, and with how photography changes what it means to cope. Most of my students in sunny southern California did not seem to me marked by loss, and I wondered if this was a book that just wouldn't speak to them.

I had asked the students to each bring in a photograph that was important to him or her (almost all the students were women). We were to analyze these pictures with the phenomenological categories that Barthes makes use of early in his essay. The discussion was excellent. We were all interested in seeing the pictures, and also in hearing about who had what kind of pictures near to their beds, their desks, their phones. One woman spoke shyly and with an air of semiembarrassment as she talked about a photograph of her grandmother she kept near to the place she worked. One of the men in the class used Barthes's categories to analyze pictures of an old girlfriend, and of his father. Carol raised her hand to speak. She did not have a photograph with her, she explained, but she would like to tell us about one. There were two, really. The first was taken in the spring in her family's backyard. The trees were in bloom, her siblings were smiling. They were a family, a family all together. She explained that this was pretty special since her truck-driver father was not there much of the time. The next picture was (she laughed softly, nervously as she said this) taken almost in the same spot (she emphasized these words as if *that* was the remarkable aspect of these pictures) in her mother's backyard. But her father was not there. We could all hear the difficulty she was having in keeping her voice on the pitch of the carefree young girl that she was so adept at adopting in class. You see, she tearfully explained, her father had left the family, her parents were split now. She tried hard to smile, "*Sorry, it was just that those photos occurred to me*," she said as if she needed to excuse herself, "*when we all started talking about photography and loss.*" She had lost her father and, in a way, her family. "*Funny,*" she said, "*there were no flowers in the second picture.*"

Now she was looking to me for help. OK, I've said much more than I wanted to, much more than I've ever said before in a public situation. Help! I looked around the room, trying myself to regain control. Carol had clearly said something they all understood, and she had said it in such a way as to pass beyond the conventional emotional content of classroom interventions. And now the students (including Carol) were looking to me to be the teacher, to make it possible to go on as a class. Could it be done while acknowledging the steps Carol just took, or was "going on as a class" dependent on our losing the real force of Carol's narrative of loss?

While meeting to discuss a recent conference on feminism in the 1990s, a group of my students (in this group, all women) began to talk about their feelings of solidarity with other women. The Asian American and African American women were talking about how they felt more comfortable with other women of color when there was a political crisis on campus or in the region. The white women (who were a minority in this class) nodded affirmingly, but one of them, Beth, asked with real intensity: "*Are Jews white?*" I was struck by the force of this question. What was she asking? As I thought about the query and the puzzled response to it, it seemed to me that Beth wanted to know if she was to be allowed into the circle of solidarity; if being a Jew was enough to gain her access to those who believed they "knew how it felt to be oppressed."

One of the issues at stake in Beth's question was what it meant to claim a legacy of oppression and who was entitled to do so. Why would one want to make such a claim? The students were saying that this enabled them to connect with others who would understand them and on whom they could count. Claiming a legacy of oppression thus established what moral philosophers like to call a "we-group," people with whom one identifies and with whom one feels connected. Establishing a "we-group" can be a source of comfort, of defense, and of pleasure. In this regard my students reminded me of my parents, who, when traveling anywhere would immediately search out a "Landsman" with whom they could sit, eat, or kibitz. These people were no longer perfect strangers. When Beth asked "Are Jews white?" she was asking the others if they considered her a stranger. She wanted into the group, and claiming a Jewish legacy might have been just the ticket.

There are many ways to discuss the politics of education in the United States today. Indeed, participating in these discussions (in blogs, on panels, at faculty meetings) have for many taken the place of both serious scholarship and genuine inquiry. Instead, we see well-worn ideological positions refurbished with a university coating. The results are predictable and marketable. Current debates about the canon (canons), about diversity, and about freedom of inquiry and expression are not responses to the so-called politicization of the university but attempts to steer education in particular political directions. Who should be served by the university and how? This would be an important question to pursue, but do we even have the intellectual tools to do so now? Where would we begin?

In the current debates about the lost soul of American politics, "political education" usually means a politicized or ideological education, one based more on prejudice than on reason or facts. This discourse about the university is blind to the necessity and desirability of political education. Citizens are not born, they are made, and education in being political is crucial for a healthy democracy. Universities, to be sure, have only a very small role to play in an individual's political formation, and their place in the polity's development of an active citizenry is limited. But they can have an important political function for those who work within them. How can we ensure that this function fosters democratic political education rather than political corruption? Perhaps my three narratives can help us reflect on this question.

The first two stories evince the attempt to carve out a space in which education takes place. This is not exactly a separate, disconnected space, but it is a protected one. When Eve told me that she knew she would be in the hospital before Christmas she was trying (at least in part) to break that space. *How are we going to talk seriously about Flaubert, Michelet, and Marx when it is clear that I am sinking into madness? How can you go on teaching about representing the truth when I have stopped taking the drugs that might keep me from falling apart?* I imagine that almost every teacher hears this question in some form: *What can you possibly have to teach ME?*

Reading Nietzsche with Eve was in no way an attempt "to deal with her problems," if by "problems" we mean her manic-depression. But it was not a denial of her fears about this condition, nor was it an escape from her questions about why she was sinking into a pit she knew and detested. (This was an aspect of Eve's knowing that I found most disturbing. She could see where she was going, but seeing it made no difference in her capacity to change. And her incapacity to change did not block—at least at this moment—her lucidity.)

Nietzsche provided us with a language, a rich, complex network of issues to which Eve could connect herself but which did not merely reflect her own, immediate personal concerns. There came a time, I later learned, when Eve could no longer speak a language that anyone else could understand. But for a few months, reading Nietzsche allowed us to think together about issues that were of vital importance to her in a way that was open to others. Reading together provided a *mediation* of the personal into the public. Finding one's issues acknowledged in some public way (even if the representative of the public is a notoriously antidemocratic philosopher or merely a teacher in an independent study) is to experience an aspect of the mediation of politics, and perhaps of the attraction of democracy. Finding one's issues acknowledged in some public way is also to experience a crucial aspect of education. (Is it necessary to say that this finding, this acknowledgment, is only a beginning of politics, only an aspect of education?) Of course, acknowledgment alone does not solve problems; public recognition is not a substitute for power or for knowledge. There were moments when I believed that our discussions were going to make an important difference in Eve's battle to stay afloat. That was a mistake, or rather it turned out to be a mistake.

Carol's declaration in class about her family pressured the boundaries of the "public way" we had adopted in the seminar. Was she allowed to talk this way in class, was she allowed to appear this way to her fellow students and her teacher? When Carol and the other students looked to me to reestablish the class after she had said her piece, I'd like to think that what they were looking to me for was mediation. Was there a way of acknowledging what she said while still continuing with the task at hand: the understanding of the representation of the past on film, especially as Barthes had conceptualized it? Obviously, there is no formula for doing this. One wants to provide the student(s) with the sense that their concerns count in the public context of education, not that any particular student or students dictate the context of education. Barthes, too, throughout *Camera Lucida* is struggling to find a way to address his longing for his recently deceased mother, to use the language of understanding to speak his feelings of loss, and to use his feeling of loss to deepen his understanding. So to reestablish the class or the public dimension of the class, I only had to read Barthes's responses, his calls, back to Carol. She was surprised, I think, to realize that she was already in conversation with the text of this French poststructuralist.

Might this story be relevant to some debates about multiculturalism and diversity? What would happen to our curricula and our teaching if they were capable of responding to the issues and concerns of those students who feel outside of the conversation? Responding to these issues and concerns does not mean focusing the course on a specific politics of identity in order to meet a group's demands to be represented in the class. It means finding a way to enhance our students' capacities to read and think allegorically: to find in a particular set of issues an acknowledgment of their own deepest concerns. Barthes was not speaking directly about divorce nor Nietzsche about mental illness, but their texts could be read to respond to Carol and Eve. There is no formula for this kind of reading either, but it does seem that some of the claims being put forth for participation in education are calls for acknowledgment. For acknowledgment of this kind to take place, one has to want to be part of the conversation, and one has to want to expand the conversation. This will is often lacking on the different sides of recent debates about the university and politics, and without it there is no possibility of a more inclusive political education. An educational system in a democracy cannot afford to be blind to the efforts of citizens to enter and alter the conversation that comprises an important part of political education.

When Beth asked "Are Jews white?" she was clearly calling for acknowledgment. She wanted to be recognized as someone who also suffered from oppression, and thus as someone whom the other students would not consider a stranger. The students were talking about solidarity among women of color as a resource for fighting against social injustice. Their shared identities as victims of historical and ongoing oppression was both a tool for politics and a comfort in the face of continued victimization. How was one able to participate in this sharing in the service of changing the patterns of injustice? Was there a form of allegorical thinking that would enable these students to connect with one another without a racial or ethnic common marker?

In the past few years, claiming a legacy of oppression has come to be used not only as a tool to escape from cycles of oppression, but as a vehicle for maintaining one's connection to—even identification with—it. In attaching oneself to a legacy of oppression one may reach for a moral superiority that our culture often awards to victims (that it recognizes as such). This award of moral superiority is no real substitute for justice, but it can be a powerful balm in a world of continued economic, social, and political inequality. Universities and the media have become specialists in providing feelings of moral superiority to people instead of intelligent responses to demands for real social change. In these cultural arenas, officially sanctioned marginality has become a moral high ground, the latest opiate of the people. How can we know if Beth wanted solidarity as a badge of righteousness, or if instead solidarity was to be a "haven in a heartless world" or even a tool for political change?

In 1899, William James published *Talks to Teachers on Psychology: And to Students on Some of Life's Ideals.* The second of the talks to students is called "On a Certain Blindness in Human Beings." The blindness James refers to is our inability to see the values and meaning that other people attribute to their experience of the world (including their experience of us). We are external to one another: "The meanings are there for others, but they are not there for us." James tells of his own wandering in the hills of North Carolina, and his perception of the blight the settlers had brought to the land.

> The forest had been destroyed; and what had "improved" it out of existence was hideous, a sort of ulcer, without a single element of artificial grace to make up for the loss of Nature's beauty.
>
> "What sort of people are they who have to make these new clearings?" [James asked the "mountaineer" who was driving him].
>
> "All of us," he replied; "why, we ain't happy here unless we are getting one of those coves under cultivation." I instantly felt that I had been losing the whole inward significance of the situation. Because to me the clearings spoke of naught but denudation, I thought that to those whose sturdy arms and obedient axes had made them they could tell no other story. . . .
>
> I had been as blind to the particular ideality of their conditions as they certainly would also have been to the ideality of mine, had they had a peep at my strange indoor academic ways of life at Cambridge.

James talked to students about how people often are blind to one another, closed into their own world of experience, and only capable of (mis)translating the experiences of others into their own terms. He saw a recognition of this blindness as "the basis of all our tolerance, social, religious, political. The forgetting of it lies at the root of every stupid and sanguinary mistake that rulers over subject peoples make."

In his talk to students, James does not discuss how he came to recognize his own blindness, how he came to see how much he was missing. In teaching, we find ourselves blind in some of the same ways that James discussed. We also find ourselves in a position to overcome this blindness (in ourselves and in our students), or at least to recognize it in the public space of education.

For Eve, Nietzsche was the vehicle for recognition, for moving from private pain to a kind of public acknowledgment. For Carol, something about the seminar and about photography enabled her to represent her past to others, and to find that the other participants in the conversation were capable of responding to her as a member of the group. For Beth, there was a strong desire to see her fellow students overcome what she thought of as their blindness to her and her commonality with them. Can my experience count for you, and can you possibly see how it counts for me?

Teachers are in a privileged position to help others recognize the ways in which we all fail to see, pay attention to, and connect with the experiences of others. This is not only because we can give our attention to those groups and issues that have been underrepresented within academia, although this is often a significant task. We can teach students to make use of the levels of mediation provided by education, to think allegorically, and to try to puzzle out the diverse ways that people give significance to their lives. Forgetting the blindness of which James spoke remains a dangerous possibility in teaching, leading to solipsism and to dogmatism rather than to thinking. As teachers, we find ourselves (or should I say we *can* find ourselves) in a position to call attention to this blindness, to show how it works, whom it serves. Remembering to look for the "whole inward significance" of another's situation is a crucial dimension of any inquiry that takes us beyond the comfortable borders of our own we-groups. In crossing these borders we need not only confront strangers; we can also find people who desire acknowledgment and who are capable of returning recognition. In so doing, we can teach our students to become teachers of themselves and others, and to become citizens eager to understand those around them as they understand themselves. Although this is not the only kind of understanding that can be produced in the classroom, it is a crucial one for citizens in a democracy.

18. Beyond Critical Thinking

The antivocational reputation of the humanities has been a source of pride and embarrassment for generations. The persistence of this reputed uselessness is puzzling given the fact that an education in the humanities allows one to develop skills in reading, writing, reflection, and interpretation that are highly prized in our economy and culture. Sure, specific training in a discrete set of skills might prepare you for Day 1 of the worst job you'll ever have (your first), but the humanities teach elements of mind and heart that you will draw upon for decades of innovative and focused work. But we do teach a set of skills, or an attitude, in the humanities that may have more to do with our antipractical reputation than the antivocational notion of freedom embedded more generally in the liberal arts. This is the set of skills that usually goes under the rubric of critical thinking.

Although critical thinking first gained its current significance as a mode of interpretation and evaluation to guide beliefs and actions in the 1940s, the term took off in education circles after Robert H. Ennis published "A Concept of Critical Thinking" in the *Harvard Educational Review* in 1962. Ennis was interested in how we teach the "correct assessment of statements," and he offered an analysis of twelve aspects of this process, organized into three dimensions: logical, criterial, and pragmatic, all of which allowed one to assess the coherence, evidentiary soundness, and purpose of any particular claim. Ennis and countless educational theorists who have come after him have sung the praises of critical thinking. There is now a Foundation for Critical Thinking and an industry of consultants to help you enhance this capacity in your teachers, students, or yourself.

A common way to show that one has sharpened one's critical thinking is to display an ability to see through or undermine statements made by (or beliefs held by) others. Thus, our best students are really good at one aspect of critical thinking—being critical. For many students today, being smart *means* being critical. To be able to show that Hegel's concept of narrative foreclosed the non-European, or that Butler's stance on vulnerability contradicts her conception of performativity, or that some tenured professor failed to account for his own "privilege"—these are marks of sophistication, signs of one's ability to participate as a mature member of the academic tribe. But this participation, being entirely negative, is not only seriously unsatisfying; it is ultimately counterproductive.

The skill at unmasking error, or simple intellectual one-upmanship, is not completely without value, but we should be wary of creating a class of self-satisfied debunkers or, to use a currently fashionable word on campuses, people who like to "trouble" ideas. In overdeveloping the capacity to show how texts, institutions, or people fail to accomplish what they set out to do, we may be depriving students of the capacity to learn as much as possible from what they study. In a humanities culture in which being smart often means being a critical unmasker, our students may become too good at showing how things don't make sense. That very skill may diminish their capacity to find or create meaning and direction in the books they read and the world in which they live. Once outside the university, our students continue to score points by displaying the critical prowess for which they were rewarded in school. They wind up contributing to a cultural climate that has little tolerance for finding or making meaning, a culture whose intellectuals and cultural commentators delight in being able to show that somebody else is not to be believed.

I doubt that this is a particularly contemporary development. In the eighteenth century there were complaints about an Enlightenment culture that only prized skepticism and that was only satisfied with disbelief. Our contemporary version of this trend, though, has become skeptical even about skepticism. We no longer have the courage of our lack of conviction. Perhaps that's why we teach our students that it's cool to say that they are engaged in "troubling" an assumption or a belief. To declare that one wanted to disprove a view would show too much faith in the ability to tell truth from falsehood. And to declare that one was receptive to learning from someone else's view would show too much openness to being persuaded by an idea that might soon be deconstructed (or simply mocked).

In training our students in the techniques of being critical, we may be giving them reasons to remain guarded—which can translate into reasons not to learn. The confident refusal to be affected by those with whom we disagree seems to have infected much of our cultural life: from politics to the press, from siloed academic programs (no matter how multidisciplinary) to warring public intellectuals. As humanities teachers, however, we must find ways for our students to open themselves to the emotional and cognitive power of history and literature that might initially rub them the wrong way, or just seem foreign. Critical thinking is sterile without the capacity for empathy and comprehension that stretches the self.

One of the crucial tasks of the humanities should be to help students cultivate the willingness and ability to learn from material they might otherwise reject or ignore. This material will often surprise students and sometimes upset them. Students seem to have learned that teaching-evaluation committees take seriously the criticism that "the professor, or the material, made me uncomfortable." This complaint is so toxic because being made uncomfortable is a necessary component of an education in the humanities. Creating a humanistic culture that values the desire to learn from unexpected and uncomfortable sources as much as it values the critical faculties would be an important contribution to our academic and civic life.

But the contemporary humanities should do more than supplement critical thinking with empathy and a desire to understand others from their own point of view. We should also supplement our strong critical engagement with cultural and social norms by developing modes of teaching that allow our students to enter in the value-laden practices of a particular culture to understand better how these values are legitimated: how the values are lived as legitimate. Current thinking in the humanities is often strong at showing that values that are said to be shared are really imposed on more vulnerable members of a particular group. Current thinking in the humanities is also good at showing the contextualization of norms, whether the context is generated by an anthropological, historical, or other disciplinary matrix. But in both of these cases we ask our students to develop a critical distance from the context or culture they are studying.

Many humanities professors have become disinclined to investigate with our students how we generate the values we believe in, or the norms according to which we go about our lives. In other words, we have been less interested in showing how we make a norm legitimate than in sharpening our tools for delegitimization. The philosopher Robert Pippin has recently made a similar point, and has described how the sciences, particularly evolutionary biology and psychology, have moved into this terrain, explaining moral values as the product of the same dynamic that gives rise to the taste for sweets. Pippin argues, on the contrary, that "the practical autonomy of the normative is the proper terrain of the humanities," and he has an easy task of showing how the pseudoscientific evolutionary "explanation" of our moral choices is a pretty flimsy "just so" story.

If we humanities professors saw ourselves more often as explorers of the normative rather than as critics of normativity, we would have a better chance to reconnect our intellectual work to broader currents in public culture. This does not have to mean an acceptance of the status quo, but it does mean an effort to understand the practices of cultures (including our own) from the point of view of those participating in them. This would include an understanding of how cultures change. For some, this would mean complementing our literary or textual work with participation in community, with what are often called service-learning courses. For others, it would mean approaching our object of study not with the anticipated goal of exposing weakness or mystification but with the goal of turning ourselves in such a way as to see how what we study might inform our thinking and our lives.

I realize that I am arguing for a mode of humanistic education that many practice already. It is a mode that can take language very seriously, but rather than seeing it as the master mediator between us and the world, a matrix of representations always doomed to fail, it sees language as itself a cultural practice to be understood from the point of view of those using it.

The fact that language fails according to some impossible criterion, or that we often create misunderstandings in our use of it, is no news, really. It is part of our finitude, but it should not be taken as the key marker of our humanity. The news that *is* brought by the humanities is a way of turning the heart and the spirit so as to hear in the languages people use the possibilities of various forms of life in which we might participate. When we learn to read or look or listen intensively, we are not just becoming adept at exposing falsehood or at uncovering yet more examples of the duplicities of culture and society. We are partially overcoming our own blindness by trying to understand something from another's artistic, philosophical, or historical point of view. William James put it perfectly in a talk to teachers and students entitled "On a Certain Blindness in Human Beings": "The meanings are there for others, but they are not there for us." James saw the recognition of our blindness to one another as key to education as well as to the development of democracy and civil society. Of course hard-nosed critical thinking may help in this endeavor, but it also may be a way we learn to protect ourselves from the acknowledgment and insight that humanistic study has to offer. As students and as teachers, we sometimes crave that protection because without it we risk being open to changing who we are. In order to overcome this blindness, we risk being very uncomfortable indeed.

It is my hope that humanists will continue offering criticism, making connections, and finding ways to acknowledge practices that seem at first opaque or even invisible. In supporting a transition from critical thinking to practical exploration, I am echoing a comment made by my undergraduate philosophy teacher Louis Mink, and echoed by my graduate mentor, Richard Rorty. Years before Dick Rorty deconstructed the idea of the "philosopher as referee," Louis Mink suggested that critics "exchange the judge's wig for the guide's cap." I think we may say the same for humanists, who can, as he said in a lecture at Wesleyan's Center for the Humanities, "show us details and patterns and relations which we would not have seen or heard for ourselves."

My humanities teachers enriched my life by showing me details and pattern and relations. In so doing they also helped me to acquire tools that have energetically shaped my scholarship and my interactions with colleagues and students. It is my hope that as guides, not judges, we can show our students how to engage in the practice of exploring objects, norms, and values that animate diverse cultures. In doing so, students will develop the ability to converse with others about shaping the objects, norms, and values that will give substance and character to their own lives. They will develop the ability to add value to (and not merely criticize values in) whatever organizations in which they participate. They will often reject roads that others have taken, and they will sometimes chart new paths. But guided by the humanities they will increase their ability to find together ways of living that have meaning and direction, illuminating paths immensely practical and sustaining.

19. Good and Risky

On the Promise of a Liberal Education

On the very first page of her slim book *Not for Profit: Why Democracy Needs the Humanities*, philosopher Martha Nussbaum warns, "we are in a crisis of massive proportions and grave global significance."[1] She's not talking about a calamity caused by climate change, nor is she referring to nuclear proliferation, global poverty, or unchecked population growth. No, the worldwide crisis that frightens Nussbaum is the decline of a model of liberal education based on the arts and humanities. Although a liberal arts education has never been common in most of the world, she thinks that this decline puts contemporary industrial societies at risk of "producing generations of useful machines rather than complete citizens who can think for themselves" (2). On the final page of Diane Ravitch's book, *The Death and Life of the Great American School System*, the historian of education notes "at the present time public education is in peril. Efforts to reform public education are, ironically, diminishing its quality and endangering its very survival."[2]

Both Nussbaum and Ravitch see a crisis in education brought on in part by the emphasis on testing and corporate management techniques. For both, the crisis in our education systems is a crisis for our democracy. For several years now, Martha Nussbaum has been arguing for a mode of understanding human beings (and some other animals) that would emphasize holistic cultivation of diverse capacities. Critical of philosophical perspectives that pay attention to only one mode of understanding or to only a narrow band of cognition, she has advocated an approach to philosophy that takes emotion seriously, and an approach to understanding that is more open to literature and the arts than analytic philosophy has typically been. Diane Ravitch's career as a historian of education has taken her into the highest reaches of policy making. Having documented the failure of well-intentioned efforts at decentralization in the 1970s, she became an advocate for accountability and school choice during the Clinton and Bush administrations. Her new book, however, is severely critical of the methods of tracking school performance she once favored, and of the unintended consequences of forcing an ethos of consumer choice into the public realm of the local school.

Both *Not for Profit* and *Death and Life* argue that it is an educational and political disaster to continue the retreat from broad humanistic study in favor of rote learning that can be evaluated in multiple-choice tests. Although there are significant differences between the two authors' approaches to education, their rejection of the corporatization of learning allies them with the work of the cultural literacy advocate E. D. Hirsch. Ravitch and Hirsch have been strong critics of the Bush-era school reforms whose spirit of hollow but well-funded accountability persists in the Obama era. In *Death and Life* Ravitch shows in detail how efforts to save our public schools through market-based policies and supposedly data-driven decision making have succeeded only in further degrading our ability to offer a quality education to American youngsters. The "No Child Left Behind" emphasis on accountability was supposed to give states the ability to identify problems and address them in measurable ways, but instead it created a culture of strategizing for tests and of blaming teachers.

Ravitch had once supported opening school districts to market forces like parental choice and visible performance data, but now, like Nussbaum, she worries that these reforms have taken the joy and purpose out of learning. As Hirsch and others have pointed out, instead of giving students the opportunity to have strong emotional and cognitive encounters with well-told stories, we have drilled them into thinking that effective reading is a technique with measurable outcomes to be evaluated on standardized tests.

The antidote to rote learning and narrow skill building is the cultivation of curiosity through active learning. For Nussbaum this means a reflexive, Socratic pedagogy emphasizing the critical examination of oneself as well as what is taken for granted in the opinions of others. For Ravitch, it means developing a vision of broadly practical educational purpose and a curriculum "responsible for shaping character, developing sound minds in healthy bodies . . . and forming citizens for our democracy" (167). Hirsch opts for a more direct approach in identifying the knowledge base all citizens should have: "Giving everybody more knowledge makes everybody more competent, and creates a more just society. Since knowledge is the great equalizer, the schools have a huge opportunity and responsibility to provide more equal life chances for all students, no matter where they come from."[3]

Nussbaum's orientation is toward process rather than content, and she draws on the work of theorists like Froebel and Dewey who emphasized "children's own activity as the source of their learning" (60). Education creates autonomy, thus preparing citizens for political participation. This means learning to abandon passivity, as Dewey said, changing from a position of "inert recipiency and restraint to one of buoyant outgoing energy" (65). Hirsch is at the other end of the educational reform spectrum. He doesn't want to depend on the buoyant energy of children to dictate what the curriculum should look like; he wants us to reach some consensus on what we think it important for our compatriots to know. Ravitch agrees that standards with content are crucial for educational reform, and that a discussion of what we consider essential knowledge is healthy for our common culture.

Although Nussbaum, Ravitch, and Hirsch have very different views of what comprises a liberal education, they do agree that such an education is crucial for a polity of citizens rather than of subjects. The goal, both reflexive and pragmatic, is for students to become independent thinkers and autonomous subjects whose independence and autonomy are not compromised by interaction with others. Kant's notion of enlightenment as "emergence from self-imposed immaturity" suits their views very well. Education should prepare students to become citizens capable of civil disagreement. On the one hand, this purpose seems like common sense, but these days it also seems utopian given what passes for discourse in our decidedly uncivil public sphere.

Nussbaum's optimistic view of liberal education doesn't just aim to produce civility; it winds up having a specific political content. It seems fair to say that if we cultivate a Socratic spirit of argument and reflexive self-examination, the result will be better thinkers and citizens able to advance their own individual projects even as they contribute to progress toward the common good. But she goes on to claim that if we cultivate a rich experience of the arts, the result will be more men and women who are caring, who have the imagination to understand the dilemmas and opportunities of others and will therefore work to support more opportunity for everyone. A skeptic might sum up the argument this way: a good education based on the liberation of a child's capacity for action and an innate aversion to seeing others suffer just happens to produce people who resemble contemporary American liberals, people much like Martha Nussbaum herself. This is not, we are told, an education with the crass goal of producing individuals who can succeed economically; that's why her book is called "not for profit." This is not, we are told, an education focused on content. But this supposedly process-oriented education would in the United States produce individuals with political views that ensure that they will vote with the Center-Left section of the Democratic party.

Not all defenders of a broad education equate learning with developing cosmopolitan liberals exhibiting great sensitivity to suffering. Peter Berkowitz, writing on liberal education in the *Wall Street Journal*, bemoans the infringement of speech on university campuses stemming from a fear that one might offend a group on the lookout for insults to its identity. He has argued that "our students and faculty need to learn to be less sensitive. . . . The cultivation of sensitivity sharpens antennae for hurtful words and ideas, and encourages complaining whenever they sting."[4] For Berkowitz, politically correct sensitivity can be a weakness and not just a virtue. A senior fellow at Stanford's Hoover Institution, he thinks it essential that citizens study the great works of literature, philosophy, and religion, and that they acquire a sense of both the capacity and limitations of the sciences. Although he disagrees with Nussbaum about the type of citizen a liberal education produces, he does emphasize that such an education "represents the culmination of a citizen's preparation for freedom."

With regard to teaching art to produce the right kind of sensitivity, Nussbaum seems to realize that one will have to censor the content of the art that the students encounter: "The imaginative component of democratic education requires careful selectivity" (109). Indeed, she puts scare quotes around the word "literature" when she uses it to refer to those books that just don't teach the right kind of activity or play. Rousseau, an author she is fond of quoting, was also sensitive to this selectivity, but he was clear about the illusions that his Emile would have to swallow in order to become a good citizen and not just an educated individual. In other words, Rousseau acknowledged the tension between the flourishing of the person and the formation of the citizen. This is a tension missing in many of those who defend the positive political import of liberal education. Ravitch writes that a "democratic society cannot long sustain itself if it citizens are uninformed and indifferent about its history, its government, and the workings of its economy." Nussbaum, Berkowitz, Ravitch, and Hirsch all seem convinced that if you just teach the correct version of the truth, and the correct version of art, then education will lead to "responsible citizenship" without personal (or philosophical) loss.

I wish this were so, for I, too, am a strong advocate of the potentially positive social outcomes of a liberal education. I, too, believe that the liberal arts have pragmatic import, and that an education in the humanities, arts, and sciences is healthy for modern representative democracy because it creates citizens more capable of making thoughtful decisions about their representatives or about key issues. But we must also recognize that even though education may be salutary for a republic, it doesn't follow that all those who are educated will become defenders of the educator's policies. Cosmopolitanism can be stimulated through active learning, but so can nationalism; partisans of equality can mount their arguments more strongly because of their liberal education, but so can defenders of hierarchy. It is at best disingenuous (and probably counterproductive) to defend a liberal education because it will produce people whose opinions the defender finds congenial.

The humanities are rightly seen as the heart of a liberal education, and in recent years many have bemoaned their decline at the university level. The rise of interdisciplinarity has not diminished the hyperspecialization in the academy, and the resultant pursuit of status through esoteric language has deepened the gulf between humanists and the public. Advanced work in literature, the arts, and critical theory—although it may reject profit and standardized testing—has certainly not been promoting the education of citizens for responsible participation in representative democracies. The ironic sophistication that ruled universities in the 1990s and early 2000s and the development of theoretical "posthumanism" today aren't especially fertile soil for planting trees of freedom and responsible citizenship.

Notwithstanding their theoretical and ideological differences, the commentators cited here all urge that we not abandon the humanistic foundations of education in favor of narrow, technical forms of learning intended to give quick, practical results. It's an important and timely plea because the pursuit of so-called useful educational results continues apace, and because the threats to humanistic education are indeed profound. But "uncritical group think," to use Nussbaum's phrase, isn't to be found only among the test designers evaluating No Child Left Behind statistics. Groupthink can also be found in humanities departments. As Louis Menand has recently noted, our system of graduate education, though it pays lip service to critical thinking, "is not reproducing itself so much as cloning itself."[5] Don't let the verbal iconoclasm fool you: "[a]cademics don't want to appear to be conformists: their success depends on it."[6]

An honest defense of liberal learning must be prepared to acknowledge the extraordinary variety of ways in which the arts and sciences can be taught or put to use. We cannot promise specific political and social results without undermining our credibility as humanists (or even posthumanists) willing to critically examine our own presuppositions. A pragmatic, reflexive approach to liberal arts (including the sciences) would be open to political irrelevance as well as to making a contribution to the public good. A pragmatic, reflexive approach would allow for profit as well as for self-examination—for practical, measurable success at specific tasks as well as self-consciousness and empathy. A pragmatic, reflexive approach to education would enable students to discover what they love to do, to get better at it, and then to be able to explain why what they love to do might be of interest to somebody else. This approach to education might not produce compassionate, cosmopolitan liberals, nor practitioners of what the Hoover Institution calls "the virtues of a free society." But a pragmatic, reflexive approach to the liberal arts would give us an enhanced opportunity to experience the world without undue reliance on unquestioned authority while creating an opening through which we can share that experience with others. And that still sounds like "emergence from self-imposed immaturity" to me.

Notes

Introduction

1. In addition to writing essays concerning fairly specialized topics in history and philosophy, during the period in which I have worked on these pieces I have translated my scholarly concerns into projects aimed at a wider audience by preparing two exhibitions at major cultural venues and writing in magazines, newspapers, and, more recently, websites, and blogs. The exhibitions were *Sigmund Freud: Conflict and Culture*, originating at the Library of Congress in 1998, and *Irresistible Decay*, one of the exhibitions that opened the Getty Museum in Los Angeles. I edited companion volumes to each show. I have written for *Tikkun*, *Bookforum*, *The Los Angeles Times*, *The San Francisco Chronicle*, and *The Huffington Post* with some regularity during this period.
2. *Psycho-Analysis as History: Negation and Freedom in Freud* (1987; Ithaca, N.Y.: Cornell University Press, 1995); *Knowing and History: Appropriations of Hegel in Twentieth Century France* (Ithaca, N.Y.: Cornell University Press, 1988); *The Ironist's Cage: Trauma, Memory and the Construction of History* (New York: Columbia University Press, 1995).
3. "Tradition, Memory and History: On Edward Shils and Yosef Yerushalmi," in *The Ironist's Cage*, 177–85.
4. See, for two examples that can stand for many others, *The American Historical Review*, "Forum on Memory and History," 102 (December 1997); and Allan Megill, "History, Memory, Identity," in *Historical Knowledge, Historical Error: A Contemporary Guide to Practice* (Chicago: University of Chicago Press, 2007), 41–59.
5. See Hayden White's collections of essays and his *Metahistory: The Historical Imagination in the 19th Century Europe* (Baltimore: Johns Hopkins University Press, 1975); and Peter Novick, *That Noble Dream: The Objectivity Question and the American Historical Profession* (Cambridge: Cambridge University Press, 1988).
6. Patrick Hutton, *History as an Art of Memory* (Hanover, N.H.: University Press of New England, 1993), 71.

7. Susan Crane, "Writing the Individual Back into Collective Memory," *American Historical Review* 102 (1997): 1382.
8. Kerwin Klein, "On The Emergence of 'Memory' in Historical Discourse," *Representations* 69 (Winter 2000): 130. Saul Friedlander, Dominick LaCapra, and I are the targets for Klein's criticism.
9. Ibid., 142. On a similar topic, see Wulf Kansteiner, "Finding Meaning in Memory: A Methodological Critique of Collective Memory Studies," *History and Theory* 41 (2002): 179–97.
10. Megill, *Historical Knowledge, Historical Error*, 22.
11. Hacking's historical-philosophical work was important to me in working on the essays in this section, and it has continued to inspire productive research and reflection. See, for example, his *Rewriting the Soul: Multiple Personality and the Sciences of Memory* (Princeton: Princeton University Press, 1995), and my review of the book, "The Memory Politics of the Soul," *The Kenyon Review* 19, no. 1 (Winter 1997): 158–61. See also Ian Hacking, *Historical Ontology* (Cambridge, Mass.: Harvard University Press, 2002). After I began working on section 1 of this book, historians Jan Goldstein, Matt Matsuda, and Jerrold Seigel published important books on the history of the self, and on the relation of memory and modernity in nineteenth-century France.
12. Ruth Leys, *Trauma: A Genealogy* (Chicago: University of Chicago Press, 2000); and Ann Kaplan, *Trauma Culture: The Politics of Terror and Loss in Media and Literature* (New Brunswick, N.J.: Rutgers University Press, 2005). The literature on trauma and culture is by now enormous. For a fairly recent survey of the field in relation to history and critical theory, see Dominick LaCapra, "Traumatropisms: From Trauma via Witnessing to the Sublime?," in *History and Its Limits: Human, Animal, Violence* (Ithaca, N.Y.: Cornell University Press, 2009), 59–89.
13. Giorgio Agamben, *Homo Sacer: Sovereign Power and Bare Life*, trans Daniel Heller-Roazen (Stanford: Stanford University Press, 1998); Remnants of Auschwitz: The Witness and the Archive, trans Daniel Heller-Roazen (Boston: Zone, 2000); The Open: Man and Animal, trans. Kevin Attell (Stanford: Stanford University Press, 2004).
14. "[T]he decisive fact is that, together with the process by which the exception everywhere becomes the rule, the realm of bare life—which is originally situated at the margins of the political order—gradually begins to coincide with the political realm, and exclusion and inclusion, outside and inside, *bios* and *zoē*, right and fact, enter into a zone of irreducible indistinction." Agamben, *Homo Sacer*, 12
15. Agamben, *State of Exception*, trans. Kevin Attell (Chicago: University of Chicago Press: 2004).

16. Agamben, *Homo Sacer*, 72–73.
17. Ibid., 95.
18. Ibid., 99.
19. Agamben, *Remnants*, 72.
20. Ibid., 50.
21. Ibid., 104.
22. Ibid., 107.
23. Ibid.
24. Ruth Leys, *From Guilt to Shame: Auschwitz and After* (Princeton: Princeton University Press, 2007), 133–56.
25. Douglas Crimp, "Mario Montez, for Shame," in *Regarding Sedgwick: Essays on Queer Culture and Critical Theory*, ed. Stephen M. Barber and David L. Clark (New York: Routledge, 2002), 65. Quoted in Leys, *From Guilt to Shame*, 152.
26. Leys, *From Guilt to Shame*, 153.
27. Walter Benn Michaels, *The Shape of the Signifier: 1967 to the End of History* (Princeton: Princeton University Press, 2004). On the moral-political judgments at work (and obscured) by the trauma concept, see Didier Fassin and Richard Rechtman, *The Empire of Trauma: An Inquiry Into the Condition of Victimhood*, trans. Rachel Gomme (Princeton: Princeton University Press, 2009). On the construction of the idea of the victim and the ways the backlash against this idea erases actual suffering see Carolyn J. Dean, *Aversion and Erasure: The Fate of the Victim After the Holocaust* (Ithaca, NY: Cornell University Press, 2010).
28. In addition to his recent collection cited above, see his *History in Transit: Experience, Identity and Critical Theory* (Ithaca, N.Y.: Cornell University Press, 2004); *Writing History, Writing Trauma* (Baltimore: Johns Hopkins University Press, 2001); *History and Memory After Auschwitz* (Ithaca, N.Y.: Cornell University Press, 1998).
29. LaCapra, *History and Its Limits*, 118.
30. Cited in "The Ticklish Object," www.lacan.com/zizparallax.htm (accessed July 2010). See also *The Parallax View (Short Circuits)* (Cambridge, Mass.: MIT Press, 2006), 25.
31. Slavoj Žižek, "Neighbors and Other Monsters: A Plea for Ethical Violence," in *The Neighbor: Three Inquiries in Political Theology* (Chicago: University of Chicago Press, 2005), 161.
32. Ibid., 163.
33. Ibid., 162.
34. Slavoj Žižek, "You May!," *London Review of Books*, March 18, 1999, www.lrb.co.uk/v21/n06/print/zize01_.html (accessed July 2010).

35. LaCapra, *History in Transit*, 103–4.
36. The journal *Rethinking History* (8, no. 4 [2004]) published a group of essays on LaCapra in response to his own reflections on his career ("Tropisms in Intellectual History").
37. See, for example, *The History Wars: The Enola Gay and Other Battles for the American Past*, ed. Edward T. Linenthal and Tom Engelhardt (New York: Henry Holt, 1996). On the Freud exhibition itself, see Steven Dubin's account (mostly informed by local New York sources) in *Displays of Power: Controversies in the American Museum from the Enola Gay to Sensation* (New York: NYU Press, 2001), 118–51.
38. Peter Kramer, *Listening to Prozac: A Psychiatrist Explores Antidepressant Drugs and the Remaking of the Self* (New York: Viking, 1993).
39. Žižek, "You May!," 5.
40. I draw here on my "Psychoanalysis and Nature: Commentary on Papers by Bodnar and Stantostefano," *Psychoanalytic Dialogues* 18, no. 4 (2008): 536–40.
41. Ralph Waldo Emerson, "Experience," in *Selected Writings of Emerson*, ed. Donald McQuade (New York: Random House, 1981), 329.

1. Remembering Forgetting

1. See, for example, George Johnson, "Memory: Learning How It Works," *New York Times* August 9, 1987; and Hervé Ponchelet, "Les Secrets de la mémoire," *Le Point*, April 4, 1988. This essay was originally written for a special issue of the journal *Representations* concerned with "memory and counter-memory" that appeared in 1989. I have not tried to update the bibliography on memory and forgetting, but I have discussed some of the issues that have arisen in the historical study of memory in the introduction to this book.
2. Sander L. Gilman, *Disease and Representation: Images of Illness from Madness to AIDS* (Ithaca, N.Y.: Cornell University Press, 1988), 1.
3. The first use of *amnésie* is 1803. *Amnésique* is first used in 1898. See, for example, *Grand Larousse de la langue française* (Paris, 1971).
4. On the place of memory in d'Alembert and Diderot's organization of knowledge in the *Encyclopédie*, see Robert Darnton, "Philosophers Trim the Tree of Knowledge: The Epistemological Strategy of the *Encyclopédie*," in *The Great Cat Massacre and Other Episodes in French Cultural History* (New York: Basic, 1984). Amédée-Marie-Paulin Rouillard's thesis has perhaps the best documentation of the resurgence of interest in amnesia in late nineteenth century. In it he claimed

that before the first half of his century all who spoke of amnesia were really only describing aphasia. See his *Essai sur les amnésies, principalement du point de vue étiologique* (Thèse pour le doctorat en médecine, Faculté de médecine de Paris, 1885), 7 and passim.

5. Some important works in the period include Jean-Pierre Falret, "Amnésie," in *Dictionnaire* in *des sciences médicales*, vol. 3 (1865), 725–42; Eugène Azam, *Amnésie périodique, ou dédoublement de la personnalité* (Bordeaux, 1877); José Miguel Guardia, "Les Maladies de la mémoire," *Revue scientifique*, 3rd ser., 1, no. 24 (1881): 738–47; Sigismund Zaborowski, "La Mémoire et ses maladies," *Bulletins de la Société d'anthropologie de Paris*, 3rd ser., 4 (1881): 514–16; Charles Richet, "La Personnalité et la mémoire dans le somnambulisme," *Revue philosophique* 15 (1883): 225–42; Henri Legrand du Saulle, "Les Maladies de la mémoire," *Gazette des hôpitaux* 57, no. 139 (1884): 1105–7; Rouillard, *Essai sur les amnésies*; Paul Auguste Sollier, *Les Troubles de La mémoire* (Paris, 1892). Henri Bergson's *Matière et mémoire: Essai sur la relation du corps à l'esprit* (Paris, 1896) should be read in relation (and in opposition) to much of the psychological literature on memory of the preceding three decades.

6. Jan Goldstein, *Console and Classify: The French Psychiatric Profession in the Nineteenth Century* (Cambridge: Cambridge University Press, 1987), passim.

7. See Robert M. Young, *Mind, Brain, and Adaptation in the Nineteenth Century: Cerebral Localization and Its Biological Context from Gall to Ferrier* (Oxford: Oxford University Press, 1970), especially chapter 1 and the conclusion. Rouillard stresses the importance of Gall's work for moving away from a conception of *the* memory to a conception of *memoires* in *Essai sur les amnésies*, 16, 32. On English psychiatry and phrenology, see L. S. Jacyna, "Somatic Theories of Mind and the Interests of Medicine in Britain, 1850–1879," *Medical History* 26 (1982): 233–58; Roger Cooter, *The Cultural Meaning of Popular Science: Phrenology and the Organization of Consent in Nineteenth-Century Britain* (Cambridge: Cambridge University Press, 1984).

8. Young, *Mind, Brain, and Adaptation*, 235. For a very brief treatment of this history in the context of contemporary debates about memory, see Israel Rosenfield, *The Invention of Memory: A New View of the Brain* (New York: Basic, 1988), 12–96.

9. On the debates between the spiritualist tendency in French psychiatry and the positivists, see Goldstein, *Console and Classify*, chapter 7.

10. Théodul Ribot, *Les Maladies de la mémoire* (Paris, 1881), 55–56. Ribot takes the case from Benedict Auguste Morel, *Traité des maladies mentales* (Paris, 1860), 695. Henceforth references to Ribot will be given in the text. With the exception of the epigraphs from Nietzsche and Proust, all translations are my own unless otherwise noted.

11. The original source for this case is *Lettre de Charles Villiers à G. Cuvier* (Paris, 1802).
12. Ribot would publish such a book in 1885.
13. Ribot, *Maladies de la mémoire,* 82. See Ian Hacking, "The Invention of Split Personalities: An Illustration of Michel Foucault's Doctrine of the Constitution of the Subject," in *Human Nature and Natural Knowledge: Essays Presented to Marjorie Grene on the Occasion of Her Seventy-Fifth Birthday,* ed. A. Donagan, A. N. Perovich, Jr., and M. V. Wedin (Boston: Reidel, 1986), 63–85. I return to a case of periodic amnesia below.
14. Hacking, "Split Personalities," 83–85.
15. Ribot goes on to talk about a basic sentiment of life and of the body that underlies our conscious sense of identity.
16. Bergson, *Matière et mémoire,* 36.
17. The critical (but appreciative) review of Bergson's *Matière et mémoire* by Gustave Belot in the *Revue philosophique de La France et de l'étranger* 44 (1897): 182–99 was entitled "Un Nouveau Spiritualisme."
18. Auguste Motet hypnotized the patient in court to prove his point. See his "Relation médico-légale d'un cas d'accès de somnambulisme spontané et provoqué: Prévention d'outrage public à la pudeur," *Annales d'hygiène publique,* March 1881, 124; cited by Rouillard, *Essai sur les amnésies,* 122. On legal responsibility and amnesia, see Eugène Azam, *Hypnotisme et double conscience: Origine de leur étude et divers travaux sur les sujets analogues* (Paris, 1893), 120–22; Louis Benoit, *Contribution à l'étude des amnésies traumatiques au point de vue clinique et médico-légal* (Lyons, 1899); Falret, "Amnésie"; Firmin Lagardelle, *Affaire Caillot: Double assasinat, amnésie simulée, epilepsie, alcoolisme, et monomanie allégués, condamnation à mort* (Paris, 1877); Joseph Maxwell, *L'Amnésie au point de vue la médecine judiciaire* (Bordeaux, 1902); Rouillard, *Essai sur les amnésies,* 227–37.
19. Alfred Fouillée, "La Mémoire et la reconnaissance des souvenirs," *Revue des deux mondes* 70 (1885): 139. See also his "Le Mécanisme de la mémoire," *Revue des deux mondes* 69 (1885): 357–89.
20. Fouillée, "Mécanisme de la mémoire," 139.
21. The dispute between Fouillée and Ribot was fundamental, and one can still find echoes of it today in theories of narrative and history. Do historical events have any meaning and direction before we organize them into a narrative? Are historical events by virtue of their status as events necessarily narrativized, thus having meaning and direction? See, for example, Hayden White, "The Value of Narrativity in the Representation of Reality," in *The Content of the Form* (Baltimore: Johns Hopkins University Press, 1987); Paul Ricoeur, *Time and Narrative,* vol. 1

(Chicago: University of Chicago Press, 1984); David Carr, *Time, Narrative, and History* (Bloomington: Indiana University Press, 1986); and "The Representation of Historical Events," *History and Theory*, Beiheft 26 (1987). (See the discussion of photography and continuity in "Photographic Ambivalence" below.)

22. Hippolyte Taine, *De l'intelligence*, 16th ed. (Paris, n.d.), 153.
23. Albert Guillon, *Les Maladies de la mémoire: Essai sur les hypermnésies* (Paris, 1897), 59. Henceforth references to this volume will be made in the text. Guillon dismisses as unscientific the much more cursory treatment of hypermnesia made by Edmond Antoine-Emil Blandet in his thesis *De l'hypermnésie, ou l'exaltation de la mémoire* (Thèse pour le doctorat en médecine, Faculté de médecine de Paris, 1840).
24. Emphasis in the original.
25. Guillon quotes Emmanuel Régis, "Les Aliénés peints par eux-mêmes," *L'Encéphale* 2 (1882): 548. We should note that the tailor wrote his history twelve years after the war.
26. This is even clearer in an account given of the symptoms of this patient in Régis, "Les Aliénés peints par eux-mêmes," 547–64.
27. On French psychiatry and the courts, see Goldstein, *Console and Classify*, 162–78, 292–97.
28. Hacking quotes the lecture in "Split Personalities," 74.
29. As Paul Janet noted, "If the ego can feel itself to be double, in what consists its unity, which the spiritualist psychologists consider as the fundamental base of their doctrine"; "La Notion de la personnalité," *La Revue scientifique de la France et de l'étranger*, 2nd ser., 10 (1876): 574. Hacking's account of this use of Félida for such "proof" is particularly persuasive. See his *Rewriting the Soul: Multiple Personality and the Sciences of Memory* (Princeton: Princeton University Press, 1995), especially chapters 10 and 11.
30. Eugène Azam, "Le Déboublement de la personnalité et le somnambulisme" (1890), in *Hypnotisme et double conscience* (Paris, 1893), 149–50. Azam presented a more complete description of Félida through 1877 to the Bordeaux Académie des médecines morales et politiques, published as *Amnésie périodique, ou dédoublement de la personnalité* (see note 5 above). In this version he reports Félida's reaction to her pregnancy as follows: "Her pregnancy did not bother her; and she resigned herself to it rather cheerfully" (12).
31. Azam, *Amnésie périodique*, 150. Despite the predominance of the second personality, Félida's eleven childbirths or miscarriages took place in her "normal" personality. We are not told in which condition the last ten conceptions occurred, but we are told in the 1877 version (16) that only two children were then living.

Pierre Janet notes a case in which a woman, Léonie, is hypnotized at the beginning of childbirth. She is mother in personality 2—the personality in which she does not recognize her husband; *L'Automatisme psychologique*, 2nd ed. (Paris, 1893), 132–33.

32. Félida is discussed, but not named, in the 1860 publication "Sommeil nerveux ou hypnotisme," *Archives générales de médecine*; the article is reprinted in Azam, *Hypnotisme et double conscience*, 13–33, with the subtitle "Première publication faite en France sur l'hypnotisme." Azam's hypnotic work with Félida is described in *Amnésie périodique*, 12–13.
33. Azam, *Amnésie périodique*, 48. Pierre Janet agreed that somnambulism is always distinguished by some alteration of memory, although for him only "*le dernier somnambulisme*" is characterized by an absolute memory; *Automatisme psychologique*, 75.
34. Azam, *Hypnotisme et double conscience*, 95. In the 1877 version (28–29), he insisted on the primacy of the amnesia in Félida's condition. Ludovic Dugas would later call the phenomenon of "*la fausse mémoire* a special case of *dédoublement de la personnalité*." See his articles "Sur la fausse mémoire," *Revue philosophique de la France et de l'étranger* 37 (1894): 34–45; "'L'impression de 'l'entièrement nouveau' et celle du 'déjà vu,'" *Revue philosophique de la France et de l'étranger* 38 (1894): 40–46; and "Dépersonnalisation et fausse mémoire," *Revue philosophique de la France et de l'étranger* 46 (1898): 423–25. These articles include references to a debate on paramnesia and the self that continued throughout the 1890s.
35. Azam, *Hypnotisme et double conscience*, 106.
36. Freud's notion of the unconscious, of course, made disunity or division a necessary component of his topography of the psyche. For him, the story of Félida was an example of "oscillating between two different psychical complexes which become conscious and unconscious in alternation"; "A Note on the Unconscious in Psychoanalysis" (1912), in *Standard Edition of the Complete Psychological Works of Sigmund Freud*, ed. and trans. James Strachey, 24 vols. (London: Hogarth Press, 1953–74), 12:263.
37. Sigmund Freud, "On the Theory of Hysterical Attacks," in *Standard Edition*, 1:152.
38. Sigmund Freud, "Project for a Scientific Psychology," in *Standard Edition*, 1:350. Freud writes: "For every excessive intrusion into consciousness there is a corresponding amnesia."
39. See, for example, Freud's treatment of Frau Emmy von N., described in *Studies on Hysteria*, in *Standard Edition*, 2:48–105, esp. 60 and note. See chapter 6 for a discussion of this case.

40. See Michael S. Roth, *Psycho-Analysis as History: Negation and Freedom in Freud* (Ithaca, N.Y.: Cornell University Press, 1987), passim. See also chapters 6 and 7 below.

41. Even the *Revue des deux mondes* got in on the act. See the impressive, thorough articles of Fouiltée, "Le Mécanisme de la mémoire" and "La Mémoire et la reconnaissance des souvenirs" (note 19 above).

42. Pierre Nora, "Entre mémoire et histoire: Les Problématiques des lieux," in *Les Lieux de mémoire*, vol. 1, *La République* (Paris: Gallimard, 1984), xvii; translated as "Between Memory History: *Les Lieux de Mémoire*," in *Representations* 26 (1989): 7–24.

43. Dugas, "Sur la fausse mémoire," 41. See also Rouillard, *Essai sur les amnésies*, 29.

2. Dying of the Past

1. Jean-Baptiste-Felix Descuret, *La Médecine des passions* ou *les passions considérées dans leurs rapports avec les maladies, les lois et la Religion* (Paris: Béchet Jeune et Labé, 1841), 716–18. The cases are not dated.

2. For a detailed account of the history of medical discussions of nostalgia, see Klaus Brunnert, *Nostalgie in der Geschichte der Medizin* (Dusseldorf: Triltsch Druck und Verlag, 1984). See also Edward Casey, "The World of Nostalgia," *Man and World* 20 (1987): 361–84; George Rosen, "Nostalgia: A 'Forgotten' Psychological Disorder," *Glio Medica* 10, no. 1 (1975): 28–51; Jean Starobinski, "Le concept de nostalgie," *Diogène* 54 (1966): 92–115; Susan Stewart, *On Longing: Narratives of the Miniature, the Gigantic, the Souvenir, the Collection* (Baltimore: Johns Hopkins University Press, 1984); and the special issue on memory in the *Bulletin de Psychologie* 42, no. 389 (1988–89), especially the articles by André Bolzinger, "Jalons pour une histoire de la nostalgie," 310–21; and Gilles Micouin, "De la nostalgie à la neurasthénie: une rupture epistemologique," 322–27. Since this essay was first published, there have been various studies on nostalgia. I'll cite a few here: Svetlana Boym, *The Future of Nostalgia* (New York: Basic, 2001); Peter Fritzsche, *Stranded in the Present: Modern Time and the Melancholy of History* (Cambridge, Mass.: Harvard University Press, 2004); Susan J. Matt, "You Can't Go Home Again: Homesickness and Nostalgia in U.S. History," *The Journal of American History* 94, no. 2 (2007): 84, www.historycooperative.org/journals/jah/94.2/matt.html (accessesd June 15, 2010).

3. However, there have been periodic reconsiderations of nostalgia as a medical category throughout the late nineteenth century through recent years. See, for example, M. Bachet, "Étude sur les états de nostalgie," *Annales Médico-psychologiques*

108 (1950): 1:559–87, 2:11–34; Bolzinger, "Jalons pour une histoire de la nostalgie," 320–21; J. P. Porchet, "La Nostalgie: À partir de jeunes militaires" (Thèse de médecine, Lille, 1979).

4. Descuret, *La Médecine des passions*, 715.
5. See "Remembering Forgetting," chapter 1 of this volume.
6. George D. Sussman, *Selling Mother's Milk: The Wet-Nursing Business in France, 1715–1914* (Urbana: University of Illinois Press, 1982), 112. See also Elisabeth Badinter, *L'Amour en plus: Histoire de l'amour maternel* (Paris: Flammarion, 1980); Joan Scott and Louise Tilly, *Women, Work and the Family* (New York: Holt, Rinehart and Winston, 1978); Edward Shorter, *The Making of the Modern Family* (London: Collins, 1976).
7. D.-F.-N. Guerbois, "Essai sur la nostalgie: appelée vulgairement maladie du pays" (Thèse de médecine, Paris, an XI [1803]), vol. 31, no. 290, 13.
8. Ibid., 14. The final sentence of this quotation is repeated in Delmais-Eugène Pinel's article, "Nostalgie," in the *Encyclopédie méthodique*, "Médecine," vol. 10 (1821), 662. See also H.-J.-M. Hyacinthe Musset, "Essai sur la nostalgie" (Thèse de médecine, Paris, 1830), vol. 9, no. 292, 10.
9. Guerbois, "Essai sur la nostalgie," 3.
10. M. Reynal, "Dissertation sur la nostalgie" (Thèse de médecine, Paris, 1819), vol. 2, no. 35, 9; J. J. A. Martin, "Dissertation sur la nostalgie" (Thèse de médecine, Paris, 1820), vol. 8, no. 250, 13; Julien-Vincent Huet-Bienville, "Dissertation sur la nostalgie" (Thèse de médecine, Paris, 1821), vol. 6, no. 190, 5; Jules Yvonneau, "Considérations medico-philosophiques sur la nostalgie" (Thèse de médecine, Paris, 1821), vol. 1, no. 34, 8; José-Feliciano Castilho, "Dissertation sur la nostalgie" (Thèse de médecine, Paris, 1831), vol. 7, no. 235, 24–25; Auguste Benoist de la Grandière, *De La nostalgie ou mal du pays* (Paris: A. Delahaye, 1875), 3.
11. François-Théophile Collin, "Considérations sur la nostalgie" (Thèse de médecine, Paris, 1832), vol. 9, no. 271, 8. Gilles Micouin, "De la nostalgie à la neurasthènie," emphasizes that nostalgia was part of the early-nineteenth-century tradition of psychosomatic medicine, which was willing to consider the effects of ideas or emotions on the body. According to Micouin, the disease was later removed from the concern of doctors, who only wanted to consider the effects of the body on ideas or emotions.
12. Reynal, "Dissertation sur la nostalgie," 8.
13. On natural desire turned bad, see Reynal, "Dissertation sur la nostalgie," 7. Several dissertations repeat the idea that without the desire at the root of nostalgia peoples from all over the globe would flock to the most temperate zones. For an

early expression of this idea, see Remi-Victor Allard, "Dissertation sur la nostalgie" (Thèse de médecine, Paris, 1820), vol. 5, no. 139, 6–7.

14. Collin, "Considérations sur la nostalgie," 10.
15. Several writers thought that women were less vulnerable to the disease because their way of life was less likely to lead them away from home than the ways of life open to men. All agreed that girls who moved to cities for domestic work were particularly vulnerable to the disease.
16. Castilho, "Dissertation sur la nostalgie," 13–14. (This list of causes follows the order of the original.)
17. Ibid., 15.
18. Sava Petrowitch, "De la nostomanie" (Thèse de médecine, Paris, 1866), 42. The term "Nostomania" was an attempt to create a technical word for nostalgia. C. Castelnau, in opposition to the "distractions of Paris," recommends religion's promise of other-worldly satisfactions: "Considérations sur la nostalgie" (Thèse de médecine, Paris, 1806), 19. Castilho advises the doctor to provide a passion for something else, little matter what: "Dissertation sur la nostalgie," 27. Cyr. Ducrest de Lorgerie prescribes an even more general treatment. In language that recalls Homais's sage counsel to Emma Bovary, he writes that the doctor should excite the patient's imagination in order to destroy the effects of a diseased imagination: "Dissertation sur la nostalgie" (Thèse de médecine, Paris, 1815), 18.
19. Louis-Alexandre-Hippolyte Leroy-Dupré, "De la nostalgie" (Thèse de médecine, Paris, 1846), no. 134, 26.
20. Martin, "Dissertation sur la nostalgie," quoting Tourtelle (author of a treatise on hygiene), 22–23. Pilet, "De la nostalgie: considérée chez l'homme de guerre" (Thèse de médecine, Paris, 1844), vol. 12, no. 43, 29.
21. See Louis-Jacques Begin, "Nostalgie," in *Dictionnaire de médecine et de chirurgie pratique* (Paris: Gabon, Mequignon-Marvis, J. B. Baillière, 1834), 12:84.
22. Ibid., 79. See also Castilho, "Dissertation sur la nostalgie," 21. (The epigraph of this chapter is from this source, 17.)
23. See Gilles Deleuze, *Présentation de Sacher Masoch* (Paris: Éditions de Minuit, 1967), 32–33, 119–22, 126–29. Susan Stewart states that "[t]he nostalgic is enamored of distance, not of the referent itself" (*On Longing*, 145). According to Grandière, the person with nostalgia "becomes at the same time the artisan and the victim of his own suffering" (*De la nostalgie ou mal du pays*, 103).
24. Stewart, *On Longing*, 23.
25. Rue de la Harpe, in the Fifth Arrondissement, has a long history of being reshaped to fit the modernizing city. Later in the nineteenth century it would be almost

entirely transformed by Haussmann's reconstruction of the city. See Jacques Hillairet, *Dictionnaire historique des rues de Paris* (Paris: Éditions de Minuit, 1963), 621–22.

26. See, for example, Allard, "Dissertation sur la nostalgie," 6–7; Raoul Chenu, *De La nostalgie* (Paris: Parent, 1877), 30.

27. On patriotism and nostalgia, see Musset, "Essai sur la nostalgie," 6. Perhaps it is significant that this thesis was presented in December 1830, just months after the July Revolution brought Louis-Philippe to power. On colonization and nostalgia, see V. Widal, "Nostalgie," in *Dictionnaire encyclopédique des sciences médicales* (Paris: Asselin, 1879), 13:361; Brunnert, *Nostalgie in der Geschichte der Medizin*, 177–79.

28. Pierre-Urbain Briet, "Essai sur la nostalgie" (Thèse de médecine, Paris, 1832), no. 162, 8.

29. Rousseau is explaining that as the Swiss lose their "première simplicité" they become less vulnerable to the dangerous effects of the music of the "Ranz des vaches." Of course, for Rousseau the price paid for this increased immunity is extremely high.

30. Leroy-Dupré, "De la nostalgie," 28n.

31. Pilet, "De la nostalgie," 19. The point about the inverse relation between civilization and susceptibility to nostalgia is often made by citing examples of non-Europeans. Pilet mentions the North American Indian who asked how he could move to a place where his ancestors were not buried, unless their bones would follow him. Another example repeated in the literature is that of Assan, a young Chinese man, who embraces a tree in Paris that reminds him of his homeland.

32. Allard, "Dissertation sur la nostalgie," 9. See also Brunnert, *Nostalgie in der Geschichte der Medizin*, 177. In summarizing earlier discussions of women and nostalgia, Théodule Ribot writes of a greater natural plasticity among women: *Problèmes de psychologie affective* (Paris: F Alcan, 1911), 66.

33. Musset, "Essai sur la nostalgie," 38. He recommends education as protection against the disease. Education should make people more stoic, enabling them to cope with the difficulties that would otherwise destroy them.

34. Morin, "De la nostalgie aux points de vue philosophique et médical," *La France médicale et pharmaceutique* 3, no. 26 (1856): 204.

35. Charles-François-Alexandre Gueit, "Quelques considérations sur la nature de la nostalgie, ses causes et son traitement" (Thèse de médecine, Montpellier, 1874), no. 74, 36.

36. Widal, "Nostalgie," 380.

37. "De la Nostalgie," manuscript no. 3 Pour le prix fondé par M. le Docteur Lefèvre, Archives de l'Academie de la Médecine.

38. Grandiere, *De la nostalgie ou mal du pays*, 182–85.
39. Charles Lasègue, review of A. Haspel, *De la nostalgie*, in *Archives générales de médecine*, 6th ser., 25, no. 1 (1875): 760.
40. Ibid., 762.
41. Ibid., 763.
42. Widal, "Nostalgie," 366.
43. Ibid., 380. Ribot's late, brief discussion of nostalgia is intended to provide evidence for the importance of affective memory, an important topic in early-twentieth-century psychology: *Problèmes de psychologie affective*, 63–67.
44. See Jan Goldstein, *Console and Classify: The French Psychiatric Profession in the Nineteenth Century* (Cambridge: Cambridge University Press, 1987), 324, 328. For a description of Lasègue's work on hysteria, see Etienne Trillat, *Histoire de l'hystérie* (Paris: Seghers, 1986), 122–25.
45. Trillat, *Histoire de l'hystérie*, 126–79; Ilza Veith, *Hysteria: The History of a Disease* (Chicago: University of Chicago Press, 1970), 228–56; Elizabeth Roudinsesco, *La bataille de cent ans: Histoire de la psychanalyse en France* (Paris: Éditions du Seuil, 1982), 1:21–49; Phillip R. Slavney, *Perspectives on "Hysteria"* (Baltimore: Johns Hopkins University Press, 1990), 131–32. The literature on hysteria is enormous, and I cite here a few more recent studies by way of orientation: Mark Micale, *Approaching Hysteria: Disease and its Interpretations* (Princeton: Princeton University Press, 1994); Janet Beizer, *Ventriloquized Bodies: Narratives of Hysteria in 19th Century France* (Ithaca, N.Y.: Cornell University Press, 1994); Jan Goldstein, *Hysteria Complicated by Ecstacy: The Case of Nanette Leroux* (Princeton: Princeton University Press, 2009); Andrew Scull, *Hysteria: Biography of a Disease* (Oxford: Oxford University Press, 2009). See also chapter 3 of this volume.
46. Sigmund Freud, *Beyond the Pleasure Principle* (1920), in *Standard Edition of the Complete Psychological Works of Sigmund Freud*, ed. and trans. James Strachey, 24 vols. (London: Hogarth Press, 1953–74), 18:38.

3. Hysterical Remembering

1. Pierre Janet, *L'État mental des hystériques* (Paris: Felix Alcan, 1911), 215; hereafter abbreviated *EMH*.
2. Quoted in Etienne Trillat, *Histoire de l'hystérie* (Paris: Seghers, 1983), 211.
3. See the introduction and other essays in this section, and Ian Hacking, *Rewriting the Soul, Multiple Personality and the Sciences of Memory* (Princeton: Princeton University Press, 1995), especially 154–209.

4. I have discussed these issues in the introduction to *The Ironist's Cage: Memory, Trauma, and the Construction of History* (New York: Columbia University Press, 1995), and in "Victims, Memory, History," *Tikkun*, March/April 1994, 59–60. For strong contrast, see Judith Herman, *Trauma and Recovery* (New York: Basic, 1992), and Frederick Crews, *The Memory Wars* (New York: New York Review of Books, 1995).
5. The best general survey is Mark Micale, *Approaching Hysteria: Disease and Its Interpretations* (Princeton: Princeton University Press, 1995). See also Elaine Showalter, *Hystories: Hysterical Epidemics and Modern Media* (New York: Columbia University Press, 1998).
6. On Félida X and Doctor Azam, see Roth, "Remembering Forgetting," chapter 1, and Hacking, *Rewriting the Soul*, 159–170.
7. Henri Legrand du Saulle, *Les Hystériques: État physique et état mental, actes insolites, délictueux et criminels* (Paris: Libraire J.-B. Bailliere, 1883), 3.
8. The work of Josef Delboeuf is a good example of this tendency. See his "De l'Analogie entre l'état hypnotique et l'état normal," *Revue de l'hypnotisme* 3 (1888): 289–92.
9. This had to do with Briquet's insistence on male hysteria. In this regard, see Jan Goldstein, "The Uses of Male Hysteria: Medical and Literary Discourse in Nineteenth-Century France," *Representations* 34 (Summer 1991): 152. Also see Mark S. Micale, "Charcot and the Idea of Hysteria in the Male: Gender, Mental Science and Medical Diagnosis in late-nineteenth century France," *Medical History* 34 (October 1990): 363–411; Mark S. Micale, *Hysterical Men: The Hidden History of Male Nervous Illness* (Cambridge, Mass.: Harvard University Press, 2008); and Elaine Showalter, "Hysteria, Feminism, and Gender," in *Hysteria Beyond Freud*, ed. Sander Gilman et al. (Berkeley: University of California Press), 286–344.
10. On Charcot's medical work and cultural importance, see, for example, Micale, *Approaching Hysteria*; Georges Didi-Huberman, *L'Invention de l'hystérie: Charcot et l'Iconographie Photographique de la Salpêtrière* (Paris: Macula, 1982); Jan Goldstein, *Console and Classify: The French Psychiatric Profession in the Nineteenth Century* (New York: Cambridge University Press, 1987); Georges Guillain, *Charcot: Sa Vie-Son Oeuvre* (Paris: Masson, 1955); Martha Noel Evans, *Fits and Starts: A Genealogy of Hysteria in Modem France* (Ithaca, N.Y.: Cornell University Press, 1991), 9–50; Debora L. Silverman, *Art Nouveau in Fin-de-Siècle France: Politics, Psychology, and Style* (Berkeley: University of California Press, 1989),75–106.
11. Micale, "Charcot and the Idea of Hysteria in the Male," 385, and Micale's recent edited collection with Paul Lerner, *Traumatic Pasts: History, Psychiatry, and*

Trauma in the Modern Age, 1870–1930 (Cambridge: Cambridge University Press, 2010). See also Esther Fischer-Homberger, *Die traumatische Neurose: vom somatischen zum sozialen Leiden* (Bern: H. Huber, 1975).

12. See, for example, George Frederick Drinka, *The Birth of Neurosis: Myth, Malady, and the Victorians* (New York: Simon and Schuster, 1984), 108–22.
13. Jean-Martin Charcot, *Leçons sur l'hystérie virile* (Paris: Le Sycomore, 1984), 36.
14. For all his emphasis on traumatic events as the precipitating causes of hysteria, Charcot firmly believed that degenerate heredity left one vulnerable (predisposed) to such events. On the popularity of degeneracy as a category in late-nineteenth-century medical and social texts, see, for example, Debora Silverman, *Art Nouveau*; Robert Nye, *The Origins of Crowd Psychology: Gustave Le Bon and the Crisis of Mass Democracy in the Third Republic* (Beverly Hills, CA: Sage, 1975); and Susana Barrows, *Distorting Mirrors: Visions of the Crowd in Late-Nineteenth-Century France* (New Haven: Yale University Press, 1981).
15. See Charcot, "Sur un cas d'amnésie rétro-antérograde," *Revue de médecine* 12 (January 1892): 81–96; Janet, "L'Amnésie continue," *Revue générale des sciences* (March 30, 1893): 167–69; and A. Souques, "Essai sur l'amnésie retro-antérograde dans l'hystérie, les traumatismes cérébraux et l'alcoolisme chronique," *Revue de médecine* 12 (May 1892): 366–401; (November 1892): 867–81.
16. But Mme. D. did recognize Charcot when she would be reexamined by him. The doctor concluded that this was because she had seen André Brouillet's much-reproduced painting of Charcot, *Une Leçon Clinique à la Salpêtrière*, prior to the July 14 of her trauma.
17. Adam Crabtree regards Charcot's paper delivered to the Académie des Sciences on February 13, 1882, as decisive. This was published as "Sur les divers états nerveux déterminés par l'hypnotisation chez les hystériques," *Comptes-rendus hebdomadaires de séances de l'Académie des Sciences* 94 (1882): 403–5. In 1881, Charcot had already published *Contribution à l'étude de l'hypnotisme chez les hystériques* (Paris: Progrès médical, 1881). See Adam Crabtree, *From Mesmer to Freud: Magnetic Sleep and the Roots of Psychological Healing* (New Haven: Yale University Press, 1994), 166–67.
18. Anne Harrington, "Hysteria, Hypnosis, and the Lure of the Invisible: The Rise of Neo-Mesmerism in Fin-de-Siècle French Psychiatry," in *The Anatomy of Madness: Essays in the History of Psychiatry*, vol. 3, ed. W. F. Bynum, Roy Porter, and Michael Shepherd (New York: Routledge, 1988), 227. Harrington has returned to these issues recently in *The Cure Within: A History of Mind Body Medicine* (New York: Norton, 2009), 31–66.
19. Charcot, "Sur un cas d'amnésie rétro-antérograde," 85.

20. Marcel Gauchet, *L'Inconscient Cérebral* (Paris: Seuil, 1992), 65. Gauchet discusses Charcot's relationship with Luys, 111–19.
21. Pierre Janet, *L'automatisme psychologique* (Paris: Félix Alcan; 1889); parts of this study had already appeared from 1886–1888 in the *Revue Philosophique*.
22. Pierre Janet, "L'Anesthésie hystérique," *Archives de Neurologie* 69, no. 70 (1892): 32. This publication was based on a series of lectures given by Janet at the Salpêtrière. In the first lecture, he makes a case for the psychological understanding of the disease, which he calls a *maladie de la personnalité*.
23. Janet, "L'Anesthésie hystérique," 40.
24. Pierre Janet, *Névroses et idées fixes*, 4th ed. (Paris: Félix Alcan, 1925), 127; hereafter abbreviated *NIF*.
25. Janet writes: "Nous voyons bien par ces faits et bien d'autres du même genre que les souvenirs des événements récents existent même pendant la veille, mais qu'ils existent d'une manière toute particulière; ils semblent sinon inconscients, du moins subconscients, c'est-à-dire *en dehors* de la conscience des maladies." Ibid., 130; my emphasis.
26. Ibid., 135.
27. Ibid., 138. For an approach to amnesia which also emphasizes the integration (or association) of memories but does so on the level of neuro-anatomy, see Korsakoff, "Étude Médico-Psychologique sur une forme des Maladies de la Mémoire," *Revue Philosophique* 28 (May 1889): 501–30.
28. Janet discusses Marceline in detail in *EMH*, 545–688, under the title of a "Félida Artificielle." He had earlier published this account in the *Revue Philosophique* in 1909.
29. Pierre Janet, *The Major Symptoms of Hysteria: Fifteen Lectures Given in the Medical School of Harvard University* (New York: Hafner, 1965), 88; hereafter abbreviated *MSH*.
30. *EMH*, 371.
31. Jules Janet, "L'hystérie et l'hypnotisme, d'après la théorie de la double personnalité," *Revue scientiftque* 20 (May 19, 1888): 617–23.
32. Ruth Leys has discussed Janet's emphasis on forgetting in the context of debates on memory in the beginning of this century and in recent psychological treatments of posttraumatic disorders, in "Tramatic Cures, Shell Shock, Janet, and the Question of Memory," *Critical Inquiry* 20 (Summer 1994): 623–62. This material is integrated in her book, *Trauma: A Genealogy* (Chicago: University of Chicago Press, 2000).
33. Friedrich Nietzsche, "Redemption," in *Thus Spake Zarathustra*, trans. Thomas Commons (New York: Modern Library, 1970), 153.

34. See in this regard the important work of Jan Goldstein, *Console and Classify* (New York: Cambridge University Press, 1987); and Debora Silverman, *Art Nouveau in Fin de Siècle Paris: Politics, Psychology and Style* (Berkeley: University of California Press, 1989).
35. See Charcot, "Spiritisme et hystérie," in *Oeuvres Complètes*, vol. 3, *Leçons sur les maladies du système nerveux* (Paris: Lecrosnier et Babè, 1890), 229–38; and "Une lettre de M. Charcot au sujet des séances publiques d'hypnotisme," *Revue de l'hypnotisme* (1886): 380. Carnival performers were well aware of Charcot's reputation as an expert hypnotist and even imitated him in their performances. See A. R. G. Owen, *Hysteria, Hypnosis, and Healing: The Work of J. M. Charcot* (London: Dennis Dobson, 1971), 204.
36. On the two-way street between French psychiatry and the occult, see Harrington, "Hysteria, Hypnosis, and the Lure of the Invisible," 226–46.
37. For biographical information, see Marilisa Juri, *Charles Richet, physiologiste, 1850–1935* (Zurich: Juris Druck & Verlag, 1965); and Stewart Wolf, *Brain, Mind, and Medicine: Charles Richet and the Origins of Physiological Psychology* (New Brunswick, N.J.: Transaction, 1993). More recently, see Jacqueline Carroy, "Playing with Signatures: The Young Charles Richet," in *The Mind of Modernism: Medicine, Psychology and the Cultural Arts in Europe and America, 1880–1940* (Stanford: Stanford University Press, 2004), 217–49.
38. Richet writes, "Ainsi la conscience de la personnalité dépend de nos souvenirs. . . . Mais que ces souvenirs personnels se dissipent; que cette conscience du moi d'il y a une minute, du moi, d'il y a un jour, du moi d'il y a un an, du moi d'il y a vingt ans, vienne à s'effacer; alors, je n'aurai plus d'autre moi que celui qui résultera des conditions extérieures." Charles Richet, *L'Homme et l'Intelligence, Fragments de physiologie et de psychologie* (Paris: Félix Alcan, 1884), 248.
39. Charles Richet, "De la Mémoire Elémentaire," *Revue Philosophique* 11 (June 1881): 545.
40. Richet, *L'Homme et l'Intelligence*, 537.
41. Joseph Maxwell, Les *Phénomènes psychiques: recherches, observations, méthodes* (Paris: Félix Alcan, 1903), 16
42. Both Richet and Janet worked with the woman that Janet named "Leonie," after first having named her "Mme. B." See Janet's discussion of Mme. B. in "Notes sur quelque phénomènes de somnambulisme," *Bulletin de la société de psychologie physiologique* (1885): 24; and *L'automatisme psychologique* (Paris: Félix Alcan, 1889), 49. See also Jacqueline Carroy, *Hypnose, suggestion et psychologie: l'invention des sujets* (Paris: Presses Universitares de France, 1991), 84–86. Charcot's discussion of faith healing is in his *La foi qui guérit* (Paris: Félix Alcan, 1897).

43. See, for example, Richet's preface to Maxwell, *Les phénomènes psychiques*, ix: "Il y a dix ans on ne soupçonnait pas l'existence des rayons Roentgen. Avant la photographie, on ne savait pas que la lumière réduit les sels d'argent. Les ondes hertziennes ne sont connues que depuis trente ans à peine. Il y a deux cent ans, on ne connaissait de cette force immense électrique que la propriété de l'ambre frotté."
44. Charles Richet, "A Propos du mysticisme moderne: réplique à M. Rosenbach," *Annales des sciences psychiques* 2 (1892): 292–301.
45. See Juri, *Charles Richet*, and Wolf, *Brain, Mind, and Medicine*.
46. Charles Richet, "Lettre à M. Dariex," *Annales des sciences psychiques* 1 (1891): 4
47. Charles Richet, préface to *Les Hallucinations télépathiques*, by Edmund Gurney, F. W. H. Myers, and Frank Podmore, trans. L. Mariller (Paris: Félix Alcan, 1891), xiii.
48. Gabriel Delanne, *Le Phénomène spirite: témoinages des savants*, 4th ed. (Paris: Chamuel, 1893), 192, 264.
49. H. Fourtier, "Les Joyeusetées de la photographie, photographies spirites," *Photo-Journal* 8 (1891): 243.
50. Aleksandr Aksakov, *Animisme et spiritisme: Essai d'un examen critique des phénomènes médiumiques*, trans. Berthold Sandow (Paris: P. C. Leymarie, 1895).
51. Baraduc writes: "Je reste donc bien cantonné dans le domaine de l'iconographie de l'invisible. . . . J'ai surtout cherché à obtenir les signatures de forces *cachées, forces vitales et psychiques*, niées jusqu'à present." Hyppolite Baraduc, *L'Ame humaine: ses mouvements, ses lumières et l'iconographie de l'invisible fluidique* (Paris: Carre, 1896), 34.
52. Baraduc, *L'Ame humaine*, 40.
53. See Fourtier, "Les Joyeusetées de la photographie," 241–45.
54. See Ulrich Baer, "Photography and Hysteria, Towards a Poetics of the Flash," *Yale Journal of Criticism* 7 (spring 1994): 41–77.
55. Jean-Martin Charcot, *Leçons du mardi à la Salpêtrière: Policlinique, 1887–1888* (Paris: Delahaye & Lecrosnier, 1888), 178; quoted in Didi-Huberman, *L'Invention de l'hystérie*, 32.
56. See the excellent discussion in Didi-Huberman, *L'Invention de l'hystérie*, 119–25; and Baer, "Photography and Hysteria," which provides a powerful interpretation as well as an excellent bibliography. See also Baer, *Spectral Evidence: The Photography of Trauma* (Cambridge, Mass.: MIT Press, 2002). There is by now an enormous literature on photography, hysteria and the paranormal. I cite here only a few works, in addition to the collections on hysteria, medicine, and modernism cited above. Robert A. Sobieszek, ed., *The Ghost in the Shell: Photography and the Human Soul, 1850–2000* (Cambridge, Mass.: MIT Press, 1999); Geoffrey

Batchen, *Burning With Desire: The Concept of Photography* (Cambridge, Mass.: MIT Press, 1997); and Geoffrey Batchen, *Each Wild Idea: Writing, Photography, History* (Cambridge, Mass.: MIT Press, 2001); Jennifer Tucker, *Nature Exposed: Photography as Eyewitness in Victorian Science* (Baltimore: Johns Hopkins University Press, 2005); and Corey Keller, ed., *Brought to Light: Photography and the Invisible, 1840–1900* (New Haven: Yale University Press, 2008).

57. See Rae Beth Gordon, "From Charcot to Charlot: Unconscious Imitation and Spectatorship in French Cabaret and Early Cinema," *Critical Inquiry* 27, no. 3 (2001): 515–49.
58. See the Collection Bourneville in the Archives de l' Assistance Publique, Paris.
59. As quoted in Owen, *Hysteria, Hypnosis, and Healing*, 247.
60. From *Le Gil Bias*, August 25, 1887, in Press Clippings collection on Bourneville in the Archives de l'Assistance Publique: M24 234–5.
61. See Michael S. Roth, "Freud's Use and Abuse of the Past," in *The Ironist's Cage*, 186–200; and *Psycho-Analysis* as *History: Negation and Freedom in Freud* (Ithaca, N.Y.: Cornell University Press, 1995). Also see Patrick Hutton, *History an Art of Memory* (Hanover, N.H.: University Press of New England, 1993), 59–67.

4. Trauma, Representation, and Historical Consciousness

This chapter was first presented at the Zentrum für inrerdisziplinäre Forschung in Bielefeld. The author is grateful to Jörn Rüsen for his invitation and his comments.

1. In "Hysterical Remembering," chapter 3 of this book, I discuss Charcot's and Janet's approaches to hysteria, memory, and trauma. In the original published version of this essay, I recapitulated much of that presentation, but here I have edited this section so as to avoid repetition as much as possible.
2. On Félida X, see "Remembering Forgetting," chapter 1 of this book; and Ian Hacking, *Rewriting the Soul: Multiple Personality and the Sciences of Memory* (Princeton: Princeton University Press, 1995), 159–70.
3. See, for example, Richard Terdiman, *Present Past: Modernity and the Memory Crisis* (Ithaca, N.Y.: Cornell University Press, 1993); Matt K. Matsuda, *The Memory of the Modern* (Oxford: Oxford University Press, 1996); Laura Otis, *Organic Memory: History and the Body in the Late Nineteenth and Early Twentieth Centuries* (Lincoln: University of Nebraska Press, 1994); and Mark Micale and Paul Lerner, eds., *Traumatic Pasts: History, Psychiatry, and Trauma in the Modern Age, 1870–1930* (Cambridge: Cambridge University Press, 2010).

4. Ruth Leys has discussed Janet's emphasis on forgetting in the context of debates on memory in the beginning of this century and in recent psychological treatments of posttraumatic disorders. See Leys, "Traumatic Cures: Shell Shock, Janet, and the Question of Memory," *Critical Inquiry* 20 (1994): 623–62. This material is integrated in her book, *Trauma: A Genealogy* (Chicago: University of Chicago Press, 2000). In this regard, see also Judith Lewis Herman, *Trauma and Recovery* (New York: Basic, 1992), 34–35; Bessel A. van der Kolk and Onno van def Hart, "The Intrusive Past: The Flexibility of Memory and the Engraving of Trauma," in *Trauma: Explorations in Memory*, ed. Cathy Caruth (Baltimore: Johns Hopkins University Press, 1995), 158–82; Daniel L. Schacter, *Searching for Memory: The Brain, the Mind, and the Past* (New York: Basic, 1996), 231–33.
5. Sigmund Freud, *Introductory Lectures on Psycho-Analysis*, in *The Standard Edition of the Complete Psychological Works of Sigmund Freud*, 24 vols. (London: Hogarth Press, 1953–74), 16:275.
6. Van der Kolk and van der Hart, "The Intrusive Past," 176.
7. See Roth, "You Must Remember This: History, Memory, and Trauma in *Hiroshima Mon Amour*," in *The Ironist's Cage: Memory, Trauma and the Construction of History* (New York: Columbia University Press, 1995), 201–13.
8. Carl E. Schorske, "History and the Study of Culture," in *History And . . . : Histories Within the Human Sciences*, ed. Ralph Cohen and Michael S. Roth (Charlottesville: University of Virginia Press, 1995), 390.
9. Hans Kellner, "Beautifying the Nightmare: The Aesthetics of Post-Modern History," *Strategies* 4/5 (1991): 292–93
10. Robert Dawidoff, "History . . . But," in *History And . . .*, 395–406.
11. Hayden White, "The Politics of Historical Interpretation: Discipline and Desublimation," in *The Content of Form: Narrative Discourse and Historical Representation* (Baltimore: Johns Hopkins University Press, 1987).
12. The literature on this subject is enormous. Some important statements of the key issues are found in Saul Friedlander's edited collection, *Probing the Limits of Representation: Nazism and the "Final Solution"* (Cambridge, Mass.: Harvard University Press, 1992); Dominick LaCapra, *Representing the Holocaust: History, Theory, Trauma* (Ithaca, N.Y.: Cornell University Press, 1994), hereafter cited in the text as *RH*; Lawrence L. Langer, "What More Can Be Said about the Holocaust," in *Admitting the Holocaust: Collected Essays* (New York: Oxford University Press, 1995), 179–84. See the discussion of photography in this regard in "Why Photography Matters to the Theory of History," chapter 14 of this volume.

5. Trauma

1. Alexandre Kojève, *Introduction à la lecture de Hegel*, 2nd ed. (Paris: Gallimard, 1968), 436n; *Introduction to the Reading of Hegel*, trans. J. H. Nichols, Jr. (Ithaca, N.Y.: Cornell University Press: 1980), 160–61. The translation has been somewhat altered.
2. See Strauss's letters to Kojève, published in Leo Strauss, *On Tyranny*, revised and expanded, ed. Victor Gourevitch and Michael S. Roth (Chicago: University of Chicago Press, 2000), 208; 239 (August 22, 1948); 291 (September 11, 1957). The Nietzsche reference is to *Thus Spake Zarathustra*, 1:3–5.
3. In the preceding section I have drawn on my work with Victor Gourevitch in our preparation of the revised, expanded edition of *On Tyranny*.
4. I have discussed this contemporary version of Weber's iron cage in *The Ironist's Cage: Memory, Trauma and the Construction of History* (New York: Columbia University Press, 1997), 148–62.
5. Sigmund Freud, *Introductory Lectures on Psycho-Analysis*, in *The Standard Edition of the Complete Psychological Works of Sigmund Freud*, 24 vols. (London: Hogarth Press, 1953–74), 16:275.
6. I have discussed this issue in "You Must Remember This: History, Memory, and Trauma in *Hiroshima Mon Amour*," in *The Ironist's Cage*, 201–213, and more generally in "Trauma, Representation and Historical Consciousness," chapter 4 of this volume.
7. On this and related topics, see Wendy Brown, *States of Injury: Power and Freedom in Late Modernity* (Princeton: Princeton University Press, 1995).
8. Carl E. Schorske, "History and the Study of Culture," in *History and . . . : Histories Within the Human Sciences*, ed. Ralph Cohen and Michael S. Roth (Charlottesville: University of Virginia Press, 1995), 390. Also cited above, 83.
9. Hayden White, "The Burden of History," (1969) in *Tropics of Discourse: Essays in Cultural Criticism* (Baltimore: Johns Hopkins University Press, 1978), 27–50; and "The Politics of Historical Interpretation: Discipline and De-Sublimation," (1982) in *The Content of the Form: Narrative Discourse and Historical Representation* (Baltimore: Johns Hopkins University Press, 1987), 58–82.
10. Hayden White, "Modernist Event," in *Figural Realism: Studies in the Mimesis Effect* (Baltimore: Johns Hopkins University Press, 1999), 74.
11. Ibid., 82.
12. This is the course charted quite self-consciously by Saul Friedländer. For example, see his *Memory, History and the Extermination of the Jews of Europe* (Bloomington: Indiana University Press, 1993).

13. A point made long before the trauma vogue by Christopher Lasch in *The Minimal Self: Psychic Survival in Troubled Times* (New York: Norton, 1984).
14. See, for example, the discussion of the "age of testimony" in Elie Wiesel, "The Holocaust as Literary Inspiration," in *Dimensions of the Holocaust* (Evanston, IL: Northwestern University Press, 1977), 9; Shoshana Felman and Dori Laub, *Testimony: Crises of Witnessing in Literature, Psychoanalysis and History* (New York: Routledge, 1992), passim; Cathy Caruth, *Unclaimed Experience: Trauma, Narrative and History* (Baltimore: Johns Hopkins University Press, 1996), 26–27, 106–7; and Judith Lewis Herman, *Trauma and Recovery* (New York: Basic, 1992), 181–83. The literature in this area has grown enormously in the last decades. See Michael S. Roth and Charles G. Salas, eds., *Disturbing Remains: Memory, History and Crisis in the Twentieth Century* (Los Angeles: Getty Research Institute, 2001); E. Ann Kaplan, *Trauma Culture: The Politics of Terror and Loss in Media and Literature* (Piscataway, N.J.: Rutgers University Press, 2005), 24–41; Carolyn J. Dean, *Aversion and Erasure: The Fate of the Victim After the Holocaust* (Ithaca, NY: Cornell University Press, 2010), 1–30, 178–83; and the discussion of trauma, shame, and witnessing in the introduction to this volume.
15. Peter Novick, *The Holocaust in American Life* (New York: Houghton Mifflin, 1999), passim.
16. The key text remains Judith Herman's *Trauma and Recovery*. But see also Frederick Crews, *The Memory Wars: Freud's Legacy in Dispute* (New York: New York Review of Books, 1995).
17. See in this regard, Walter Ben Michaels, *The Shape of the Signifier: 1967 to the End of History* (Princeton: Princeton University Press, 2004).
18. Mark Seltzer, *Serial Killers: Death and Life in America's Wound Culture* (New York: Routledge, 1998), 254–92.
19. See, for example, Novick's discussion of responses to the TV-movie *Holocaust* and Spielberg's *Schindler's List*, 209–214.
20. Hal Foster, *The Return of the Real: The Avant Garde at the End of the Century* (Cambridge, Mass.: MIT Press, 1996).
21. Foster, *The Return of the Real*, 168. More recently, artists (especially those marked by queer theory) have emphasized shame as an aspect of trauma. See the introduction of this volume.
22. Geoffrey Hartmann, Shoshana Felman, Dominick LaCapra, and Cathy Caruth are some of the most important examples in this regard.
23. See Judith Butler's framing of the "ethical turn" in the humanities in relation to the de Man scandal: "Ethical Ambivalence," in *The Turn to Ethics*, ed. Marjorie Garber, Beatrice Hanssen, Rebecca L. Walkowitz (New York: Routledge, 2000), 20.

24. Seltzer, *Serial Killers*, 284n31.
25. Seltzer's goal is not, however, only to demarcate this fit but to develop a theory of violence and public life out of concepts of mimesis and identification.
26. Cathy Caruth, *Unclaimed Experience*, 18.
27. Ibid., 91–92.
28. Ibid., 18 and 92, respectively.
29. Ibid., 108.
30. See the introduction to this volume for a brief discussion of LaCapra's more recent work in this area.
31. See Dominick LaCapra, "Acting Out and Working Through," in *Representing the Holocaust: History, Theory, Trauma* (Ithaca, N.Y.: Cornell University Press, 1994), 205–23.
32. Leo Strauss, *Thoughts on Machiavelli* (Chicago: University of Chicago Press, 1995), 298. I consulted Kojève's own copy of the book in his library, thanks to Mlle. Nina Ivanoff.

6. Falling into History

1. The case of "Frau Emmy von N." is case 2 of Josef Breuer and Sigmund Freud, in *Studies on Hysteria*, in *The Standard Edition of the Complete Psychological Works of Sigmund Freud*, trans. and ed. James Strachey, 24 vols. (London: Hogarth Press, 1953–74), 2:48–105, here at 61. Hereafter references to this volume of the *Standard Edition* will be given in the text.
2. Jules Janet, "L'hystérie et l'hypnotisme, d'après la théorie de la double personnalité," *Revue Scientifique* 20 (1888): 618.
3. Ibid.
4. Pierre Janet, *L'État mental des hystériques* (Paris: Felix Alcan, 1911), 618.
5. Ibid., 429.
6. Ibid., 423.
7. J. B. Pontalis, "Le Sèjour de Freud à Paris," *Nouvelle Revue de psychanalyse* 8 (1973): 236.
8. *L'État mental des hysteriques*, 479.
9. Ibid., 478.
10. On these general themes in psychoanalysis, see my *Psycho-Analysis as History: Negation and Freedom in Freud* (1987; Ithaca, N.Y.: Cornell University Press, 1995); and "Freud's Use and Abuse of the Past," in *The Ironist's Cage: Memory, Trauma and the Construction of History* (New York: Columbia University Press, 1995), 186–200.

11. The case is discussed in the "sensitivity" chapter of Kramer's *Listening to Prozac* (New York: Penguin, 1994), 67–107. Hereafter references to this book will be given in the text.
12. Kramer cites, among other sources, two key articles: Donald F. Klein, "Cybernetics, Activation, and Drug Effects," in R. H. Van den Hoofdakker, ed., "Biological Measures: Their Theoretical and Diagnostic Value in Psychiatry," in *Acta Psychiatra Scandinavia*, vol. 77, suppl 341 (1988), 126–37; Donald F Klein, "Anxiety Reconceptualized," in *Anxiety: New Research and Changing Concepts*, ed. D. F. Klein and J. G. Rabkin (New York: Raven, 1981), 235–61.
13. See Paul H. Wender and Donald F. Klein, *Mind, Mood and Medicine: A Guide to the New Biopsychiatry* (New York: Farrar, Strauss, Giroux, 1981), 334–35.
14. Peter Kramer, *Freud: Inventor of the Modern Mind* (New York: Penguin, 2006), 98–100. Kramer draws especially from the work of Patrick Mahony, *Freud's Dora: A Psychoanalytic, Historical and Textual Study* (New Haven: Yale University Press, 1996).

8. Why Warburg Now?

1. See for example, Ethan Kleinberg, "Interdisciplinary Studies at a Crossroads," *Liberal Education* 94, no. 1 (2008).
2. Carlo Ginzburg, "From Aby Warburg to E. H. Gombrich: A Problem of Method," in *Myths, Emblems, Clues*, trans. John and Anne C. Tedeschi (London: Hutchinson Radius, 1990).
3. I was Associate Director of the Getty Research Institute from 1995–2000. Its first two directors, Kurt Forster and Salvatore Settis, had enormous sympathy for and interest in Warburg's work, and saw the GRI as continuing that legacy. Thomas Crow, the first American to head the Institute, saw no reason, as far as I know, to depart from this Warburgian stream. One would be hard pressed, I think, to find many other areas of overlap in the scholarship of these three influential art historians. Warburg was a name they could share.
4. See the *London Review of Books* 21 (April 29, 1999), and letters on June 10 and July 1, 1999.
5. Kurt Forster, introduction to *The Renewal of Pagan Antiquity*, by Aby Warburg, trans. David Britt (Los Angeles: Getty Research Institute, 1999), 2.
6. Edgar Wind, "Warburg's Concept of *Kulturwissenschaft* and its Meaning for Aesthetics," in *The Art of Art History*, ed. Donald Preziosi (New York: Oxford University Press, 2009), 192.

7. This was one of Ginzburg's concerns in 1966. See his remarks on analogy and parallelism.
8. Forster, introduction to *The Renewal of Pagan Antiquity*, 6.
9. The German text was published as *Serpent Ritual: An Account of a Journey* (*Schlangen-ritual: Ein Reisebericht*), with an afterword by Ulrich Raulff (Berlin: Klauss Wagenbach, 1988). See Aby M. Warburg, *Images from the Region of the Pueblo Indians of North America*, ed. Michael P. Steinberg (Ithaca, N.Y.: Cornell University Press, 1995).
10. Georges Didi-Huberman, *Image survivante: histoire de l'art et temps des fantômes selon Aby Warburg* (Paris: Minuit, 2002).
11. Carlo Severi, "Warburg Anthropologue ou le déchiffrement d'une utopie—De la Biologie des images à l'Anthropologie de la mémoire," in "Image et Anthropologie," ed. C. Severi, special issue, *L'Homme*, 165 (2003): 77–129.
12. Salvatore Settis, *The Future of the Classical*, trans. Allan Cameron (London: Polity, 2007), 83–90.
13. Wind, "Warburg's Concept of *Kulturwissenschaft*, 193.
14. Juliet Koss, "On the Limits of Empathy," *The Art Bulletin* 88, no. 1 (March 2006): 139–57.
15. Matthew Rampley, "From Symbol to Allegory: Aby Warburg's Theory of Art," *Art Bulletin* 79, no. 1:52.

9. Classic Postmodernism

1. This chapter was originally a review essay on Keith Jenkins, *Refiguring History: New Thoughts on an Old Discipline* (London: Routledge, 2003). Hereafter references to this work are cited in the text.
2. Peter Novick, *That Noble Dream: The "Objectivity Question" and the American Historical Profession* (Cambridge: Cambridge University Press, 1988), 410.
3. Frank Ankersmit, "Statements, Texts and Pictures," in *The New Philosophy of History*, ed. F. R. Ankersmit and H. Kellner (Chicago: University of Chicago Press, 1995), 212–40; *Historical Representation* (Stanford: Stanford University Press, 2002), passim.
4. See, for example. David Carr, *Time, Narrative, and History* (Bloomington: Indiana University Press, 1986); Hans Kellner, "However Imperceptibly: From the Historical to the Sublime," *PMLA* 118, no. 3 (2003): 591–96.
5. This is clear even in the passages on inheritance that Jenkins quotes. See also Jacques Derrida, *Specters of Marx: The State of the Debt, The Work of Mourning,*

and the New International, trans. Peggy Kamuf (London: Routledge, 1994), passim; and Derrida, *The Work of Mourning*, ed. Pascal-Anne Brault and Michael Naas (Chicago: University Press of Chicago, 2001).

6. Stanley Fish, "Truth but No Consequences: Why Philosophy Doesn't Matter," *Critical Inquiry* 29, no. 3 (2003): 415.
7. See, for example, Richard A. Posner, *The Problematics of Moral and Legal Theory* (Cambridge, Mass.: Belknap Press of Harvard University Press, 2002); Jeremy Waldron, "Redressing Historic Injustice," *University of Toronto Law Journal* 52 (Winter 2002): 153–60.
8. One might look at the interesting revival of the historical novel with Pat Barker, or in regard to questions of history and memory in the work of Ian McEwan, W. G. Sebald, and many others. On the powerful detail, see Christopher Lane, "The Poverty of Context; Historicism and Nonmimetic Fiction," *PMLA* 118, no. 3 (2003): 450–69.
9. See Elazar Barkan, *The Guilt of Nations: Restitution and Negotiating Historical Injustices* (New York: Norton, 2001).
10. This is a central theme of *Disturbing Remains: Memory, History, and Crisis in the Twentieth Century*, ed. Michael S. Roth and Charles G. Salas (Los Angeles: Getty Research Institute, 2001). The essays in this volume explore how events of catastrophic intensity are transformed into memory and history in different times and places.

10. Ebb Tide

1. Ankersmit, "Invitation to Historians," *Rethinking History* 7 (2003): 419. This is an essay on F. R. Ankersmit, *Sublime Historical Experience* (Stanford: Stanford University Press, 2005). References to this book will be given parenthetically in the text.
2. For another attempt to preserve the distinctiveness of historical practice from Rorty's deflationary mode, see John H. Zammito, "Rorty, 'Historicism' and the Practice of History: A Polemic," in *Rethinking History* 10, no. 1 (2006): 9–48. See also my "Thin Description: Richard Rorty's Use of History" in *The Ironist's Cage: Memory, Trauma and the Construction of History* (New York: Columbia University Press, 1997).
3. Collingwood is a theorist of history for whom the category of experience is most important, but he receives no attention in this volume. Perhaps this is because

Collingwood focused on the possibilities of reexperiencing the past, not on a notion of a experiential, ecstatic union with the past.

4. Martin Jay, *Songs of Experience: Modern American and European Variations on a Universal Theme* (Berkeley: University of California Press, 2005).
5. See ibid., 344–46.
6. See the introduction to *Disturbing Remains: Memory, History, and Crisis in the Twentieth Century*, ed. Michael S. Roth and Charles G. Salas (Los Angeles: Getty Research Institute, 2001); see also Roth, *The Ironist's Cage*, and "Trauma Representation and Historical Consciousness" (chapter 4 of this volume) and the introduction to this volume.
7. Eelco Runia, "Presence," *History and Theory* 45, no. 1 (2006): 4.
8. Jay, *Songs of Experience*, 390.
9. See for example, "Trauma, Representation and Historical Consciousness," and "You Must Remember This: History, Memory and Trauma in Hiroshima Mon Amour," in *The Ironist's Cage*. See also Robert Dawidoff, "History . . . But," in *History And . . . : Histories Within the Human Sciences*, ed. Ralph Cohen and Michael S. Roth (Charlottesville: University Press of Virginia, 1995), 3 70–81.
10. For a historical account of this issue in Western Europe and the United States, see Peter Frizsche, *Stranded in the Present: Modern Time and the Melancholy of History* (Cambridge, Mass.: Harvard University Press, 2004).
11. Ankersmit, "Invitation to Historians," 421.

12. Inquiry as Hope

1. Richard Rorty, "Anticlericalism and Atheism," in *The Future of Religion*, ed. Santiago Zabala (New York: Columbia University Press, 2005), 40.
2. Richard Rorty, *Philosophy as Cultural Politics* (Cambridge: Cambridge University Press, 2007). Hereafter references are given parenthetically in the text.
3. There has also been civil and serious engagement with Rorty's work by some of the major figures in Anglo-American philosophy. The volume *Rorty and His Critics* is a model in this regard. Robert B. Brandom, ed., *Rorty and his Critics* (Malden, Mass.: Blackwell, 2000).
4. Ibid., 124.
5. Hegel, *Philosophy of History*, trans. J. Sibree (New York, 1956), 79.
6. Ibid., 19.

7. "[Hegel's] System was no sooner published than it began to be read as a *reductio ad absurdum* of a certain form of intellectual life" (92). In conversation the philosopher Victor Gourevitch has called this a "decapitated Hegelianism," an appellation I think Rorty would have found apt.
8. Alan R. Malachowski, ed., *Reading Rorty* (Malden, Mass.: Blackwell, 1991), 62.
9. Ibid., 13.
10. Ibid., 15.
11. "On Ethnocentrism: A Reply to Clifford Geertz," reprinted in Richard Rorty, *Objectivity, Relativism and Truth: Philosophical Papers, Volume 1* (Cambridge: Cambridge University Press, 1991), 203–10.
12. Rorty quoting John Rawls's exchange with Habermas published in *The Journal of Philosophy* 92, no 3 (1995), 49n9.
13. Richard Rorty, *Achieving Our Country: Leftist Thought in Twentieth-Century America* (New York: Columbia University Press, 1998), 36.
14. Ibid., 37.
15. Ibid.
16. Ibid., 140.
17. Ibid., 84–88.
18. Ibid., 101.

13. Photographic Ambivalence

1. Stanley Cavell, *The Word Viewed: Reflections on the Ontology of Film*, enlarged ed. (Cambridge, Mass.: Harvard University Press, 1979), 23.
2. Roland Barthes, *Camera Lucida: Reflections on Photography*, trans. Richard Howard (New York: Hill and Wang, 1982), 65.
3. Stephen Bann, "'When I Was a Photographer': Nadar and History," *History and Theory*, Theme Issue 48 (2009): 95–111. The phrase "the rim of ontological uncertainty" is from this paper, p. 101. I participated in the *History and Theory* conference "Photography and Historical Representation" as a respondent to Stephen Bann. The present essay grew out of the conversations at the conference, and I am grateful to other participants, and particularly to the organizer, Jennifer Tucker, for creating this occasion to think about photography in relation to the theory of history.
4. G. W. F. Hegel, *The Philosophy of History*, trans. J. Sibree (New York: Dover, 1956), 79.
5. See, for example, Nancy Armstrong, *Fiction in the Age of Photography: The Legacy of British Realism* (Cambridge, Mass.: Harvard University Press, 2000).

6. Henri Bergson, *An Introduction to Metaphysics*, trans. T. E. Hulme (New York: Liberal Arts Press, 1955), 42.
7. Anson Rabinbach, *The Human Motor: Energy, Fatigue, and the Origins of Modernity* (New York: Basic, 1990), 113; see also Stephen Kern, *The Culture of Time and Space: 1880–1918* (Cambridge, Mass.: Harvard University Press, 1983), 25–26.
8. Henri Bergson, *Time and Free Will*, trans. F. L. Pogson (New York: Macmillan, 1910), 115.
9. Ibid., 76.
10. Mary Ann Doane, *The Emergence of Cinematic Time: Modernity, Contingency, the Archive* (Cambridge, Mass.: Harvard University Press, 2002), 77. See also Henri Bergson, *Matter and Memory*, trans. N. M. Paul and W. S. Palmer (New York: Zone, 1988), 76; Marta Braun, *Picturing Time: The Work of Etienne Jules Marey, 1830–1914* (Chicago: University of Chicago Press, 1992), 280–82.
11. Michel Frizot, in *Photography Theory*, ed. James Elkins (New York: Routledge, 2007), 180.
12. Roland Barthes, "The Discourse of History," trans. Stephen Bann, *Comparative Criticism* 3 (1981): 5.
13. Susan Sontag, *On Photography* (New York: Farrar, Straus, Giroux, 1977).
14. Thierry de Duve, "Time Exposure and Snapshot: The Photograph as Paradox," in Elkins, *Photography Theory*, 113.
15. Video recording, though, would seem to work in the opposite direction because it shows the flow of time without breaking it into frames. But this would be an illusion. Videos do extend the episode. The video recording is an elongated snapshot, but even a lengthy recording is ripped out of historical continuity. Photographic and video reproduction are *interruptive yet precise* modes of representation. Their accuracy is twinned to their breaking apart continuity.
16. Bann, "When I Was a Photographer," 77.
17. Susan Stewart calls the photograph as souvenir "the logical extension of the pressed flower." See her *On Longing: Narratives of the Miniature, the Gigantic, the Souvenir, the Collection* (Baltimore: Johns Hopkins University Press, 1984), 138.
18. See Barthes, *Camera Lucida: Reflections on Photography*, trans. Richard Howard (New York: Hill and Wang, 1982), 95. Stephen Bann discusses a parallel lithographic image in "When I Was a Photographer," 100–101. Geoffrey Batchen has drawn interesting parallels with the "dizzying temporal convolution" found in Walter Benjamin's "Little History of Photography": *Camera Lucida:* Another Little History of Photography," in *The Meaning of Photography*, ed. Robin Kelsey and Blake Stimson (Williamstown, Mass.: Sterling and Francine Clark Art Institute, 2008), 77–78.

19. Barthes, *Camera Lucida*, 87.
20. Indeed, I would make use of some of the unpublished material as heuristic devices and then publish the correspondence with Leo Strauss. See Michael S. Roth, *Knowing and History: Appropriations of Hegel in Twentieth-Century France* (Ithaca, N.Y.: Cornell University Press, 1985); and Leo Strauss, *On Tyranny: Including the Strauss-Kojève Correspondence*, ed. Victor Gourevitch and Michael S. Roth (Chicago: University of Chicago Press, 2000).
21. Eelco Runia, "Presence," *History and Theory* 45, no. 1 (2006): 5.
22. Dominick LaCapra, "Is Everyone a *Mentalité* Case? Transference and the 'Culture' Concept," *History and Theory* 23, no. 3 (1984): 310, n. 17.
23. See the sharp critical perspective on this trend by Ethan Kleinberg, "Presence *In Abstentia*," *Storia della Storiografia* 55 (2009): 43–59.
24. Frank Ankersmit, *Sublime Historical Experience* (Stanford: Stanford University Press, 2004), 125. See my discussion in "Ebb Tide," chapter 10 in this volume.
25. Walter Benn Michaels, "Photographs and Fossils," in Elkins, *Photography Theory*, 445.
26. Ibid., 434. Michaels is quoting other essays from the *Photography Theory* volume.
27. Michaels's essay explores how bypassing intentionality presents a challenge to the category of art. He is especially interested in Michael Fried's recent analyses of this same issue: Michael Fried, *Why Photography Matters as Art as Never Before* (New Haven: Yale University Press, 2008). See my discussion in, "Why Photography Matters to the Theory of History," chapter 14 in this volume.
28. Eelco Runia, "Burying the Dead, Creating the Past," *History and Theory* 46, no. 3 (2007): 323.
29. Cora Diamond, "The Difficulty of Reality and the Difficulty of Philosophy," in *Philosophy and Animal Life*, ed. Stanley Cavell et al. (New York: Columbia University Press, 2008), 43–46. Hereafter references to this work are in the text. I am grateful to Kari Weil for calling my attention to this essay. See also Ian Hacking's comments on the political-national aspects of reading the poem in the same volume, 156–60. The poem can be found in Ted Hughes, "Six Young Men," in *The Hawk in the Rain* (London: Faber and Faber, 1957), 54–55.
30. Jacques Derrida and Bernard Stiegler, *Echographies of Television*, trans. Jennifer Bajorek (Cambridge: Polity, 2002), 117. I was alerted to this text by its citation in Carey Wolfe, "Introduction: Exposures" in Cavell et al., *Philosophy and Animal Life*, 31.
31. For White the synecdoche is not just a part substituting for the whole (like metonymy), but also an essential aspect substituting for the whole. See the introduction to *Metahistory: The Historical Imagination in Nineteenth Century Europe*

(Baltimore: Johns Hopkins University Press, 1973), especially 34: "With Synecdoche . . . a phenomenon can be characterized by using the part to symbolize some *quality* presumed to inhere in the totality, as in the expression 'He is all heart.' . . . Metaphor is essentially *representational*, Metonymy is *reductionist*, Synecdoche is *integrative*, and Irony is *negational*."

32. Roland Barthes, "Rhetoric of the Image," in *Image, Music, Text*, trans. Stephen Heath (London: Fontana, 1977), 44.
33. Marianne Hirsch and Leo Spitzer, "Incongruous Images: 'Before, During, and After' the Holocaust," *History and Theory*, Theme Issue 48 (2009): 9–25. Hirsch and Spitzer delivered this paper at the conference at which I first discussed the issues in this chapter.
34. Mary Ann Doane, "Indexicality and the Concept of Medium Specificity," in Kelsey and Stimson, *The Meaning of Photography*. She is referring to Didi-Huberman's "The Index of the Absent Wound (Monograph on a Stain)," *October* 29 (1984): 63–82. See also his *Images in Spite of All: Four Photographs from Auschwitz*, trans. Shane B. Lillis (Chicago: University of Chicago Press, 2008); and my essay "Why Photography Matters to the Theory of History," chapter 14 in this volume.
35. Carl E. Schorske, *Fin-de-Siècle Vienna: Politics and Culture* (New York: Knopf, 1980); Debora Silverman, *Art Nouveau in Fin-de-Siècle Paris: Politics, Psychology, and Style* (Berkeley: University of California Press, 1989).
36. Stephen Kern, *The Culture of Time and Space, 1880–1918* (Cambridge, Mass.: Harvard University Press, 1986); Rabinbach, *The Human Motor*.
37. Jennifer Tucker, *Nature Exposed: Photography as Eyewitness in Victorian Science* (Baltimore: Johns Hopkins University Press, 2006).
38. Mary Ann Doane, *The Emergence of Cinematic Time: Modernity, Contingency, the Archive* (Cambridge, Mass.: Harvard University Press, 2002), 11.
39. Ibid., 12.
40. Siegfried Kracauer, "Photography," in *The Mass Ornament: Weimar Essays*, trans. and ed. Thomas Y. Levin (Cambridge, Mass.; Harvard University Press, 1995).
41. Doane notes that: "Historical analyses of photography consistently demonstrate photography's inclination toward the contingent, the particular, the detail. . . . Photographic technology is the automatic, unthinking guarantee of the predilection for the contingent." Doane, *The Emergence of Cinematic Time*, 142.
42. Robin Kelsey, "Photography, Chance, and *The Pencil of Nature*," in Kelsey and Stimson, *The Meaning of Photography*. Kelsey discussed "photographic madness" at the conference at which I first talked about the issues in this chapter.
43. Doane, *The Emergence of Cinematic Time*, 144.

44. Ibid., 140.
45. Hacking's work is important to both Doane and Kelsey. See *The Taming of Chance* (Cambridge: Cambridge University Press, 1990).
46. Doane, *The Emergence of Cinematic Time*, 208.
47. Ibid., 220.
48. See Michael S. Roth, "Hysterical Remembering" (1996), chapter 3 in this volume; Clement Cheroux, *The Perfect Medium: Photography and the Occult* (New Haven: Yale University Press, 2005); and *Brought to Light: Photography and the Invisible, 1840–1900*, ed. Corey Kellor (New Haven: Yale University Press, 2008).
49. Barthes, *Camera Lucida*, 118.
50. Bann, "When I Was a Photographer," 103.

14. Why Photography Matters to the Theory of History

1. Jacques Ranciére, "S'il y a de l'irreprésentable," in *L'art et la mémoire des camps: représenter, exterminer* (Paris: Seuil, 2001), 96.
2. Stanley Cavell, *The World Viewed: Reflections on the Ontology of Film* (Cambridge, Mass.: Harvard University Press, 1971), 23.
3. Georges Didi-Huberman, *Images in Spite of All: Four Photographs from Auschwitz*, trans. Shane B. Lillis (Chicago: University of Chicago Press, 2008); and Michael Fried, *Why Photography Matters as Art as Never Before* (New Haven: Yale University Press, 2008).
4. There is by now a significant body of work on the photographic representation of the Shoah. See, for example, Andrea Liss, *Trespassing Through Shadows: Memory, Photography and the Holocaust* (Minneapolis: University of Minnesota Press, 1998); Teresa Swiebocka, ed., *Auschwitz: A History in Photographs* (Bloomington: Indiana University Press, 1993); Barbie Zeller, *Remembering to Forget: Holocaust Memory through the Camera's Eye* (Chicago: University of Chicago Press, 1998); Clément Chéroux, ed., *Mémoire des camps: Photographies des camps de concentration et d'extermination Nazis (1933–1939)* (Paris: Marval, 2001); Marianne Hirsch, "Surviving Images: Holocaust Photographs and the Work of Postmemory," *Yale Journal of Criticism* 14, no. 1 (2001): 5–37.
5. I quote this passage in my essay "Shoah as Shivah," reprinted in Michael S. Roth, *The Ironist's Cage: Memory, Trauma and the Construction of History* (New York: Columbia University Press, 1997), 203.
6. The literature on this subject is massive. See Peter Novick, for example, on evolution of historical representation of these events in an American context: *The*

Holocaust in American Life (New York: Houghton Mifflin, 1999), passim. See also Daniel Levy and Natan Sznaider, *Holocaust and Memory in the Global Age* (Philadelphia: Temple University Press, 2006); and Jörn Rüsen, "Holocaust Memory and Identity Building: Metahistorical Considerations in the Case of West Germany," in *Disturbing Remains: Memory, History and Crisis in the Twentieth Century*, ed. Michael S. Roth and Charles Salas (Los Angeles: Getty Publications, 2000), 252–70. Saul Friedlander has been one of the most thoughtful commentators on the changing nature of historical representation of the Shoah: *Memory, History and the Extermination of the Jews of Europe* (Bloomington: Indiana University Press, 1993); "History, Memory and the Historian: Facing the Shoah," in *Disturbing Remains*, 271–82.

7. See, for example, Cathy Caruth, *Unclaimed Experience* (Baltimore: Johns Hopkins University Press, 1996); Ruth Leys, *Trauma: A Genealogy* (Chicago: University of Chicago Press, 2000); Dominick LaCapra, *Writing History, Writing Trauma* (Baltimore: Johns Hopkins University Press, 2000); Roth and Salas, *Disturbing Remains*; E. Ann Kaplan, *Trauma Culture: the Politics of Terror and Loss in Media and Literature* (Piscataway, N.J.: Rutgers University Press, 2005); and the introduction to this volume.
8. See the distinction between bearing witness and giving testimony in Michael Bernard-Donals and Richard Glejzer, *Between Witness and Testimony: The Holocaust and the Limits of Representation* (New York: State University Presses of New York, 2001). For a careful discussion of the issues involved for historians and critical theorists in regard to "unrepresentability," see Dominick LaCapra, *History and its Limits: Human, Animal, Violence* (Ithaca, N.Y.: Cornell University Press, 2009), especially chapters 1 and 3.
9. Jean-Francois Lyotard, *The Differend: Phrases in Dispute*, trans. Georges Van Den Abbeele (Minneapolis: Minnesota University Press, 1988), 56–58. See also *Heidegger and "the Jews,"* trans. Andreas Michel and Mark Roberts (Minneapolis: University of Minnesota Press, 1990). For a powerful critique of Lyotard's position (a critique used cited by Didi-Huberman), see Jacques Ranciére, "S'il y a de l'irreprésentable," passim.
10. From Hannah Arendt, "Le procès d'Auschwitz," in *Auschwitz et Jerusalem* (Paris: Deuxtemps Tierce, 1991), 257–58.
11. Bruno Chaouat, "In the Image of Auschwitz," *diacritics* 36, no. 1 (2006): 89.
12. Claude Lanzmann, interview in *Le Monde* January 19, 2001.
13. Gerard Wajcman, "De la croyance photographique," *Les temps modernes* 56, no. 613 (2001): 47–83; Elizabeth Pagnoux, "Reporter photographique à Auschwitz," *Les temps modernes* 56, no. 613 (2001): 84–108. Hereafter references to Wajcman are given in the text.

14. Even Spielberg's film is attracting more nuanced readings. See, for example, Christoph Classes, "Balanced Truth: Steven Spielberg's *Schindler's List* Among History, Memory, and Popular Culture," *History and Theory*, Theme Issue 47 (2009): 77–102.
15. Two essays recently appearing in *History and Theory* concerning photography and the Holocaust should be mentioned as also refusing the false choice between radical skepticism and simple empiricism. Susan Crane raises important questions concerning the desensitization that can stem from repeated viewings of atrocity photographs: "Choosing Not To Look: Representation, Repatriation and Holocaust Atrocity Photography," *History and Theory* 47, no. 3 (October 2008): 309–30. Judith Keilbach takes a balanced, pragmatic approach to the use of photographs in this context: "Photographs, Symbolic Images, and the Holocaust: On the (Im)Possibility of Depicting Historical Truth," *History and Theory*, Theme Issue 47 (2009): 54–76.
16. Most famously in "Art and Objecthood" originally published in 1967 and now found in Michael Fried, *Art and Objecthood: Essays and Reviews* (Chicago: University of Chicago Press, 1998).
17. Michael Fried, *Absorption and Theatricality: Painting and the Beholder in the Age of Diderot* (Chicago: University of Chicago Press, 1980); *Courbet's Realism* (Chicago: University of Chicago Press, 1990); *Manet's Modernism, or, The Face of Painting in the 1860s* (Chicago: University of Chicago Press, 1996).
18. See Jeff Wall, *Selected Essays and Interviews* (New York: Museum of Modern Art, 2007).
19. James Elkins, "What Do We Want Photography to Be? A Response to Michael Fried," *Critical Inquiry* 31, no. 4 (2005): 938–56.
20. Quoting Ludwig Wittgenstein, *Wiener Ausgabe*, ed. M. Nedo (Vienna: Springer, 1994–95), MS 109 28:22.8.1930
21. Fried, "Art and Objecthood," 163. "Theater and theatricality are at war today, not simply with modernist painting . . . but with art at such—and to the extent that the different arts can be described as modernist, with modernist sensibility as such."
22. Michaels writes: "The repudiation of the photographer's intentions is in itself the appeal to the beholder's experience. Once the structural (or theoretical) indifference to the beholder that Fried identified as absorption appears as indifference, not just to the performance of the person being photographed but also to the performance of the photographer, its meaning is completely inverted. Instead of being irrelevant, the beholder is the only one who matters." Quoted from "Photographs and Fossils," in *Photography Theory*, ed. James Elkins (New York: Routledge, 2007), 439. Fried and Michaels remain in a very interesting dialogue, some of which can be found in the notes to *WPMANB*.

16. Graves of the Insane, Decorated

1. This essay was written in response to David Maisel's photographs published in his *Library of Dust* (San Francisco: Chronicle, 2008). The cover of *Memory, Trauma, and History* is based on a photograph by Maisel, and one can see many of his images at www.davidmaisel.com (acccessed February 2011).
2. Carla Yanni, *The Architecture of Madness: Insane Asylums in the United States* (Minneapolis: University Of Minnesota Press, 2007).
3. Sue Bell, "Oregon State Hospital," *Salem Online History*, http://www.salemhistory.net/places/state_hospital.htm.
4. Thomas W. Laqueur, "Spaces of the Dead," *Ideas from the National Humanities Center* 8, no. 2 (2001): 4.
5. For more on Ben Tabler's search, see www.cartercenter.org/health/mental_health/archive/documents/dark_corner_roberts.html (accessed February 2011).
6. I've written about this effort to materialize the world of mental illness and death through photography in "Hysterical Remembering," chapter 3 of this book.

19. Good and Risky

1. Martha Nussbaum, *Not for Profit: Why Democracy Needs the Humanities* (Princeton: Princeton University Press, 2010). Hereafter references are given parenthetically in the text.
2. Diane Ravitch, *The Death and Life of the Great American School System: How Testing and Choice are Undermining Education* (New York: Basic, 2010). Hereafter references are given parenthetically in the text.
3. E. D. Hirsch, "Why General Knowledge Should Be a Goal of Education," *Common Knowledge* 11 (1998).
4. Peter Berkowitz, *The Weekly Standard* 15, no. 33 (May 17, 2010). See also "Why Liberal Education Matters," *Wall Street Journal*, May 15, 2010.
5. Louis Menand, *The Marketplace of Ideas: Reform and Resistance in the American University* (New York: Norton, 2010), 153. See my review in the *Los Angeles Times*: www.latimes.com/entertainment/news/arts/la-ca-louis-menand10-2010jan10,0,2507744.story (accessed February 2011).
6. Ibid., 116.

Index